THE CLASH

lbans City Hall – BANNED
Hempstead Pavilion – BANNED
ble Civic Hall – BANNED
bury – ????????????????????

the Clash get banned tonight in Aylesbury it will mean that th
nowhere left in the Home Counties for them to play as every
hall has now banned them. This would be a total drag as they ar
arly one of the most important British bands of the seventies.

please don't damage the place or each other or attempt to get
ge and please be reasonable to the bar staff. Other than that –
DAMN GOOD TIME!

's make it so the Clash can return to Aylesbury!
future is in your hands. Ta.

Stardate Concerts presents

isco

WN HALL

Open 7.15 p.m.   Bar
DRESS AS YOU LIKE
ADMIT
ONE   £2.00

POLLO THEATRE, Manchester

M.C.P. presents—
THE CLASH AND GUESTS
aturday, 11th February 1984
vening 7.30
ALLS
4.00
13

FAIRDEAL THEATRE
(ex. Brixton Astoria)
211 Stockwell Road, S.W.9

IN MCP, PIMPS, PUNKS, HUSTLER
GOODTIME GIRLS &
THE CLASH
Down at the Kasbah Club
FRIDAY JULY 3
at 8.00 p.m.
STALLS

Nº 1260

No cameras or recorders
This portion to be retained (P.T.O.)

MUSIC MACHINE
CAMDEN HIGH ST. Opp. Mornington Cresc.
LONDON. N.W.1   Tel: 01-387 0428/9

Wednesday 19th
SORE THROAT
plus Blazer Blazer
Admission £1.00

Saturday 22nd
GONZALEZ
plus 13
Admission £2.00

Thursday 20th
MERGER
plus Little Bo Bitch
Admission £1.50

Monday, Tuesday, Wednesday, Thursday, 24th, 25th, 26th & 27th July
THE CLASH
plus the Specials
Advance tickets £2.50 from Box Office

Friday 21st
LAST LONDON APPEARANCE OF
'THE DICKIES'
from U.S.A.
plus The Edge
Admission £2.00

plus From New York 'Suicide'

LICENSED BARS — LIVE MUSIC — DANCING — FOOD
8 p.m.-2 a.m. MONDAY TO SATURDAY
PLAYING TIMES 10.30 & 12 MIDNIGHT

APOLLO THEATRE, GLASGOW
STRAIGHT MUSIC PRESENTS
THE CLASH
Monday, 21 January 1980
at 7.30 p.m.
STALLS
Nº 28
TICKET £3.00
TO BE RETAINED
TICKETS CANNOT BE EXCHANGED

LONDON AGAINST RACISM
GLC
rking for Housing in London

ALL THE YOUNG PUNKS: A PEOPLE'S HISTORY OF THE CLASH

IAIN KEY

First published in Great Britain 2025 by Spenwood Books Ltd
1 Totnes Road, Manchester, M21 8XF

Copyright © Iain Key 2025

The right of Iain Key to be identified as author of this work
has been asserted in accordance with Sections 77 & 78 of
the Copyright, Design and Patents Act 1988.

All rights reserved. No part of this book may be reproduced in any form or by any electronic or mechanical means, including information storage or retrieval systems, without permission in writing from the publisher, except by a reviewer who may quote brief passages.

A CIP record for this book is available from the British Library.

ISBN 978-1-915858-37-5

Hardback printed and bound in the Czech Republic by Akcent Media

Design by Bruce Graham, The Night Owl

All image copyrights as captioned

spenwoodbooks.com

ALL THE YOUNG PUNKS:
A PEOPLE'S HISTORY
OF THE CLASH

IAIN KEY

Spenwood Books
Manchester, UK

ALSO PUBLISHED BY SPENWOOD BOOKS

Cream – A People's History

Queen – A People's History

Thin Lizzy – A People's History

Goin' Down De Mont – A People's History of Rock & Pop Concerts at Leicester's De Montfort Hall

The Rolling Stones in the Sixties – A People's History

All Down The Line – A People's History of the Rolling Stones 1972 North American tour

Gonna See All My Friends – A People's History of Fairport Convention

All The Songs Sound The Same – The Wedding Present

Tell Everyone – A People's History of the Faces

Wild! Wild! Wild! A People's History of Slade

All Our Loving – A People's History of The Beatles

Wish You Were Here – A People's History of Pink Floyd

This Guitar Has Seconds To Live – A People's History of The Who

Cropredy Capers – Another People's History of Fairport Convention

Just Backdated – Melody Maker: Seven Years in the Seventies

The Ukrainians – From Kyiv to the Kosmos

Solid Bond in Your Heart – A People's History of The Jam

Magical Highs – Alvin Lee & Me

Jimi Hendrix – The Day I Was There

Prince – The Day I Was There

The Stranglers – Live (Excerpts)

Sometimes These Words Just Don't Have To Be Said – The Wedding Present

Simple Minds, Heart of the Crowd – A Fan History

Led Zeppelin: Whole Lotta Love – A People's History

FOREWORD

Year Zero. I was there. Monday 7th May 1977. At the Rainbow Theatre in Finsbury Park on the night that punk rock was ripped from the arms of the art school provocateurs who surrounded Malcolm McLaren. Here was the proof that punk was more than a west London clique. Sure, those pals of McLaren, the Subway Sect, were on the bill, but The Prefects from the English Midlands kicked things off, and Manchester's Buzzcocks took it up a gear. And then The Jam came on to remind us all that there was life to be lived in the satellite towns beyond the Westway.

It was those sterling sons of the suburbs that me and my bandmates had come to see. Having spent a couple of years bashing out Stones, Faces and Who tunes in my mum's backroom, The Jam's Mod-inspired style appeared more accessible to us than the art school imagery that accompanied early features on The Clash. Painted trousers?? Never mind the Pollocks!

Having witnessed The Jam in the sweaty confines of a packed Nashville Rooms the week that their debut single 'In The City' came out, we were here to see our heroes claim the crown of punk from Bernie Rhodes' boyos. But it didn't quite work out that way. The vast expanse of the Rainbow stage seemed to intimidate The Jam. Maybe it was the first time that they had played such a huge venue, but the explosive energy they were famed for fizzled but never caught fire in the way it had at the Nashville.

When The Clash hit the stage, however, the whole venue took to their feet and remained there for the rest of the evening. In many ways, what they were doing was not 100 miles away from the music me and my mates had been playing. Paul Simonon was the most visually compelling bass player I'd seen since Jimmy Lea of Slade. Mick Jones was throwing Keith Richard shapes while playing Pete Townsend riffs. And Joe Strummer… well, he was genuinely different. We were up in the balcony, yet the intensity of his performance was like nothing I had ever witnessed before.

I came home with my ears ringing and my perspective changed. Suddenly, my generation were visible, liberated from the long hair and flares that had signified rebellion since 1967. While the hippies and their fellow travellers rebelled against what they referred to as 'The Man', we were in revolt against the bloated toothless carnival of egotism and excess that rock culture had become. And, more than any other band, The Clash embodied this revolution.

Where the Stones had become complacent, The Clash played with an urgency that grabbed you by the lapels. The heroes we had looked up to were middle-aged, but the bands playing at the Rainbow were our age. And perhaps the most significant moment in any artist's career comes when they see someone just like them creating something amazing. The penny dropped for me that night: I realised that you didn't need any justification to make the music you want to make. The core message of punk rock was self-empowerment – 'here's three chords, now form a band' – and it finally made sense to me as I rode home from Finsbury Park on the Tube.

The Sex Pistols had opened the doors of punk rock for those willing to pierce their cheek with a safety pin and shop at Sex on the Kings Road. At the Rainbow that night, The Clash let everyone else into the punk rock scene through the toilet windows. While Johnny Rotten's cynical sneer made great headlines, The Clash defined themselves by their principles.

Their first great single – and, not coincidentally, Topper's first appearance on the drums – was 'Complete Control', a polemical pushback against their management, promoters and record company's attempts to curb the band's determination to do things differently. For any kid struggling against authority – of parents, teachers, older siblings – this song told them that they were not alone, that they belonged to a rejectionist pop-art movement called Punk.

If the Rainbow ignited my love of The Clash, it was their appearance at the Rock Against Racism/Anti-Nazi League Carnival in April 1978 that defined them in my eyes as a genuinely radical group that wanted to change the world. I marched that day with my bandmates through the streets of London's East End and experienced another Clash-induced epiphany in the concert in Victoria Park.

Seeing an estimated one hundred thousand kids just like me packing the park in opposition to the fascist National Front, I realised that this was my generation taking sides. Just as protests against the Vietnam War had come to define the previous generation, so we were going to be defined by our opposition to discrimination of all kinds – racism, sexism, homophobia, xenophobia. We would be the generation of 2-Tone, of Artists Against Apartheid, of women's peace camps and Gay Pride.

When they followed their appearance at RAR with '(White Man) In Hammersmith Palais' it seemed to me that The Clash were taking on the mantle of leadership in this movement, but their second album was a disappointment. The first-person narrative that worked so well on 'White Man' took an insular turn as song after song drifted into self-mythologising.

I continued to follow them avidly and my faith was paid off when *London Calling* was released. Expansive in every sense of the word, this was The Clash hitting their stride, moving beyond punk, beyond rock itself to find their own space in a multicultural medium that lived up to the promise of that day in Victoria Park.

However, their fourth album, *Sandinista!*, wasn't the record I needed at the end of 1980. The guys that I'd been playing with since I learned how to strum a chord had gone their separate ways and the venues where we used to play were no longer interested in guitar bands. The wheel of pop culture was turning again and style was reasserting its domination over content. In that state of mind, a triple album by The Clash felt like a betrayal of everything we'd fought for in the Punk Wars.

The egotism and excess that punk had revolted against seemed to be creeping into the band that had led the charge. There were more songs about being in The Clash and too many tracks that should have been kept for the 25th anniversary boxed set. And there was a whiff of complacency too. Making a double album out of *London Calling* had been totally justified, as there was so much great material. *Sandinista!* had too many fillers.

They tell me there is a really good single album hidden in *Sandinista!* but I wouldn't know as I've never felt able to listen to the whole thing. I was once invited to join The Levellers onstage at their *Beautiful Days* festival to play 'Police On My Back' and had to bluff my way through it. There were baffled to discover that I wasn't familiar with what they considered a classic Clash cover version. I guess you had to be at the Rainbow in 1977 for my stance to make sense.

By the time *Combat Rock* came out, I was already on my own post-punk trajectory, playing my first solo shows around London. The Clash were still a major influence, a fact underscored by reviewers referring to me as a 'one-man Clash'. Despite this, I didn't really connect with the album. 'Straight To Hell', in my opinion the record's stand out song, is yet another Strummer/Jones riff on *Apocalypse Now*. And I can't help but note that the two tracks that have lodged themselves deepest into the public's consciousness – 'Rock The Casbah' and 'Should I Stay or Should I Go' – required respectively a war on a Muslim country and a Levi's advert to make them popular.

What cannot be denied, however, is that *Combat Rock* is a successful album, both artistically and commercially. Recorded with one eye on the American market, with radio-friendly production and expensive videos for the newly-launched MTV, it's a record that finally sees The Clash embracing the rock mainstream. In the months following its release, they would find themselves playing at the Shea Stadium with The Who and headlining the US festival in California in front of 140,000 people.

Yet any artist that seeks to use popular culture to express radical ideas will constantly be confronted by the contradictions inherent in such an approach.

Given the principles that Strummer, Jones, Simonon and Headon professed in their interviews, was there ever a band so well named? The clash between what they believed in and what the music industry required them to do was a constant challenge throughout their career.

The success of *Combat Rock* only heightened the contradictions in The Clash's stance. Can punk rock survive being played in the stadium where The Beatles once shook America? How much genuine connection can you have with a crowd of 140,000? Finding themselves in the belly of the beast, The Clash, fearful of being digested, shattered.

That the band which once meant so much to me should come to such an ignominious end was heartbreaking, yet none of the post-*London Calling* mis-steps detracted from the continuing influence The Clash had on me. Far from it. When it was my turn to be tagged as a 'spokesman for my generation', I learned a lot from the mistakes that the band made.

The failure of their brand of radicalism and the disappointments of their career choices were highly instructive. The message I took from their struggle with the contradictions of pop stardom was that you cannot change the world by just playing songs. Slogans on t-shirts will only get you so far. If you really want to have any kind of agency, you have to engage with the mainstream politics of the day.

It was this insight that led me to co-found the Red Wedge initiative in 1985, joining forces with my other hero from that night at the Rainbow, Paul Weller, in an effort to defeat the government of Margaret Thatcher at the 1987 general election. The record shows that we failed in our efforts and others will doubtless draw their own lessons from our mistakes. But I would never have undertaken such a crusade were it not for The Clash.

For all their contradictions, they played with a passion that few have matched, then or since. To see them live was to believe that you were witnessing the arguments and provocations that occur in the place where generational forces confront one another. I would wish that every nineteen-year-old could feel as empowered as I did that night at the Rainbow. It marked my coming of age.

Are they still the only band that matters? For the many people who have contributed to this book, they were undoubtedly the band that mattered the most.

Ladies and gentlemen - *Ther* Clash!

BILLY BRAGG

INTRODUCTION

I was born a decade too late to appreciate the punk explosion first hand. However I have spent many years since making up for this. My introduction to The Clash was a battered cassette of *London Calling* handed down by my sister Cathy in early 1982 which I went to play on repeat, loving the variety of styles on the album. I was 13 years old and until that point had been listening to the likes of Shakin' Stevens and whatever was in the Top 40 charts.

Many bands I discovered in my teens were on the verge of splitting up, or had split up, and I only discovered their back catalogues out of sequence. With The Clash, I heard 1978's *Give 'Em Enough Rope* and 1982's *Combat Rock* before 1977's self-titled debut and 1980's *Sandinista!* I am ashamed to admit that I didn't even hear some of the non-album singles until *The Story Of The Clash (Volume 1)* was released in 1988!

Over the years I've collected all The Clash's music, sourced numerous bootlegs, read countless books and seen many documentaries. But it's only been through editing this book, reading people's contributions, hearing stories first hand and in some cases seeing the sheer exhilaration, whether on Zoom or in person, as they revisit their heady days of youth that I've really understood why they were 'The Only Band That Matters'.

Releasing five studio albums in six years between 1977 and 1982 is some going by anyone's standard, but when you also factor in that one of these was a double and another a triple, with the sound evolving on each, it's all the more incredible.

All The Young Punks is the story of The Clash through the eyes of their fiercely loyal followers, from their earliest days travelling around the UK, taking punk to the provinces, to switching many onto politics, through to bringing New York to a standstill, whilst soaking up reggae, hip hop, rap…

I think it's safe to say The Clash were unique.

IAIN KEY

ALL OTHERS ARE SHIT
THE ONLY BAND THAT MATTERS
IS, OF COURSE, THE CLASH
JONNY 'ITCH' FOX

⭐ THE ROUNDHOUSE
5 SEPTEMBER 1976, LONDON

KEVIN PIKE

My first encounter with The Clash was at the Roundhouse. I was a new punk on the scene. The Clash were just pure energy, the lyrics hit right at the core of how the youth of the day and the punk movement were feeling. It's like they were writing our diaries, noting our very existence, and telling the world exactly how we felt. Joe's high-energy performance was just an adrenalin rush, and you couldn't help but get swept up and pogo your head off to the exciting sounds battering your ear drums. From then

Kevin Pike couldn't wait to get his next adrenaline fix

on, you knew The Clash was the only band that mattered, and as the years passed, were proved right. It was always essential to find and attend the next gig to get your adrenalin fix.

⭐ INSTITUTE OF CONTEMPORARY ARTS
23 OCTOBER 1976, LONDON

ROADENT

I got my travel warrant from HMP Birmingham to London. I'd only been there for a short visit. Miscarriage of justice, of course, and I went to the ICA where The Clash were playing. I was over early doors, and I met Joe. I asked, 'Do you know anywhere I can sleep?' and he said to come and sleep at the rehearsal room. Then I asked if I could carry boxes and get into the gig for nothing… and so I became their road filth!

I know that people talk about all that 'last gang in town' thing, but we were a very close-knit bunch. Joe, Paul and I spent a long time sleeping

Roadent went from HMP to meet The Clash at the ICA

in Rehearsal Rehearsals. I think we had something like four sheets, one blanket, one sofa, two cushions and a one bar electric fire, and we'd take turns in having the blankets. Paul was lucky – he didn't have a sense of smell!

Joe used to spend a lot of time at Sebastian Conran's flat, or the house when Sebastian was meant to be looking after it for his father. His allowance was meant to be the rent he collected, which wasn't a great deal because Joe certainly never paid very much!

With punk we couldn't quite believe the moral panic that was being caused. I remember me and Joe discussed it, once saying that if a band hadn't made it after two years you may as well knock it on the head because you're never going to make it, but The Clash did. We did think we were something special. You know, all of us did. We knew Siouxsie from going down Club Louise's on Poland Street. Everybody used to be down there and at the 100 Club. We all thought we were special because we weren't of the same ilk as everything that was gone before.

Certainly, with The Clash there was no feeling they'd go on to become this sort of massive thing and there was no feeling of Joe that would be canonised into St Rummer, but we did feel we were special.

LACY LADY
11 NOVEMBER 1976, LONDON

MIKE HERBAGE

I saw The Clash live a fair few times back in the day. The last was the disaster version after Mick Jones had got the sack. That was at Brixton Academy in '84 or '85. It was appalling, like watching a once mighty lion in its dying embers. We left after four songs.

But there was the good stuff too. I saw them in '76 at a club in East London called the Lacy Lady. It was only their sixth or seventh gig. Subway Sect were supporting. There weren't many people there – maybe 40 tops – and I wasn't exactly blown away. I went out of curiosity more than anything. It took me another six months or so to see them…

But this time it was with 2,500 other people at the Rainbow. How did that happen? They'd improved immensely, as you'd expect, and the addition of Topper on drums lifted it to a different level. This was the *White Riot* tour. Now they were the real deal. The buzz at the venue was amazing. It was punk's first coming out to the mainstream rock world.

This gig was a real revelation for me. I'd been to see other bands at The Roxy and The Marquee and the scene was great. But this is the gig where you really felt the power. Not just of the music but the movement itself.

I then saw them again at the Rainbow at the end of the year. We went for two of the three nights. I can't remember the support for these though, I've been told since it could have been Penetration.

As we went into '78, I saw them at The Music Machine three or four times over the summer and winter. '(White Man) In Hammersmith Palais' had been released and they were really hitting their stride. I can't imagine there was a better live band on the planet. (Both Richard Hell and Suicide got bottled off stage at the Music Machine gigs. Richard Hell FFS! The bloke all but invented punk. I was appalled.) To be honest, the scene had changed hugely by March of '78. All the *Sun* readers had tagged along and read that punks were meant to gob at bands and it was all 1-2-3-4 ramalama. It ruined it really. But we still had The Clash and they were monsters by this stage.

ANARCHY TOUR

ELECTRIC CIRCUS
9 DECEMBER 1976, MANCHESTER

AK MCALLISTER

I first saw The Clash on the infamous *Anarchy* tour. A tour that pretty much didn't happen in many places it should have, but it did happen in Manchester, twice. And what an impact they made on me! It's proved to be lifelong. I was 16 then, I'm 64 now and the impact is still there, resonating like a life force that hit and never left. The energy, the pure unadulterated energy emanating from the stage was tangible. Joe Strummer with his 'electric leg' fronting a gang of noise and rhythm, Mick Jones weaving his melodic solos through their sound wall. Paul Simonon, looking like the maestro of cool playing his bass with the notes written on the neck, over Rob Harper's steady and effective pulse-beats. This was a noise for a new generation, and, significantly for me, it was a white noise I could connect with. I grew up on a diet of Black music; soul, funk and reggae provided the meat 'n' gravy for my daily musical menu. When the music, now known as 'punk', first appeared to me, I found some white youths with guitars I felt I could connect with. I'd already tried and rejected Genesis, Pink Floyd and The Beatles. I did like The Kinks though. I'd found some common ground there.

Visually, The Clash looked original and fantastic in their painted clothes, and there was some kind of movement all over the stage from all of them. In my mind now it's like a moving portrait. The tight stage of The Electric Circus suited them, framing them in a compact proscenium vignette. I always felt they worked better in smaller venues rather than the big open stages of the Manchester Apollo for example.

But what I really remember is 'feeling' The Clash live – just as much as 'watching' them. The Clash were a very visceral experience. It wasn't just a visual or cerebral event. They offered hearts, souls and muscles and if you were willing to share with them, you could experience a connection, maybe the best band connection you might ever experience.

When they played 'White Riot' the place went wild. Everybody was

AK McAllister remembers the audience going wild at 'White Riot'

jumping around, joining in, dancing and singing along. 'White Riot' is a masterpiece of the punk era for me. Simple in its structure, immediate in its 'feel-appeal', energy, pace and attack. It sends its political message directly out to those of us who come from working class backgrounds, from the estates, the terraced housing and the terraces. It's a song for the disenfranchised and a call to arms, particularly for white working-class youth to not be too chicken to try to make changes. And it's a mighty moment live!

I was never one for getting right to the front of the stage. I occupied a space just at the back of the mayhem, close enough to take it all in but crammed in with the pogo jumpers. I was moving, couldn't not move, but couldn't look away. Strummer was like a magnet pulling us in. His presence was a force.

Pretty much everyone I knew, and any face I recognised from the scene in Manchester was there. My friend, Ian Dalglish, and I had already formed a band. We were inspired by the Detroit bands, MC5 and The Stooges. I was just following Ian's lead at that time; I hadn't really had time to think about what kind of band we should be. I couldn't play an instrument, and Ian already had the guitar,

Poster for the ill-fated *Anarchy* tour with The Clash bottom of the bill

15

chords and lyrics, but I knew I would write songs. I was already thinking politically and was aware of the idea of anarchy as a construct, but punk would prove my most effective art and politics teacher.

Ian had seen me dancing to Northern Soul in a local youth club and asked me to join his 'punk' band, solely based on the notion that I would make a good front man. To explain it to me, he played me some of his records, but I only said yes after hearing The Stooges, especially 'Search and Destroy'.

The Clash, of course, were also a socio-political outfit, particularly Joe Strummer. This became more and more evident throughout his life. I connected with this. I was aware and had been educating myself about global politics, especially thinking about South Africa and its apartheid system, the USA and segregation, Northern Ireland, and about the freedom fighters in Angola. (This had been brought to my attention through music via reggae band The Twinkle Brothers.) The Clash brought politics and music together in a very earthbound way, the music was robust and direct, and you couldn't separate the message from the music. And, like myself, they all shared a great love of reggae music. The influences from world music would, of course, creep into their sounds very quickly and surface more fully formed in later albums. This was also true for me. I got heavily into Latin jazz, and went on to play trumpet, for a short time, with Manchester band The Jazz Defektors.

GARY HOUGH

I was lucky enough to catch The Clash a few times back in the day, starting at Manchester's Electric Circus on December 9th, 1976. The Damned had been booted from the *Anarchy* tour, and through a tip off from Pete Shelley of Buzzcocks, I knew they were stepping in to replace them. Buzzcocks didn't have their best night due to some technical difficulties and they were clearly under rehearsed, but it still ended up being one of my favourite gigs. The place was heaving, full of energy, and it had a kind of wildness to it that captured the heart and spirit of punk. It is why to this day I still go out to watch and photograph the underground bands, as it brings that similar excitement as anyone who's seen 'Girls In Synthesis' or any number of other bands on the current live circuit can attest.

After that gig finished, I remember trudging back to Manchester in my donkey jacket and Doc Martens, sweating like mad and having dodged some of the local lads who weren't exactly fans of us punks.

IAN MOSS

I have mixed feelings and emotions about The Clash. Whilst recognising that they were an excellent band possessed with intelligence and insight, I alas also found them to be often contradictory and overly concerned with image. I saw them on half a dozen occasions and was progressively less impressed, but they also provided me with one of those rare lightning bolt experiences where I felt as one with the band. That was the first *Anarchy* tour date at the Electric Circus in late 1976.

I'd heard about The Clash but of course I'd never heard them and I was interested enough to wander right up to the lip of the stage (no crush for a bottom of the bill band). I stood directly in front of Joe Strummer as The Clash seemed to erupt from the first moment of their appearance. They were amphetamine fast, the front three of Jones, Simonon and Strummer a blur of constant motion. Their DIY paint splattered and stencilled attire was eye catching and, for a teenager, highly impressive.

Their sound was thin, wired and speedy. Speed was my drug of choice. It was obvious that it was their choice too. I was open-mouthed, gleefully happy. Most songs were a blur but as Strummer less than a yard away from me launched into 'Cheat' I was rocked on my heels:

I get violent when I'm fucked up
Get silent when I'm drugged up
Want excitement don't get none
I go wild

Those words seared into my brain. I felt complete connection with them. They perfectly described my state of mind at that point of my life.

I was won over absolutely. They played 'Police And Thieves' and it was an unexpected masterstroke. I loved them.

I saw them again a few weeks later when the *Anarchy* tour returned. I liked them a lot but understandably their impact on me was reduced.

Months later came 'White Riot' the single followed by their debut album and I gobbled them both up. I still believe the thin reedy sound of their album to be one of the most authentic and honest capturing of what early punk sounded like.

Their second album came along, and the overly produced Americanisms turned my stomach. It sounded like corporate trad rock to my ears. I was hugely disappointed and felt slightly betrayed. In the future, I could enjoy the music of The Clash, but I ceased to believe in them and perceived them as following the lineage of The Who and the Stones, 'corporate rockers' rather than a band who represented an alternative.

JIM FRY, EARL BRUTUS

I was absolutely the right age for punk rock. I left school in 1976 and went to Stockport Technical College to do graphic design. The first records I bought were things by the likes of Alice Cooper and Queen (when they were a heavy metal band) but my great obsession was Sparks, the first band I ever saw live when I was 13 or 14 in 1974.

ALL THE YOUNG PUNKS

I have an older brother, Martin, which meant I could do things an 18-year-old would do when I was just 15. For example, we took the National Express down to see Bowie on the *Thin White Duke* tour. And I saw The Who with Keith Moon at Belle Vue in Manchester. Then we got wind of a gig by a band that were meant to sound like the New York Dolls playing in Manchester. That was Sex Pistols. We went to the second of the Lesser Free Trade Hall shows. It was about 50p to get in.

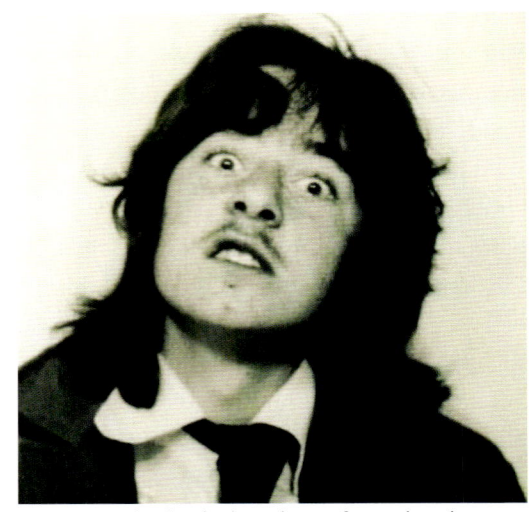
Jim Fry was absolutely the right age for punk rock

There's a lot of snobbery in Manchester about this kind of thing, that the people who went to the first one now are the key people, and those at the second aren't so important. Which is typical, but we saw the first Buzzcocks gig with Steve Diggle, and then Slaughter and the Dogs and then we saw the Pistols. It was, as people say, a real light bulb moment. A real watershed moment. I'd assumed that you had to be talented and musical to be in a band, but it became apparent you didn't!

On 9 December came the *Anarchy* tour. We bought tickets from Virgin Records in Manchester. I don't think I'd been to the Electric Circus before. I saw Buzzcocks, Johnny Thunders and The Heartbreakers, The Clash and then the Pistols. By then the Bill Grundy thing had happened and they were Public Enemy Number 1!

It was very exciting and quite dangerous. Manchester was quite a hostile place if you walked into the wrong street. We were suburban kids, posh kids, and we'd have to be on the last train. If not you were stuck and would have to walk about ten miles home.

That was the first time I saw The Clash. We got to see the whole bill again ten days later, played on a Sunday night when the *Anarchy* tour was back. I was immediately drawn to them, and I bought 'White Riot' and the debut album pretty much the day it came out. I was an avid *NME* reader so was ripe for the whole thing.

ROXY
1 JANUARY 1977, LONDON

DARYL HUMPHREYS

In 1976 we used to travel to various clubs and venues around London. The Kings Road in Chelsea was the place to buy alternative clothes at shops like Seditionaries, which was run by Malcom McLaren and Vivien Westwood, or at ACME Attractions, run by John Krivine. One night at The Global Village (a large nightclub under the railway arches in Charing Cross) we noticed a group who looked and acted very differently. We later knew them to be members of the Sex Pistols and their entourage and we recognised the faces of soon-to-be punk celebrities including John Ritchie, Jordan, Siouxie Sioux, Billy Idol and Adam Ant.

At the weekends we'd hang around the King's Road and if you looked right, you'd get invited to the cool parties where early in-the-know punks gathered. You'd also pick up flyers for punk gigs and the first band I remember seeing were Chelsea in the Chelsea Potter pub on the King's Road. Home-made fanzines like *Sniffin' Glue* were where you learnt about the new bands and discovered the DIY ethos of punk.

Three main bands emerged as the clear frontrunners of punk: the Sex Pistols, The Clash and The Dammed. The Dammed were the first to make it onto vinyl with the independent label Stiff Records. I can remember intently listening to their album when it came out in early '77, soaking up the energy of songs like 'New Rose' and 'Neat Neat Neat' which were like nothing we'd ever heard before.

The underground London punk scene surfaced in December of 1976 with the launch of the Roxy Club in London's Covent Garden. Suddenly, there was a dedicated venue where you could go and see all the bands you'd been hearing about. The Roxy was started by ACME Attractions staffer Andy Czezowski with shop assistant and Rastaman Don Letts on the turntables. Seeing as there were hardly any punk records available at the time, Don played mainly heavy Jamaican dub reggae, which was all right with us. Drinks were cans of Colt 45 lager, accompanied by ready-rolled spliffs and various amphetamines, all available from the bar.

On my first visit to the Roxy in December of '76, I saw Generation X and The Banshees. Gen X were nothing special and the Banshees were still learning how to play but they did an interesting cover of the *Captain Scarlet* TV puppet show theme, plus their own punk version of 'The Lord's Prayer'! It's hard nowadays to imagine how intimate things were at the Roxy back then. Everyone knew each other and there was no 'us and them' between the bands and audience. You'd see Johnny Rotten hanging out by the decks chatting to Don Letts and I remember seeing Joe and Paul from The Clash who'd dropped in to check out the bands that first night.

A PEOPLE'S HISTORY OF THE CLASH

The Clash played The Roxy at the official launch party on a cold New Year's Day in 1977. It wasn't easy to get there due to the lack of public transport. I have a vivid recollection of their performance but I can't remember where I slept that night, although it wasn't unusual for us to head to the train station in the early hours and doze until we could catch the milk train home. The Heartbreakers also played that evening although I have no recollection of seeing them, so they obviously didn't make much of an impression!

There was a huge buzz around The Clash appearing at The Roxy and they did not disappoint. We'd positioned ourselves at the back, standing on seats to get a good view of the action in anticipation of what was about to unfold.

Following a casual introduction from Joe, the band immediately burst into the blistering punk classic 'London's Burning'. The first impression was that they looked fucking amazing! Joe's shirt was emblazoned across the front with the year 1977, which in itself was a bold statement confirming that we were at the start of the new year, at ground zero, in what was about to become the year of punk and that we were witnessing first-hand the launch of something very special.

It was unusual back then to see a punk band that was musically tight with a full set of their own songs. Most bands relied on covers because they lacked original material. But The Clash performed their own songs, written about their own experiences. They were songs that we could easily identify with. Standouts from the set were 'I'm So Bored With The USA', 'White Riot' and the awesome 'London's Burning'. The entire performance was a fast-paced onslaught of energy from start to finish and Joe was the perfect frontman with his unassuming laid-back attitude.

It felt much more co-ordinated compared to other bands we'd seen, which could have been a bad thing because the core appeal of punk was that it was spontaneous and unpolished. But these elements were retained with an overtone of confidence, underscored with pure raw energy. It was the moment The Clash transformed in front of our eyes from being like any other fledgling punk band, who could just about manage three chords, to being a tight entity with their own distinctive sound and attitude, all of which was very much of the time.

We learnt later that Clash manager Bernie Rhodes had a lot to do with mentoring the attitude of the band but he couldn't have done it without having the right material. Paul Simonon influenced their unique take on punk style with his improvised clothing designs, using spray-painted provocative slogans.

Joe Strummer was quoted as saying 'like trousers, like brain' ie. you either wore the narrow trousers worn by punks or you wore the wide hippy flares that were worn by the majority of people in 1977. According to Joe, you were either on one side or the other; one side was young, forward thinking and innovative while the other was stuck in the past and unable to think for themselves.

 THE CLASH SIGN TO CBS
25 JANUARY 1977

DARYL HUMPHREYS

When The Clash signed to CBS and released their first album in '77, it was a bittersweet moment for punk. In many ways it was a triumph that one of the first bands had achieved a major deal with a major label but many saw signing with American label CBS as a total sell-out. A more philosophical view is that they had to go with a big label in order to reach a wide audience and it had to be a label with clout. All the labels at the time were run by 'suits' with a few independent exceptions, and CBS could be said to be the best of a bad bunch.

Did the album capture the live sound and rebellious spirit of The Clash? Not entirely is the answer. Some of the songs lost impact in production which could be down to the band's lack of recording experience and the label not knowing how to deal with punk. Creative interference was rife and some of the songs felt like they'd been artificially speeded up, which had the effect of losing some of the edge. But at the end of the day, it remains one of the greatest albums of all time and it changed the face of music forever.

 'WHITE RIOT' RELEASED
18 MARCH 1977

MARTIN RYAN

This is already being hailed as the most important event of the year. I hope that this is only the first of many, and we can expect more goodies like it. However this is a great single, it overspills with chaos. One snag though, the words are almost impossible to decipher. OK so maybe that was deliberate, but for us Clash fans outside London, who don't see them as often and don't know the words, your best bet is to get hold of *London's Burning*, Clash's own mag, and read along with it. The B-side, '1977', is just as good, in fact better. This has to sum it all up. Look, this record explains what is happening, much better than I can. Get it now, as it's not likely to be on their LP, either 'Riot' or '1977'. What Clash say is truth, they are totally dedicated. If you don't believe it, then you should stick to one of the national pop papers, because we are not writing this review for you.

A PEOPLE'S HISTORY OF THE CLASH

WALLACE DOBBIN

During 1976 reports had reached us up in the far north, through music papers and magazines, about the future of rock 'n' roll. Not the guy from New Jersey, but a band from the Westway, 'the only band that mattered'.

I didn't to get to see or hear The Clash until John Peel played both sides of their debut single, 'White Riot' c/w '1977', on his show. My diary says it was 8th March. I loved the A-side, but for me it was Joe Strummer's banshee wail of '1977' and that strident proclamation of the new order: no Elvis, Beatles or the Rolling Stones.

I remember release day, queuing outside Virgin Records in Newcastle with a small group of fellow would-be revolutionaries, waiting for the shop to open. Open it did and in we piled (well, walked respectfully in) to the strains of '1977' playing on the shop's stereo system. My turn at the counter arrived and I handed over my money and was given what felt like the most precious and dangerous thing I'd ever owned. The picture sleeve (only three band members) spreadeagled against a wall and that pink banner announcing the arrival of the last gang in town.

I still have that worn out copy, scratched and bruised with a now torn and scarred sleeve, a living 'record' of those halcyon days. I'd go through the same process again when the album was released a month or so later, only this time I had the added incentive to get there really early. If you were lucky enough to get one of the first copies, you might find a red sticker inside which meant you could send off a coupon in the *NME* to have a chance of getting the otherwise unavailable *Capital Radio* EP. And I did.

About a month after the album came out, I saw The Clash live for the first time at Newcastle University, the *White Riot* tour. I remember much discussion about what they'd open with. It had to be '1977', what else? But it wasn't, as U-Roy's 'Natty Rebel' faded out and the lights dimmed, the band shuffled on, and Strummer yelled 'Newcastle's Burning!' Now it might well have been 'London's Burning', but in my mind, it will always be Joe's empathetic connection with our regional isolation. He was talking to us.

I'd see The Clash many more times over the years, the last at the Lyceum in London towards the end of 1981, but never again did I feel the same excitement or connection as I'd done back in 1977. They were the spark that lit the rock 'n' roll flame that still burns so fiercely to this very day.

The Clash. Definitely the only band that mattered.

IAN MOSS

I saw The Clash a couple of times in 1976 before they had released a record. They were fierce and fiery. They impressed me with their passion and clearly there was an intelligence about them that many other sound-a-likes lacked (although, in the maelstrom of noise, this intellect was quite difficult to pinpoint, one had to sometimes rely on intuition about these things).

Fast forward a little while and The Clash, despite much revolutionary rhetoric, signed a big bucks contract with the giant CBS label. They were accused of being sell-outs; maybe they were... but even if they weren't they were certainly hypocrites.

What, though, of the music?

Thankfully, that did not disappoint; produced by their live-sound engineer Mickey Foote, their authentic punk sound was replicated in the studio. With wailing police sirens announcing the intro, the band wade in as if their lives depend upon it, accusing the white British populace of being mere spectators of their own subjugation. It goes on to encourage revolt in the same manner as the oppressed black youth who had rioted at the 1976 Notting Hill Carnival. This song signalled an end to passivity and the acceptance of the status quo; it ignited feelings of justice and equality, and set off thought processes that found their ultimate expression in the Rock Against Racism movement which ultimately won the argument against the rising fascist organisation, The National Front.

THE COLISEUM
15 MARCH 1977, HARLESDEN, LONDON

STEVE PALMER
I've still got the flyer for this which I picked up on the night. It was The Slits' first ever show. Viv Albertine wasn't in the band but she was in the audience, and asked to join them the next day. My recollection is that Subway Sect were pretty awful, as were Buzzcocks, because of sound problems which also affected The Clash at first. But it was a very powerful performance and they were in their 'space cadet' outfits after ditching the Jackson Pollock garb. My mate and I were chased by huge Teddy Boys after the show, as was often the case. They were much older than us.

THE CLASH RELEASED
8 APRIL 1977

MARTIN RYAN
This album just has to be one of the most essential statements ever made. To call it brilliant is just taking a short cut. This is real music in that its heart felt. Music born of frustration.

A PEOPLE'S HISTORY OF THE CLASH

The Clash is a pop album, right? The trouble with most intellectual (or so-called) musicians is that they try to pretend you've got to be a genius to understand where they are at. Not The Clash, they speak everyone's language, your language! This album needs no analysis, it's so straight up. The rip-offs are good.

The Gary Glitter-type intro to 'Police And Thieves', better still the 'Autobahn' bit at the end of 'Cheat'. You've gotta cheat to survive, even in rock 'n' roll. If nothing else, it proves that The Clash can play.

'White Riot' is here. Unfortunately for them who bought the single, it's slightly better though, the words are clearer; I think it's faster even. I just hope people listen and act now. Everything they sing is last resorts, when all else fails. There's a lot of irony too. It's a warning of what might happen. This LP rules OK.

ANDREW STREHLER

I was a Canadian kid dropped into Chislehurst, a satellite of South London, in 1975. For my thirteenth birthday in May 1977, I went to WH Smith in Bromley, cash in hand, to buy my first record. I knew of punk as my neighbour had regifted me his 'Anarchy' single for Christmas 1976. I was unaware of *Sounds*, *NME* or *Melody Maker*. Any info I got was from listening to the older boys at school.

Walking into WH Smiths there was this garish green cover with three guys who looked like they were staring into my soul saying, 'Kid, if you buy this record, we will change your life.' I stared at them and at the back cover and back at them and I thought 'this is the most exciting thing I've ever seen' so I walked up to the till and paid for it.

The excitement grew on the bus ride home. Flipping the record over and over again. Strummer/Jones/Simonon. Who the hell were these guys? And, if I had the slightest idea about 'cool', these guys were the coolest!

Record home, sitting on the floor, needle at the ready… crackle and then… kick snare kick snare and then an almighty Mick Jones power chord and we were off and running. The record ended too quickly so had to be played again. The lyrics? Well to a 13-year-old it meant jack shit at the time… but I explored, I asked questions and in time things began to unravel.

The Clash were the most important band of my life at 13. At 60, The Clash are still the most important band in my life. They shaped me into who I am today. For that, I am forever grateful.

ALL THE YOUNG PUNKS

WHITE RIOT TOUR

BARBARELLA'S
3 MAY 1977, BIRMINGHAM

KARL STATTON

My first Clash gig should have been at Birmingham Town Hall, supporting the Pistols on the *Anarchy* tour. Like 75 per cent of that tour, the show was cancelled in the wake of the filth and the fury of the Grundy incident. I had to wait approximately four months until the second night of the *White Riot* tour. The venue was Barbarella's, one of my all-time favourite venues. Placing myself in front of the stage, dead centre, I patiently waited for showtime. First up were the Subway Sect and they did not disappoint. I don't recall much of their set ('Eastern European' being the only title I can remember). Next up? The moment I'd been waiting for since December. The Clash!

(Approximately one month earlier, myself and some mates ended up at Dingwalls, watching the Heartbreakers. I was stood talking to Palmolive from the Slits when we were interrupted by someone claiming to be the new drummer with The Clash. Mine and my mate's reply to this announcement? 'Yeah, course you are!' I seem to remember a shrug of the shoulders before walking off. We felt a bit stupid when we read the

Karl Statton saw The Clash at Birmingham's Barbarella's nightclub

Poster for the *White Riot* tour

A PEOPLE'S HISTORY OF THE CLASH

following week's *NME* and discovered it was true. (Yes folks, we accused Topper of bullshitting!)

We happened to see him some time prior to The Clash taking the stage at Barbarella's. We apologised and he couldn't have been more of a gent. Anyway, after apologies were accepted, we continued to wait and then came the moment that changed my life.

They walked on, Strummer stepped up to the microphone and suddenly it happened.

'BIRMINGHAM'S BURNING!' complete with the second lyric change, 'Up an' down the Bullring, it's so bright.' Like I said before, what happened over the next hour or so changed my life forever.

I went on to see the Clash another 16 or so times, and although I saw them play much better, and longer, etc., that night in Birmingham will always hold a special place in my heart.

⭐ THE AFFAIR
4 MAY 1977, SWINDON

DAVID MARX

When 'White Riot' catapulted The Clash into the consciousness of Jim Callaghan's Britain during the spring of 1977, the band toured extensively; with one of their ultra-high-octane gigs having taken place in Swindon, where my band, The Aggravators, played support.

Paul Simonon (above) and Mick & Joe (below) in action in Swindon

The idea was for us, along with Subway Sect, to kick start the evening at Swindon's then equivalent of the Cavern Club, The Affair, with The Clash performing just across the road in what was then called Central Hall. But amid more than spurious circumstances, the latter burnt down that very afternoon – along with some of The Clash's equipment – which entailed all three

27

bands playing said tiny club (with a maximum capacity of perhaps 250) with The Clash using our backline and drums.

I was still at school and remember catching the bus into town with my guitar, before succumbing to a bout of nerves at the mere sight of the queue (which had already stretched right around the block by half-past five in the afternoon). I don't really recall any of Subway Sect's set, as the place was so packed, we couldn't even get out of the dressing room, but when we did, the place went super bonkers. It seemed Swindon was proud to have its very own punk band opening for The Clash, who, suffice to say, quintessentially ticked all the necessary boxes.

Due to us all sharing the very small dressing room and spending a bit of time together, we accompanied all four members of The Clash onto the miniscule stage. Well, I say walked, the place was so packed, it took about ten minutes to literally prise our way through both the darkness and the heaving throng of sweat and anticipation. Upon arrival, The Clash kicked off with 'London's Burning' (Joe Strummer having unsurprisingly altered some of the lyrics to 'Swindon's Burning') while I stayed ensconced at the very front between Strummer and bassist, Paul Simonon.

Joe in action at The Affair, Swindon

Paul in action at The Affair, Swindon

Photos David Marx

What followed was a nigh incendiary execution of The Clash's entire debut album – all fast and furious, suave and snarling – replete with another reference to the town during 'Police and Thieves' ('Walking down Swindon High Street') and an unsuspecting compliment by way of Strummer dedicating 'Garageland' to The Aggravators.

Ending with 'White Riot' and encoring with 'Janie Jones,' I have to say the gig still stands as one of the finest and most blatantly memorable I have ever witnessed, and I saw The Clash on numerous occasions thereafter.

The acute adrenaline rush of the whole evening may have played a part, as might the graciousness of The Clash themselves. Apart from inviting us to support them the following night in Liverpool, Simonon endeavoured to ply me with white wine after the gig, Strummer gave me a t-shirt and Topper Headon talked endless drums with our drummer. Mick Jones, who, having used my amp, had all the controls cranked up to number ten (which I only noticed when I was packing away) was more than complimentary about my guitar playing. Having got them all to sign their autographs in one of my school notebooks, Jones wrote 'Hendrix Lives!'

NICK KEEN

I was working as a seasonal deck chair attendant on Bournemouth's golden beaches during the glorious sun-soaked summer of 1976, before starting my first proper job in the September. I was just 19 years old and, like many of my contemporaries, I was lapping up the freedom of living away from home.

From a very young age I'd worshipped the trinity of music, clothes and football. It was probably around 1970, just as The Beatles separated and disbanded, that my passion for music raced up to fifth gear. Saturday jobs, several paper rounds and diligent thrift paved the way for a serious record-collecting addiction; singles apart, my first contemporary album was T. Rex's 1972 *Bolan's Boogie* release. As with so many like-minded 1970s teenagers, I was utterly consumed by the wonder of music and dead serious about it too. I felt I had a hunch on what was happening and hip, and what was dull and dated, lapping up anything from the likes of Mott the Hoople, James Brown and Be Bop Deluxe in a home-taping frenzy of late-night radio and borrowing music from mates. My bible was the *NME* and the influential prose of Nick Kent and Charles Shaar Murray. And radio presenter John Peel was my apostle.

By 1976 I was heavily into the Stones, The Who, Led Zeppelin and The Wailers. I'd witnessed The Temptations, Can, The Kinks, Dr Feelgood and Graham Parker among other illustrious line-ups. There was a sense that the times were a-changing as voiced by Peelie, viewed by the press and validated by the embryonic bands shaking up the system. Almost without knowing I was all-consumed by punk. It was an easy and natural transformation; it just happened, and for eighteen months it was my life. The loons were binned, Yes albums hidden and small sweaty venues frequented.

Bournemouth was a gig haven and had a glut of spot-on independent record shops. My home town was the great railway metropolis of Swindon which, much

ALL THE YOUNG PUNKS

to my delight and warped amusement, was also part of the punk trailblazers circuit too. In May 1977, it was there that I first saw The Clash at the Affair club on their *White Riot* Tour. I was desperate to see the band and disappointed that the 1976 Bournemouth Village Bowl gig was cancelled – as was most of the Sex Pistols doomed *Anarchy* tour. I can't recall the song running order that night, but I do remember the lyrics from 'London's Burning' being changed to 'Swindon's burning'! The Affair was an extremely small club, and hilariously called a ballroom, where bands had to parade through an excited and cheering crowd having exited the shoe-box size changing room to reach a cramped stage. I witnessed many legendary red-hot punk performers there.

I'd religiously bought the 'White Riot' single as a confirmation of my commitment to the cause and played the self-named debut album like a boy possessed. Disappointingly, I was too late in applying for the free Capital Radio *NME* disc – it costs an arm and a leg to buy now.

ERIC'S
5 MAY 1977, LIVERPOOL

BANJO

The Clash were undoubtedly Liverpool's favourite punk band. While the Sex Pistols' debut gig at Manchester's Lesser Free Trade Hall has been acknowledged as the starting point of that city's punk scene, The Clash's first gig at Eric's performed a similar magic for Liverpool. The gig was witnessed by Jayne Casey, Julian Cope and Ian McCulloch, who went on to form Big in Japan, Teardrop Explodes and Echo & The Bunnymen respectively. Also in attendance was one Pete Wylie of Wah! fame who, legend has it, approached The Clash's Mick Jones after the gig to tell him how he had been inspired to form a band. The story goes that Jones handed Wylie his guitar with the words, 'Pay me back when you're famous.' Wylie later stated, 'That day everything changed… nothing in Liverpool was ever the same again'.

It wasn't that Liverpool didn't love Sex Pistols, but that, apparently, they just weren't that good when they played Eric's, for what would be the only gig the band ever played in the city. Also, it was only the third gig at Eric's, so both band and venue were still unknown quantities, which meant that only around 50 people were present. Of course, over the years the number of people who have since claimed they were there is probably over 100 times the number that attended, such is the impact punk has made on history.

By the time The Clash played on May 5, 1977, things had changed. Punk was exploding all over the country, attracting the outcasts, the curious and those in search of *something* to match how they felt and to give voice to the noises in their heads. Liverpool was not in a particularly good place; financially in the trough of an economic slump following the decline of its docks and shipping industries and culturally still looking for a way out of the shadow cast by The Beatles' unprecedented success.

Musically, Liverpool had yet to find a post-Beatles identity, although The Real Thing had kept the city's flame burning in the charts. When Roger Eagle and Ken Testi decided to open Eric's, Roger, perhaps sensing that change was in the air, asked those members of his club he took under his wing not to listen to The Beatles, for fear that the past would infiltrate the new present.

Jayne Casey, one of those who were so instructed, remembered:

'A couple of years ago we'd been to a funeral, and we were all sat round a table. There was me, Ian McCulloch and Pete Wylie. Ian looked at me and said, 'Have you listened yet?' And I said, 'No, have you?' And he said, 'No' and we both looked at Wylie and said, 'Have you?' And he said 'no' and we both in the same second said, 'Yes you have! We know you have!' And he was like 'I haven't, I haven't' but we were like, 'We can tell from your composition that you've listened to them for years!' So, we're convinced that he listened, he pretends he didn't, but he did.'

But the music that was being made by the new generation paid no heed to the likes of The Beatles. The Clash themselves penned a song called '1977' that famously claimed, 'No Elvis, Beatles or The Rolling Stones in 1977.'

The Clash were everything a band should have been at that point and place in music. Young, good looking, well dressed, confused and even contradictory.

Their songs combined political thrust with killer riffs, signing about hate, war, being bored and riots. Live they were described as like 'three James Deans coming at you', as the front line of Mick Jones, Joe Strummer and Paul Simonon charged and attacked, backed up by the mighty Topper Headon.

That gig revitalised the city's music scene. People met there and were jointly inspired to *do something*. What nobody could have predicted was how much they could go on to do. There are times in life when the stars just seem to line up and things work out right, a one in a billion meeting of minds and talents, and this seems to have been one of those occasions.

People formed bands before they knew what kind of musicians they would turn out to be, taken by The Clash's messianic call. We can thank the gods of chance, or perhaps some other agent of destiny, that this crowd included the extraordinary voices of Ian McCulloch, Pete Burns, Pete Wylie and Holly Johnson, along with the mercurial talents of guitarist Will Sergeant, drummer extraordinaire Budgie and art prankster/cultural terrorist Bill Drummond.

It may be the case that this astonishing pool of talent would have come together regardless of this gig, but the point remains that The Clash lit the touchpaper, and the firework duly went into the higher atmosphere and exploded.

The Clash were one of the first bands this writer saw at Eric's, a few months on from their debut appearance, on their *Tommy Gun* tour. As confession is alleged to be good for the soul, I will hold my hand up and say that I was never a massive fan after their initial run of singles, nailing my colours to the Pistols' mast instead. That said, this was without question one of the most thrilling gigs I have ever seen. The Clash were undoubtedly at their best live, unmarred by the poor production of their first album and the American sheen of their second.

To this day I can remember the energy of the gig, along with the heat, the packed crowd and the feeling that, somehow, this was a gig that would stay with you long after we had left the venue. I had never seen Eric's so crowded, perhaps the fullest I ever saw it, apart from Iggy Pop. The size of the crowd was such that people had spilled out from stage front through to the bar area, making even a glimpse of the stage tricky.

The Specials were supporting them on this tour (under their earlier name The Coventry Automatics) and although I tell people I saw them it is probably more honest to say that I glimpsed them, through a doorway and over people's heads. The crowd looked hot, and we didn't fancy getting caught up in the heat and mess of it, just for a support band.

If I had the chance, I would tell my teenage self to get in there and catch one of our era's most important bands while they were still unknown. I was amazed at how popular they seemed to be despite few people in my social circle having heard of them.

As the band left the stage and people headed to the bar, we saw our chance and pushed our way in. Thankfully we got to within a few people of the front of the stage and The Clash burst forth and blew our teenage minds, playing their first album and early singles. They already had a run of songs to make most new bands weep with envy.

With the Sex Pistols banned from almost everywhere and soon to split up, The Clash were head of the punk pack at this point, and made a nonsense of the myth that punk bands couldn't play their instruments. The people inspired by their first Liverpool gig have achieved much in the years since and have doubtless inspired other people in their turn.

Perhaps this is the ultimate compliment for a gig, or even a band – that they create these ripples in a pond to such extent that they are still being felt all these years later.

Liverpool, and indeed the whole world, would be so much worse without them.

GRANT MCPHEE, FILMMAKER

Almost everybody has witnessed a life-affirming musical experience. Certain gigs, however, transcend being merely a reciprocal transaction between fan and performer. These rarified events symbolise a moment of change, become a flagpole in the ever-evolving story. Bob Dylan 'going electric' at the Newport Folk Festival, the Stones sacrificial death-to-the-sixties at Altamont and of course, the infamous Sex Pistols religious North-West year zero at Manchester's Lesser Free Trade Hall. These moments all stand as exemplars of the power of the musical experience, the unwitting evangelist to the convert, empowering them to 'go forth and testify'. The Clash created two such explosive moments and these were, amazingly, only two days apart.

Musical change, movements, scenes, whatever you wish to call them are much like chaos theory. The complexities of the constituent components which create them are so bafflingly complex as to become indefinable and impossible to predict. Only in Tony Wilson's theory of Praxis may we try and look back and attempt to glean some explanation as to 'why it happened'. Sometimes though, it's best to refrain from analysis and simply appreciate that these moments thankfully happened.

The Clash's May 1977 *White Riot* tour was the vector that kickstarted a new musical revolution in two different cities, two days apart. The DNA from those events still percolates through music made to this day.

Date One: 5th May 1977, Eric's, Liverpool. The Sex Pistols had performed at Eric's a few months previously. Unlike when they had first played Manchester in June though, there was bafflingly no immediate explosion of activity in their aftermath. 'Anarchy In The UK' was yet to be released but the band had performed on Granada's *So It Goes* on the 26th August, broadcast to both Manchester and Liverpool. The complexities and precise alignments required for pop-change would have to wait for their allotted time.

Date Two: When the time eventually arrived, two symbolic conduits of change had also been waiting for this coming moment. Waiting 13 years to be precise, the time elapsed since The Beatles left Liverpool. These conduits were former Beatles manager Allan Williams and Cavern DJ Bob Wooler. They were sitting, along with Deaf School guitarist Clive Langer, in The Grapes pub, which was situated next door to Eric's. In there they met three previous students of Liverpool School of Art, about to have a quiet pint before The Clash. These students were Phil Allen, Kevin Ward and Bill Drummond. 'You three should form a band,' the students were told. After witnessing The Clash on 5th May 1977, they did. Big in Japan formed, birthing Zoo Records. And next door to The Grapes, in amongst the hordes at Eric's were Pete Wylie, Julian Cope, Ian McCulloch, Paul Simpson, Dave Balfe, Jayne Casey, Holy Johnson and Pete Burns. Many would meet for the first time, and together they would form the majority of Liverpool's hugely influential post-punk music scene.

PLAYHOUSE THEATRE
7 MAY 1977, EDINBURGH

GRANT MCPHEE

On 6th May, The Clash would play in Aberdeen and no band of note was formed.

On the 7th May 1977 at Edinburgh's Playhouse Theatre, it was a different story. Starved of punk music, Scotland was ready for a change. Although The Sex Pistols had also played in Dundee, much like with Liverpool there was no Lesser Free Trade Hall moment. In fact, the ignition point of the Edinburgh *White Riot* tour was not The Clash themselves. It was their support acts – namely The Slits and Subway Sect. In attendance on that night were Alan Horne and Edwyn Collins, who would form Postcard Records and Orange Juice, arguably birthing the 'indie-pop' movement. While Postcard Records represented Glasgow, Edinburgh itself was represented by the future members of Fire Engines, Josef K, Scars and the vast majority of teenagers who would form the nucleus of Fast Product, the record label which would form in the aftermath and release the debut singles of Gang of Four, Mekons, Human League and Dead Kennedys.

Both of these record labels would give Scotland a significant kickstart in becoming a nation associated with independent music. This would almost certainly not have happened had the precise people not been there on that date with the precise people playing at that date. The Clash themselves cast their approval on what they had helped create by featuring both Postcard and Fast Product on the sleeve of 'Hitsville UK' (with Fast being name-checked in the song).

On 8th May 1977, the *White Riot* tour headed to Manchester. It was a tremendous success and had the punk ignition not been already lit, perhaps that too would have been Manchester's moment. The rarified moments of change are unpredictable and unknowable but they happen, and The Clash will forever be part of the cosmic chaos that creates them.

ELECTRIC CIRCUS
8 MAY 1977, MANCHESTER

DAVID LANGFIELD

The first concert I ever went to. I went to Oxfam in my dinner hour and bought some black straight leg trousers, white shirt and black shoes, my punk gear for The Clash gig at the Electric Circus in Manchester. The line-up was The Clash, Buzzcocks, The Slits and Subway Sect. We queued up for an hour and had never seen so many punks in one place. When we got in it was full to the brim, sweating, boiling hot with reggae playing in the background. The Clash started off with 'Manchester's Burning'. I'd never seen anything like it in my life. The crowd went mental, beer spilt, bottles everywhere. 40 minutes of pure energy. Not a bad first gig for an 18-year-old punk.

GARY HOUGH

I saw them in May 1977, memorable in that I spent part of my mum's birthday money that I'd saved that month to go to this gig, which was worth every penny, because I saw a brilliant new all-girl band, The Slits. Ari Up was jumping about just to the side of me with not a lot on that I recall. They were brilliant live and another support band that went on to be legendary (in their own right), Subway Sect, were on too. I never got into them at all. In fact I was bored when they were on, to be honest. The Clash, however? Well they were insane! Fast, frenetic and the sound and lyrics were sharp, and they did one of the best versions of 'White Riot' ever.

MARTIN RYAN

For the first time that I could recall, accessing the Electric Circus involved standing in the famous/infamous queue that stretched down the side of the venue and, depending on the draw of the band, behind the iconic building. Despite the average Mancunian punk looking far from outrageous, the queue drew the attention of a handful of the kids from the neighbouring flats who appeared each Sunday to watch the curious patrons stand in line. The term 'feral youth' had yet to be coined by politicians and in fairness, on the one occasion the youths created the slightest of conflicts, the distressed minor returned in the company of his mother who remonstrated with his adversary.

   The queue was more a ritual than a necessity, as even the possession of a ticket would not fast-track your entry. For those who preferred a cosier wait, there was a pub just around the corner on neighbouring Rochdale Road where you could wait for the queue to abate whilst being entertained by an organist whose act seemed to consist mainly of playing *Opportunity Knocks* winner Bernie Flint's current breakthrough, 'I

ALL THE YOUNG PUNKS

Don't Want To Put a Hold On You'. Although it was a traditional pub with family entertainment, we did encounter a friendly gentleman who had presumably deduced that this watering hole was a stopover for fans en route to the nearby rock venue and who offered to sell us some 'gear'.

The visit of The Clash, who had previously appeared as part of the *Anarchy* tour, also attracted the attention of the police as they monitored the situation. The sight of uniformed police around the building was somehow fitting. The queue tonight was at least apposite for one of the top Manchester gigs of all time. I had seen The Who in 1975 when they generously bequeathed the cream of much of their back catalogue and there was the earth-shattering appearance by Johnny Thunders and the Heartbreakers earlier in the year.

I was to witness the double bill of the Ramones and Talking Heads later that month and David Bowie's post-'Heroes' showing at Stafford the following year. Whichever of those occasions was the gig of my lifetime still varies daily but the appearance at the Electric Circus of The Clash on their *White Riot* tour remains an abiding memory.

For what seemed like the first time, the Circus DJ played an exclusively punk soundtrack mixed with early stirrings of the obligatory dub reggae that would become punks' brother-in-arms courtesy of Donn Lett's role as DJ at London's Roxy, reinforced by Mark Perry's command in punk bible *Sniffin' Glue* to 'try to listen to reggae'.

The Slits' short set confirmed Pete Shelley's description of the all-girl band. There was none of the restraint in which women in rock tended to engage; the solid guitar bass drum sound supplying a portent force behind Ari Up's equally uninhibited vocals. The singer roared her musical preference whilst returning via the crowd to the dressing room with a cry of 'reggae reggae reggae'. Local fanzine writer Steve Shy (Shy Talk) candidly described them as 'amazing'.

A PEOPLE'S HISTORY OF THE CLASH

There was a suitable congeniality to Subway Sect. Less direct than most of their contemporaries, singer Vic Godard emphasised their unpolished approach by referring to a piece of paper before announcing each number. Despite the lacklustre presentation, there was clearly a level of sophistication to this band. Like fish out of water, the exuberant response to the structured arrangements seemed almost to mystify the band and their deadpan approach.

Unlike both support bands whose sets I had to learn on the night, The Clash set had been pre-burned into my memory, with the 'White Riot' single, debut album and the *NME* freebie 'Capital Radio' ensuring there would be no musical surprises.

The question mark over their decision to spout their political dogma via the international set up of CBS was still a hot topic and their contemptuous re-reading of 'London's Burning' as 'Manchester's Burning' for the opener should have raised further questioning of The Clash's stance. But now The Clash seemed untouchable, with the music press collectively assessing them as the only band that mattered.

Once the band hit their stride, which was almost instantaneously, it was quickly obvious that they were firmly in the driving seat of the punk revolution. The Clash had certainly benefited from the notoriety that the Sex Pistols had sown but the latter's refusal, or probably their overbearing manager's refusal, to exploit them as a live act, left the way clear for The Clash to rise to the top of the pile. The Clash's standpoint as people's champions may have been compromised by their choice of a major record label and their manager's personalised CLA5H number plate on his limousine, but their willingness to deliver their music to the masses in all its power and glory, both in the flesh and via their quickly released debut album, seemed to earn them clemency from the judgemental punk audience.

Whether there was much truth in Malcolm McLaren's claims that there were insurmountable obstacles to his band playing live remains questionable given that both The Clash and Johnny Thunder's Heartbreakers had both been quarries for the kind of self-righteous indignation that had annihilated much of the *Anarchy* tour. Then there was the fact that the Circus had hosted the *Anarchy* tour twice and would surely throw the doors open to a further showing as would many other venues across the nation. Either way, it was The Clash who fired the warning shots and sent us back to our cosy existence in a state of delirium. I am not sure I had yet come to regard any punk band as the greatest band in the world, but on tonight's showing maybe it is The Clash.

RAINBOW THEATRE
9 MAY 1977, LONDON

CHRIS HILDER

I saw the 101ers as a support act in December 1975 at the theatre in what is now London Metropolitan University on Holloway Road, Islington. It was the North London Polytechnic where I was doing my bachelor's degree. The gig was with the Mickey Jump Band and Be-Bop Deluxe as the main act. I remember the 101ers and enjoying the performance, especially the energy, and I recall within my group of friends that we said we should watch out for them as they were sure to break out. I specifically remember Joe Strummer (as he became known) who was quite extrovert. But I don't remember much else about that gig.

A couple of years later I came across a copy of The Clash's debut album at a record stall on Portobello Road. It was marked as 'Not for Resale' and I smiled at the irony.

The first time I saw The Clash perform was at the Rainbow in Finsbury Park on the *White Riot* tour. Also on the bill were The Prefects, Subway Sect, Buzzcocks and The Jam. We were up on the balcony, and during The Clash's set I remember watching the mosh pit at the front of the stage. It was heaving and people were pogoing and I wished I could get down and join in, although there was also some fighting which I was less enthusiastic about.

After the gig I was exuberant and walked out of the Rainbow utterly convinced that prog rock (which is what I'd previously enjoyed) was dead and punk was where my heart lay.

STEVE PALMER

This is the night that punk really kicked off, literally. We trashed the seats in the stalls and threw them onstage.

DARYL HUMPHREYS

When the infamous Bill Grundy/Sex Pistols TV incident took place in December 1976, it had a very negative impact on the development of punk. Had it not happened, I am certain the music would have taken a different course, for better or for worse. The Grundy incident unexpectedly thrust punk into the public eye and no one was prepared for the reaction. The gutter press savaged the movement, claiming that punks showed their appreciation by spitting and throwing stuff at their bands and each other, which was total nonsense. Punks were being harassed up and down the country and at the same time, the main bands set out warily on the nationwide *Anarchy* tour. The tour never really got off the ground because gigs were cancelled left right and centre by the authorities who were by this time running scared. Those that did happen were beset by gangs of marauding 'straights' who turned out in force to spit, chuck stuff at the bands and beat up the punks.

There were still punk-friendly venues dotted about such as London's Nashville Rooms where I saw the original line-up of Adam and The Ants in 1977 (they were excellent) but at other venues like The Marquee in Wardour Street, punk bands were being trashed by non-punk audiences who came to bait and hate. When X-Ray Spex played there in '77, I remember a spit-soaked Poly Styrene bravely completing the set, despite the abhorrent behaviour of the audience. It was a sad sight to see and it felt like it could be the end for punk.

This was the atmosphere in which The Clash launched their nationwide *White Riot* tour in May 1977. They had experienced the *Anarchy* tour and knew what to expect from hostile crowds, but there were also many emerging punks around the country who had heard of The Clash and were eager to see them live.

The *White Riot* tour peaked at the Rainbow Theatre in London's Finsbury Park on May 9th 1977 with the band performing on their home turf supported by The Jam, Buzzcocks and Subway Sect. The Rainbow was a seated venue with a capacity of just under three thousand. It was not a performance to be missed and I still have my ticket stub from that day.

After bunking the Tube, we arrived early and were met with many familiar faces from the Roxy days, along with new faces of fans that had come in from the suburbs. There were also some well-known punk personalities there who had turned out to see the triumphant homecoming.

The Jam put in a half-decent performance for a band that was more Mod than punk, although they were dwarfed by the size of the stage. Buzzcocks and Subway Sect were on good form, with both bands confidently thrashing out their unique take on punk music. The atmosphere was taut with anticipation in the build-up to the headliners and when they finally appeared, The Clash simply owned the stage.

Joe was in his element as the laid-back charismatic front man and the band seemed more mature, more experienced and even tighter than before. From our vantage point up in the balcony, we could see the crowd occupying the small space between the stage and the seating as they began to surge violently backwards and forwards. At one point Joe paused and appealed to them to stop pushing from behind as the people down the front were being crushed against the stage.

The song 'White Riot' was written following the Notting Hill Carnival of 1976 when carnival goers reacted violently against police harassment. Several members of the band attended the carnival and witnessed the civil unrest first hand.

Their subsequent song became a nationwide call to arms for a disaffected youth, amplified on vinyl and via live regional performances during the *White Riot* tour.

When The Clash struck up the opening chords of 'White Riot' that night at the Rainbow, the crowd at the front erupted into a wild frenzy. They literally tore up several rows of seating, hurling an entire row onto the stage where it landed at the feet of Joe Strummer. Make no mistake, these were heavy old school hardwood theatre seats, bolted together and firmly secured to the floor. They must have weighed a ton! The hair on the back of my head stood up as I glanced sideways to see the astonished look on other people's faces which was as if to say, 'Did we really see what just happened?' The band carried on playing without missing a single a beat.

I learnt later that the tour ultimately lost money due to property damage, with the band having to foot the bill.

 NOTTINGHAM PALAIS
12 MAY 1977, NOTTINGHAM

PHIL CURME

I'd heard 'Career Opportunities' on the John Peel show and had never heard anything like it before. Everyone was listening to increasingly pretentious prog rock which said nothing to the average bored teenager in depressed, monochrome Britain. The new music Peel was playing was exciting and spoke to people like me. It is impossible nowadays to articulate how impactful punk was in those early days – it was like a tsunami crashing onto our shores and sweeping away previous conceptions of what rock and roll was all about.

I was at Trent Poly and bought a ticket to see The Clash as soon as I heard they were heading for the Midlands. The original gig was cancelled because Joe Strummer had contracted hepatitis – the spitting thing had got him! It was rescheduled for May 12, 1977 – the evening before an important exam I needed to take. I went anyway and dragged my reluctant flatmates along with me.

The Buzzcocks supported… and they were great. Pete Shelley had replaced Howard Devoto and the crowd were sceptical at first… but not by the end. The Clash came on and Joe shouted, 'Nottingham's burn-ing!' and the place burst into life. I'd never experienced anything like it. Someone on stage made a giant paper plane out of a giant poster of the cover for the forthcoming first album – Joe, Mick and Paul on the steps of Rehearsal Rehearsals in Camden. I caught it and still have the poster.

The first album came out and it felt like the soundtrack to what was going on in my head. I knew every word, every riff, and played it until I wore the record out.

My copy was one of the first, so I got a free EP featuring 'Capital Radio' and an interview with the boys recorded by Tony Parsons on the Circle Line.

 'REMOTE CONTROL'/'LONDON'S BURNING' (LIVE) RELEASED
13 MAY 1977

MARK CARTWRIGHT

Where do I start without boring you all too much? Let's go back to the moment in my life that kicked off the chain of events leading up to hearing The Clash for the first time, understanding what they meant to me and why they helped change/shape my life from then on.

It was around the beginning of 1977. I was 13 and still at school. I'd been a bit of a wrong 'un and landed myself in what was known then as borstal. Many things led up to this, but the state of the country, boredom and peer pressure were definite contributors. I was at a crossroads and thinking 'which way do I go? Where does the rest of my life take me?'

The Clash themselves weren't the catalyst for change. The Sex Pistols took that spot, after I heard 'Holidays In The Sun' and went out with my pocket money (yes, you got that when you were at Her Majesty's Pleasure) and bought the single. Things were never gonna be the same. The anger and the need to have direction were being channelled now.

It was in late '77, after I'd latched onto the scene and found people who felt the same, that someone played me 'White Riot'. 'OMG! Who, what, why haven't I heard these until now?' By this time I was out of borstal but in a care home, so moving in the right direction at least. After feeding my hunger for the band with everything they had released by then, it was evident that this having a life-changing effect on me.

The politics, the social awareness, the anti-racial sentiment, all resonated with how I was feeling, a perfect storm of music and words. Having grown up in what could only be described as a 'non-tolerant', and by today's standards, backward thinking environment, The Clash's music started to make things much clearer for me.

Having a band with a lead singer like Joe Strummer, a man who had no fear of sharing the words that meant more to him than just song lyrics, with an audience who, whether he knew it or not, needed someone's direction. This was a band that had so much more to give to myself than they would ever have known.

If I had to pick one song that gave me the need and the fight to become more than I was at that point, 'Remote Control' would be it. The verse:

Can't make no progress
Can't get ahead
Can't stop the regress
Don't wanna be dead

said to me, 'No I can't stop anything or get ahead unless 'I' do something, no one will do it for me, and I don't wanna be dead!'

So yes, The Clash did save my life. More than that, they gave me a reason to try and help save more people's lives, and never give up trying. Beyond all that though, they gave us all some of the best music and words ever recorded.

The future is unwritten, but at least I still had a future to write, thanks to Strummer, Jones, Simonon and Headon.

ROCK GARDEN
19 MAY 1977, MIDDLESBROUGH

MICHAEL TODD

In 1977 my life was changed like many others of similar age to myself by the impact that punk made on the music industry and society in general. I was 19 years old, living with my parents in Redcar, Cleveland, and working at the local steel works. As a young teenager I was a glam rock kid, very much into Bowie and Roxy Music with a little bit of Deaf School and Split Enz as variation. Gigs wise, I'd only seen two groups live – Status Quo at Stockton's Globe Theatre when I was still a school kid, and then, when I was 17, I managed to get into a nightclub called Club Fiesta, also in Stockton, to see Slade.

By the time 1976 arrived, things were getting a bit boring within the music scene. Supergroups and their stadium rock were putting a huge distance between groups and fan bases. Disco was on the rise and kids were bopping along to the likes of The Bay City Rollers and watching the *Donny & Marie* Osmond show on TV. Things were ripe for a shake up and thankfully punk arrived to put everything in the mixer.

One Sunday morning my interest was aroused by an article in the *News of the World* about how this abomination called 'punk rock' was putting the youth of the day in danger by exposing them to anarchy and rebellion. It was being spearheaded by groups with subversive names such as The Damned, Sex Pistols and The Clash. The monikers of the band members also gave the paper a field day, Johnny Rotten, Sid Vicious, Rat Scabies to mention just a few. They couldn't even play their instruments and only knew three chords at best. The fans of punk music, aptly named 'punk rockers', wore ragged clothes festooned with safety pins and swastikas and went around intimidating the public while smelling like a tramp's vest.

Did the article put me off as intended? Hardly! In fact, it had quite the opposite effect, as the next day I was causing havoc in the house listening to my newly bought long player, the self-titled first Clash album. 'Turn that rubbish down,' me mam said. I replied, 'Bugger off. Go and play yer Val Doonican shite in the front room if you don't like it.' Rebellion was afoot. Well, small steps to begin with.

A few weeks later, I found myself in Middlesbrough, on my lonesome, at The Rock Garden. Why? The simple answer to that is, The Clash were in town.

On entering the venue, I nearly turned around to walk straight back out. To be honest, being a bit of a shitty arse due to having led a sheltered life up to that point, my first glimpse of punk rockers put the willies up me. There were only four of them, two lads and two lasses. They were by themselves in the middle of the room. Everybody was staring at them like they had the bubonic plague. They may as well have been ringing bells, shouting out 'Unclean! Stay away! Unclean!' Well what reaction would you expect if you turned up in Middlesbrough on a Saturday night festooned in safety pins and swastikas, dragging along your girl with a dog lead and studded collar? I ask you. You'd hardly expect someone to come up to you and have a general chit chat about the weather, would you?

I bought myself a pint to steady the nerves and enjoyed listening to all the loud new music that was booming out from the DJ's speaker system while taking in my surroundings and waiting for the support act, Subway Sect, to come on. I thought they were awful. To me it was just a loud incoherent noise, and they went down like a lead balloon with most of the crowd.

The Clash were amazing. I'd never seen anything like it in my life. From the first drum beat of 'Janie Jones', I was drawn in hook, line and sinker. I also travelled to see them at Newcastle University but couldn't get in as I didn't have a student's union card. Plenty were dragged in through windows by the band though! I did see them at Leeds' Queens Hall though, but the most I remember of that gig is hitchhiking home with two lasses. Unfortunately, our truck driver was the Yorkshire Ripper (for definite, as I've never felt so intimidated in my life plus I recognised him when he was finally caught!).

NEWCASTLE UNIVERSITY
20 MAY 1977, NEWCASTLE-UPON-TYNE

PETER SMITH

This was the night that punk truly arrived in Newcastle, and the first time I saw The Clash. It was the first big punk gig in Newcastle, and it sold out well in advance. Most of the tickets had been sold to students through the student's union;

in fact, if I remember correctly you had to be a student to buy tickets, which was the source of some aggro and trouble on the night of the gig. Luckily, I was a student at Sunderland Poly and I used my union card to buy a couple of tickets for Marie and I.

When we arrived at the Union building on the night of the gig, the entrance was surrounded by a group of local punks who were trying to get in. There were a few scuffles between the doormen and the punks, who were angry because they couldn't get in to see 'their band' who (in their eyes) were playing for a group of middle-class students. In 1977, Newcastle University ballroom was in a smallish room up a flight of stairs, with the main bar being down on a lower level. The union building was a maze with several bars, a pool room, and several lounges. You could wander around the building and dip in and out of the gig in the main ballroom. There was a great sense of anticipation that night. The Northeast had missed out on the Sex Pistols *Anarchy* tour which had been booked to visit Newcastle City Hall and had been cancelled because of the controversy around the band. So, this was the first chance for local punks to see a 'big' punk band.

The place with packed, however the audience was largely students with a smattering of local punks who had somehow managed to buy tickets and were crammed around the stage upstairs. I sensed that these guys didn't really know much about punk but had decided that it was right for them. They were probably much more into the image, the concept of anarchy and rebellion, than they were into The Clash's music. The first Clash album had been released a few weeks before the gig, and the audience were there as much out of curiosity and because of reports that they had read in the *NME* and *Sounds* than as result of the music. I'd read reports that The Clash were *the* new punk rock band to out-punk (and out rock) the Pistols, so I had to see what these guys were like.

Support came from The Prefects (replacing The Jam, who had just left the tour), Subway Sect and The Slits. Marie and I made a point of making our way from the bar up to the ballroom to see each of the bands. The sound wasn't great for any of the support acts, who all seemed a bit amateur and ramshackle, but I guess that's what punk was about in those early heady days. There was a lot, and I mean lots, of spitting at the band. This was one of the first times I'd seen a crowd spit at the stage and it's difficult to imagine how prevalent the practise was in those days. The Clash were just streets ahead of the support acts. For their set there was lots of pogoing, but the spitting was relentless. Poor Joe Strummer was covered in spit. They looked great; just like their pictures on the cover of the first album. I'd heard some of the tracks from the first album, including new single 'White Riot', and loved Janie Jones and 'Police And Thieves', which were played a lot at punk gigs at venues like Middlesbrough Rock Garden in 1977 and 1978. The set was short, as were each of the songs, and consisted of tracks from the first album. The sound was a bit murky, but the atmosphere, the band's passion and the power of delivery made up for it.

We'd seen a few punk bands during 1976, including Sex Pistols at a small gig in a pub in Whitby, but this was the first sold out and wild punk gig that we had attended, and it was just great. It set me off going to lots of punk gigs over the next few years. Don Letts, who managed The Slits, was wandering around with a massive video camera, filming the event. The music between the bands was very heavy, loud dub and reggae, which was quite new to all of us. There were further scuffles around the entrance area throughout the night, with punks fighting with the guys on the door to get in, and there were a few fights inside the gig. As I had very long hair, so I could easily have been a target. I was always careful to avoid trouble, and always managed to do so.

The day after the gig Joe Strummer and Topper Headon were arrested, in true punk fashion, for stealing pillowcases from a hotel room in Newcastle and spent some time in the cells. Great memories of an era that now seems so long ago. Where did all the time go?

CITY HALL
21 MAY 1977, ST ALBANS

TIM COOPER

I saw them about a dozen times. I went to a few dates on the *White Riot* tour and later that one at the Rainbow (where all the seats got ripped out). At St Albans, between the support acts, Buzzcocks, Subway Sect and Slits, you could see out of a huge picture window upstairs by the bar loads of 'Teds' (Teddy Boys) converging on a kind of grass mound outside, swinging bike chains in readiness to attack us at the end. I legged it at the end to my own pathetic Honda 70 scooter with the key in my hand, hoping it would start first time, as they began chasing everyone.

The weird thing about the Teds is that their antagonism was a one-way street. There was no enmity on our side – to us they were just old blokes in fancy dress. When my mates and I went to see Bo Diddley in Southgate, in 1978, we had to get a couple of mates who were psychobillys to chaperone us, so we didn't get beaten up by all the Teds... even though we liked the same music.

At Chelmsford, just over a week later, 29 May, although I had my own fanzine (*Cliché*) and always got in free to gigs, I hadn't arranged anything, so I said I was on the guest list and when the guy got it and asked my name I said, 'I'll show you.' He turned it round and I spotted 'Johnny Rotten' on there and said I was him, safe in the knowledge John would get in anyway – if he was even there!

Then there was the Music Machine gig with Suicide and Coventry Automatics in July 1978. It was really depressing, with loads of skinheads in polo shirts and DMs who came for the would-be Specials and chucked (full) beer cans at Suicide. One hit Vega and he just walked over to Martin Rev with blood on his face and turned the keyboard up as high as it would go. Funny but The Clash had become a different beast by then, with the mainstream rock sound of the second album, and were attracting a different crowd – lots of football hooligans who had 'read' tabloid tales of violence at punk gigs and hoped for a scrap.

 MANDELA HALL, UNIVERSITY OF SUSSEX
25 MAY 1977, BRIGHTON

SIMON BAIN, AGE 15

My first connection with The Clash was on the *White Riot* tour in Brighton. It was one of those pivotal moments and the first band I got to see. Being relatively young, I couldn't get into clubs to see bands, but Sussex University was like a hall. Seeing them was a revelation to me, and that was it, I was off. I started stage crewing for bands. I would haul all the gear in at various venues and then haul all the gear out. I used to get paid to do that whilst I was still at school. I wasn't working directly for the band, just humping boxes. The bands would still have their stage crew, but in each venue there'd be a local crew who worked directly for the promoter. At Brighton Top Rank you had eight flights of stairs. The actual band crew wouldn't want to do any of that, they just wanted to look after the actual equipment once it's on stage. I think we got about £10 a day.

I ended up living in London because I connected with a t-shirt company called Fifth Column who were instrumental in those early days. They created all those iconic t-shirt designs that you see now from the early days. Robin Richards was the main designer. Some of their guys had come down to Brighton for the Bank Holiday, I bumped into them on the seafront. After helping them out of a spot which involved a clash between Teddy Boys and some football hooligans they invited me up to London.

Little did I know beforehand that these guys were seriously connected. They had a squat in Kentish Town on Castle Road, just around the corner from Camden Market, and used to do all the t-shirts for bands. There weren't any royalties to be paid or copyright. You could just make a t-shirt and sell them at

Portobello Market. The bands didn't care and would come along and ask for a few of theirs! Fifth Column would eventually end up printing t-shirts for bands for their concert tours.

I suddenly found myself right in the mainstream. We were going to gigs every single night, printing t-shirts all through the night and then selling them on the market. I also got a job working at Better Badges who used to make all the badges for concerts.

On one trip home to see my mum down in Brighton I bumped into a guy loading some sound equipment into the Polytechnic on his own. The students hadn't turned up to unload, so I gave him a hand. I think that may have been for Throbbing Gristle. The following week he contacted me back in London as he was doing Holly and the Italians at the Hope & Anchor and asked if I would help. From that, the band offered me a job as their roadie. I'd never touched a musical instrument in my life, but they said they'd teach me what to do… I ended up helping these guys out, them showing me how to handle guitars and all that kind of stuff, and then before I knew it, they had a hit called 'Tell That Girl To Shut Up'.

Next thing I know we were on tour with The Clash on the *16 Tons* tour, all the way around England. The Clash were my absolute favourite band!

Later, I was working for The Bodysnatchers who also went on tour with The Clash, in Europe. I knew the band from their previous tour and remember a gig in Paris. It was an amazing gig in a tent, the Hippodrome de Pantin, a huge venue holding a few thousand.

I bought The Clash a round of drinks after that, even though I had no money. A round of drinks in a French nightclub was an absolute fortune then! My whole week's wages gone, but it was cool. The Bodysnatchers turned into the Belle Stars, who then ended up supporting The Beat. The Beat offered me the opportunity to work with them, and then they ended up doing seven nights with The Clash at the Mogador Theatre in Paris!

Whilst I was on those shows, The Beat used to have t-shirts for sale. Bernie Rhodes came up to me asking about them and why the band did them. All this time The Clash had been touring but they'd never done any merchandise. Bernie was all about trying to be this cultural revolutionist but he overlooked the basic things. The band needed to earn some money. I remember saying, 'Get good quality t-shirts, good quality print, give value for money.' I think that, after that day, they started selling t-shirts. I'm not saying it was me, but you think about all those tours that they did where they never used to sell merchandise…

I became a regular face. I'd occasionally show up for rehearsals and sometimes help on stage too, doing the smoke machines and various other bits and pieces, fixing things every now and again…

DE MONTFORT HALL
28 MAY 1977, LEICESTER

GLENN WILLIAMS

Lance 'Butch' Clark was the kid in our year who was in the know about punk. He read the *NME* front to back every week and was the first to start wearing safety pins and ripped clothes. He looked like a punk as well.

We were never mates, but then punk rock came along, and we both saw the Pistols on the *Today* show in December 1976. I went to him for all my punk news as I was still more into heavy and prog rock, and it was him who told me the Sex Pistols were going to play at Leicester University one Friday night.

It never happened, so the first concert by a real punk band was to be The Clash at De Mont. I was going, so was Butch, and so were Andy 'Man' Haley and Andy Merriman. Both were also big Pistols fans.

We got to the De Mont in the afternoon and hung around the backstage door. Butch was messed up and dressed down and looked the part, something that could not be said for the other three of us. After an hour, a coach arrived and off stepped some punkish-looking people who we took to be the support bands (Buzzcocks and Subway Sect) followed by a few – it must be said – rather uncouth-looking women who later turned out to be the opening band, The Slits. They were followed by Joe Strummer, Topper Headon, Paul Simonon and Mick Jones, the latter of which belched at us with a grin.

Andy Merriman suggested that Butch looked like one of the band, and Andy Haley then urged him to follow the band in, which Butch did. The stage door closed behind him. We were quite stunned and expected the doors to open any minute and for Butch to come flying out. He didn't.

The three of us remaining bought tickets and went in. It was a great gig. Buzzcocks were probably the best and I doubt there were 300 people inside. We caught up with Butch, who told us that he hung around backstage after he got in, wondering what to do until one of the grey-haired De Mont staff asked if he was looking for something. Quick as a flash, Butch asked him where the bar was. 'Don't you know?' asked the geriatric.

'Course not. I haven't fackin' been 'ere before, 'ave I?' Butch said, after which he was left alone, chatting occasionally to the band members who no doubt wondered who the hell he was. Then he slipped into the audience as the doors opened. Walking into a gig as one of the band members. Sheer class, Butch.

CHANCELLOR HALL
29 MAY 1977, CHELMSFORD

STEVE PALMER
Four mates and I drove there. Queuing up outside, some local herberts were opposite trying to break a chain off a fence to attack us punks. They soon scarpered when the train arrived from London and a load of punks came round the corner.

RAG MARKET (CANCELLED)
17 JULY 1977, BIRMINGHAM

PAUL PANIC
My first gig was Slade in Birmingham Odeon in 1975, when I was 12. My parents dropped me off and picked me up afterwards, because none of my mates were into going to see music live. I used to listen to John Peel every night. When he was crossing over from the old stuff that he used to play into punk and new wave stuff, I would record it religiously. I didn't have that much money to spend, so I'd make lists voraciously of the records that I wanted.

I remember being on my Sunday paper round and seeing this little article on the front of *The Sunday Times* about this record that was due to be released called 'Anarchy In The UK' by the Sex Pistols. I thought it sounded amazing but the article talked about how it was a disgrace, blah-blah-blah. I went to a local music shop in Shirley, in Solihull, and tried to order this record. For a start, they said they'd never heard of it, and then they said it couldn't be ordered because it had been banned, and that really got me interested!

Birmingham had a famous punk club called Barbarella's. When I was about 16, we used to dress up in punk stuff and go there. We'd get in even though you had to be 18, and that's where I first started seeing bands, people like Suburban Studs and The Killjoys with Kevin Rowland, who later went on to Dexys.

One day I read that there was going to be a big punk festival at the Birmingham Rag Market, which was going to be headlined by The Clash, and with Subway Sect, Spizzenergi and a few other bands, including a band from France called Stinky Toys. The idea was that they'd take over the whole market and do this gig, but when it was publicised the vicar of the church in the Bull Ring put up some objections. I think it got cancelled on the morning of the gig. By this time The

Clash were already in Birmingham.

Bernie Rhodes was big friends with a local promoter in Birmingham called Dave Cork who ran a company called Midnight Music. He and Bernie used to work together, as far as I understand, and he had something to do with The Clash coming to Birmingham quite a lot. The Clash apparently went around Birmingham with the help of Dave and some contacts he had, got some equipment from a local heavy metal band and played an unannounced gig at Barbarella's that night.

I didn't go to that, but when they came back later that year, I went to the next gig at Barbarella's. Barbarella's was this tiny little club owned by a guy called Eddie Fewtrell, who used to run all the Birmingham clubs. It was hot and sweaty, a typical small gig type thing, but it was electric.

In those days there were no pretensions. I remember standing behind Captain Sensible in the café at one gig. The bands just used to mix with the audience before and after the gigs. It wasn't a star trip, it was like everybody was friends really, at least until a lot later on when it became a bit more elitist.

 VORTEX CLUB
16 AUGUST 1977, LONDON, UK

DARYL HUMPHREYS

On the evening of 16th August 1977, Mark P (AKA Mark Perry, founder of punk fanzine *Sniffin' Glue* and member of punk band Alternative TV) got up on the stage at the Vortex Club to announce the death of Elvis Presley. The response was not what he expected as the crowd went wild with jubilation, raucously celebrating the death of The King. Mark did his best to try and explain Elvis's legacy and his importance to music but he was shouted down. Looking back, it typified the punk attitude at a time when everything from before was being cancelled. The Clash had made this sentiment clear in their song '1977' when they said there was to be 'no more Elvis, Beatles or the Rolling Stones.' Looking back, it was a pretty extreme attitude to say the least but it's how people felt at the time.

That same evening, I got talking to Sebastian Conran who was living at his parent's house in Portland Square. Sebastian was working with The Clash at the time doing a variety of things. What I didn't know was that members of the band were also staying at the house and when we went there for a drink later, I was surprised to walk in on Paul Simonon practising bass in one of the rooms. We shared a few beers and had a good chat about the early gigs at The Roxy and what it was like doing the *White Riot* tour. We were both reggae fans and we swapped stories about how we got into the music and which bands we'd seen. Paul made a big impression in that he was very approachable with no airs and graces.

 'COMPLETE CONTROL'/'CITY OF THE DEAD' RELEASED
23 SEPTEMBER 1977

GARETH ASHTON

NO ELVIS, BEATLES OR THE ROLLING STONES. Ironic really, because The Clash, Sex Pistols, The Jam, Buzzcocks and The Damned became my generation's version of all three of them. Forget Year Zero and look to the future was, and still is, my mantra.

I was 13 years old, living in the sticks, armed only with my older sibling's record collection and a love of T. Rex, when I saw The Jam on the *Marc* show in 1977. Fuse lit.

A little late to the punk party perhaps, but it was a different world back then. Punk was my own Beatles, my personal Rolling Stones, and as musically and as culturally exciting as Elvis must have been in the beginning. But punk had an extra string to its bow: politics. Of all the bands to come out of the class of '76, The Clash were by far the most eloquent, demanding that you listen and listen good. They introduced me to reggae and taught me tolerance and intolerance in equal measure.

But none of those influences would have been ignited if it wasn't for the fact that they were also an excellent rock and roll group. 'Complete Control' and '(White Man) In Hammersmith Palais' are just two examples of my life's soundtrack.

Like all the best bands, they progressed from album to album, perplexing and vexing their fan base along the way. I remember we had discussions at school about how we thought that *London Calling* wasn't 'punk' enough and even incorporated disco into the eclectic mix of tracks. But it sold for £5 for a double album which was very punk. They repeated the act on *Sandinista!* a year later. They may have sold out to some people after signing to CBS, but now they were getting their own back. Biting the hand that fed them.

The Clash left more than a musical legacy. They influenced the rest of my life politically, furnishing me with an attitude of individuality and the open mindedness to seek out new musical genres. I feel so blessed to have caught them in the most informative years of my life, and they were such inspirational messengers.

RIP Joe, and thank you boys.

IAN MOSS

Were The Clash so stupid? They'd signed to CBS and now they were whinging about corporate interference. DJ John Peel, for one, was unimpressed. 'Surely, they must have realised CBS were not a foundation for the arts?' he opined. Still, at least the puppies were showing their teeth and beginning to growl at their masters, rather than rolling over to have their tummies tickled. Megalomaniac manager Bernie Rhodes was also attacked in the song; indeed, he gave the track its title, after calling a band meeting to announce, to the great astonishment of Strummer and Co, that he wanted 'Complete Control'.

On the musical front, this was the first single that genius drummer Topper Headon played on, and he provided a solidity they had previously lacked. The overall sound here is much more powerful than on their first recordings, and Joe Strummer sounds magisterially commanding as he expresses his indignation at the position the band were in.

One might be tempted to thank Lee Perry for this, since he receives the nominal production credit; but the finished product that the great Jamaican provided was far too radical for The Clash. So they tampered with his mixes and pushed the guitars up in trad-rock style, eliminating the heavy, echoing bass in favour of a sound that – ironically, due to the subject matter of the song – would be much more acceptable to the men in suits at CBS.

MICHAEL MULLIGAN

The Clash could be pigeonholed by the expression, 'Q. What are you rebelling against? A. Well, what have you got?' No target was off limits – the wealthy, the media, the church, other punk and pop acts, and – come September 1977 – their major label record company, an arrangement that had already been lambasted by *Sniffin' Glue* founder Mark Perry, with his 'big quote': 'Punk died the day The Clash signed to CBS.'

When CBS opted for 'Remote Control' as the follow-up to the band's March debut 'White Riot' (the band reportedly wanted 'Janie Jones'), it was enough of an excuse for Joe and Mick to 'stick it to the man', and they did it with three minutes and fifteen seconds of self-eulogising, anthemic, passionate lyrics, driving melodies (plural) and elevated musicianship, at a time when dumbing it down was all the rage (be careful what you wish for, kids – we got Sham 69).

It was a statement that – unlike some of their peers – the band were not afraid to align themselves with punk. The line, 'This is your punk rocker' sits on a list with 'punk rocker in the UK' from '(White Man) In Hammersmith Palais', 'When some punk sees some rock-olla' from 'Last Gang In Town', and more obviously 'All The Young Punks' on *Give 'Em Enough Rope*, and 'Dirty Punk' on *Cut The Crap*.

With the wonderful 'You're my guitar hero' they began a run of memorable ad-libs/non-sequiturs that would crop up in songs like 'Last Gang In Town' ('Come on, yeah, Kentucky Fried Chicken'), and 'The Magnificent Seven' ('News Flash, Vacuum cleaner sucks up budgie', and many more...).

John Peel supposedly rolled a proverbial eye at the song's sentiments, but it didn't stop him playing it, nor his listeners championing it – it ranked ninth on his Festive 50 for 1977 (behind Neil Young's 'Like A Hurricane'), rising to No. 2 the following year, with only 'Anarchy In The UK' by the Sex Pistols ahead of it. It even entered the UK Top 40 at No. 28, where it sat between Bob Marley and The Wailers with 'Waiting In Vain', and George Benson with 'The Greatest Love Of All'.

Perhaps having nailed my own colours to the punk mast (in a restrained, middle class, teenage schoolboy way) I identified with the lines, 'They're dirty, they're filthy, they ain't gonna last.' But The Clash did last, and this song excites the older but not much wiser me almost as much today as it did 40 plus years ago.

NEIL MARSDEN

I was 14 when I first heard 'White Riot' and 'Complete Control' at the local youth disco. We pogoed frantically to them and also to Buzzcocks, Sex Pistols and later Joy Division. This led me and my mates to form our first bands. The first two singles I bought were The Clash's 'Complete Control' and The Adverts 'Gary Gilmores Eyes.' A pair of classics from my local Discount Records shop in Sale.

EUROPEAN TOUR 1977

PARADISO
26 SEPTEMBER 1977, AMSTERDAM, NETHERLANDS

LUUK VERSLUIJS

In 1976 and 1977 I was reading the *NME*, the *Melody Maker* and *Sounds*, which were available in the Netherlands, and I listened to the *John Peel Show*. That's how I got acquainted with the punk rock and new wave movements from the UK and the USA.

The main venue in 1977 in the Netherlands was the Paradiso in Amsterdam. I lived in Amsterdam as a student and visited the Paradiso regularly. The first punk concert in Paradiso was the Sex Pistols in January 1977 with support acts Johnny Thunders and The Heartbreakers and The Vibrators. I was there, but the show was not a big success. There were only about 300 people in the 1,500-capacity venue and the audience response was lukewarm.

This had all changed by the time The Clash arrived at the Paradiso in September. This was the second show by The Clash in Amsterdam. The first had been in a small venue in May 1977 and was a private gig for a music magazine. I had heard of this show and thought it was odd that a music magazine (*Muziekkrant Oor*) could book The Clash for a private gig for its employees.

Since the Sex Pistols show, I had seen many punk and new wave bands at the Paradiso, including The Police, The Damned, The Stranglers, The Boys, Ramones, Talking Heads, Television, Blondie, Tom Petty and The Heartbreakers, The Saints, Mink Deville and Jonathan Richman and The Modern Lovers. But I attended these shows alone, as no friends of mine were into punk or new wave.

But numbers attending the Paradiso were growing and audiences became more and more enthusiastic. For The Clash (the first of four times I saw them), the venue was almost sold out. Support acts were the Dutch punk band The Flyin' Spiderz and Siouxsie and The Banshees. Siouxsie and The Banshees used The Clash's backline and after a few songs, their bass player blew up Paul Simonon's bass amp. It took 20 minutes to fix or replace the amplifier, after which Siouxsie and The Banshees continued their set.

The Clash were fast and furious. The audience went wild. It was the best audience in the Paradiso at that point. During the last song of the set, members of the audience climbed onto the stage and sang along with the band. They weren't thrown off. It was a memorable end to a great show.

⭐ SALLE DES FÍTES DE TINQUEUX
30 SEPTEMBER 1977, REIMS, FRANCE

MICHEL JOLYOT

I was a student in Reims, and I was going to many concerts, as many as concerts as I could. There were supposed to be two concerts, one with The Clash and the day after The Damned, but they split the day before in Lyon, so only The Clash came.

The room where it was held was split in two and they used only used half a room for the gig. There were only about 150 people there. We didn't know much about The Clash in 1977. We knew it was punk, but that's all.

It was in this little room in the suburbs, a room where generally there were never any other concerts. I was more of what we used to call in France 'baba cool', meaning still a little bit hippy, even though it was in 1977. I was listening to a different kind of music, especially Gong, I was much more inspired by their founder Daevid Allen and Genesis. The ticket cost 22 francs which is

Michel Jolyot's ticket for The Clash in Reims

about three Euros.

The first act was The Lou's, who were a group of girls from France. I went there with a Canadian from Quebec; he was French speaking and had just come back from India. Imagine the shock for anybody coming from India seeing The Clash for the first time in 1977! I was shocked too. I must confess we left before the end, because it was very noisy, very violent and very hard to listen to. There were only one or two spotlights and there was a big photo at the back with something like policemen running on it. Joe Strummer had some Coca-Cola, and he poured it on the audience.

GET OUT OF CONTROL TOUR

ULSTER HALL
20 OCTOBER 1977, BELFAST (CANCELLED)

BRIAN YOUNG

Mid-1976. I'm sweet 16 and like every other hot-blooded, crazy mixed-up teenager I'm going quietly off my rocker, torn apart by raging hormones while trying to make some sense out of the competing pressures and demands of normal everyday life – school, friends, family, drink, drugs and the opposite sex. Unlike others of the same age, I'm stuck here in Belfast searching for a way out of the daily mayhem of 'the troubles' in an abnormal society mired in the past and riddled with bigotry, sectarianism and prejudice. For me music provides that escape.

'Jeepster' was the first record I bought. Marc Bolan turned me on to both seventies glam rock and fifties rock 'n' roll. Via Bowie, Lou Reed and Iggy Pop, I'd become obsessed with the New York Dolls – even trying to start a fan club with another oddball, one Steven Morrissey in Manchester. I'd travelled to see T. Rex play in the Isle of Man in '75 with my delinquent chums and even got to meet the band. Marc Bolan handed me a signed T. Rex songbook and I returned home vowing to follow in his footsteps. By the time I'd gotten to see David Bowie at Wembley in May '76, I'd formed a band with my pals. That band was RUDI and we pretty much singlehandedly kickstarted punk in these parts – and if anywhere was primed for and needed punk rock, it was Belfast.

The weekly music papers were our lifeline and kept us up on what was hip and happening. As a result, I'd picked up a US import copy of the Ramones debut album in April '76 when it first hit the racks and it changed everything. I remember devouring all the early punk articles – like *Sounds* 'A-Z of Punk' in July '76, back when there were only about three modern punk combos. They had to include sixties bands like ? and the Mysterians to pad out the feature. (In RUDI we played '96 Tears' and I still love the song.)

Alongside the Ramones, in the early days it was largely American acts like Tuff Darts, the Modern Lovers, Mink Deville, Television and (of course) my favourites, The Heartbreakers, who were making the running and dominating the column inches. The first UK bands I recall reading about were The Sex Pistols and The Damned. The Clash were very much seen as late comers. I knew Strummer had been in pub rockers the 101ers, which I'd seen sprayed under the Westway in May '76 as the coach we were on drove into London en route to see the Thin White Duke at Wembley.

And I also remember the *Sounds* write up of a Clash press junket in Rehearsal Rehearsals where Mick Jones looked more like Keith Richards than Keith did! But stuck here in Belfast, I couldn't see any of the bands I was reading about. And as none had records out yet, I couldn't hear them either! John Peel tried his best but in 1976 punk vinyl was thin on the ground. In that pre-internet age, it was incredibly frustrating to read all about the 100 Club Punk Festival but not to be able to see or hear any of the bands who played it.

December '76 saw the ill-fated *Anarchy* tour decimated following the Grundy debacle. I'd have crawled over broken glass to have seen the Pistols, Damned, Clash and Heartbreakers in action. As reports filtered back, the Pistols may have snagged the column inches but everyone I spoke to confirmed that onstage The Heartbreakers wiped the floor with the competition every time. I still have a ticket for the Manchester *Anarchy* tour date Morrissey sent me with 'souvenir?' scribbled hastily across the bottom.

I was finally able to hear what all the fuss was about after picking up copies of the first ever UK punk bootleg albums – The Clash's *Take It Or Leave It* and The Pistols' *The Good Time Music Of* from a local bootlegger here who advertised in *Sounds*. Remember those awful, oversized sleeves that had pictures of The Worst and their mates on the front? Rumour had it that the manager of either the Buzzcocks or Slaughter And The Dogs was behind this dodgy enterprise.

This was my very first taste of The Clash and I was very impressed. Nevertheless, I was kind of suspicious of The Clash at first. For sure, Paul Simonon always was the walking epitome of cool – and Mick Jones was clearly from the Richards/Thunders school of rock 'n' roll, which was fine by me – but Joe Strummer just didn't ring true. I got the impression he was trying too hard. He looked decidedly uncomfortable in his spiffy new punk threads and brand-new bleached crop, obviously dumbing down and trying to act hard, even talking absolute bollocks about stabbing people in some early interviews! In hindsight, I reckon he was trying to overcompensate for the fact that he'd been a well-known pub rocker in the 101ers and was now slated by the press for having been a public schoolboy. Like so many feted UK punksters, he too was obviously much older than he claimed and had been round the block several times already. There was never any mention of Terry Chimes either, which I found strange.

Regardless, I snapped up 'White Riot' the day it came out in a shop on the Albertbridge Road – but I gotta fess up that it certainly didn't knock me for six the way 'Anarchy' or 'Neat Neat Neat' did. ('New Rose' was always much too close to the 'Jetboy' riff for me…) and I really didn't (and still don't) like the ridiculous 'No Elvis, Beatles or Rolling Stones' of flip side '1977' – a tuneless rant of a song with gormless lyrics. I also loathed Strummer's 'Chuck Berry is Dead' shirt as I learned guitar playing along to a Chuck Berry hits album, and without Mr Berry's efforts rock 'n' roll as we know it would simply not exist.

Weirdly, I much preferred follow up 45 'Remote Control' to 'White Riot', and never understood why the band seemed so annoyed at its release. What really swayed me though was the first Clash album. When the Pistols' LP finally hit the racks, it sounded plodding and over produced – like just another mainstream rock band. Yaaawn! I much prefer the *Spunk* recordings. The Damned's debut was a full-on energy rush for sure – but where could they go next?

In contrast, *The Clash* was a proper album… with proper songs! I still thought the group looked somewhat gawky on the front cover – and their image was still scrappy and all over the place – but they had such killer songs; real catchy tunes with melodies and singalong choruses. From the first blast of 'Janie Jones' I was hooked! On top of the strength of the material, Mick Jones's inspired arrangements, clever guitar parts and trademark 'woo… oo… ah' backing vocals lifted them into another dimension. Lyrically too they were writing about real things we could relate to – and did. I played the album to death and many a night we staggered drunkenly home from our usual watering hole, the notorious East Belfast dive the Glenmachan, bellowing 'Garageland' at the tops of our voices… Heaven help the neighbours! *The Clash* remains my favourite album by any UK punk combo to this day.

One reason I preferred The Clash to the Pistols or Damned was that I always was a sucker for that twin frontman attack… Johansen/Thunders, Jagger/Richards and now Strummer/Jones… It was no accident that in RUDI we had a similar line-up, with both Ronnie Matthews and I sharing lead vocals.

It soon became apparent that The Clash were coming on in leaps and bounds

– especially in comparison to their safety-pinned contemporaries who shot their load and had nothing to follow it up with. They began to dress better too, looking much more like a proper band with their own image and identity – Joe Strummer was much more assured and comfortable in his role. Once Topper Headon joined on drums everything fell into place – and his inventive and assured drumming propelled them to new heights. 'Complete Control' was the first record he played on and still sounds as anthemic and awe inspiring today as the day I first heard it. It's possibly my favourite Clash song ever.

Ironically, for a band who preached revolution at every turn, they were probably the most old-fashioned and traditional punk combo musically – and that's no doubt why they appealed to me so much! In (the still hugely under rated) Mick Jones they had a tunesmith second to none and his guitar playing remains unrivalled for inventiveness and melody. I sat up and took note – and I wasn't the only one.

And when we heard that our favourite UK punk combo was to play the Ulster Hall here in Belfast on October 27th, 1977, we couldn't wait...

Arriving early in the day, we sat outside the Ulster Hall knocking back our usual carry out of Olde English cider and Mundies wine. All our usual mates were there, but as literally hundreds of fledgling punky wavers we'd never seen before started to appear, many from much further afield, it slowly dawned on me just how big punk was becoming here in Belfast.

The concert had been arranged by the Ents Team from Jordanstown Polytechnic and as far as I know they had never staged a gig as big as this before – nor had they staged any previous punk gigs. The Clash were big news and the local media turned up to see this new punk rock phenomena for themselves. Disappointingly, much of the local media coverage of the event replicated the shock horror 'must we fling this filth at our pop kids' approach typical of the scummy UK tabloids – spending more column inches poking fun at these ridiculously dressed kids with funny haircuts and gleefully poking fun at the fact that one resourceful punkette was using a kettle for a handbag! (Sheer genius!)... So much for the local press!

> **I ALWAYS WAS A SUCKER FOR THAT TWIN FRONTMAN ATTACK...**
>
> **BRIAN YOUNG**

Meantime, at the Ulster Hall everything was going fine and there was a palpable air of excitement and anticipation amongst the gathered throng. The Clash had apparently set their gear up and sound checked, when word arrived that either the insurance cover for the gig had been cancelled or (as was rumoured later) the promoters never had proper insurance in place and couldn't arrange any at the last minute due to outstanding claims from the damage caused at The Clash's recent Rainbow gig, when hundreds of chairs were trashed.

There was also talk that Belfast City Council, who owned the Ulster Hall, didn't want a nasty punk rock band to sully the walls of their famous venue and had withdrawn permission for the gig to take place – though I'm not sure how much truth there is in that.

For whatever reason, the gig was cancelled at the very last minute, leaving hundreds of disgruntled teens, many of whom had downed a few alcoholic beverages, royally pissed off and unwilling to disperse from outside the venue. On cue, the cops arrived in Land Rovers to clear away the hundreds of angry punks. Some folk sat down in the road and refused to budge, and others threw a few beer cans – tame stuff compared to a 'proper' Belfast riot. Regardless, more used to dealing with hardened rioters than garishly dressed teens, the cops simply went into their normal heavy handed 'riot' mode and started laying into people.

My wee brother had a Kodak camera with him and took some snaps of the cops beating up some kid with their truncheons. The cops spotted his camera, pulled him into the back of a Land Rover and wouldn't let him out until they had ripped the film out of the camera. Way over the top for some kids who just wanted to see their favourite band! There were a couple of arrests too, before most people reluctantly dispersed. Many of us rushed round to the swanky Europa hotel, where the Clash were staying and where Joe Strummer came out to remonstrate with the angry fans, many of whom blamed the band for not playing.

Eamonn McCann, the Ents manager for Queens University then appeared and apparently tried to get the gig rescheduled to one of the venues within Queens University Students Union – so we all then raced excitedly up to Queens. For whatever reason the band weren't permitted to play there either, returning to the Europa.

Next day, of course, the local media whipped up the usual punk 'shock horror' stories and showed brief interviews with Joe Strummer. Even then, no one really seemed to know why the gig had been cancelled and the band left for Dublin where they were booked to play in the prestigious Trinity College. Of course, that gig took place without a hitch!

In hindsight, I think the reason people remember that event so much is that it was the first time that we began to realise just how popular punk was becoming here. We were now all part of something that was big and getting bigger by the day – and was now making front page news locally and nationally. The very fact too that the gig had been cancelled combined with the brutal behaviour of the RUC both outraged and kind of united folk in an 'us against them' situation. It acted as a catalyst for the local scene, galvanising many people who were there into action. For example, in RUDI we straightaway wrote the song 'Cops' as a pure gut reaction to the events of that night. It started off with the well-known Belfast street chant 'S! S! R! U!C!' with a chorus of 'we hate the cops!' No beating about the bush there, bub! – and it (rightly) became the first Belfast punk anthem!

The 'Incredibly Boring Band' changed their name to Protex (Blue) and came up with their own song 'Black Riot' on the same subject. Even Jake Burns from still long-haired, K-Tel, wannabe punks Stiff Little Fingers was interviewed on local radio alongside other frustrated punters after the no show. Ironically the week before the aborted Clash gig, the new line up of Dr Feelgood with Gypie Mayo had played to a packed Ulster Hall in front of many of the same audience that turned up to see the Clash without any trouble or insurance hassles… That concert went off without a hitch! (It was a different promoter – who doubtless had arranged the necessary insurance cover.) As a postscript of sorts, the Polytech team had booked the Stranglers to play the Ulster Hall a week later. After the furore over the Clash gig, this too was cancelled…though the band did get to play Coleraine Polytech, and that gig went off without any trouble too. You couldn't make this stuff up!

I did see The Clash on the night of the aborted gig – but didn't get to chat to them properly, face to face, until the next day. One of my best mates, Wee Gordy Owens, managed to sneak into the Europa and stayed in Joe's room. Gordy was, and is, a diehard Clash fan and used to ring up Rehearsal Rehearsals almost every day to talk to the band – or, often, Johnny Green, for an update on their current activities.

Gordy rang me first thing the next morning, told me he'd stayed in Joe's room and urged me to get down to the Europa right away if

> **NO ONE KNEW WHY THE GIG HAD BEEN CANCELLED…**
>
> BRIAN YOUNG

I wanted to meet the band as they were all about to come down for breakfast. I raced down, clutching all my Clash record sleeves as well as the 101ers Chiswick picture sleeve. I got to meet first Joe and then Mick. Both were very friendly and approachable. Joe autographed all my sleeves and then told me to get Mick to sign them, insisting the 101ers picture sleeve was slipped in amongst the Clash ones. When Mick was signing them, he reached the 101ers sleeve and looked at it with absolute disdain, exclaiming 'that's one of his', and put it deliberately to one side. Joe was in stitches! I think he was kind of flattered that someone had bought the 101ers 45! (It's still a killer 45 by my reckoning!)

I can't remember much of what we chatted about, but they did seem distressed and disappointed at not getting to play and were also genuinely interested in what was happening in Belfast and how people coped with the day-to-day hassle of normal life under difficult circumstances. They were keen to find out what the local punk scene was like too. They certainly didn't act much like big time rock stars – unlike almost every other English punk rock notable I was to encounter in later days…

As a footnote, like so many NI punk rockers, Gordy moved to London for a couple of years in the early 80s…and Joe Strummer always put him on the guest list! (If you've seen the *Good Vibrations* film – the character in it called 'Fangs' who drags Terri down to see RUDI play is based on Wee Gordy – Fangs was one of his nicknames due to his dilapidated dental work.) Gordy and I are still good mates, and he still worships The Clash!

What impressed me then, and still does to this day, was that at least The Clash had made the effort to come and play here – which no other big punk outfits had done. That meant a lot to me then and still does now. Personally, I was prepared to give them the benefit of the doubt – and better still, they did keep their promise to return to play here as soon as possible, at Queens University on 17 December 1977.

STUART CLARK, *HOT PRESS*

Joe Strummer's first visit to Belfast was in 1978 when the City Council, God bless 'em, forced the eleventh hour cancellation of The Clash's Ulster Hall gig. The riot that resulted from the RUC's heavy-handed treatment of the punks outside remains a part of local rock 'n' roll folklore, and led to them being given the benefit of the doubt when they posed for pictures in front of the Long Kesh cages. People were altogether less forgiving when a couple of months later their hero took to wearing an H-Block t-shirt. Forget the cause, there was huge resentment over The Troubles being co-opted into The Clash's guerrilla chic. This is our everyday reality, the reasoning went, not the latest Vivienne Westwood creation.

'Hey man, look it!' Strummer protests. 'If I go to Spain, I'm going to stand in front of an El Greco hamburger stand. If I go to Belfast, I'm going to stand in front of one of those cages, cos to me it's all about showing people what's going on. You think everybody in the world knows what's going on in Belfast? No, they don't. We didn't construct that cage on the corner or have it flown in. We just fucking walked up to it and stood there. This is reality, let's have it out. No way, in 1978, would that picture have appeared on the front of *The Daily Telegraph*. Y'know, 'We can't be showing that to the people of Tiddlesborough or Braintree, Essex.' I had no trouble with that at all. If we were in Sardinia now, I'd get out and stand in front of the Sardinian Office of Sardines, or whatever.'

The word in Derry is that The Clash subsequently wouldn't play there because they'd received Loyalist death threats. 'C'mon, we're poseurs anyway,' says Strummer, neatly side-stepping the question. 'We're rock 'n' rollers. We get on stage. Don't think that we're shrinking violets or intellectuals. We're all hair gel missionaries.'

Now you know where those situationist slogans like 'Sten Guns In Knightsbridge' came from! Later, when a good deal more booze and spliff has been consumed, Joe admits that the picture and t-shirt furore 'taught me a lot about shutting up, really. If you don't know all the details, shut up. This is a conflict that's been going on for over 700 years, and we've only been alive for a microscopic amount of that time. The one thing I would like to say in relation to Northern Ireland, is that whatever we did there was always well-intentioned. I know I'm contradicting myself all over the shop, but I never saw our actions as being exploitative.'

APOLLO THEATRE
25 OCTOBER 1977, GLASGOW

RON WILLIAMSON

I was brought up in a place called Helensburgh, an hour on the train from Glasgow. The only record shops we had were not the sort who broke new music trends, so we had to get all our records in various shops in the city. A mate brought a copy of The Clash's 'Remote Control', who I hadn't heard at this point. I had a listen and liked it but wanted to hear more. The next week I went to Glasgow and was in Listen, a brilliant record shop, where I bought the debut album. When I got home, I put it on the turntable and was blown away by it, consequently playing it to death.

The first time I saw The Clash was at the Glasgow Apollo, one of the best gigs I have ever been to. Luckily, they came back in December 1977 so off I went to see them again, another totally amazing experience. Going to see The Clash was not just a gig, it was an event.

I moved to London in October 1978, having now seen the Clash four times in a year. When I arrived in my new flat in Harlesden, London, one of my flat mates asked, 'Do you fancy seeing The Clash? They're playing tomorrow at The Roxy.' We went to the Roxy the next morning and got tickets. Again, what a performance. By 1982, I'd seen them a further five times. Getting into The Clash was a life-changing experience.

After they broke up, I was able to see Joe Strummer perform at Glastonbury Festival, where I also saw Big Audio Dynamite with Mick Jones, and then Gorillaz with Mick Jones and Paul Simonon.

When Joe died, it felt like the end of an era. I lived in Somerset by then, quite close to Glastonbury, and was able to go to the festival 19 times. The one band I would have loved to see headline the Pyramid stage was The Clash. Alas, it was never to be.

DONALD HAMILTON

I first saw The Clash in 1977 when they first played the legendary Glasgow Apollo, and it remains the most awe-inspiring gig of my life.

Hearing 'Anarchy In The UK at the end of 1976 had turned my view of music around completely, and when I heard 'White Riot' and then The Clash album, I knew that something seismic was happening. I listened to it almost non-stop for months, and even now, hearing the drums at the beginning of 'Janie Jones' gives me goosebumps.

As the support band's kit was cleared off the stage and the Clash backdrops of the police photo from the back of the first album and a German bomber appeared, the atmosphere was electric. Then the muffled dub reggae that had been blasting over the PA stopped and it was time for The Clash. I was beside myself with excitement. I thought I knew what to expect as the band ran on stage.

As Strummer came up to the mic, I was waiting for the traditional, 'Hello Glasgow, we're The Clash, this song's called....'. Instead he screamed 'London's Burning' and the band exploded into a riot of movement, colour and noise. I had never experienced anything like it, and probably haven't since, except at my second Clash gig (but I knew what to expect then). The place just went mental with arms, legs and bodies flying everywhere.

My memories of the gig itself are just a jumble – Strummer's left leg pumping like mad, his arm thrashing away at his Telecaster, Jones and Simonon racing back and forward across the stage, their guitar leads getting tangled, the roadies running on trying to untangle them, Simonon hunched over his Rickenbacker looking both cool and menacing, Jones a blur of movement as he ran and leapt all over the stage, Strummer putting every ounce of passion into every number, Topper pounding the drums like his life depended on it, little or no chit chat between numbers – just straight from one into the next. Everything fast and furious. 'Police And Thieves' at breakneck speed. The place going even more mental to 'White Riot'. 'What's My Name' with an intensity that turned an okay album track into a piece of musical brilliance…

I went on to see them many more times at the Apollo, including the 'Closing down the Apollo' gig in 1978, which was just as manic but with violence erupting everywhere, as the bouncers and the punks tried to settle old scores, all as captured in Rude Boy. I clearly remember when Strummer stepped in with the call to the bouncers 'simmer down, control your temper…' just before they went straight into 'White Riot' and everything kicked off again with double the intensity.

I truly believe that these early gigs were the finest experience you could have of The Clash live – the power, the intensity and the rawness – and I'm glad I saw them like that. Don't get me wrong, the later gigs were great, but a lot of the edginess and the sense of danger lurking just around the corner had gone.

CLOUDS
26 OCTOBER 1977, EDINBURGH

ROADENT

I stopped working with them when we were on tour. I can't remember what tour it was, the one with Richard Hell on it. Me and Richard had been getting on well since the gig at Edinburgh Clouds Club. None of the bands had sponsorship or anything in those days so I was going out to do a shopping run for strings, picks, sticks, skins, all those sorts of things. I'd asked Richard Hell's people as well, asking if they wanted me to get anything while I was out. When I got back, Mick was like, 'Have you got me strings? Have you got me strings? I suppose you've got Richard Hell all this stuff.' That was it, just Mick Jones. Just him as a person. That's when I came up with a famous quote, 'You need a valet, not a roadie.'

I went to Bernie and asked for my train fare back to London. I went to Malcolm the next day and asked if he needed someone to work for him? I moved from Rehearsal Rehearsals to 6 Denmark Street. You too can stay there now, with the rooms costing a few hundred quid a night!

I was friends with Joe and Paul thereafter and I've reconciled with Mick as well. I became a journeyman sound engineer, and I did do a tour with The Clash later. I remember the people from the PA company saying, 'You know we've got this tour with The Clash,' and asking would I do it? They knew about the history between me and them, but I was quite happy to do it and we got on, up to a point.

I called Joe 'Woody' which he took great umbrage at, and Topper and Paul had to pull us apart because Joe took a swing at me. The next day Joe was sore. He came in and said, 'I must have really clocked you, cause my hand's so swollen I can't hardly hold a pick.' It was soon forgotten.

Many, many years later, we I bumped into Mick in Notting Hill, and we discussed the possibility of a Clash reunion and saying they would have to take a leaf out of the Pistols book and say you're just doing it for the money. I've seen Mick on a few occasions since, and had a few drinks. I did bump into Joe occasionally up until his sad demise. We were good friends; everybody was very close at that beginning. I didn't actively maintain contact, but whenever we saw each other, that thing, you know, kicked in again.

LEEDS UNIVERSITY
27 OCTOBER 1977, LEEDS

GARY LONGDEN

The Clash have now assumed legendary status from the punk era. They were a remarkable band. Some of the myths surrounding them are at odds with reality. Many of their achievements are often under-appreciated.

I saw them first at Leeds University in 1977 on the *Out Of Control* tour. They were supported by The Lou's, who were terrible, and Richard Hell and the Voidoids, who were (very) good (by comparison) with a great rabble rouser in 'Blank Generation'. The gig was a 2,000 sell out with a suspiciously high guest list inflating the figure further. It was dangerously packed.

The Lous came on at 7.45pm and were canned off at around 8.10pm, a mercy killing. Richard Hell appeared at 8.30pm and blazed, impressively, through to 9pm leaving everyone wanting more. Then we waited and waited. The crowd became more impatient, surges became more threatening, fights first broke out amongst the fans and then frustration became focussed on the empty stage. A few tried to clamber onto the stage. Nervous bouncers repelled them, punches were exchanged, the fans came off worst, and a terrace roar arose, combined with an almighty surge. Dozens began to scale the barriers, fighting the bouncers back who were unsure whether they should flee or protect the equipment. At that precise moment, the house lights went down, the stage lights came on, and The Clash appeared to 'London's Burning'. Cynical. Stage managed. Magnificent.

It was a visceral, muscular, loud, performance, but it was not musically accomplished. It was like watching an 800m runner sprinting the first 100m. After that there was nowhere to go. Even 'Police And Thieves', which in theory should have provided band and audience with a breather, was played twice as fast as the recorded version.

Contemporaneous performances by the Buzzcocks, Jam, Stranglers and The Boomtown Rats were far better musically, and more enjoyable gigs, even if they lacked the outlaw chic of The Clash.

 NEWCASTLE POLYTECHNIC
28 OCTOBER 1977, NEWCASTLE-UPON-TYNE

PETER METCALFE

This was the gig where some idiot at the front of the crowd grabbed hold of Mick's guitar (a much-loved Les Paul Junior), and the neck smashed. Until then it had been great, but Mick stormed off when this happened and he was obviously mega pissed off. The thing I remember most is that Joe and the rest of the band carried on to the end of the song but didn't really know what to do and kept looking at each other.

PETER SMITH

In October 1977, The Clash returned to Newcastle. There was violence and fighting at the gig which took place at the Students' Union. Being a weekend gig meant it was a party night for the students. Admission was 'students only' which was a source of anger and in direct contravention of The Clash's tour policy which guaranteed access to non-college students. Richard Hell had a firework thrown in his face at the gig, which took place a few days before Bonfire Night. These were crazy nights of excitement with excellent rock music despite the violence and clashes between rival gangs.

 APOLLO THEATRE
29 OCTOBER 1977, MANCHESTER

AK MCALLISTER

The first thing I remember about this Apollo gig is Richard Hell bouncing his bass from the stage right down into the orchestra pit and the thing coming back so quickly, like an Exocet land-to-air missile, and comically almost knocking him over and out. This may well have been a regular trick of his, but it felt spontaneous and genuine.

Musically, The Clash were much tighter than the Electric Circus gig. Brilliant drumming from Topper Headon was allowing the others more interaction and freedom. Years later, Topper talked about how Paul's playing of simple bass lines allowed him to be freer on the drums and really be able to add more intricate and interesting layers. They were getting to know each other now. They were getting better at their instruments and their songs. This was an outstanding set, one of the best I saw.

A PEOPLE'S HISTORY OF THE CLASH

DAVID LANGFIELD
Supported by Richard Hell and the Voidoids, by October The Clash were sounding more like the band we now know. They were fantastic live. Loads of fans got in by climbing up the drainpipe and into the gents' toilets and then onto the first balcony. By the following week, the staff had put black grease on them! The touts selling badges outside were doing a roaring trade.

MARTIN RYAN
The Clash's *Out Of Control* tour arrived in Manchester at the Apollo Theatre. Like the Electric Circus and the universities, the Apollo was situated a drive or a bus ride away from the city centre and, despite its location in the satellite district of Ardwick, the all-seater Apollo was set to depose the Free Trade Hall as Manchester's calling point on UK tours.

The Clash had much to prove this Saturday night. 'Out Of Control' was a reference to their recent 'Complete Control' single, a riposte to their record label for lifting 'Remote Control' as a single from the debut album. As Mark Smith wryly observed, the punch line to the whole episode was that the single was released on CBS. A more crucial issue was the £2.50 ticket price, which represented a 60 per cent increase on the £1.50 charged at the Electric Circus back in May.

Before a note was played it was clear the cavernous Apollo was never going to match the condensed atmosphere created within the Electric Circus. There was none of the usual interaction and swapping of notes with the regulars. We were in a large auditorium watching a show on a distant stage. The surge from the seats that greeted the opening band quickly receded when it was noticed that the act on stage was not Richard Hell and the Voidoids, but a group of females. The Lou's were a French all-girl group who Mick Jones apparently rated highly and who made all the right noises. They were politely applauded, but this was a night when the audience had bigger fish to fry.

What exactly the issue with the sound was during Richard Hell's first attempt to play was unclear but his tetchy response in throwing his guitar aside and storming off prompted a chorus of 'I'm So Bored With the USA'. In an act of diplomacy to the American guests, or maybe a jokey slight on the audience's xenophobia, Joe Strummer would later introduce the same song as 'I'm So Bored With The UK'.

The Voidoids ultimately returned to complete their set with Hell offering an overly courteous 'thank you' after each number, but the damage had been done long before they closed with a rendition of The Stooges 'I Wanna Be Your Dog', complete with dog howling backing vocals.

The way was clear for The Clash to make a further conquest. Whether the excitement generated by the music justified the level of exuberance that saw rows of seats smashed was doubtful but, in an act that mimicked the scenario when The Clash played the Rainbow on the *White Riot* tour, the front rows of seats were forcibly ripped from their anchors. Still playing the insurgent, Strummer advised to pass the seats forward and out of the way. There was little to fault The Clash for within their set, although Mick Jones and Paul Simonon employing the big stage to strike guitar hero poses only compounded the shattered myth that the band were now force-feeding music that had been so unaffectedly vibrant the last time around. There was no air of bewilderment outside after the gig.

The Apollo is situated on a main bus route by the Ardwick roundabout, and, in the first real act of camaraderie, the crowd made their way to whatever mode of transport would ferry them home.

TONY HOLT

My wife (to be) called at the box office in Ardwick on her way home for work to buy four tickets a few days before the concert. I parked my MGB GT (blue, rusty and unreliable) in the small car park in front of the Apollo. I was 25 and semi-respectable and we went to the Apollo to view the punks. We were not disappointed by the other attendees. We were seated in the side stalls and recall Richard Hell and the Voidoids and Penetration were on the bill. Many seats were ripped up and thrown. We saw Tony Wilson with a scarf artistically round his neck running up and down the aisles.

Afterwards, having carried three passengers, the exhaust dropped off during the return journey, a regular occurrence due to ridiculously low ground clearance, and my future father-in-law provided something out of his shed to repair it.

VICTORIA HALL
30 OCTOBER 1977, STOKE-ON-TRENT

CHRIS JONES

I first saw The Clash on a Sunday night in October 1977. The backdrop was the Brixton Riots one. Bang on 10.30pm the city council turned off the electricity to the stage and turned the lights on – curfew hit the band in the middle of the encore.

The next time they played in Stoke was on the same day I had to go on a school trip to London. I was in sixth form. The 'highlight' of the trip, and the teachers were trying to do us a favour and give us a treat, was England vs Czechoslovakia at Wembley. All through this utterly dire game, all I could think of was that at this very moment, The Clash were playing in my hometown. I wasn't exactly tearful,

A PEOPLE'S HISTORY OF THE CLASH

but it was an emotional ordeal. It would have given me a tremendous thrill seeing them play live, and it was the opposite having to miss them!

The next scheduled tours both had the gigs in Stoke cancelled. I only saw them once more, on the *London Calling* tour at Manchester Apollo. I was in the centre of row FF, 32 rows back, so when the lights dropped, I climbed onto the top of the back of the seat in front and walked to the front row, across the backs of the seats. I don't remember any details, just the energy and excitement and the buzz.

TOP RANK
1 NOVEMBER 1977, SHEFFIELD

JUNCO PARTNER

My introduction to The Clash, other than small bits on the punk explosion in the *NME*, came on a coach travelling to a Sheffield Wednesday away match in 1977, where I was taken with the older scruffs on the back seats talking about going to see the band in Leeds on the *White Riot* tour.

My first purchase was 'White Riot' along with the usual punk singles coming out at that time – Sex Pistols, Damned and Buzzcocks, then The Clash's debut album. The energy they had on that first album was incredible. It helped if you got the accompanying songbook a few months later, so gnarled were Strummer's words.

NME and *Sounds* were a must every Thursday, if you were lucky, in the north of England. A poster in the weeklies declared The Clash's *Out Of Control* tour with all the tour dates so it was noted in the diary. Expectations were high.

My first Clash gig was also my first ever gig. 1st November 1977 at Sheffield Top Rank along with a couple of friends who had cottoned on. It was a Tuesday, so it was a case of getting home from work, changing and then getting the bus to Sheffield. I was still underage but had been dabbling with alcohol in my local on the quiet and at football.

The Claymore outside the venue was a blur of Lewis Leather, Doc Martens and crazy colour, with lots of food colouring. I managed a couple in the pub, and we made our way up the steps and in. We didn't get advance tickets, but just paid on the door. Safely in, we managed another drink as Richard Hell was coming on.

I can't remember much about him; I was more people watching and remember thinking that the front stage area was a bit like a football crowd. Shouts of 'Clash, Clash, Clash' boomed out as the lights dimmed and then they were on, opening with 'London's Burning' and 'Complete Control', which had been released a couple of months before and was already a favourite.

I can't remember much else from the gig apart from gyrating bodies and that the band never stood still for a minute, although I do recall walking out in just a sweat-soaked t-shirt and a bomber jacket (which was to become de rigeur for a couple of years) on a winter's night. Thankfully the bus was warm. I'd got the bug, and it was to be another six months or so until they returned to Sheffield. We arranged to go to as many gigs as we could on the next tour.

Having grown up with northern soul, glam and Bowie, it may be a cliche now to say this was a progression. The whole punk thing was something special: the music, the clothes, the attitude and the camaraderie. The Clash were of course the darlings of the press at that time, but the press would fall in and out of love with them. For most fans it was a love affair that probably ended when Mick Jones got sacked. Interviews in the press were regular and relevant for the times. The band always had something to say on current affairs and that was echoed in all our daily lives. The Clash were the real deal as far as I was concerned. They all looked great. They had the clothes, the graphics and the stage presence of a juggernaut.

Live they were devastating. I always loved the fact that until later years they didn't walk on – they ran. After my baptism of fire at Sheffield Top Rank, gigs came fast and furious, with me attending most gigs in Sheffield and at Doncaster Outlook and Retford Porterhouse. I saw most of the original wave, the newer bands and then with post punk, a whole new era.

I saw The Clash a total of 22 times, mostly in the north of England, in Sheffield, Leicester, Derby, Blackburn, Bradford, Leeds, Birmingham, Manchester and Bridlington. On most occasions, my mate Dale had a works van, so we were lucky to be able to go straight from work to northern gigs, leave after the gig, rob some snacks in the services and be home in the early hours in time for work the next day. The journeys to these places are probably a book in themselves. What I can say looking back is that the venues were totally different everywhere we went, from the Top Rank format to the grandeur of Bridlington and Leicester; the modernity of Derby Assembly Hall and the cavern that was Birmingham Bingley Hall (a gig we only saw the last half hour off due to Spaghetti Junction playing a mean trick on us and sending us towards Bristol!).

A highlight was a doubler on the *Radio Clash* tour, seeing them at Bridlington Spa and Sheffield Lyceum with Theatre Of Hate as support. We followed other bands as well, including the early Adam and the Ants, and we'd been following Theatre Of Hate so it was a bonus to see them support The Clash. The Clash were on fire at that time. The sets were touching two hours, with a lot of new songs that would end up on *Sandinista!* being played along with the older favourites.

I started picking memorabilia up from gigs and using the back pages of *NME*.

A PEOPLE'S HISTORY OF THE CLASH

We'd get stuff from our local record shops as well. We would even try and peel posters from the advertising hoardings, no mean feat as there were layers of old posters underneath. Success was rare in this case, and you'd often end up with a ripped corner. My original collection was lost in a house move as I'd left the tubes in the van I'd hired. When I went back to the depot the day after, the van had been hired out again and my tubes were never to be seen again. Whoever found it would be sitting on a fortune now.

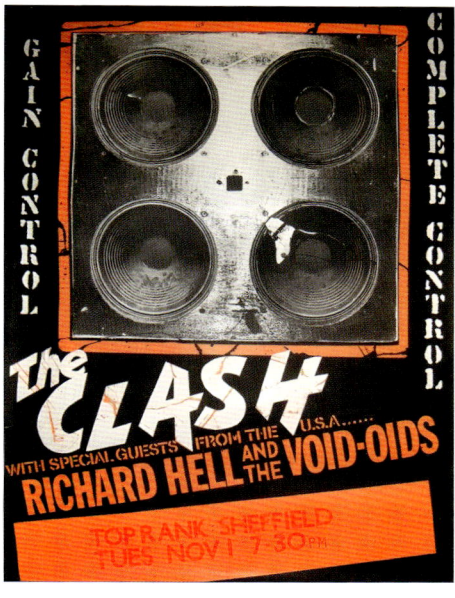

The advent of the internet and eBay meant I could start picking bits I'd lost up again so it's slowly built back up again over the years. I still add items occasionally if it's something different, but the days of spending a lot on collectables has waned, more due to space than not wanting anything.

The Clash have probably been my only constant through my life for the last 47 years. They outlived every girlfriend, which is probably why those relationships didn't last. The Clash are never far away to this day, with me attending Clash nights in the UK and Europe and with my involvement with Strummercamp Festival, another long relationship since 2005.

There's still some great music out there to listen to and still plenty of gigs to go to, so the legacy of punk is still with me today. There's even a trickle of Clash live albums filtering out and we are all kept up to date on the Clash City Collectors Facebook page, a stunning timepiece for all Clash fans.

 KING'S HALL
2 NOVEMBER 1977, DERBY

PHIL CURME

I got a ticket for their next tour and saw them at the King's Hall, Derby on 2 November 1977. I dragged along some mates, and I remember one – Rob – being so stoned he couldn't stand up. When The Clash came on, he burst into life as though someone had put 1,000 volts through him! I remember a fight breaking out and the band stopped playing whilst Mick tried to sort it out. After the gig a bloke chucked a load of 'Complete Control' badges into the crowd, and I still have a couple of them. 'Complete Control' reinforced my love of dub reggae.

 TOP RANK
7 NOVEMBER 1977, BIRMINGHAM

ALAN RODGER

I moved to the West Midlands in 1975 and began to pick up on punk in 1976. I was always a big fan of the music press. I won tickets to see Hawkwind at Birmingham Odeon in 1976, so I suppose that was probably the first big gig I went to.

The next time I went to Birmingham Odeon was to see The Damned on the T. Rex tour in March, six months later. John Peel was the only source of the music really whilst I was still at school. Although I was a former T. Rex fan – the first single I ever bought with my own money was 'Hot Love' in 1971 – I mainly went to see The Damned, because hearing New 'Rose' when it came out was massive. It was a real moment, seeing one of the leading punk bands live at the age of just 16.

I went to the record department in Boots after school one day and picked up 'Anarchy In The UK', but as I was wearing school uniform the woman took it off me! I could have had that for 45p. The Clash was the next big one, one of the big three or four punk bands that I went to see early November 1977. I'd heard the first album by then. My mate had it and played it regularly.

They were playing a couple of thousand capacity venues by this stage, and they were brilliant, coupled with the fact that one of our local punk heroes, Spizz, was also on the bill. He knew the promoters used to put on the big names.

The Clash that night were just electric to watch. The stage was only a couple of feet high and I spent the whole time down the front, which I didn't normally do. My abiding memory is of them starting 'Police And Thieves'. Suddenly all the power went off on stage in the middle of their set – no instruments, no amps, no lights or anything – and all that was left in were the emergency lights in the venue. But Topper kept playing, which was amazing. Eventually, they got the rest of the instruments started up and continued. I managed to stay behind and talk to talk to Strummer after being let in the dressing room. I chatted with him for a while. He was a nice guy to talk to.

I saw The Clash lots more. They did another big tour in the summer of 1978 with Suicide supporting (who had the same format as Soft Cell, but much weirder). I didn't go down the front for The Clash that night, but they were very good. After six months of constant touring they were more polished and not quite as raw, and the songs were very different; much more rock n' roll. It was great to see them again.

The next time I saw them was about 1982. I'd sworn I would never see The Clash again because they could never be as good as those first times. That might seem a bit strange, but it was that special.

TIFFANY'S
8 NOVEMBER 1977, COVENTRY

PAUL PANIC

After they'd done the *Anarchy* tour and got a bit of press, they were playing bigger venues. The Top Rank in Birmingham was quite a large venue. I went back there just a few years ago when they opened it up for bands again and it still had the same blooming carpets it used to have in '77. You just walked in and your feet would stick to the carpets.

I think The Slits supported them again at that gig. I went with a couple of mates, and then the next night they were playing at Tiffany's, a big ballroom-type venue right in the middle of Coventry. In those days you used to be able to get a 10p bus ride to Coventry from Birmingham. Everyone was queuing for ages on the stairs outside before the gig and I remember everyone dressed up in their punk finery. Once inside, we were down the front.

Some bands would just amble on and start tuning up or whatever, but The Clash were always right on the nail. They'd come rushing on like a military unit. It'd be Paul Simonon with his legs apart stance and with the bass, Strummer would stand there looking like he's having an epileptic fit, sort of angsty, and Mick Jones would be running about everywhere. They were a very, very tight band and very high energy and full on. At that time, they were a very full-on punk band. They sounded very raw, but not in an unrehearsed way. They were obviously very well-rehearsed.

You can rehearse as much as you want, but you can only get a certain type of tightness in a rehearsal room. The rest of it is learned on the road, doing it night after night. The only other band I can think of that would probably be like that would be the Ramones, because they were just a band who came on and never stopped. It was just one, two, three, four, and into the next one. The Clash were proper hard-hitting.

I saw them again at Coventry, a couple of years after, and again, they were good, but by then the songs were starting to get more sort of melodic and more experimental. When they played the song 'London Calling', I remember thinking, 'Oh, this is a slight letdown compared to something like 'Janie Jones' or 'White Riot' in terms of power.' But obviously it's got a power in a different way. I love it now. But they were always, always a great live band.

WINTER GARDENS
9 NOVEMBER 1977, BOURNEMOUTH

NICK KEEN

The Clash's *Out Of Control* gig at Bournemouth's beautiful deco Winter Gardens in the November was the moment that I fell head over heels in love with the band. A blitzkrieg assault of the senses: Stukas, gobbing, Richard Hell as support, Pollock-inspired paint splashes, bondage trousers, battered guitars, riots and a set of short dynamic songs performed by four guys each with their own vision. I couldn't take my eyes off them.

I passionately followed The Clash from their primitive early first tour gigs until the very last UK performance in August 1982 at Bristol Locarno, with Terry Chimes sitting in on the drums due to the sad sacking of Topper. It was a rearranged gig as Joe went mysteriously AWOL a few months earlier and returned to the stage cheered on by the expectant audience and sporting a radical Mohican haircut. I feel lucky to have witnessed them progress from a year zero punk band to the only band that mattered. For six years, everything they mythologised was integrally wrapped up in my life. The Clash were innovative, many of those great singles never originally appearing on any of their five albums.

I don't have a favourite single or album, they all excited me. There was always so much going on. A heady concoction of ground-breaking artwork, Ray Lowry graphics and Pennie Smith showcasing photography. Where do you start? The anthemic power of 'Complete Control' whipped up by Mick's guitar hero fretwork, the reggae greats namedropped in '(White Man) In Hammersmith Palais', the 'Magnificent Seven' wordplay – for a short while, I believed that Pepe Unidos really did exist and produced the remix – and the 'Know Your Rights' single with its free sticker are just snippets. Every majestic release packed a considerable punch.

I was buying a glutton of punk albums over this period, so I can't remember when exactly I bought their eagerly anticipated debut album. It was all a blur. Their second album, *Give 'Em Enough Rope*, received mixed reviews. The impression was that they'd sold out by hiring an American to produce the album, but I loved the big guitar production. *London Calling* blew my mind and still does. The triple album cheek of *Sandinista!* astonished me. They were on a roll. Ploughing through it was a spiritual awakening. I've since heard they earnt very little from it at the time, but that wasn't the point. The band were literally creating a legendary piece of art in front of our very eyes. For me *Combat Rock* really holds up, and I love the experimental new world approach. It's stunning.

Mick and Topper got the questionable boot. The Clash limped on with a new-fangled line-up that was destined for failure. *Cut The Crap* was the result of the implosion and it's rarely mentioned in The Clash canon. I saw every UK tour, collected stacks of t-shirts, pinned on all the tin badges and sellotaped up all the posters. For me, they were just the coolest band on the planet in every possible sense.

ELIZABETHAN BALLROOM
15 NOVEMBER 1977, MANCHESTER

AK MCALLISTER

Oh wow! For many of us this was home turf. Belle Vue was the first theme park-style thing most of us had witnessed – a zoo, a fairground, a boating lake, roller coasters, and a speedway track that was also the former home of Manchester City during their days of transition from Ardwick FC. It was also the home of the under 18s Sunday night disco called the Zoo B Doo, where I used to dance with my first girlfriend. But it was also a place for tribal wars. It was a bit like the film *The Warriors*. There were certain tribes from certain areas present, and they were always ready to fight.

The aggression in the air was evident from the moment we arrived. Firstly, there were many locals there without tickets. Plans to crash the doors had been discussed well in advance, and this was now definitely going to happen. And on the night, it did. Within minutes of the doors opening there was a swell in the waiting queue and many people pushed forwards until the doors, and the bouncers, gave way and everybody was in. The bouncers made a token effort to keep up appearances and maybe threw a couple of people out again, but they knew it was too late. Everybody who was jibbing in had already jibbed in.

The Clash played a great set. They were on top of their game. 'Who wants it to sound like the record? Me neither,' were the words Strummer began the set with that night. The videos from this gig, recorded on an old VCR machine, really capture the energy the band delivered onstage and the sheer vibrancy of the audience close to it.

Outside, after the gig, the local tribal rivalries did erupt, and we had to stand our ground against some West Gorton meatheads who'd decided to come 'a punk-bashin''. Targeted just for dressing alternatively, but particularly wearing anything immediately identifiable as punk clothing, you were seen as a legitimate target by 'the straights'. We usually held our own though, and we all made it out safely from the local rednecks in their flares, Penny Round collared shirts and platform shoes.

As The Clash sang in 'City Of The Dead', 'What we wear is dangerous gear, get you picked up anywhere.'

ALL THE YOUNG PUNKS

GARY HOUGH

I loved this gig, despite getting a bit crushed as it was rammed. Granada TV had sent a film crew, which added to the excitement that I might appear on TV.

Picture the scene, like a seventies football crowd at Old Trafford when you were tight against each other in the Stretford End. Funnily enough, there was a couple of lads who wore their United scarves around their necks, as if it wasn't dangerous enough getting targeted after you came out for being a punk!

GED DUFFY

It was a wild night and as we were queuing up to pay our 90p to get in, a large gang of punks charged the doors and smashed their way in, so we just followed them. Slim and I got the taste for free gigs after that. The Clash were brilliant, a total visual three-pronged attack of Jones, Strummer and Paul Simonon. They started the gig with 'London's Burning' but Joe Strummer changed the opening line to 'getting in for nothing' as a nod to all of us who had stormed in for free.

MARTIN RYAN

The Elizabethan Ballroom in the Belle Vue Amusement Park was an event which would be preserved in part by the Granada TV cameras, here to capture footage of Siouxsie and the Banshees and The Clash for Tony Wilson's second series of *So It Goes*. Subway Sect had returned to The Clash fold but were not on the agenda for the TV show, or if they were, their support slot ended up on the cutting room floor.

Attempts to collect the admission charge were abandoned almost immediately. I don't recall the level of destruction being on the scale reported, such as all the glass doors being shattered. I am sure a few managed to tender the admission charge before the door security became resigned to letting the majority in for free. Whether the cost of seeing The Clash was less than the exorbitant £2.50 at the Apollo I don't recall, not being one of the handful who paid.

The whole debacle could have been a preconceived stunt. Presumably Granada TV's funding of the event ensured there would be no financial loss and, anyway, were the audience not effectively extras? Mick Hucknall's visible presence has been pinpointed on numerous re-runs of the footage.

Joe Strummer was quick to garner integrity from the proceedings, announcing the opener 'London's Burning' as 'Getting In For Nothing'. Despite the guileless politics to which Strummer sometimes religiously adhered, this was an incontestable return to form for The Clash, who regaled the swaying masses throughout with most of the debut album and the customary stage reworking of 'Capital Radio' with Strummer announcing that 'twenty-five English pounds' was being offered for the *NME* giveaway single of that title.

To mask any wrongdoing for their co-operation with the big business that this TV company constituted, the by now guitar-less Strummer pointed to a cameraman with the rationalisation, 'See that, that's money talking. Your money.' Or maybe the singer was attempting to divert the beer and glasses and the obligatory phlegm away from the band as the cameramen were suddenly fair game. A further petty act saw Strummer revise the lyrics of 'What's My Name' to 'Here we are on TV, what does it mean to me? What does it mean to you?... Fuck off,' again pointing his wrath at a (no doubt) union card holding cameraman.

But this was a night of payback as the underwhelming appearance at the Apollo was displaced by what was, for all the questionable political sloganeering, a spirited performance played to a once more upright audience allowed to dance without the bouncers throwing them back into their seats. There was talk of some rough handling of fans at stage side, which Tony Wilson insisted was the work of The Clash entourage, but as a live rock band The Clash were once again back among the elite.

Probably the most tellingly political statement of the night was Joe Strummer questioning if the audience thought punk was dead. The inquiry brought a vociferous response, although the follow up question delivered a more rousing thumbs up to confirm punk was alive and well as Strummer added, 'Thank God for that.'

QUEENS UNIVERSITY
17 DECEMBER 1977, BELFAST

BRIAN YOUNG

Originally, two shows were planned but logistics dictated that there would be just the one gig. After the previous Ulster Hall furore, Queens University Students Union held a ballot to see if nasty punk bands should even be permitted to play within their hallowed walls! What a sign of the times, huh? (Remember, it wasn't that long since The Clash had been branded racists and banned by other students unions who insisted that 'White Riot' was a racist white power diatribe. Typical students. Talk about missing the point.) Thankfully, punk rock won out!

Arriving early, we queued up at the back of Queens Students Union under the watchful eye of the RUC, who had turned up to keep a wary eye on any punky troublemakers. Thankfully, this time they kept their distance and didn't try to interfere with the mass consumption of alcoholic beverages by clearly underage teens. Queens, on the other hand, were taking no chances – everyone was searched on the way in, and all sorts of studded belts and punky paraphernalia was confiscated. Hilariously, there were boxes and boxes of the stuff, and it must have looked like a BDSM convention to the bewildered door staff! The actual venue, the McMordie Hall, wasn't that big but was packed. It wasn't yet set up as a permanent concert venue and the stage looked ramshackle and slung together at the last minute. Support was French band The Lou's, who looked better than they sounded – and frankly the audience didn't pay them much attention.

From the minute The Clash came onstage they were treated like conquering heroes. With Topper in the line-up, they were simply unbeatable live and the whole gig passed in a white-hot blur of excitement. Joe even dedicated a song to RUDI and at the end of the night I managed to scramble onstage alongside a couple of other determined punters in time to join in on backing vocals on their last number, 'White Riot'. It was a great night – memorable for all the right reasons – and as we spilled outside afterwards under the hostile glare of the ever-present RUC, nothing could dampen our spirits. It was a gig which cemented a longstanding devotion to The Clash in these parts.

QUEENSWAY HALL
25 JANUARY 1978, DUNSTABLE

GARY CONNOLLY

I have many great memories of The Clash. My earliest memory of the band was in 1977. A friend of my Mum's son lent me the debut album to listen to. It was a life changing moment hearing that record.

In early January 1978, The Clash came to play my hometown of Dunstable for the second time at the now demolished Queensway Hall. The first time they had played here was in 1977 on the *White Riot* tour, at the California Ballroom which I didn't know about, another venue sadly no longer with us.

The Queensway Hall gig was infamous and described by Mick Jones as 'one of their best gigs' to date. The place was packed, and it seemed fans had come from everywhere to see them play. The atmosphere was electric. Unfortunately, there was an undercurrent of violence running through the gig all night, with fights breaking out and support bands being canned off the stage. The Clash were brilliant however and revelled in the atmosphere, producing a stunning performance which included a couple of new songs given an airing ahead of their second album.

Everything that happened that night was another life changing moment for me as a 15-year-old. I had never witnessed anything like it, the crowd especially, although punks behaved more like the football hooligans which I had seen first hand.

'CLASH CITY ROCKERS'/'JAIL GUITAR DOORS' RELEASED
17 FEBRUARY 1978

MARTIN BLENCO

You can make a case for any one of half a dozen singles as being the best the Clash ever released, and in reaching such a judgement you have to bear in mind what was on the flip side of each 45. The Clash got stick for the rather posy nature of the 'Clash City Rockers' lyric, but to my 17-year-old heart and brain this was pure poetry. And I was a Rolling Stones fan too, so Mick singing on the B-side about Keith Richards' ongoing drug problems and his upcoming trial was another plus point. There was probably no real prospect of such a high-profile rocker ending up in the slammer, but you couldn't be sure. Clang clang go the jail guitar doors indeed!

A PEOPLE'S HISTORY OF THE CLASH

ROCK AGAINST RACISM CARNIVAL
30 APRIL 1978, VICTORIA PARK, LONDON

'ON RESISTANCE STREET' BY TONY FLETCHER

I grew up in a racist society.

Thankfully, the formative years of my London life were relatively free of prejudice. In the early seventies reggae and soul music had as big a presence on the British pop charts as glam. My mum made friends with the West Indian and Asian immigrants she taught in South London comprehensive schools, my surrogate big brother Jeffries did his best to turn me on to influential new Black music, and no one around me at my primary/elementary school (which took in kids of all demographics) was ever heard spewing racist slurs.

That changed when I went to secondary school in Kennington, just south of the Thames, in 1975, aged 11. Despite (because?) of the presence of a few Black kids at our school – and there would have been more, given our location in Kennington/Brixton, had we not been attending a selective grammar school – several pupils were vocally supportive of the National Front, the openly racist, pro-repatriation political party. In many ways, this just reflected wider society, in which the NF was gaining steady strongholds at the polls and in the streets, preying on White working-class football supporters and anyone else who wanted scapegoats for their problems in life. These racist pupils around me probably learned the insults and lies at home where, quite apart from possible parental influence, all they had to do was switch on the TV, where BBC and ITV hosted shows like *Love Thy Neighbour* and *Till Death Us Do Part*, which utilised every racist colloquialism under the sun (any retroactive claims at satire going well above the audiences' heads), and 'comedians' like Bernard Manning told jokes about Pakis and odour-eaters and everyone laughed. No wonder a lot of these kids at school turned out racist. They didn't know any better.

Somehow, I did. While I don't remember my own family having discussions around the dinner table about skin colour, it seemed to go unsaid that racism was wrong, like stealing and killing was wrong. I'm not suggesting for a moment that we were holier than thou, that we weren't capable of generalisations and occasional lapses of terminology, and I have horrible memories of how my school class bullied a frail, timid Indian kid when he showed up around our fourth year (I probably took personal relief in the fact that at least someone was being treated worse than me). But generally speaking, my personal clan knew where it stood.

This might explain why the first issue of my fanzine – called *In The City* that one time out – contained a stick-figure drawing by YT of the infamous NF March through South London's Lewisham in the summer of 1977, at which it was confronted by a solid wall of anti-racists who had decided it was finally time to meet force with force. And it certainly explains why I attended the Anti-Nazi League / Rock Against Racism rally in Trafalgar Square on April 30, 1978, before joining the march to Victoria Park in Hackney where a crowd of up to 80,000 eventually gathered to hear music by The Clash, Steel Pulse, the Tom Robinson Band, X-Ray Spex and Patrik Fitzgerald. The Clash performance was incendiary, going down in history as one of the most momentous moments in punk rock history.

But while the music that day was memorable, the Carnival Against the Nazis was also a watershed moment in British racial politics. As one of the many voices heard in the new film *On Resistance Street* explains, and I paraphrase but mildly, 'Some people may have come 'only' for the music, some because it was a free festival, but not one of them would have left without understanding the message.' All over the UK, you can still meet people for whom the March to Hackney was their own Road To Damascus.

Billy Bragg, who himself is featured briefly in *On Resistance Street*, is just the first name that comes to mind. Unfortunately, the success of April 30, 1978, and the other RAR/ANL carnivals and club and college shows that followed, did not eliminate the threat of the National Front overnight, and there were some horrendous years to follow as an outwardly Nazi skinhead revival gathered steam and served to terrorise gig-goers and everyday people for the next several years. Indeed, if the election of Thatcher's rightward-lurching Conservative Party in May 1979 served to dissipate the National Front's own appeal at the polls, it also led to a more overtly violent street movement called the British Movement, for which these skinheads were the stormtroopers, often to the point of sporting BM and swastika tattoos, as well as DM boots with steel toe caps that they were all too willing to test on the skulls of their victims.

We can look back on the peak period of 2-Tone as cultural glory years if we want to, but for anyone who witnessed these skins 'Seig Heiling' while dancing to The Selecter (a band that had only one white member), as I did in the summer of 1979 at the Electric Ballroom, those

> **THE CARNIVAL WAS A WATERSHED MOMENT IN BRITISH POLITICS...**
>
> TONY FLETCHER

memories are laced with a form of nostalgic arsenic.

Nonetheless, as Thatcherism came to dominate the 1980s, combining a directive of up-by-your-bootstraps self-serving capitalism with a calculated decimation of working-class institutions, the new wave moved leftwards accordingly.

The Jam dropped the Union Jack, sang about impending nuclear war and claimed to embrace socialism. The 2-Tone groups fought, sometimes literally in self-defence, to unite black and white, and launched an unprecedented number of home-grown inter-racial bands into the Top 10. Political bands like Hull's The Housemartins topped the charts, singing openly socialist anthems while demanding nationalisation of the record industry. The miners' strike of 1984 further galvanized musicians up and down the land. And the decade ended with an embrace of Chicago house music and Detroit techno, the birth of the Balearic/Acid House/Madchester/rave movements, and the near-universal embrace of ecstasy, which not only united kids on the dancefloor without the hassles of the 2-Tone era, but temporarily turned the football terrace fighters into inflatable-banana-waving loved-up charmers.

Still, you can safely argue that before the events of this previous paragraph, and influencing so many of them, there was The Clash. The same group that had the audacity to cover Junior Murvin's 'Police and Thieves' on their debut album, proving that punk and reggae could mix musically as well as culturally, and who followed it up with '(White Man) In Hammersmith Palais,' still one of the most important singles in British history, then headed to the States and embraced hip-hop, electro, the blues and all other forms of influential Black music. (I have been listening to *Sandinista!* while writing this review; it gets better every year.) And in case anyone still got the wrong end of 1977's breakout single 'White Riot,' Joe Strummer was unequivocal in his own beliefs:

'We're anti-fascist, we're anti-violence, we're anti-racist and we're pro-creative' he told the *New Musical Express* in 1976. 'We're pro-creative.'

PHIL CURME

The National Front were making inroads into politics, thanks to Martin Webster and John Tyndall, and Sham 69 were trying to shake-off their racist followers. The Rock Against Racism concert in Victoria Park was a magnet for disaffected youth and I travelled down in a bus from Nottingham. I remember walking past Nazi thugs mouthing threats behind ranks of policemen. It felt like we were taking back territory from the far right but it also felt like mainstream politicians were doing nothing in the face of the fascist threat. My abiding memory is of Jimmy Pursey coming on during 'White Riot' and my thinking, 'This is him disavowing Sham's skinhead following and nailing his colours to the Anti-Nazi League / Rock Against Racism mast.'

CHRIS HILDER

I saw The Clash at the Rock Against Racism following the Anti-Fascist League march at Victoria Park in Hackney. We didn't go to see the bands; we went to protest. The bands were a welcome 'thank you' after the march. We assembled in Trafalgar Square at a very early hour on a soggy but not terribly wet morning. Some friends came down overnight from the north of England and they woke us up early in our lodgings in Crouch End.

After walking from Trafalgar Square to Victoria Park, we ended up lined up with the left-hand bank of speakers 40 – 50 yards away. We had a great view of the stage and enjoyed seeing the bands. Tom Robinson wasn't that 'big' for me, so for me The Clash were my headliners. Their set was very energetic and exciting. I can't remember the individual songs apart from 'White Riot'.

The first Clash album had hardly left my turntable and that was (still is) my favourite song from that album. Jimmy Pursey from Sham 69 joined them on stage. I would have preferred it to have been Strummer singing on his own as Pursey, to me, was shouting. Regardless the energy was brilliant and the whole crowd was up for it.

Tom Robinson's set was a bit of a come down, but we all enjoyed singing along to '2-4-6-8 Motorway' and 'Glad To Be Gay'.

CRAIG EDWARDS

The first time I saw The Clash. They were marching from Trafalgar Square to Victoria Park. I had all my punk gear on and a pigeon shat on my black PVC motorcycle jacket as I was leaving Trafalgar Square. The Clash were playing just as we arrived in the park, and there was a big marijuana cloud hanging above the park. There were punks, Rastas and all sorts of people there, and it was like a holiday atmosphere. Jimmy Pursey came out and sang 'White Riot' with The Clash. X-Ray Spex were on, and Steel Pulse, who were absolutely brilliant. I also saw The Clash at Sheffield Top Rank. They played all the old favourites. The Slits were support. They were absolutely shite.

DYLAN WHITE

This was an Anti-Nazi League rally with a gig in Victoria Park in the East End at the end of it. Me and a few friends went to a packed Trafalgar Square, and we had these big yellow ANL signs. There was a load of Anti-Nazi rallies all through '78, '79. The whole punk movement was into it, as was the 2-Tone movement.

There were bands like The Ruts playing on trucks as we did the long march

A PEOPLE'S HISTORY OF THE CLASH

to Victoria Park. Thankfully, it wasn't raining and there was Patrik Fitzgerald, playing 'Safety Pin Stuck In My Heart'. We got X-Ray Spex, the Tom Robinson Band, Steel Pulse and then The Clash, and it was fantastic. It was a big crowd. It was like being at the Reading Festival. You felt you were part of something. Growing up in South-West London, I'd never been to Victoria Park before, so it was like, 'Wow where are we?' There were thousands there. It was a great day out. It didn't finish that late. The Clash were at the top of their game. The second album wasn't out yet, but they'd had the success of the first album. They delivered. Jimmy Pursey got up at some point and did something. Whether he got on for the encore with The Clash I can't remember. And then we had to work out how to get a Tube home…

Dylan White remembers the long march to Victoria Park

ED SILVESTER

Although we were always going to the *Rock Against Racism* event at Victoria Park, primarily to see X-Ray Spex and Steel Pulse, we were excited to hear that The Clash were to be a late inclusion. Getting to Victoria Park was easy for us Eppingites, as it was a short trip on the Central Line to Mile End underground station. We then followed the slow moving and excited crowd to the park.

First up were those Day-Glo punks, X Ray-Spex. Poly Styrene had shaved her head before the gig and was wearing a woolly scarf wrapped around her head. I wondered whether this was an anti-sex symbol stance, or was she just feeling ill? All afternoon the bands were plagued by poor sound quality. But Poly's distinctive vocals and saxophone-driven sound were going down well with the crowd. Unfortunately, Patrik Fitzgerald, the next act, was canned off stage by Clash fans at the front of the stage. His weedy pop wasn't appreciated by the crowd, and with hindsight he shouldn't have been on the bill.

Next up, the main course and the band that everyone was eagerly waiting for, The Clash. Joe Strummer came on stage wearing a red t-shirt, with a Red Brigade slogan on the front, and white drainpipe jeans. He looked the business, and in sharp contrast to the long-haired Mick Jones. They kicked off their set with 'Complete

ALL THE YOUNG PUNKS

Control' and finished with Jimmy Pursey jumping on stage and singing 'White Riot' with them.

Occasionally, I watch the film *Rude Boy* to gaze at the vast crowd that day, and to feel and recreate some of that youthful energy. I couldn't stand the film; the main character came across as a moron to me, but I have always loved the band's live performances in the movie.

Being a punk and watching hippies collecting money in buckets was certainly a strange contradiction. Hadn't Johnny Rotten said, 'Never trust a hippie?' The idea was to run the Nazis out of town, but my one abiding memory is of watching small groups of skinheads sticking the boot in and pocketing the cash. No one lifted a finger. Too scared, I guess.

Ed Silvester was excited to hear that The Clash were added to the Victoria Park bill

The Tom Robinson Band were the headlining act, and it felt like an anti-climax after The Clash and X Ray-Spex. I seem to remember someone saying that The Ruts were performing somewhere in the park, on the back of a lorry. But I didn't see them.

GARETH THOMAS

I first went to see The Clash in Victoria Park. There was a sense of occasion, with the politics, etc., and I'm not saying we weren't sensitive to the political issues once we were there, but if I'm totally honest I went because The Clash were playing. We ended up going on the march and doing all these chants along with the people carrying banners.

I went to four Clash gigs in the space of five months during 1978. I used to bunk off school and follow The Clash around the country. They were at the peak of their powers. At this point The Clash were just unbeatable; they were the only band in town, all those clichés – they were the last gang in town. They looked the part. They had the energy. They had the songs. They had everything going for them.

DARYL HUMPHREYS

By 1978 I had begun to drift away from the scene. Things had moved on and the music had lost much of its original appeal as it gave way to new wave and post punk. We'd also grown dissatisfied with attending gigs, mainly because the bands and audience were increasingly dominated by what we called 'pin punks' or even worse, the resurgent skinheads who seemed to be everywhere you went at that time.

In the spring of '78, we heard about an anti-racism festival taking place at Victoria Park in the East End of London. The event consisted of a protest march from central London to the venue, followed by performances from several well-known bands. The organisers of the march were the Anti-Nazi League and the concert was to become known as 'Rock Against Racism' (RAR). The movement was a direct response to the rise of the National Front (NF) and a reaction towards some of the rock hierarchy who held racist views (in particular, Eric Clapton who came out as an Enoch Powell supporter at one of his concerts). The Clash were to be the main band.

The Clash were always up-front about their stance against racism and one of the most powerful images I can remember of that time was when they protested outside NF leader Martin Webster's home in Teddington. They were joined by members of the British reggae band Steel Pulse and by ex-Sex Pistols bass player Glen Matlock. Considering the violent reputation of the NF it took some real guts to stick your neck out and protest like that.

Supporting at RAR were an array of well-known bands including X-Ray Spex, The Buzzcocks and Sham 69. The punk bands were augmented by the excellent British reggae bands Aswad and Steel Pulse. It was a gig not to be missed.

The march was well attended with coachloads of protesters arriving in London from far and wide. We'd heard there was likely to be trouble with NF supporters along the route and had decided to head early to the venue to get a good position to see the bands. Looking back, I've got mixed feelings about the day; there was a tension in the air between the event organisers and the punks, plus there were other factions present which made for a potential melting pot of trouble. However, in the end the event went off peacefully and the atmosphere was brilliant.

There were the usual high expectations of The Clash and they played true to form, although they were beset by sound problems. We heard later that the organisers had tried to pull the plug when they were due to play 'White Riot', which summed up the gulf between the killjoy Leftie activists and the anarchistic punks. When they did finally play the song, it was duly received with the expected jubilation from the crowd.

I've never been a fan of Sham 69 and Oi music, but to give Jimmy Pursey some credit, he did make a stand against racism by performing at RAR which contrasted starkly with his core fan base who consisted mainly of racist skinhead types.

ALL THE YOUNG PUNKS

X-Ray Spex and the Buzzcocks were on form as usual and the British reggae acts were superb live. Steel Pulse's seminal 'Ku Klux Klan' was the standout anti-Nazi anthem of the day.

HÉLÈNE GIB

I was 14 in 1978 and in middle school. A trip was planned to England, travelling by bus to Northampton. When we arrived, I discovered people with incredible looks: Iroquois punks of all colours with pins in their noses, and skinheads wearing pork pie hats, braces and Doc Martens all together in the town centre.

I quickly met other young people including two brothers, Nigel and Tim, who drove an MG. They invited me to join them at a concert in London: *Rock Against Racism*. It was the first time I'd found myself in a crowd with so many people, punks and Rastas all in the same place for a great gig. There was a wonderful mix of people and musical culture.

As a young French girl, I didn't realise where I was and what that gig was to become. I remember Steel Pulse, and of course The Clash. After the concert, I studied Joe Strummer's lyrics. They have influenced me, my humanist awareness and punk attitude for the rest of my life.

Later I organized hundreds of concerts over ten years with my friends in a little town in France (Diff'Art) and painted a lot, including many portraits of famous people, but not all mainstream! I was invited to exhibit at the first Strummer Fest in Agen, in Southern France in 2014. The festival organiser asked me if I could pick up a guy at the Toulouse-Blagnac airport. I learned at the last moment that it was Ray Gange, so I found myself with the guy who was on the wall of my teenage room, featured on the poster of the *Rude Boy* film.

We are still friends, and I firmly believe in the fact that people are put in our way not by chance.

Hélène Gib had never been in such a big crowd as the one at Victoria Park

PAUL LYMN

It's Sunday April 30th, 1978, and a 14-year-old me gets out of bed at 6.30am and jumps on my bike to get the Sunday papers for my morning round. My mind really isn't on the job in hand though, as at 8am the coach leaves for London for the *Rock*

A PEOPLE'S HISTORY OF THE CLASH

Against Racism carnival at Victoria Park, Hackney. My father is the branch organiser for the Anti-Nazi League in Leicester, and responsible for the two coaches that leave Humberstone Gate in Leicester city centre.

We arrive a bit early and it's total chaos. People have shown up who've not bought tickets but somehow everyone who wants to go seems to get a seat! Not long after 8am, the two coaches are away and joining the M1. There seem to be endless other coaches on the motorway, all heading to the same destination. The excitement mounts the more coaches we see! The guy sat in the seat in front of me pulls a Spanish onion from his bag and begins eating it as if it it's an apple. At least half the people on the coach have streaming eyes! (It's funny looking back now, but at the time it was awful!)

Around three hours later we arrive somewhere near to Trafalgar Square where the march begins. Around an hour later, the march sets off but one of the lads I'm with suggests that if we march the entire route, we will end up missing all the bands. We leave the march at the first Tube station we see.

Eventually we arrive at Victoria Park. Being from Leicester, we then realise that none of us know how to use the London Underground, so it takes us ages, heading in the wrong direction and choosing the wrong lines. The park is heaving, and I feel quite intimidated by it all. We catch the last song in X-Ray Spex's set and the excitement grows as the stage changeover takes place.

When The Clash hit the stage, my life changes instantly. The band are the most exciting thing I've seen and heard. We are stood towards the back purely and simply because we are nervous, but it's a joyous crowd, so we need not worry. We are hanging on Strummer's every word as if our lives depend on it. The Clash's set seems to go in the blink of an eye, and all too soon it's over. The heaving crowd are baying for more, but Tom Robinson's roadies are changing the stage over, so we know Strummer and Co aren't coming back on.

It really is a life changing day. Being from the Midlands we haven't seen anything like it. Smelling Indian food for the first time in my life from stalls set up by Indian Workers Association members is truly incredible. More chaos ensues when we're looking for our bus near the park. By some miracle, we bump into my parents and we don't let them out of our sight from that point on.

We get back to Leicester at around 1am and I have to be up for school the next day, but I lay awake all night, still buzzing from what we've just witnessed!

(I went on to see The Clash nine more times and bought all their recorded output. They remain to this day the finest rock and roll band of all time, and my all-time favourites.)

ALL THE YOUNG PUNKS

PETE METCALFE

I was a student in Cardiff and the Students Union at the University arranged free coaches for anyone wanting to go to the event. A free Clash gig – count me in!

It was a strange day and not your average gig. A very early start to get the coach into London, then a couple of rallying speeches in Trafalgar Square followed by a long march to Victoria Park in Hackney where The Clash, the Tom Robinson Band, X-Ray Spex and Steel Pulse were playing live plus a 'punk poet' who got badly heckled.

Most of the marchers were either members of the Socialist Workers Party (loads of banners) or were peace-and-love hippy types. There were a few punks on the march but not too many. Along the route at various points, gangs of right-wing yobs jeered and tried to get a fight going but the police had them cordoned off.

When we got to Victoria Park there was a huge crowd. X-Ray Spex were on first and then The Clash, so it was still light when they played. They started with 'Complete Control', which was my favourite song of theirs at that time and they were up for it. At one point later in their set the power failed but they got it sorted.

Between songs you could hear over the PA occasional chants of 'Sham' from a section of the crowd. I was just thinking 'what are they doing here?' when The Clash went into 'White Riot' and Jimmy Pursey bounded on stage to guest on vocals. He was very enthusiastic but completely out of key. Thankfully Joe butted in on vocals to rescue things.

IAN WEST

The day punk entered my vocabulary and permeated my consciousness is forever etched in the upper vaults of my memory banks. By 1976 I was out of the loop with regards to rock-orientated music and I hadn't purchased one of the big three rock papers for a good long while. The sight of boring rock dinosaurs and their fans, still adorned with long straight lank hair and wearing the obligatory flared jeans did nothing to excite or inspire me, and the pretentiousness of overblown prissy prog with its classically trained and technically brilliant musicians was out of reach for any normal bloke from a council estate who aspired to learn an instrument and make music to excite and stir the soul.

Only Bowie seemed impervious to stagnation and criticism, though I still followed a few others that had rocked my world in recent years such as the early pioneering and influential era Roxy Music, Dr Feelgood, New York Dolls, Be-Bop Deluxe and a handful of other artists that still managed to tingle my spine and raise the hairs on my arms.

A PEOPLE'S HISTORY OF THE CLASH

I had become 'Soul Boy Tart' (as someone once called me), resplendent in bowling shirt and six-inch high-waist trousers. *Blues & Soul* was the magazine of choice and funk, Northern Soul and super sexy smooth sounding soul were what floated my boat. Yet the onset of plastic disco was disturbingly draining out the very soul in soul and watering down the funk in funk and made me hanker for new horizons... And unknown to me at the time, something new was already wafting in the air...

Ian West was a 'soul boy tart' until punk came along

It was on my return to day-release at George Stephenson College in Watford at the beginning of September 1976, where I was studying for a City and Guilds in Photolithography, that a fellow student looked me up and down in my soul boy clothing and quipped: 'I'm surprised that you're not into punk rock yet!'

Punk rock! What the heck is punk rock? Could the couple of students that I had noticed who had returned from summer break and stood out like a sore thumb in their tight trousers and whose ears were now noticeably and starkly apparent rather than hidden under regimental thick wavy locks be purveyors of this punk music?

Overwhelming curiosity compelled me and by the end of the year my wardrobe included a plastic sleeveless shirt with a long zip crossing from shoulder to hip and adorned with numerous safety pins and a collarless shirt nicked from my dad that I had artistically turned into a splattered 'Jackson Pollock'. Yet I dared not wear such outrageous gear out in public, on my own in the wilds of Buckinghamshire, 40 miles north of London. Especially as the Sex Pistols had recently aroused such venom and anger on the *Today* show with Bill Grundy, instigating violent retributive outpourings against what the horrified conservative public failed to understand and ignorantly feared.

By early '77 the tiny box in my local record shop in Aylesbury headed 'Punk/New Wave' held just a small smattering of seven-inch singles and even fewer LPs. Yet I eagerly spent as many pounds of my wages on punk vinyl as I possibly could. Punk sounded exactly as I had first imagined back in September: short, sharp, basic and like a stinging slap across the face! It was exhilarating and refreshingly exciting, especially in comparison with the pompous and self-indulgent home-grown conventional rock of the time and the laid-back East Coast sound currently heralding from America. That may have produced some great songs, but it didn't somehow resonate and inspire the young masses to pick up an instrument.

Two-to-three-minute songs with every precious second filled with promise and sheer spine-tingling excitement, rather than dreary three-minute guitar or drum solos, seemed like a life-saving breath of fresh air. Speed inspired pogoing like a demented meercat while at the same time strangling your mate's neck, rather than sitting cross-legged upon the concert room floor swaying dopily side-to-side, was the dance of the day to accompany punk. Year Zero had reset everything like a dinosaur-destroying asteroid!

The Damned, Pistols, Adverts, Ramones all had laid tracks to vinyl and in March I heard the single version of 'White Riot' (which I prefer by far to the album version) and somehow you immediately knew that they had something to say rather than just fashionably saying it, and that they really meant it! I purchased their self-titled album as soon as it was released in early April, when I found it propped up at the front of the 'Punk' album box in the record shop. And the solarised photo of Joe, Mick and Paul standing in a narrow alleyway on the cover seemed to accurately herald the razor sharp, angry, adrenaline-fuelled sounding contents within. The album was on almost permanent loud play on my turntable.

It was obvious from the start that The Clash would be one of punk's big players, though, as yet, only their stonking cover of Junior Murvin's 'Police And Thieves' hinted at their future progress and diversity.

The DIY punk ethos struck a chord with the disillusioned youth of the time, though perhaps I should say it struck three chords! Some fanzine or other had a produced a crude picture showing three basic chords alongside the wording: 'This is a chord. This is another. This is a third. Now form a band.'

It felt like a rallying call to arms – or guitars! In every city and town in the land, teenagers heeded the call and formed their own bands – myself, aided by my next-door neighbour Pete, did likewise! There hadn't been anything like it since kids borrowed their mothers' washboards twenty years earlier during the skiffle craze. Though both were often crude and very basic Bambi-legged-like stumbling beginnings, it didn't matter! It didn't need to be polished and professional. Being creative, having fun and doing it yourself was all that mattered.

It was to be just over a year after I saw *The Clash* album calling to me across the record shop floor that I was to finally get to see them live at long last, at the very first Rock Against Racism gig in London's Victoria Park.

A PEOPLE'S HISTORY OF THE CLASH

My band mates (Pete, Paul and Adam – known to all as Shaker because of his epilepsy) and I boarded the London bound train departing from Aylesbury that morning, where we alighted at Marylebone and caught the Tube to Charing Cross.

We joined the brimming, colourful, banner-waving throng in Trafalgar Square, just in time to catch the back end of the speeches. Being rather cynical in my observations, it seemed like a vast opportunist recruiting ground for the Socialist Worker party despite the well-intentioned, honest and genuine anti-racist endeavours of many other parties and individuals in the square that morning. Yet I was happy to collect all the bright 'Pogo on a Nazi', 'Nobble an NF Nazi' and other badges being freely handed out.

As the march headed off towards East London, because of our position on the Charing Cross side of Trafalgar Square, we found ourselves filtering in just a few yards behind the very head of the march. Looking behind there was an impressive, seething, endless mass of huge banners all swaying to the movement of the march. All along the long route to Victoria Park the main chant bellowed out by us all was: 'The National Front is the Nazi Front. Smash the National Front!'

Rumours abounded of an expected ambush somewhere en route by the National Front. Thankfully the rumours were just that, and I very much doubt that the NF could muster up enough support to counter the tens of thousands marching the six or seven miles that day.

Being brutally honest we, like so many others converging on Victoria Park that day, were mainly there to see the bands, and especially The Clash. Yet I couldn't help but be caught up and swept along by the chanting mass and I felt quite proud and emotional at voicing and showing my own support against something that I'd always found abhorrent and beyond my own comprehension.

It seemed to take hours to reach our destination. When we finally arrived and stepped onto soft grass after all those miles of trudging upon hard tarmac, everyone rushed to be at the front of the stage area. It seemed like only minutes before one of punk's greatest heroines, Poly Styrene, graced the stage with her band, X-Ray Spex. Most of the marching mass

Ian West's badges reflected the punk sentiment towards Britain's far right

were still yet to arrive. I can clearly recall being caught in the jostling, jarring throng as everyone at the front pogoed in unison at the onset of the first song.

Next up were the superb Steel Pulse with their own British Brummie brand of political roots reggae. I loved them! And it was only a couple of months later, whilst journeying up to Scotland, that I bought a cassette of their excellent debut *Handsworth Revolution* from an M1 service station.

Sometime later that afternoon I needed to use the public convenience situated just behind the back of the stage and who should I bump into strutting alongside me towards the same destination but Mick Jones. I felt too awed to think of anything to say other than something that would sound embarrassingly sycophantic and it was hardly the place to utter something that could be misconstrued such as 'have a good one!'

I joined my mates somewhere among the trees behind the main crowd and in line with the centre of the stage. With the appearance of The Clash imminent, we decided to negotiate a path through the throng towards the front. As we wound a winding path, we spied fellow Aylesburians Kris Needs (editor of *ZigZag* magazine) and his band The Vice Creems (whose infamous second single was reputed to have an uncredited Mick Jones and Topper Headon plus Tony James from Gen X playing all the instruments) sitting in a circle on the grass. Shaker shouted out loudly their name followed by something rude and we ducked down as their heads popped up and they swivelled around in response.

We finally settled in a suitable position about thirty yards from the front just minutes before The Clash bounded onto the stage. Absolute mayhem ensued from the very first note as everyone violently bounced up and down and the atmosphere and energy was scintillatingly electric. It was as if everyone was joined together by an invisible live wire that sent pulsing shock waves throughout the audience. I wish that I could recall each song in order and with clarity, and I've obviously since watched the two songs recorded for the *Rude Boy* film to bolster my memory, though I can clearly recall Jimmy Pursey joining them on stage for 'White Riot' at the end. Yet it's the pure vibrant energy that remains the strongest memory from that day, and the thrill of seeing, at last, what would become one of punk's finest and most enduring bands.

PETER STRIKE

I was only 19. I got the coach up from Norwich, met at Trafalgar Square and set off. I lost my mates and wasn't sure how to get to the park so I followed the march for hours with the police escort through east London. The National Front and skinheads were at every corner pub, pelting us with bricks, etc! We got to Victoria

Park to see the Tom Robinson Band headlining but bloody missed The Clash, X-Ray Spex… I was pissed off, to say the least, but I've still got the poster/flyer from that day.

SUE TERRY

I was 15 in 1975 and living in Cheltenham, Gloucestershire. We all used to moan like hell about how boring it was but we had an art college that had always put on good gigs. I met my boyfriend, who is now my husband, there. The pair of us were in the right place at the right time for the first stirrings of punk. When we first heard The Clash, Sex Pistols and The Damned on the John Peel show, my goodness! My head exploded. There was nothing like it, it was a

totally different landscape. I remember getting the *NME* and reading the very first review of The Clash, possibly after supporting Sex Pistols. I think it was written by Charles Shaar Murray and we were intrigued. I loved reading about them, I loved the music, I thought it was great.

When I first heard 'White Riot' I thought, 'Oh, what's going on here?' I couldn't quite understand the lyrics at first, I must admit, but I understood once I got to know the story behind it and after reading interviews with Joe. In 1976, he came out with that great quote, 'We're anti-fascist, anti-violence, anti-racist, pro-creative, and we're against ignorance.' What's not to like in a band that has that as their driving force?

We saw The Clash for the first time in April 1978 at the Anti-Nazi League Carnival in Victoria Park. I was at the local technical college to do my A-levels and the students union organised a bus. A group of us who were into punk instantly bought tickets, I think it was 60p. It was an incredible event. I was most drawn to the fact that The Clash were there. It was a fantastic bill with X-Ray Spex, Steel Pulse, Patrik Fitzgerald and lots of the kind of people who were on the scene who we had records by or seen in fanzines.

To suddenly find yourself with 80,000 other people, the biggest crowd I'd ever been in, was a little bit too much. I stayed on the edge with some friends, and my boyfriend and his brother and others went down to the front. There were people from all over the country there. I stood there thinking, 'Good God, this is huge.' At the end, Jimmy Pursey joined them for 'White Riot'. I think he did that to show to the skinhead following that he had that he was also kind of on the right side of things.

The Clash showed me how things could be different. When they made all their own stage gear, or were customising things, Paul Simonon said, 'It's alright for the Sex Pistols, they've got Vivian. We've got to get ours from jumble sales and then drip paint on it.' I thought, yeah, we see that! Another reason why The Clash were better than the Sex Pistols was because you could do that at home. I could get a shirt and drip paint on it. I couldn't afford the prices Seditionaries were charging.

I appreciated their creativity and their way of looking at life, in '(White Man) In Hammersmith Palais' for example. Take the 'tear it down, destroy everything' nihilism of Sex Pistols and where does that leave you? With The Clash, I always thought it was 'where does it take you?' It was like they were putting a key in the door for you.

 '(WHITE MAN) IN HAMMERSMITH PALAIS'/ 'THE PRISONER' RELEASED
16 JUNE 1978

BRIAN YOUNG
Whilst 'Clash City Rockers' had nicked its main riff from The Who and kept things moving, nothing could have prepared us for their next 45. If the Clash never made another record this alone would justify their place in the history books. For my money it was the best 45 to come out of punk anytime, anywhere. Yep, it's that good!

IAN MOSS
This was the almighty leap that The Clash needed to make to separate themselves from the constantly growing 'all sound the same' punk rock pack.

Although 'White Man' is nowadays routinely cited as the band's finest record, it was seen as a weird aberration, and it was certainly not universally loved. Starting with a fanfare of guitar, the song moves into something like a grooving ska-rhythm, a perfect backing for Joe Strummer to expound his thoughts, in what is a far-reaching and outstanding lyric. The scene is set for us when Strummer describes attending a reggae gig at Hammersmith Palais which featured Delroy Wilson, Leroy Smart and Dillinger.

He is disappointed by the way in which the artists embrace showbiz protocol, when he expected to be enthused by a rebel spirit. After this, his thoughts turn to the disillusionment he feels with the new 'power-pop' groups whom he considers to be in it solely for the money, and he rails against the sheer stupidity and ignorance of the punk rockers who are too self-obsessed with their petty squabbles to notice that the establishment is completely corrupt and has no moral compass.

Angrily, he makes the point that even Adolf Hitler would be welcomed by the Government if that happened to be expedient. This burgeoning maturity suited The Clash; they had removed their own self-imposed shackles and could now move forward free of any baggage.

CHRIS GREEN

I remember listening to the first LP shortly after it came out. I had many friends who'd seen them at Barbarella's in Birmingham in the autumn of 1976, so I knew they were something special and a bit more than just the warm up act for the Sex Pistols. But I didn't see The Clash live for the first time until 1978.

The game changing single for me – albeit the first LP is wholly visceral for many reasons – was '(White Man) In Hammersmith Palais'. The personal connection I felt to this song was from being a keen West Brom supporter at the time. We had the so-called 'Three Degrees' – Laurie Cunningham, Cyrille Regis and Brendon Batson – playing for us, three exciting British Black footballers in one high profile team. This attracted lots of unwelcome and disgusting racism from the terraces and the National Front in general (from other clubs' supporters, not West Brom I hasten to add) so 'White Man' became something of an anthem my friends and I would sing on coach trips to and from games. It was the musical backdrop to the life and times we experienced, and has had a profound influence on my outlook to life ever since.

Like many fans of The Clash, I saw them several times and bought all the records, but in 1982 I decided to follow them around the country for a large part of the *Casbah Club* tour. Each night, along with several other dedicated fans, we'd turn up at the sound check, ask one of the band members to put our names on the guest list or blag our way into the venue some other way, and after the gig itself we'd go backstage to chat to the band and drink and eat some of their rider.

How easy it was to do this – and to be able to chat to Strummer, Jones, Simonon and Chimes (and indeed members of the entourage) when they had become such a massive commercial band by this point with the success of the singles off *Combat Roc*k – still amazes me and is testimony so how close they were to their fans even when extraordinarily popular.

'(White Man) In Hammersmith Palais' was arguably The Clash's finest 45

The only other band of that time to attract a similarly dedicated following was The Jam. At times, it felt as if both bands were slugging it out to produce the best music of their era – which is why both also fondly remembered with deeper devotion arguably a strong as any other British popular music acts of all time.

When Joe Strummer died in 2002, a large group of friends met to celebrate his life and many of us either go or have been to Strummercamp for many years since.

Each Christmas for the best part of the last 20 years we also go to see a band called Take The 5th – comprised of Worcester-based Clash-inspired musicians and one of the best Clash tribute acts around – to relive some of the best music of our youth that still means so much today. Take The 5th's final gig was on 27 December 2024. Age catches up with all of us.

OUT ON PAROLE TOUR

FRIARS
28 JUNE 1978, AYLESBURY

JOHN FLEMING

I can remember it being a beautiful sunny day. I prepared for the gig by lying in the sun and getting burnt listening to The Clash on my cassette player in the back garden. We were incredibly lucky to have Friars up the road in Aylesbury, where a lot of punk bands played. After me and a couple of mates had changed into our ripped up shirts, held together with the obligatory safety pins, we jumped on the bus for a half hour ride. As 15 year olds, it was quite daunting trying to get access into the strictly over 16s venue, but in we got. We had been here previously to see Blondie, The Jam, the Ramones and the Buzzcocks, but this was a whole different experience. First up were The Coventry Automatics, but they announced that they would now be known as The Specials.

Then it was time. I can still remember the excitement of finally getting to see the greatest punk rock band ever, and boy did they not let me down. People talk about life changing experiences and this was definitely one for me. The sheer power that came from the stage with the coolest fuckers I had ever seen is a memory that will never leave me. I was lucky enough to see The Clash a few more times and they never ever disappointed. People talk about good bands, but The Clash, for me, were the greatest band who ever took to the stage. How lucky was I?

SIMON BRINKLOW

I saw The Clash twice at Friars. The first time was in 1978, around the time '(White Man) In Hammersmith Palais' came out. Me and my mates were all under age because you had to be 16 to get into Friars and we were all 15, but we managed to get in. For the gig we sat upstairs because of the reputation of the crowd and this stuff about trouble but of course we were watching everybody jumping around and then thinking we should have been there! The support band that night was the Coventry Automatics who announced onstage they were changing their name to The Specials.

The second time was January 1980, which was the first gig of the *London Calling* tour. We all had to go over to the record shop in Aylesbury at like six o'clock in the morning to get tickets!

IAN WEST

My second taste of The Clash live was in my hometown of Aylesbury at the famous Friars Club. Punk had already been embraced at Friars, most memorably for me in the form of the Ramones. In just a few months' time Stiff Little Fingers would be just as warmly welcomed and go on to form a long-lasting association that would last for decades. They would even record the magnificently powerful *Hanx* album there. I had no doubt that the Clash would also go down a thundering storm.

As I headed home from my job at the County Offices, just a stone's throw from the current home of Friars at the Civic Centre, I was filled with excitement at the imminent prospect of what would certainly be a gig to be etched into the Friars annals.

As I hurriedly marched down the Bicester Road, I spied a white transit van that slowed right down at my approach and then very deliberately made a move to park up at my side. I instantly knew it was a gig van and I was half expecting to see Joe Strummer's face peering out at me from the side window. Yet as I got a closer view, I could see that the driver was a black guy and sitting next to him at the front were two white guys with a few others sat in the back. A cheeky-looking young chap with a toothless grin wound down the window and called out to me in what sounded like a Midlands accent and asked if I knew the way to the Friars Club. The other white chap – who I'd later find out was the lead singer, Terry – poked his head over his shoulder to listen to my instructions.

I duly tried to explain directions as precisely as I could and before they headed off, I asked if they were the support band and what was their name? 'Yeah, we are. We're the Coventry Automatics.'

I met up with my mates outside the Civic and told them about my encounter and once inside we headed to near the front of the stage in readiness for the support act, as I was very keen to find out what they were like. What ensued was a wonderfully enjoyable and danceable set of what I can only describe as a mixture of punk and reggae. As they came on stage someone (possibly Dave Stopps, the promoter and founder of Friars) announced a name change and that from now on they wanted to be known as The Specials…

Their dress sense wasn't the fashion-defining sharp suits and short haircuts that would soon help spawn a new youth culture. Rather, each member was doing their own thing looks-wise.

After the break, people filtered from the bars back into the main hall and I clearly remember the palpable atmosphere and anticipation building and feeling quite intense. The Clash came on and a sea of surging pogoers started up as soon as the opening song began and continued throughout their set.

The recently released '(White Man) In Hammersmith Palais' was a highlight, as was 'Police And Thieves'. I'm sure there was quite a bit of dialogue between Joe and the crowd, and I have a vague memory of Joe asking the crowd at the front to stop gobbing. (Or perhaps that was at their next gig at Friars.) It was hardly surprising as Joe caught hepatitis that year, reputedly via a globule of spit shooting straight down his throat!

Fears of violence beforehand never came to fruition, and it was pretty uneventful as far as any antagonism was concerned, apart from the usual harsh shoving and the odd punch being thrown when over enthusiastic pogoing spread out to the more motionless parts of the crowd at the sides and back. Upon entering the venue that night, a hand out had been given to everyone asking for peace as The Clash had been banned from all other Home Counties venues due to violence. I'd never seen any major trouble at any Friars gig, and you always felt like you were part of a mostly peaceful family.

Just as with the Rock Against Racism gig, it's mostly the sheer electricity of a Clash gig that still sends shivers and resides even to this day! I'm sure that much of that was generated by Joe Strummer, whose energised style of singing and playing his Telecaster was always so frenetic it was as if he was plugged into the mains.

QUEENS HALL
29 JUNE 1978, LEEDS

BOBBY EVO

We bunked the train to Leeds and bunked into the gig. My mate said, 'We're on the guest list.' The security guy asked who we were. We just pointed at a couple of names and said, 'That's us.' We were in!

GARETH THOMAS

One of the gigs I went to in 1978 was at Leeds University. This is from my diary, obviously written by a 15- or 16-year-old!

Went to see The Clash in Leeds. Unbelievable! Me and Tim set off at about 4.30pm and got there at 8.30pm. Saw The Clash and stayed at Sally's house (my older sister). The concert was amazing and afterwards we both got Joe, Mick and Paul's autographs. They were all nice blokes. On stage, they look stunning, brilliant poses against a backdrop of tanks, troops and bombers. 'White Riot', 'Tommy Gun' and 'Complete Control' were three of the best. Joe Strummer is my hero! I got a Clash badge, autographs and ten photos. I just hope the photos come out well.

I've got no idea what those photos were or where they are now, which is a real shame.

SEAN WALKER

I loved The Clash but hadn't seen them live before, so I was looking forward to it. On first were the Coventry Automatics who were in the process of transforming into The Specials. They blew me away. Me and my group of pals who I went to gigs with agreed they were the best support band we had seen in ages. The Clash were fantastic, everything I hoped and expected them to be. I still love them and all they particularly Joe Strummer stood for. This was the best gig I saw back in the day, until Joe Strummer and the Mescaleros years later. Raw power and passion.

Sean Walker loved The Clash then - and still does

APOLLO THEATRE
2 JULY 1978, MANCHESTER

AK MCALLISTER

The Clash and Suicide at Manchester Apollo. I loved Suicide's first album, *Suicide*. The Clash, not untypically, took a risk in having a synth band as a support act in the eyes of some of their Manchester punk fans, but not for me. I was looking forward to it, and Suicide didn't disappoint. They provided a memorable synth/drama/theatre show for the masses, but it wasn't for the pogo jumpers. Their ten-and-a-half-minute classic, 'Frankie Teardrop', takes us on minimal, stark tragic tale of the struggle and demise of its eponymous hero to cope with the life struggles he is facing as a poor factory worker. They were probably the first punk synth band I heard, and one of the most interesting. All power to The Clash for that risky choice of support act.

A favourite memory of this gig is that The Clash used the song '16 Tons' by Tennessee Ernie Ford as their entrance song. It's a song I've known and sung for many years at house parties with my family, a personal favourite that I've sung in quite a few bars around Manchester since. A great choice as it is so much about what The Clash were about, a worker's song, a story of struggle and poverty song.

Musically, this was probably the best I ever saw and heard The Clash. They were flying by this time. They really were on top of their game, and everything had come together. It's no accident that the band improved when Topper joined. He was a real rhythm driver, a real Clash beat-pulser. His fills on the songs, his up-tempo playing and his relentless energy really brought all the colours of the band clashing stridently to the fore. He was a major driving force for the band's musical movements and energy and no mistake. He set their sound free for me. Topper once asked, 'Well, have you ever seen a great band without a great drummer?' The answer is always no. Great drummers know they're needed. They know what they bring. Joe Strummer would say, after the final split, 'We never did a great gig after Topper left.'

GARY HOUGH

After the Electric Circus and Belle Vue gigs, I next saw The Clash at the Apollo, just prior to my birthday. (I also would see them at Blackburn's King George's Hall on my birthday, 13th July). On this tour they were supported by Suicide and The Coventry Automatics. Suicide didn't go down well, to say the least. The crowd gave them dog's abuse the whole time, but once The Clash hit the stage, the atmosphere exploded with people pushing, shoving and tumbling over each other, trying to get closer to the action. It was chaos, but the band was electric, already on the verge of the big time. I still kick myself for missing their secret gig at Rafters afterward – there were no mobiles back then to give you a heads up!

CARL ROE

I'd seen the Boomtown Rats on the Friday evening with a pal and two young ladies, and I'd mentioned going to see The Clash on Sunday but I think stripey pyjamas were as punk as they felt. So poor me was looking at going on my own, something I've never had issues with, whether it was football, gigs, whatever.

Out of the blue I get a phone call asking 'do you want a ticket?' Blah-blah… 'I've got one…' blah-blah. Gang of lads I knew, one of them being the local – shall we say – cool bloke who got into punk before punks did. I'm invited to meet in his garage at 5pm. I suspect there are eleven of us. One of the lads' dads is offering a lift there and back. The real rebels are getting the bus but Mr Waring got seven of us in his Ford Escort and laughed at how we dressed. But he admitted his folks did the same when he went to see the Kinks. I still see Eric. He must be 90-odd.

You know when you go to a gig and kind of dismiss the support? Well the Coventry Automatics (aka The Specials) were magnificent and I was so pleased to see them make it. Suicide's set was abruptly ended by a rather intense bottling by the home crowd with one of the band sustaining an actual cut head. I remember Mick Jones introducing 'Stay Free' as 'Stay Dumb'.

GED DUFFY

July 1978 started with The Clash playing the Apollo supported by Suicide and The Coventry Automatics. The latter were the first band on, and the reception was mixed. I thought that they were great as they were different to any band around at that time with the ska beat mixed with punk guitar and their movement on stage was great to see.

Within a few months they would be massive and known by everyone. Next on were Suicide and I already owned their debut album so I was really looking forward to seeing how a Clash audience would take to them. Within a few seconds of the opening song starting, the audience were booing and shouting at them. After a couple of songs, the two guys in Suicide were shouting back at the crowd and sticking the V sign up to them. The crowd then launched an endless attack of bottles and cans at the stage until Suicide did a runner off stage which was greeted with massive cheers.

The Clash started with 'Complete Control' and 'Tommy Gun' and the Apollo went wild, with people standing on the seats on the ground floor. Seats were getting broken and there were some scuffles with the bouncers in front of the stage. They did 'Clash City Rockers', '(White Man) In Hammersmith Palais' and finished with 'White Riot', 'Complete Control' (again!) and 'Guns On The Roof'.

SIMON EASON-BROOKES

My first live gig to see The Clash. Whilst having a pint next door in the Apsley Cottage next door to the Apollo (still the main watering hole pre-gigs, and still a hole!), a big guy sat next to me, and we got chatting. 'Can you dance?' he asked. 'You bet' I replied. 'Get down the front then and I will pull you up on the stage,' he said. I wasn't sure but there he was as we took our seats. 'Get up there,' my mate Si said. So up I went, the guy hauled me up on stage and away I went, bouncing and swaying away, loving it.

The band finished and the big guy screamed at me to get backstage. 'Fuck off,' I shouted, 'I've got a ticket to see The Clash.' I scrambled down off the very high stage and rejoined my mate. The Clash were superb that night. Years later I discovered that the band I had danced with were The Specials. Wow, what a night! How much would it cost now for a ticket to see both The Clash and The Specials on the same bill (if it could happen!)?

Many years later, it was my pleasure to set up Strummercamp, a festival to celebrate the life and musical influences of the late Joe Strummer…

GUY BURKE

I was slightly late to the punk rock party, still holding onto the coattails of prog giants like Genesis and the alternative of all alternatives, Mr David Bowie (still my all-time favourite artist). By late 1977 I was beginning to waver and a trip to the Manchester Apollo around November to see The Jam was a life-changing evening. This was followed in 1978 by seeing Buzzcocks, Boomtown Rats and others, and then came The Clash…

It was Manchester Apollo again and strange, as it will no doubt appear to many, it was cash on the door, £2.50 (possibly why a recent Clash tribute I saw were offering 'limited 1978 prices of 3 quid'). It irked me slightly as it had been a lot cheaper for The Jam six months previously.

The Clash always offered value for money. The support acts were Suicide, fronted by the later legendary front man Alan Vega, who were roundly booed off stage, and the bunch of 'Coventry' Specials that followed and who didn't fare much better. Thankfully it didn't put them off from establishing themselves a year or so later! The Clash ripped through a set that lasted just over an hour including the encore of 'White Riot'.

The next time I went down to Ardwick to the same venue for The Clash (the *16 Tons* tour) I was turned away as it was 'sold out'. In some ways it felt like the day punk rock truly died!

I never saw The Clash again but did see Joe live just before he died, for which I am truly grateful.

RAFTERS
3 JULY 1978, MANCHESTER

AK MCALLISTER

I was working in Rare Records, a record shop on John Dalton Street in Central Manchester. We, alongside Virgin Records, were one of the only shops keeping pace with the rapidly developing punk scene. We had a clientele of regulars including Martin Hannett and Ian Curtis, who also worked there for a short time, and many other well-known Manchester music lovers.

The day after the Apollo gig, we had a visit from Johnny Green, the very personable road manager for The Clash, and I had a conversation with him about the previous night's gig. I told him how much I loved the band, etc. and, lo and behold, I was immediately invited to a secret impromptu gig at Rafters on Oxford Road that night. I was the proverbial Sir Chuffed of Chuffed Manor to be invited and, yet again, nobody disappointed.

Here we were again, back in a small, dark venue, a compact stage and a packed-in crowd, all feeling a bit honoured and privileged to be at a 'secret' Clash gig. (It was a bit on the elitist side, this feeling, but there we go - nobody's perfect!) What a brilliant night.

Joe was literally hanging upside down from the rafters in Rafters, like a bat. His voice was shredded from the previous night's Apollo gig, and he was swallowing honey from a jar, praising its benefits for his throat and voice. There were enough people in the place to provide the exciting atmosphere to reflect the band's presence and energy and it was reminiscent of the *Anarchy* tour gig at the Circus.

Musically, they were so much better by then. They were vibing off each other and I think the impromptu nature of the gig made this feel more like the early days of punk. They knew it, we all knew it. I remember this as another brilliant gig. There's no doubt in my mind that The Clash were more suited to the small, dark, sweaty rock 'n' roll venues than they were to the bigger stages of the big venues.

GED DUFFY

The night after the Apollo they played a secret word-of-mouth gig at Rafters.

During the day I had gone to town and walked past Rafters and there was a handwritten sign outside saying 'The Clash live here tonight'. When we got in, we'd missed Suicide, so I have no idea how they went down or how long they managed to stay on stage for, but since there were only about 80 people there, I think they must have been okay.

The Clash were amazing in a small venue and played a great set. I remember they had a banner that said 'FUCK' behind them on the stage and Joe Strummer climbed up onto the rafters and hung from them during one song.

APOLLO THEATRE
4 JULY 1978, GLASGOW

JANE DICKIE

I lived in Troon and travelled up to Glasgow by train with a crowd. This was 1978 and Suicide were supporting. The crowd didn't like them much! I'm not sure what happened but the power went off and the whole place was in darkness apart from the luminous paint on the front of my home-made Mick Jones t-shirt! He was my hero and first crush.

The Clash were late on and had only played a few numbers when the Troon crowd had to leave to catch the train. I didn't budge when my

Jane Dickie wouldn't leave until she'd heard Mick Jones sing

pal Beano said to me, 'We've got to go.' I said 'not 'til Mick sings', and he waited with me. We figured we would have to hang about Glasgow Central Station until the morning. I was 16 and Beano was 14, just kids. Finally, Mick sang and we bolted down the city street in our bondage trousers, me with hair coloured green with food colouring, and both us covered in badges and with huge smiles on our faces. We made the train.

If we'd hung around, we might have caught up with Mick as he legged it out of the Apollo as this was the night the bouncers started beating up the fans, not unusual at Glasgow, and Joe didn't like that at all... but that's another story.

A PEOPLE'S HISTORY OF THE CLASH

SAUL GALPERN, NUDE RECORDS

Without The Clash and punk, I'm not sure I'd be doing what I'm doing now. I grew up in Glasgow through the whole glam, Roxy, Bowie thing. And coming out the back of that there was a gap. I admit I did listen to Genesis and Pink Floyd for a bit as well, like everyone, but I threw the records out, or sold them at Record & Tape Exchange, when I heard The Clash. They're the band that changed my life, there's no question.

'Anarchy In The UK' was the first thing I heard living up there, and it was just like, 'Wow what is this?' Then I heard about the Grundy interview and my obsession for the whole movement began. I started buying every record I could. I just loved it. The Clash represented so much, the whole political consciousness, they had that more than any other punk band. I suppose Crass later in a very different way, but they were really a bunch of hippies.

Musically, The Clash managed to evolve and become one of the great rock bands, like the Rolling Stones of that generation. A lot of people don't like to say that, but I wanted the bands to become successful because people were like, 'Oh, it's not great, it's noisy, it's not musical, they aren't songs.' So I was so happy when The Clash did break through.

They were supposed to play Strathclyde University which would have been my first time seeing them. It was an over 18s show. On the day I turned up to hang out at the record shop. People used to do it, just hanging around outside the record shop – weird, right? There were ten to 15 kids waiting outside every day. That's what we did in that punk period.

Bruce's Record Shop was quite well-known. Bruce Findlay had two shops – one in Edinburgh, one in Glasgow – and he was the original manager of Simple Minds. Anyway, The Clash turned up and we were chatting to Joe and the rest of the band, telling them we couldn't get into the gig that night as were weren't over 18. Joe ended up going off on the back of some guy's motorbike, saying they'd cancel the gig if the kids couldn't get in… and the gig got cancelled! They never played there.

When they came back to Glasgow they played the Apollo twice. I went to both shows. It was either late in the year or just freezing cold. I was wearing a boiler suit which I'd made up with painted stuff all over: 'Clash City Rockers', 'Complete Control'. I was living in Renfrewshire and was stuck in Glasgow after the gig. Renfrewshire wasn't that far, but back then the last buses were 11pm. I thought my parents were going to go berserk. I went into a hotel and they looked at me and it was a case of 'you're not coming in here, mate.' I asked if I could call my dad and I knew he'd speak to them as otherwise I couldn't get home. My dad spoke to the concierge of the hotel and they let me stay the night. Dad had to come into Glasgow the following morning and pay the hotel!

At the Apollo was where they filmed live stuff for the film *Rude Boy*. It was absolute mayhem; the bouncers were beating people up and I got shoved down the stairs a couple of times. The hilarious thing is you look back at what happened and the band had almost incited it. They would come off after the gig and then come back on for an encore. Mick Jones would be telling the bouncers to leave the kids alone, and then say, 'We've still got another number to do…. 'WHITE RIOT'!' Absolutely chaotic!

There was a lot of violence. My mate was a hairdresser and I'd said to him, 'I want to look like this guy Billy Idol,' and I produced a photo of him when he was in Generation X. I came out of the hairdresser and was walking down the road and got punched twice by a Teddy Boy. That was a mad experience.

The Clash were the best of all the bands and the ones that continually made extraordinary records. Thinking back, the gap between the first and second albums was bizarre. It was a long time, about 18 months, which is normal nowadays, but you had The Jam putting out two albums in nine months or something.

The Clash made up for it later. The wait for that second record felt like forever. I think the reason *Give 'Em Enough Rope* got a real mix of reviews was that it had been built up for such a long time. Obviously, we got the singles like '(White Man) In Hammersmith Palais' and 'Clash City Rockers' in between.

A mate of mine called Craig worked in a record shop not far from where I lived, but not in the centre of Glasgow. When *Give 'Em Enough Rope* came out, he was my port of call. I was calling him on the day of release, asking if it had arrived. I could have gone into town and got it…. He called me around 3.30pm so I had to get on the bus to get it. I was so excited.

When *London Calling* came out, I remember the lyrics to their songs: the anthems; the attitude; the clothes, the poses. It was the belief The Clash had and the shows that they did. The energy and the anger, they were first band with any kind of rallying battle cry, with real conviction.

Thinking back musically, there weren't many bands, then or even since, that have so much diversity. Listen to things like *London Calling* and then *Sandinista!* and then *Combat Rock*. On these three albums they're moving away from the rock thing and are early adopters of rap, hip-hop and reggae. It's weird that John Peel never liked them really. For me in Scotland, he was the saviour, he was the person that you had to listen to every single night; but he didn't like The Clash. I don't think he thought they were authentic enough or maybe they were too studied for him.

A PEOPLE'S HISTORY OF THE CLASH

It was punk and The Clash that led me to the music industry. Punk laid the groundwork for me to know that this was what I wanted to do. I was so into music and buying records, collecting seven inch records. I was interested in the label and who was behind it, that whole side of it always appealed to me. I didn't know what record labels did, but I knew I wanted to get into it, and this was the catalyst for me, with punk and then of course the following on musical genres – post-punk and after that the alternative bands and electronica. I just had to move down to London.

There was a time when I was doing everything because it was based on The Clash and their influence. I went round to Paul Simonon's house like a few years ago. It was bizarre. He had all these art paintings, and he was trying to sell them, and it was fascinating trying to have a conversation with him about stuff, but I was so wary of being a bit of a fan.

I moved to London with Craig in early 1980. We had a tiny, tiny bedsit on Baker Street, in Gloucester Place. We had a tiny room, and we didn't have a kitchen or a bathroom. The bathroom was outside. Craig got a job at Virgin Megastore so I was gutted that he was there. I got a job at a record shop called Bonaparte Records. It was a bit like a Rough Trade back then and they had a couple of shops. One was in King's Cross which back then wasn't exactly a place you wanted to be seen in! They had a mail order department and used to advertise in the back of the *NME*. I started working there doing mail order, putting albums into mailers and posting them off to people.

The guy that started Human out of Bonaparte's offices used to work with Eric Clapton. We signed the Au Pairs, two girls and two guys from Birmingham. Then Chris and I, who were running it, went and started the label Kamera. He used to spend most of his time down the pub or in the bookies and he hated indie music and punk! We signed The Fall and did *Hex Enduction Hour*, which is their legendary album.

It was a good grounding for me to learn from a lot of different areas of the industry, not just the creative sides. I was going out to all these gigs, seeing these bands, and realised I needed to go and work for a bigger company. I went to Elektra who had just opened a UK office and I ended up signing Simply Red. That was my grounding. I then worked for RCA but got made redundant from RCA. Then I decided that I wasn't going to work for the man anymore, and that's when I decided to start Nude Records.

GORDON RUTHERFORD

They ruined it all. By ensuring that nothing could ever reach those dizzying heights again, they deprived me of future pleasure. I've long been envious of folk who go to random gigs and report back as though they have attended the birth of the second coming. I never could. My gratification was eternally satiated in July 1978 and The Clash must bear full responsibility.

I was incredibly fortunate to see them a few times, but that night in the middle of the school summer holidays of '78 was the first. Unless I've forgotten one, it was the third gig I had been to, after Queen (an interesting introduction to live music) and The Stranglers. Nothing was ever the same again.

Memories? Well, they are hazy now. Clouded around the edges. But, from my safe European vantage point on the balcony of the Glasgow Apollo, I do vividly remember the splashes of scarlet. My skinny white knuckles gripping the seat in front, my eyes darting between the stage and the blurred bodies exchanging punches in the aisles; limbs like whirligigs. Punks versus bouncers. Later, on the pavement of West Nile Street, more pitched battles. Punks versus cops, their frenzy mirrored in pools of blood. It was both frightening and thrilling in equal measure.

The show itself felt short and sharp, with The Clash relentlessly expelling anthem after anthem. There was no in-between-tune banter. No false plaudits about what a wonderful audience we were. This was purely business. I remember Strummer, his leg pumping like a piston as he spat out the words. To his left, legs apart and bass slung low, stood the Adonis, Simonon. Glowering. Seemingly disinterested, although we would later learn that nothing could be further from the truth. On the other side of that vast stage, throwing shapes, was Jones. The one most interested, or was it concerned, at the mayhem occurring below.

There was such an intensity, a ferocity. The sound and the fury. Oh, those songs, each one hitting you like a juggernaut. But the thing that made most impact was not the music. It was the authenticity. Nobody else in the history of rock 'n' roll meant it like The Clash meant it. They performed as though they were the last band on earth, delivering the last show ever. Perhaps they were. There was nothing artificial; they never went through the motions. In football parlance, they left everything on the pitch. And more.

In doing so, The Clash ruined it all. I attended hundreds more gigs, but I can count on one hand the number that came close to that night at the Glasgow Apollo in 1978. The Clash set a bar that was just too high; they set a standard that others couldn't reach. And I'm not that tolerant. I never forgot that night. I never will.

KINEMA BALLROOM
6 JULY 1978, DUNFERMLINE

LENNY HELSING

Like many young pop music fanatics during the seventies, when the punk explosion happened, I felt that it was something I could really belong to, much more than what had already gone before. Although I also loved loads of the glam rock and hard rock groups.

The first live gig I saw was Slade at the Leith Citadel Theatre, in Edinburgh in 1975. Because I was still at school and lived in a small village a few miles down the east coast from Edinburgh, I couldn't afford to go to lots of gigs, and I missed out on seeing a lot of the early punk gigs happening in town, including the May 1977 *White Riot* tour, and The Clash with Richard Hell and the Voidoids and the Lous at Clouds on the *Out Of Control* tour a couple of months later. But I did manage to see The Jam there on 15 July.

The next time The Clash played I was determined to go, a few weeks before turning 16. I got a ticket for their gig from Ripping Records in Edinburgh, who were running a bus for the gig, so off we went over the water into Fife and the Kinema Ballroom in Dunfermline. I'm still not sure if we arrived late or whatever but think we missed the first support band, The Coventry Automatics.

Anyway, before we knew it, the main support was up on stage doing their thing. This was notorious New York duo Suicide. They were getting some serious amounts of gob all over them, often spat out venomously by a constant stream of narrow-minded punk yobs who obviously couldn't handle all the electro-noise rock 'n' roll terrorism the group was putting out. Like many others, I felt sorry for them. Alan Vega could at least dodge some of it but Martin Rev on keyboards just had to stand there and take the brunt of it.

When it was time for The Clash to come on, the whole place just erupted and went totally mental. The floor seemed to be in constant motion, like a sea of mass pogoing for every song… You couldn't help but just get caught up in the moment; there was no other option, as I soon found out. After a while I began to feel lightheaded and then everything went blurry. I still vividly remember that I then just tumbled right to the floor. It seemed to happen as if in slow motion. There were a few people around me just trampling down on me, and some were trying to move me out of the way. I don't know how long I was

Lenny Helsing pictured in 1979

down, maybe it was only a few seconds, or at most maybe a minute or two. Then I was being helped back onto my feet and after I found my bearings, I tried to move a little further back where I could at least begin to breathe a little easier.

It was a pretty scary, but ultimately a truly exhilarating experience, my first time of being totally in the thick of it, even though I wasn't anywhere near the front. At the end of the gig, I bumped into the older brother of a friend of mine from my school and he gave me a lift home in his car.

NIGEL WELCH

At 16, I first heard 'White Riot' on Radio 1 in the summer of '77. Up until then, my musical education had been provided by Black Sabbath, Led Zeppelin, Thin Lizzy and the like. I tuned into John Peel's late-night shows to listen to all the punk that was coming out. That, and reading *Melody Maker* and *NME*.

As soon as 'White Riot' came on I was hooked. It just had a freedom about it, even though I couldn't understand all the lyrics. This was *my* music. The next album I got was *The Clash* and I didn't stop playing it all summer.

Nigel Welch was a heavy metal fan until The Clash came along

In 1978, I was in Scotland. The Clash were on the *Out On Parole* tour, before *Give 'Em Enough Rope*. The support was from The Coventry Automatics and Suicide, who spent their whole set being gobbed on. The crowd was mad, and it was packed.

It was one long adrenaline rush. I was pretty much at the front. Joe was snarling and inadvertently spitting as he sang. Simonon was a tough-looking motherfucker. Mick and Topper just went about their business. The gig went by in a flash but they couldn't have played for much more than an hour. The crowd was so whipped up that we just ended up on stage. I didn't have any choice, I just went along with the momentum.

My memories are hazy, but it was one of the greatest gigs of my life. It was also one of the sweatiest. The next morning, my blue(ish) Levi's were red from the dye from the red jeans being worn by the girl in front of me.

A PEOPLE'S HISTORY OF THE CLASH

SANDY MCLEAN

I didn't really get The Clash's first album that much. I didn't really get them until I saw them play live. I got it then. They really were a people's band. The first time I saw them was in Dunfermline. I later saw them a couple of times at the Apollo in Glasgow. I'd go whenever they came to Edinburgh or Glasgow.

They came to Dunfermline just before the second album came out. Joe and Topper had been in my shop the week '(White Man) In Hammersmith Palais' came out. They flew up to do a radio station interview, did that for an hour and then the radio DJ brought them to Bruce's (the local record shop), dropped Joe and Topper off and buggered off back to the radio station. The two of them had four hours to kill before their flight back to London so they just hung out. We left them in the wee office in the back and Joe rolled joint after joint and played records. We went to the bakers across the road and got coffee and sandwiches for them and they just chatted about music for literally hours. It was brilliant. People would come in and they could see Joe Strummer behind the counter. He would serve a few customers and signed anything they wanted. It was all very good natured, unplanned and spontaneous.

Joe told us he had a Scottish mum. It was the 1978 World Cup, and a Scottish comedian called Bill Barclay had a novelty single out called 'Hoat Pies For Us, Argentina'. We had the badges and the posters in the shop. The badge was a wee blue soccer ball saying 'Hoat Pies For Me, Argentina' and Joe thought that was hilarious, so he took one of those away with him.

About a month later, they were doing a few shows, and they came to Dunfermline to do a one-off show. They played songs from the second album that no one had heard yet, and it was pretty exciting to hear 'Tommy Gun', 'Safe European Home', 'Julie's Been Working For The Drug Squad' and all those songs that we all know so well now for the first time.

I went backstage afterwards, and Joe and Topper, both remembered me. We chatted like old friends, and they gave me a beer and I just smoked dope with them and hung out with them for ages until the venue kicked us all out a couple of hours later. For a fan it was just amazing to be treated like that, but that was the way Joe treated all the fans. They had an open-door policy in the dressing room at all their shows. Joe's charisma was just incredible. Geldof, Strummer and Ian Gillan are the only three people I've met who've just got this amazing charisma, such that when they walk into a room they just glow and make each person they talk to feel that they're special and that they have a story to tell that they're genuinely interested in. He just worked his way around the room, chatting to everybody. He would speak to all the quiet fans and say, 'Come over here, sit down, do this, do that'. He was very,

very inclusive. It was quite amazing to watch.

But Joe wasn't wearing his 'Hot Pies' badge and I asked him where it was. He said, 'someone stole it off me in Croydon.' He knew exactly where he lost it. Luckily, I had one with me, so I gave him another and he was super grateful to get it back. He said, 'I thought it had gone forever.'

SPORTS CENTRE
8 JULY 1978, CRAWLEY

DAVID WALLACE

I lost interest in The Stranglers early on as I suspected that they were old wave bandwagon jumpers to an extent, suspiciously musically competent and politically suspect. Conversely, I really bought into The Clash and especially idolised them for their political posturing and their image and attitude. It is hard for young people to understand how difficult it was for an impecunious schoolboy to even listen to the music back at that time; for various reasons, I couldn't even always listen to the John Peel Show and the £4 or so that an album cost (maybe £40 in today's money) was very hard to find, especially as the cost of attending concerts was a more reasonable £1 to £2.50. One really shopped around and weighed things up. But buying the first Clash album was a no-brainer after reading the *NME* interviews and it remains my favourite album of all time.

The first time I saw The Clash was at Crawley Sports Centre in July 1978 – the so-called *Out On Parole* tour. It's hard to describe to the uninitiated how desolate and violent late seventies Britain was. This Clash gig is well known as having been one of the most violent and intimidating music events of that whole era. Hordes of latter-day skinheads had arrived in town from London, the first time I had ever seen them en masse. They were hell-bent on destruction and had a love/hate relationship with bands like The Clash and Sham 69. The skinheads found the music and flourish exciting but the politics was anathema to them as they were far-right football hooligans at heart.

I knew my punk bands very well but was surprised that third on the bill was a band I had never heard of, The Coventry Automatics, who were later to become The Specials. They were sensational. The venue would have been half empty and not long open and it was quite easy to stand or bounce around at the front of the stage in absolute wonderment at the energy and excitement on show.

Second support band were notorious New York combo Suicide, who specialised in avantgarde keyboard noise. Their set came to an abrupt halt as the frontman was physically assaulted on stage by one of the skinheads. Not good, as I was interested in what they had to offer.

The Clash themselves played an electrifying set, the highlights of which would have been the anthems from the first album and the well-known 45s. Their image at that time had developed slightly from the early agitprop/stencil/homemade garb but they still looked and sounded like the embodiment of the punk ethos. I had to stand further away from the stage during their set as the skinheads were too dangerous to be near, and antagonistic towards spiky heads such as myself. They were even more unsafe for the female friend I was with, who was 17 like me.

I did have a ticket for The Clash concert that was supposed to have occurred at The Roxy in October of that year but I think it was cancelled and maybe rearranged. I had to cash that in as I couldn't attend the rearranged gig due to school commitments. I was absolutely gutted, although possibly partly relieved, either suspecting or knowing that Harlesden was not a safe place for me with no train home and a bed to sleep in. Sometimes we would sleep rough in that era, but I was getting in a lot of trouble at school and my mate had been very badly beaten up after a Siouxsie and the Banshees gig in Brighton earlier that year.

> **THE CLASH PLAYED AN ELECTRIFYING SET...**
>
> **DAVID WALLACE**

STEVE PALMER

They were supported by The Specials and Suicide. This is an infamous gig due to the violence from skins. Horace Gentleman from The Specials recalled this gig when I met him. Skins beat up anyone with long hair in the audience and jumped onstage to attack Suicide (they couldn't get their head round the music and reacted in the only way they knew). Amidst all the mayhem The Clash were – as always – brilliant!

RICHARD MURPHY

I was 15 and attended with two school mates, Chris and Gary. Little did we know this would become one of the most infamous Clash gigs. It was attended by hordes of skinhead gangs from London, Brighton and various other places and beset with violence as rival factions clashed with each other and roamed the hall, randomly attacking anyone who was not a skinhead. Thankfully, as young 15-year-old schoolboys we were pretty much left alone.

The support was The Coventry Automatics, followed by Suicide from the US. This is where it went wrong. Lead singer Alan Vega came on stage in a ripped-up Teddy Boy outfit. The skinheads took an instant dislike to him, and a big, meaty skinhead jumped up on stage and attacked him, punching him several times in the face. According to press reports afterwards, he suffered a broken nose and they described how Suicide bravely finished their set. My memory was them leaving the stage and refusing to come back on (and why would you with a broken nose?). Jimmy Pursey of Sham 69 then jumped up on stage and appealed to the skinheads in the crowd to 'stop fighting with everyone!'

The Clash arrived on stage and delivered their set without any problems and were excellent. It was later described as the most violent Clash gig ever, and I don't think anything surpassed it.

TOWN HALL
10 JULY 1978, TORQUAY

DAVE PORTCH

I got into The Clash through a friend's older brother in late '77 or early '78. He had an *Anarchy* tour poster from the cancelled Torquay Ballroom gig. I heard the 'White Riot' single and was starting to read the music press. I bought their debut album on the day of its release from the local record store. I got as far as 'What's My Name' whilst sat in my bedroom lacing up my DMs. I was blown away. 'Police And Thieves' was a complete eye opener and the gateway to me getting into reggae. (Later on, I heard the original on John Peel one evening.) Everything on the album spoke to me and made it perfect listening for a pissed off 15-year-old.

The Clash on the *Out On Parole* tour in Torquay was my second ever gig and is still the best ever night of my musical experiences. Whilst in the queue to get in, the doors were a little late opening and the crowd got a bit edgy and started shouting, 'We want The Clash!' Suddenly there were police on horseback – unheard of in Torquay! There was no trouble though.

I don't remember much of The Coventry Automatics, but Suicide were amazing, although I didn't 'get' them. They were so powerful and threatening despite being gobbed on and having glasses thrown at them. All I remember of The Clash is dancing non-stop with my mates and singing along to tracks.

From that day I was totally committed to The Clash. They influenced me in many ways. I gave up on the last bit of school and flunked all my exams. Music became all consuming, as did the clothes. I hung onto Joe's words of wisdom.

I saw them again in 1980 at St Austell Coliseum in Cornwall with support from Theatre Of Hate – another great band. After that I saw them again in Bristol in August 1982, Mick's last English gig. Later I went to the Brixton Academy gigs with the second-generation Clash. They were still a superb live act with fantastic supports (they always had the best support bands).

I can still remember where I first listened to every Clash release. Every album was mind blowing, and each one has grown over the years and is still regularly listened to. I have seen all the band members as solo artists, and blagged my way into a BAD gig by getting Mick to put me on the guest list.

The Clash informed my thinking, my politics, and the need to be yourself and not follow the sheep. Rotten may have said 'get up off your arse and do something' but The Clash made you do it. It is because of their attitude and inspiration that I travelled the world, became a psychiatric nurse and stood up to all the shit the system throws at you.

NOTHING stands the pressure of a Clash City Rocker!

MASSIMO PRUDENTE, AGE 16

I was 16 years old, an Italian student from Rome studying English in the UK in Torquay. I was heavily involved in the massive student and social/political movement 'movimento' in Rome whilst listening to rock music and Italian musicians with radical political views. I was very lucky, as my English teacher was also a member of the Socialist Workers Party. One day he came to me with a concert ticket. He said that 'this was a band that you have to see'. The band were The Clash, a punk band that had sprung up in West London. I was surprised by the gift but happy and excited by what was to come. The venue was close to where I was staying.

But at this time I was more of a 'fricchettone' which is slang for hippie so I dressed in my Italian military fatigues and made my way there. Outside the venue punks mingled. One struck up a conversation with me whilst we waited to get in, hanging on my shoulder, his wrist wrapped in a metal studded bracelet. My first punk experience! The concert was explosive and very exciting. I felt like something inside me was changed forever!

I didn't become a punk overnight. It was more of a collective transformation that myself and my friends made back in Rome. There was a great punk scene in the early eighties, and specifically a club called Uonna (an acronym of uomo/donna, men/women), where punks, skins, Mods and rockabillies coexisted peacefully, for the most part.

ALL THE YOUNG PUNKS

⭐ TOP RANK
12 JULY 1978, BIRMINGHAM

PAUL HITCHMAN

As a young kid in 1977 I was looking for something new. I was bored with the old wave so when punk came along, I was all over it. A lot of kids I knew were talking about the National Front but when I heard the first Clash album and read the interviews in the music press, I knew exactly whose side I was on. I felt like it was a time of taking sides, old wave or new wave, old politics or new politics. Sitting on the fence was missing the point. 'Like trousers like mind,' as Mr Lydon once said. The Clash were always my favourite band, I liked the others, but I really related to that idea that they were 'the only band that mattered'.

Paul Hitchman (right) knew it was a time of taking sides when it came to the National Front

I saw them in 1978. I had just left school and was massively into punk. Support band Suicide were brilliant although the crowd showered them with glasses throughout their set. The Clash came on late, hot, sweaty and loud! I've never seen a band with so much energy. It's been said before but they were like 'three sticks of dynamite!' I was crushed right in at the front.

That gig brought it all to life. I'd just left school and was there with my mate, both of us wearing the regulation leather jackets and DMs. It always felt like Joe was singing for the kids, like he was pointing things out that we all felt, but expressing them in a way that none of us just could find the words to describe.

'Birmingham's burning with boredom now,' he sang at the Top Rank, and nobody could've put it better. The night went by in a blur. It felt like we'd been knocked sideways by the energy in the room. I remember stepping out into the cold night air after the gig, turning to my mate and saying, 'We need to buy some guitars!'

⭐ CORN EXCHANGE
14 JULY 1978, BURY ST EDMUNDS

GARETH THOMAS

I saw The Clash again in Bury St Edmunds and they were stunning, much better than Leeds where I'd seen them previously. After the gig I got them to autograph my 'White Riot' picture sleeve. I lived in Peterborough so got the train to the venue and arrived in time to see the support act, who were this playing this reggae-type music. The lead singer had long curly blond hair. They were The Coventry Automatics, but nobody had heard of them and of course it was the band that would later become The Specials. They blew the place apart. When they played 'Dawning of A New Era', they were amazing. I'm sure I wasn't the only one to wonder how were The Clash were going to follow this.

Of course, The Clash came on and were just amazing, as they always were back then. Three guys standing at the front, legs apart, giving off determination and commitment. They played a brilliant set and once again broke down the barriers between the audience and the band. They'd always come out and meet the fans afterwards, so we waited for them to come out. When they appeared, they were like a magnet. All the girls ran towards Paul, who was mobbed. The other guys had people going over to them, and that's when I got out my sleeve of 'White Riot' signed.

ERIC'S
22 JULY 1978, LIVERPOOL

PETE BENTHAM AND THE DINNERLADIES

I saw The Clash at Liverpool's famous venue in July 1978, thanks to an older mate, Jerry, who helped me get into punk. I was messing about with guitars with a couple of mates at the local community centre in Widnes that had some amps we could use. I grew up on The Beatles, the Stones, The Who, The Kinks, etc. and on soul and Motown, which were my older brothers and sisters' records (I am the youngest of five). I was also a bit baffled by the appeal of the prog bands of the time such as Yes and Genesis. Not just the highly complex music but how terrible they looked on the *Old Grey Whistle Test*! The only contemporary band I remember liking for a while was Dr Feelgood, who had that simple rock 'n' roll appeal (and look).

One day in late 1977, we were playing guitars in the community centre when a double denim-clad older bloke, who was a local social worker, came and chatted to us about music. When I say older, he was about 25, which you think is ancient when you're a teenager. He asked us if we were into the punk thing. We had bought 'Anarchy In The UK' when it had come out and a few other punk records, and we all listened avidly to the John Peel show. So, yes, we were into it, but being from out in the sticks, we'd never been to a punk gig. (We'd been to a Thin Lizzy concert at the Liverpool Empire).

At some point, Jerry offered to drive to Liverpool to Eric's club, which was one

ALL THE YOUNG PUNKS

of the main punk venues in the country. The gig was by Magazine, the new band formed by onetime Buzzcocks singer Howard Devoto. I reckon this was early 1978. The venue made a major impression on me. It was a hot basement, a standing gig and the punters were dead young kids like me, in all manner of DIY outfits. It was so different to the Thin Lizzy gig, which was seated and where you bought a programme and sat waiting to be entertained from the big stage. In Eric's, you were almost on the stage and the volume of the music, both bands and deejays, were on another level. Several more trips to Eric's followed to see more punk bands including The Damned, Stiff Little Fingers and Wreckless Eric and the reggae band Steel Pulse.

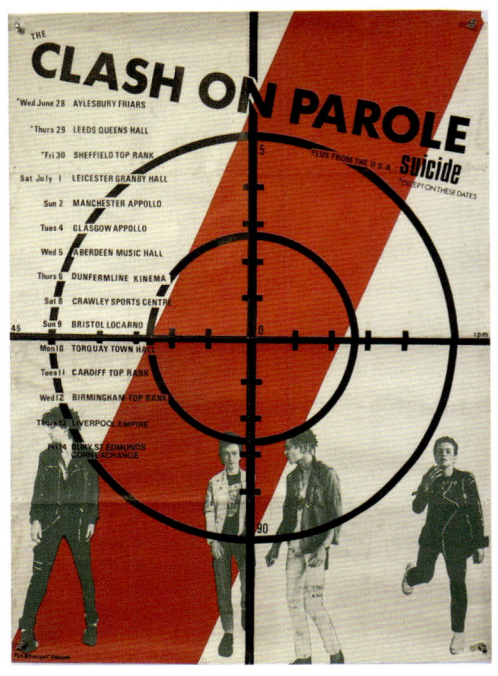

The Clash played Eric's in Liverpool after their scheduled gig at the Empire was pulled

One Saturday, when we went to the club to buy tickets for another gig, there was a piece of A4 paper stuck on the wall that said tickets for The Clash were on sale. This was when The Clash were starting to outgrow the clubs and move to bigger venues. The story was that they were supposed to play the Liverpool Empire, but the Empire had refused to take the seats out so instead they were playing two shows – a matinee and an evening gig – at Eric's. We had to get tickets for this. On the night of the gig, and after a couple of pints of Dutch courage in The Grapes pub, I seem to remember getting in the club without a problem. The first time we'd gone to Eric's, they wouldn't let me in, as I still looked about twelve when I was 18!

The support band was The Specials, but not the band we came to know and love. Singer Terry Hall had a kind of Goth haircut and they hadn't yet developed the 2-Tone sound, so we didn't really pay too much attention to them.

By the time The Clash were ready to come on, the club was absolutely packed. Being small, I had to balance precariously on a beer crate to be able to see the band. This was difficult as the crowd was like being on the Kop at Anfield in the old days. You were thrown one way and then the other. The band were explosive, starting with 'Complete Control'. It was – and still is – the most exciting gig I've ever seen, although I remember my mate Jerry being worried that Mick was becoming too much of a guitar hero. My abiding memory is of the sweat from the ceiling raining down on us. It was that hot. Internet research tells me that the set included 'Blitzkrieg Bop' by the Ramones, but I don't remember that. In fact, a lot of the details are lost in the mists of time.

The inspiration and the feeling I took away from that gig has stayed with me forever and it's fair to say it changed my life, in that I wouldn't have had the DIY spirit and confidence to do my own band if it wasn't for that club, and specifically that gig. My own band make records and constantly tour the UK and Europe, so thanks for that.

THE MUSIC MACHINE
24-27 JULY 1978, LONDON

ADAM PORGES

One of my mates had seen The Clash a couple of times in 1977 and raved about them but for some reason I hadn't gone, being not quite sold on the early days of punk and its ethos. Instead, I was hanging onto my loyalty to The Who and the Faces.

Two days shy of my eighteenth birthday, all that changed when I got to see them on the *On Parole* tour at the Music Machine in Camden, a venue right on my doorstep and one we often frequented. I don't think we bothered to get there early enough to see either of the support acts as I have no recollection of either the US band Suicide or The Coventry Automatics, but I certainly made up for it, seeing The Specials a few times not long after.

The Clash simply exploded on to stage with 'Complete Control' as the opener. In the mayhem, I got myself right down the front and into the action, with the audience going completely mental. They went straight into 'Tommy Gun', a superb live number and always much better live than on the single. They were such an exciting live act. Visually they were so captivating: from left to right across the front of the stage you had Mick Jones in red shirt and black jeans; Strummer in white cap sleeves; and Paul Simonon in black leather. They were just so damn cool, you couldn't take your eyes off them.

The set was a mixture of unheard new stuff from the soon to be released *Give 'Em Enough Rope* album, like the excellent 'Safe European Home' and Mick Jones singing 'Stay Free', interspersed with most of the classic debut album and the singles such as 'Clash City Rockers' and the majestic '(White Man) In Hammersmith Palais'. What a great night. The buzz I felt coming out into the Camden summer night still lives with me.

The Clash were at the top of their game around this period and, most importantly, they knew it and knew what was becoming possible. They were a completely brilliant live act, brimming with ideas and with their growing audience completely in their hands. *London Calling* was still 18 months away and the conquering of the US was also still to come. I saw The Clash half a dozen more times in London over the next few years, including later in 1978 at the same venue for the Sid Vicious Benefit, and they were always great but none more so than this night.

I fell in love with The Clash on that July evening and if ever asked for my best or favourite gig, for sheer excitement and adrenalin both on the stage and being in that crowd, my answer always will be 'The Clash at The Music Machine'.

ED SILVESTER

I was in awe of The Clash, and I dreamt that I'd somehow meet the band backstage, but I quickly knocked that idea on the head, as invariably meeting your idols turns into a disappointment and an anticlimax. So I'd stick to watching them live and buying their records. I'd bought tickets for this gig in advance but when I turned up, I was horrified to find out that The Clash were not going to hit the stage until almost midnight!

I was in a quandary. Did I wait and watch the first few numbers and jump on the last Tube home, thus getting into work late the next morning, or bugger off home after seeing the support bands? The desire to see The Clash perform won the day. Suicide, the American support band, didn't go down well with the partisan crowd, who had beer glasses thrown at them.

The Clash however were superb that night, the crowd having waiting were bristling with excitement before they hit the stage. Annoyingly, I ducked out before the end of the gig (to catch my last train home) and missed Steve Jones singing the encore with them. My Clash craving had temporally been satisfied, and I eagerly awaited their second album.

SORT IT OUT TOUR

ULSTER HALL
11 OCTOBER 1978, BELFAST

RORY MCDONALD

The Clash first came to Belfast in October 1977, but it was cancelled and a small riot started. My mates and I were able to get round the back of the Ulster Hall where the band were but were soon thrown out. There were only about 20 real punks in Northern Ireland in 1977 before it became the thing to be. It was soon full of posers who would dress up for a gig and then go back to grammar school. It seems funny looking back but it really was mostly working class that were the real punks we lived it and breathed it.

They came back in 1978, again to the Ulster Hall. A local band, The Outcasts, supported them. I was 16, it was my second ever gig, and as the old cliche goes it changed my life. Being a punk in Northern Ireland was a very risky business.

The Clash came back in March 1984 with the new line up. It was a good night, but it wasn't the same without Mick and Topper, and then they were gone…

 GYMNASE LE STADIUM
16 OCTOBER 1978, PARIS, FRANCE

DYLAN WHITE

In the summer of '78, I reconnected with a schoolmate I'd lost touch with when his parents moved. He'd got into punk so we became best mates, and he had the bright idea that we would go and live in Paris and form a band. I went along with this idea. I earnt a living playing guitar by busking badly and we hung out with Parisien punks. There was a record shop called Haricot Verts, which means green beans in French. You'd meet French punks there.

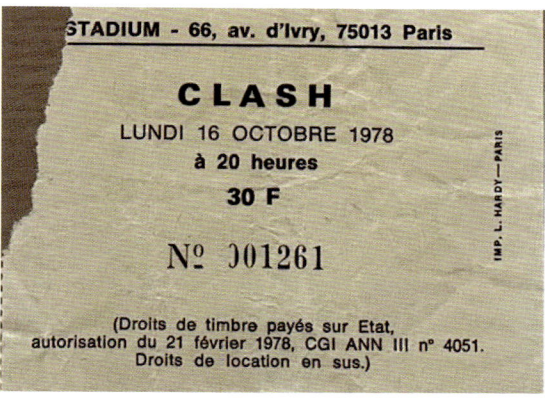

Dylan White saw The Clash in Paris with a mate he'd lost touch with

Paris was brilliant. Clubs were open, so you could get beer whenever you wanted. Bear in mind the pubs in England shut in the afternoon and they shut at 11pm at night. Paris was open. We could do what we wanted, and we were two young English fellas, so we had a ball. In the time I was there I saw the Ramones, The Stranglers – I went with a Parisien guy which was quite handy, because Jean Jacques spoke to the audience in French – and The Clash.

The Clash gig was at Le Stadium. Support was from The Lou's, a French band. It wasn't a theatre with theatre seats or a theatre bar. It was very much like some sort of indoor sports arena.

The Clash came on and were slick. They'd been touring a while now. They were now a proper rock band, and they delivered a very professional show. Mick Jones

ALL THE YOUNG PUNKS

was running from one side of the stage to the other while playing the guitar and they ran through all the singles, the first album and parts of the second album, which had just come out or was about to.

Me and this French mate had hung around earlier to try and meet them. We hung around with Johnny Green, who was their tour manager, but we didn't see them. After the show, I shouted out to Paul Simonon, 'Hey Paul, it's been worth the trip!' in an English accent and he winked at me. They were top of their game, the highest of the high. They were the top dogs all the way into *Sandinista!* No question.

⭐ PARADISO
21 OCTOBER 1978, AMSTERDAM, NETHERLANDS

ERIK VERZIJL

I have two older brothers, Peter and Rob and we lived an hour north of Amsterdam in typical middle-class suburbia. We were music lovers and got into punk/new wave around 1978. As a punk-version of Huey, Dewey and Louie, we used to travel by train to gigs in Amsterdam, primarily at the Paradiso. We saw the Ramones there in early 1978 and discovered that you could just walk into the soundcheck and chat to the bands.

So we did just that on Saturday 21 October when The Clash were playing there. The band looked amazingly cool, even in their off-stage clothes. I took along my copy of 'White Riot' and got it signed after the soundcheck. I got a bit silly and carried away, as I also asked them to sign stickers and even my Converse trainers! What was I thinking? They signed them.

I still have the sleeve and the stickers. I had a small camera with me and shot a few photos. After the soundcheck we

Erik Verzijl photographed Mick in action at the Paradiso in Amsterdam

waited outside so when we got in, we were right up front as we always wanted to stand where the action was.

First up were the Dutch punk band The Filth, who were pretty good. But we were there for The Clash. You can understand the impression it made on us. The sheer power and energy that Joe showed, the rock-star poses of Mick, the ultimate cool of Paul and the powerhouse that was Topper blew us away. We became fans for life. The set was a mix of relatively old songs and some unknown to us, including singles and some which would be released on *Give 'Em Enough Rope*.

Erik Verzijl got his copy of 'White Riot' signed

The Paradiso was sold out that night and literally packed with young punks, and a massive mosh pit was the result! Unfortunately, I never got to see The Clash again, although my brother Peter did at Jaap Edenhal in Amsterdam and The Music Machine, London. I only have good memories…

LUUK VERSLUIJS

This was the second time I'd seen The Clash, a year after my first time in the same venue. It was a sold-out show. Near the end of the set of support act, The Itch, a Dutch punk band, I noticed Joe Strummer standing next to me. I asked him, 'Do you like them?' He said, 'No'. This was the complete conversation I had with Joe shortly before the support band's set ended. I watched Joe walking out of the main hall wearing a long leather jacket. I wished I had a jacket like that.

The Clash's set list consisted mainly of songs from the forthcoming album *Give 'Em Enough Rope*. I didn't know these songs, but they sounded great live. Near the end of the gig, it got so crowded on the floor that I went to the balcony to watch the remainder of the show from there. It was very crowded there too, but I stayed there till the end.

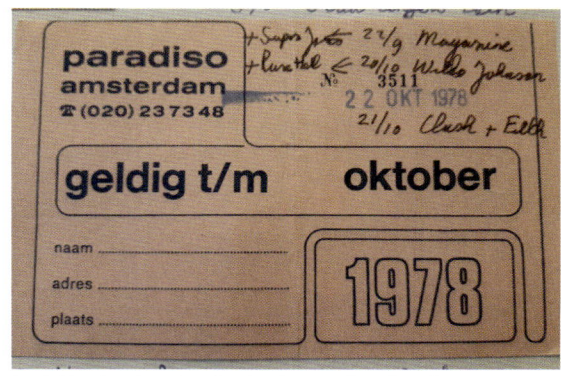

Luuk Versluijs's ticket for the Amsterdam Paradiso

ALL THE YOUNG PUNKS

ROXY THEATRE
25 OCTOBER 1978, HARLESDEN, LONDON

HARRY WANDSWORTH

The Clash at The Roxy

Initially scheduled for Saturday 9th September 1978, the gig was postponed after Bernie Rhodes infamously announced the band had gone on strike against UK radio stations for not playing their records enough on the airwaves, with a nod back to the lyrics on 'Capital Radio' stating they were in tune with nothing. Joe, Paul and Mick came out to apologise to the crowd of kids who turned up that night and they hung around for a few hours chatting to everyone.

A recently turned 16-year-old pip squeak, I approached Joe to have a natter before thinking to myself 'what the fuck do I ask him?' I piped up something completely naff along the lines of how had he found the States on the tour they'd just come back from, and was he still bored with the USA? He offered me one of his cigarettes and I puffed on half of it, before putting it out and sticking it in my pocket as a memento.

The rearranged show took place on a chilly Wednesday night in late October and I left my apprentice electrician's job in Mitcham at five o'clock sharp to get there. Every ticket holder was handed a complimentary 'Tommy Gun' t-shirt on the door to make up for the cancelled show.

This gig is one of my favourites amongst the dozen or so times I saw The Clash. The band were on fire, a burning inferno of unrivalled energy played in front of a backdrop of assorted international flags. Strummer's onstage convulsions epitomised the excitement in the crowd. Simo and Jones's guitar poses embodied a coolness not seen since the Feelgoods, with Paul's bass slung low and Mick's guitar pointing to the sky as he leapt around the stage, while Topper bashed those drums into oblivion.

A PEOPLE'S HISTORY OF THE CLASH

The whole show was absolutely electrifying, covering tracks from the first two albums and throwing in 'I Fought The Law' for the first time. Having nicked a drumstick at a Pistols gig at Brunel University a year earlier, I jumped on stage at The Roxy and added one of Topper's to my collection whilst the roadies were distracted.

MARTIN JONES

When the postponed show was meant to have taken place the band were outside talking to fans and I was listening to Mick, who was leaning against a car. He threw his cigarette butt on the ground, but instead of stamping on the butt, he stamped on my toes. Anyway, I returned the following month. The band opened with 'Complete Control'. I'd first heard the song on John Peel in and it was the best thing I had ever heard, and 48 years later it is still the best song I've ever heard in my life. The Clash would often start or end their set with 'Complete Control', but I found over the next six years that I much preferred it when they finished their set with it, saving the best till last! I would get goose bumps when I heard them play it live and occasionally it brings tears to my eyes. If I ever think about planning my own funeral, it will be on the playlist. For years, it was also the last song I would play before I went out anywhere.

Sadly, one of my memories of the night at the Roxy is the skinheads, who would go on to disrupt so many concerts over the next few years and would often make for an uncomfortable evening, especially if you were on your own.

RICH HARDWICK

I was living in Perivale and set off on the 83 bus, full of anticipation. Upon arriving, I noticed the place was in darkness and walked to the doors and a crudely written notice simply said, 'The Clash cancelled.' It was then I noticed a few people milling around in groups. As I approached one of them, I noticed it was Joe Strummer in the middle. He addressed me, saying, 'Sorry mate, the fuckin' gig is off again.' I can't remember what I uttered in my broad Scouse accent, but Joe noticed, asking, 'Where've you come from?', and I know it was a bit of a lie, but I replied

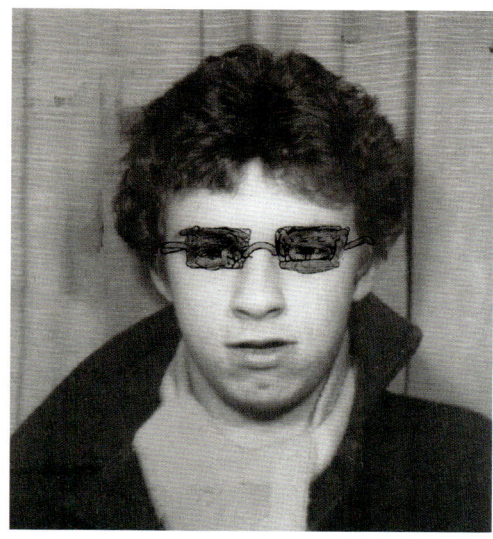

Rich Hardwick's first gig experience was Gary Glitter

'Liverpool'. He apologised even more profusely, so I said that it was ok and that I was staying at a mate's. I know it wasn't the band's fault, but in my moment of woe at missing the gig I just left it at that!

The gig finally took place at the end of October. This was my first live experience of The Clash. It was monumental. I was close to the front, stage right, and I bounced away from start to finish! We got given 'Tommy Gun' t-shirts because of the cancellation(s), and I put mine on straight away under my leather jacket. How I wish I could get into it now (although I do still have it). Apparently, some bits of the concert were used in the *Rude Boy* film, but I haven't managed to spot them. I was in a daze on the bus back home and so thankful I got to hear songs like 'Complete Control', 'Police And Thieves', 'Stay Free', '(White Man) In Hammersmith Palais' and 'What's My Name'. They even did 'Blitzkrieg Bop'!

GARETH THOMAS

Another unbelievable concert, their best yet. They looked superb. Mick Jones looking like a cowboy guitar hero, Strummer as an intense prisoner and Simonon just coolness personified. The crowd went mad as they came on stage and straight into 'Complete Control', which was a hell of a lot better than the single!

In my diary I wrote, 'They also did 'I Fought The Law', a non-original, a great song. I can't wait for the new album, *Give 'Em Enough Rope*!'

It wasn't released until 1979, so this was possibly one of the first times they played it.

 GIVE 'EM ENOUGH ROPE RELEASED 10 NOVEMBER 1978

PHIL CURME

The second album came out. I really liked it, but the adrenaline rush of the early years wasn't there. It was almost as if the first album and early gigs went beyond music – there was something much more powerful going on. I felt they had sold out for the US market and whilst I continued to really rate their music, they weren't the force in my life that they had been previously. In the early days it felt like we were all comrades in arms. When The Clash started hitting the charts it began to feel like they were public property – just another rock and roll band, albeit it one of the best. *London Calling* was great but more head than heart.

Sandinista! and *Combat Rock* are good in parts but by the time Mick was thrown out they were going into territory that didn't mean much to me, although I accept it took them to a whole new audience. I kept the faith though and bought all the Big Audio Dynamite albums, Joe's solo stuff and Paul's Havana 5am album. The latter is hugely underrated.

One of the first gigs I took my son to was Joe Strummer and the Mescaleros and The Good, The Bad and The Queen.

GREIL MARCUS

One version of rock 'n' roll, from the Official Scrapbook of the film *Sgt. Pepper's Lonely Hearts Club Band*, produced by Robert Stigwood, directed by Michael Schultz:

We decided that for the ending of Sgt. Pepper *we should create a moment of spectacular movie magic and have Peter Frampton, and the Bee Gees joined by the collective star power of scores of famed recording stars … Formal invitations were engraved… The guests were treated royally-first-class transportation to Los Angeles, limousines, luxurious hotels, the finest champagne and food-nothing but the best.*

Another version, from a report in the UK fanzine *ZigZag* on a concert that took place last year in Belgium:

Fifteen feet from the stage is the ugliest, most vicious-looking barbed wire fence you ever saw. Ten feet tall, effecting perfectly an arena within an arena, only this inner arena is where the privileged hang out, and behind this monstrosity of a fence the other arena, where the less privileged have been herded like cattle…

Suddenly, Strummer leaps into the inner arena. He streaks straight to the fence, and with his bare hands he is pulling and tugging at the bastard as hard as he can. For a second nobody knows what to do, and then all hell is let loose. Security men grab at Strummer, other people leap from the stage and grab the security men…

Joe Strummer, twenty-five, is the lead singer of The Clash. Along with guitarist Mick Jones, twenty-three, he was in San Francisco to finish of the recording of the second Clash album, as yet untitled – a record a lot of people have been waiting for. An English punk band formed hard on the emergence of the Sex Pistols, The Clash are now so good they will be changing rock 'n' roll simply by addressing themselves to the form, and so full of the vision implied by their name they will be drama-tiring certain possibilities of risk and passion merely by taking a stage.

Meeting Strummer, it's not hard to imagine him ripping down a fence separating his band from its audience. A joyful loathing of such elitism is part of what kicked off the English punk revolt in the first place, and no band has tried harder, or more self-consciously, to live up to that revolt, to keep its spirit whole, than The Clash. Built like Bruce Springsteen (a comparison Strummer, who takes Springsteen for a myth-addled softie, would not appreciate), with a James Dean haircut (no DA), black leather jacket, white t-shirt, suspenders attached with safety pins to buttonless black pegged pants, and the kind of boots they used to say your mother wore, Strummer carries himself like a man who takes nothing for granted. A few hours around him left me sorting out suppressed rage from a quick sense of humour, as in The Clash's music, you feel a wearied, bemused intolerance for frauds large and small, and a biting eagerness to wipe them out.

From the beginning, Strummer, Jones, bassist Paul Simonon and drummer Topper Headon (briefly replaced by Terry Chimes, according to the born-again spirit of punk renamed Tory Crimes) have appeared as a gang of partisans bent on the defeat of all the right enemies. They've never hedged their hatred of Britain's neo-Nazi National Front (some of Mick Jones's friends are members, as was Strummer's brother), their disgust with what Labour and the Tories have done with their power, or their embrace of reggae and its commitment to righteousness and Judgment Day. 'London's Burning,' 'White Riot' and the rave-up cover of Junior Murvin's reggae hit 'Police And Thieves' all on *The Clash*, their first album, still unissued in the United States because its sound was considered too crude, were part and parcel of a refusal of any version of the barbed-wire fence.

Middle-class in background, working-class in the themes of their songs and in Strummer's crunched accent, The Clash have been understood as 'political' for the right reasons, because, more directly than other bands, they saw in punk proof that apparently trivial questions of music and style profoundly threatened those who ran their society. That meant those who ruled were afraid, which implied that their hold on power was not so certain as it seemed. Politics thus became an intensified, eyes-open version of everyday life but if the Sex Pistols were frankly nihilistic, asking for destruction and not caring what came of it, The Clash are out for community, the self-discovery of individuals to solidarity, a new 'I' as the means to a discovery of an old 'we.'

Just as it was something punks and everybody else lived out off-stage, politics was something to dramatise onstage, until the limits and contradictions of one's life could be tensed, revealed and broken through. This was the clash the band named itself for - and acted out or played out on record or in front of audiences. What began as a stance, as a pose, was soon no act at all. The Clash didn't seek targets for protest songs, they sought a purchase on reality. They didn't carp about bad jobs - their 'Career Opportunities' was about Mick Jones's onetime job as the lowliest letter-opener, which is to say as the opener of suspected IRA letter bombs - they made noise out of their humiliations.

What has been extraordinary about The Clash is their ability to create a sound, an attack, that pushes beyond any here-and-now British specifies of race, class or culture, details that might dim their power elsewhere. Their strongest record so far, 'Complete Control,' a UK-only single, is on paper nothing more than a petulant denunciation of CBS, their British label, for releasing a 45 without first clearing it with the band. It comes across not as a naive complaint about artistic freedom but as a cosmic last stand, perhaps the most thrilling, transporting version of the punk impulse to leap from the smallest insult to greatest refusal, a definition of how much anger and determination are worth, and of how good they can feel. It's hard rock that ranks with 'Hound Dog' and 'Gimme Shelter' – music that, for the few minutes it lasts, seems to make both seem uncertain, even eager to please.

Some of the almost completed tracks I heard at The Automatt studios in San Francisco were better. Producer Sandy Pearlman, a New Yorker brought in to make The Clash palatable to American audiences, has broadened the sound – 'There are,' he announced, 'more guitars per square inch on this record than in anything in the history of Western civilization' – but he hasn't compromised The Clash's darkness, or their force.

'He couldn't,' said Strummer. 'Though he's been trying for six months to turn us into Fleetwood Mac. I think he just gave up last night.'*

The Clash have drawn on the fuck-you sound of the New York Dolls, the Stooges, the early Rolling Stones and The Who, and on the romantic populism of Mott the Hoople, but those influences long ago ceased to be more than footnotes. What you hear now in the storm of their sound is reggae, in the rhythm section, and, in Strummer's furious singing, in Mick Jones's crossing guitar lines, and in the twists and turns of the song structures, Captain Beefheart. One of many rock 'n' roll prophets-without-honour rescued from oblivion by British Beefheart is a Southern Californian who in the late punks, combined Delta blues (mostly Charley Patton and Howlin' Wolf), bebop and the sprung rhythms of American speech out of Mark Twain, Mike Fink and neighbourhood bars into awesome, and often awesomely difficult, music, caterwauls and clatter, polite greetings that hinted at obscenity, drunken curses breaking up revival meetings, preachers silencing blasphemers.

His masterpiece, the 1969 *Trout Mask Replica*, broke every rule in rock 'n' roll except one, move the listener. As Mike Bloomfield once put it, it didn't matter if it was Robert Johnson's most delicate, heartbroken guitar piece, or The Rivingtons declaiming 'Papa-Oom-Mau-Mau, Papa-Oom-Mau-Mau' again and again and again (I know it's 'Oom-Mow-Mow,' but 'Mau-Mau' is what The Rivingtons meant), it had to make you sit up and say, 'What? What?', and Beefheart's music always did.

'When I was sixteen,' Strummer mused when I mentioned the *Trout Mask* echoes I thought I heard in The Clash's new tracks, 'that was the only record I listened to for a year.' The Clash have taken Beefheart's aesthetic of scorched vocals, guitar discords, melody reversals and rhythmic conflict and made the whole seem anything but avant-garde. In their hands that aesthetic speaks with clarity and immediacy, a demand you must accept or refuse. It sounds like a promise rock 'n' roll has waited years to keep. The sense of confusion and doubt in the sound is still there, along with a sense of triumph.

There is also a claim on history, made and unmade. In 'English Civil War', which simply by its title both harks back to the seventeenth century and posits a future no one wants to think about, Strummer somehow jumps the years and takes over the voice of a twenty-year-old conscript who's stepped into the no-man's-land trenches of the Great War and now, just for a moment, speaks his piece. 'Guns On The Roof,' a song that began as an account of the arrest of two Clash members for shooting pigeons, turns into music about terrorism, and Strummer sings as a prisoner in the dock; if the fear and pride he communicates mean anything, he'll never see the streets again.

As the band uses the beat from The Who's 1965 'Can't Explain' ('Very traditional, don't you think?' said Mick Jones) to set off bombs in the courtroom, Strummer charges the bench, 'I swear by/ ALL MIGHTY GOD/ To tell the WHOLE truth/ And nothing but – the TRUTH!' Guitars rain down on every line, you're taken out into the battle outside the courtroom, back to the courthouse, and, finally, in a grand, bitter fantasy of freedom, across the world. 'I'd like to be in Af-er-ee-ca,' jibes the singer at himself. 'I'd like to be in the USA/Pretending that the wars are done.'

These songs take the harshness of the sound kicked up by the Sex Pistols and The Clash's first recordings to its limits; 'Safe European Home' shatters them. Inspired by a trip the reggae fans made to Jamaica, a pilgrimage that turned up sour ('I went to a place where every white face was an invitation to robber-ee,' runs the key line), it's a wild, self-mocking testament to the way the attempt to escape your own culture inevitably leads to being thrown back upon it. A

STRUMMER SINGS LIKE A PRISONER IN THE DOCK...

GREIL MARCUS

high, keening, up-and-down guitar line pushes Strummer's raging vocal; Mick Jones slaps him back with incessant harmonies, taunting, 'Where'd you go?' The music is almost too strong, the pace too fast; finally, it breaks, and the band changes into a new, metallic reggae as Strummer and Jones shift into a Jamaican patois as distant, and as revealing, as Strummer's borrowed cockney, the voices drifting across each other, dub style, until humour and betrayal share the song with anger and delight. The Clash make it home safe, not exactly where they want to be, but the only place they belong. They may want the world but in the heart of this song, it doesn't matter that Lee Perry, Jamaica's finest, produced 'Complete Control', or that Bob Marley said yes to The Clash in his 'Punky Reggae Party.' The Clash, this song says, must fight their own war, on their own ground.

The wars The Clash are turning into music – wars of class, race, and identity – are all too real. How they turn out will determine what The Clash, and their audiences, will make of their lives. But the war The Clash are fighting is, for better or for worse, mostly a rock 'n' roll war, a struggle to define and seize the essence of the music, to take over its history, to refashion its past and future according to what can be done by a few people, now. The Clash seem eager to get on with it.

Killing time one day before their nightly sessions in the studio, Strummer and Jones found themselves in a movie theatre, face to face with the result of all those engraved invitations and hired limousines-with platinum-coated barbed wire. 'It was unbelievable,' Jones said of the *Sgt. Pepper* finale. 'They had 'em all! Every ligger in LA! Tina Turner, Alice Cooper, Dr. John – everyone with nowhere else to go!' The film at least provided an idea for an album cover. 'These are the people who've made rock 'n' roll what it is today,' Jones said, 'and I think we owe them some sort of tribute. We'll put every one of them on the sleeve of our record, just like the faces on the Beatles' *Sgt. Pepper*, everyone hanging from –'

'Gallows,' offered Strummer.

'No,' said Jones thoughtfully. 'Lampposts.'

The choice was not without meaning; gallows are a sign of authority. Lampposts are what the kids in the Clash's streets would use, if they had the chance, or took it.

* He didn't. The album Pearlman produced, *Give 'Em Enough Rope*, came out thinned and distracted, with highs and lows missing; Fleetwood Mac's 1977 'Go Your Own Way' had far more. Mick Jones had picked up the central, explosive guitar riff of 'Safe European Home', the album's strongest song, from the live version of Sammy Hagar's 'I've Done Everything For You,' on the radio constantly as the band worked in San Francisco. Pearlman erased the riff from the final master, fearing it would sound like a cheap cop, and thus erased the voice of the tune.

ALL THE YOUNG PUNKS

GREGG JOHNSON

I guess I got into them when I was ten, when our Neil bought 'White Riot' and that (band), along with the Pistols, really got under my skin and, to be honest, changed my life forever.

   I wonder if this still happens these days to kids? There doesn't seem to be any 'youth explosion', no tribes. Maybe we can't see it cos we got old?

   I gotta say I'm a huge fan of the second album. I remember getting it for Christmas the year it came out, in '78. I loved it, and still do. Don't get me wrong. I love the first LP, the sleeve, the typography. I always rated 'Hate And War' and 'Police And Thieves' off that, but the second album? Fucking hell, it's like a jet engine going overhead when the needle hits the groove. 'Safe European Home', what a tune, what an opener…

   Of course there's our beloved 'Stay Free', 'Drug Stabbing Time', fucking 'Tommy Gun'. It's brilliant. I know it got some criticism for bringing in a big name producer, but it adds depth to the sound and with Topper on sticks they sound unstoppable.

   I submitted a version of the typography to help me get into signwriting college, and I'm still at it over 40 years later. That's the power of The Clash.

JANE SAVIDGE, PR LEGEND

When I was at school, I wrote The Clash on my schoolbag before I'd heard anything by them. That was because I thought their name sounded punk and I only wanted punk names on my schoolbag and that's presumably why Neil Young ended up on there too. I thought he must be the singer in a band called Teenage Filth - or something like that.

   Then I heard them on John Peel and I bought 'Complete Control' and I knew I'd found the band for me. Back then as a young teenager, a few months was like a ten year wait and that's why 'Safe European Home' is still my favourite song of all time; it kicked off their 'difficult' second album *Give 'Em Enough Rope* a full five months after the last thing I'd heard – '(White Man) In Hammersmith Palais' – and I must have played it fifty times that first week after I'd bought the record. I remember *Sounds* magazine gave the record five exclamation marks because it was too good to award stars to.

   Years later when I first met Joe and was about to work with him on something, I really wanted him to notice me, so I said, 'Joe, do you know how many times you refer to cash or money in the lyrics of your songs?'

   He didn't know so I said, 'Twenty-seven!'

   'Gave all his money away' ('Jail Guitar Doors'); 'You got no money' ('Complete

Control'); 'Turning rebellion into money' ('(White Man) In Hammersmith Palais'); 'And he loved to steal your money' ('Bankrobber'); 'The money feels good' ('The Guns Of Brixton'); 'I don't want to hear about what the rich are doing' ('Garageland'); 'Just because we're in a group, you think we're stinking rich' ('Cheapskates').

'And you even covered 'I Fought The Law' so you could sing 'I needed money cos I had none'.'

He laughed and my heart melted. What a beautiful man, what a beautiful band.

GARETH WILLIAMS

'I practice daily in my room…'. I've always loved songs that tell a story, and 'Stay Free' really speaks to me. To be fair, the Clash are full of songs with stories. I was too young to see them play; I was 15 when they split up and more interested in The Smiths. But politically and musically, the Clash were important whilst I was evolving into an adult human being. The first two albums, *The Clash* and *Give 'Em Enough Rope* were always on my record player and were always PLAYED LOUD! (Probably why I can't hear anything today!)

MICK COUCH, MATT MCMANAMON BAND

The vivid memory of seeing *Give 'Em Enough Rope* in the local record shop and the necessity to own it was overpowering! Getting it home and listening HARD to every track was just life modelling. The lyrics were more informative and inspiring rather than instructional.

Fast forward FORTY years and I got to meet Mick Jones and let him know his lyrics in 'Stay Free' – 'Go easy. Step lightly. Stay free,' – are just the greatest guidance any friend could give another. It's a wish, a hope, and an expression of true meaning. PROPER!

IAIN KEY

By the time I got into The Clash it was already all over bar the shouting. The first 'new' single I was aware of was 'This Is England'. However I had spent many hours over the summers of 1982 and 1983 listening to a copy of my sister's cassette of *London Calling*. I recall the edition of Radio 1's Roundtable when the Clash Mark II single was featured with the guests including Noddy Holder and Paul Weller. Holder asked Weller if he'd ever consider reforming The Jam, to which he replied, 'No, and I'd have not reformed The Clash either.'

Over the years I've become a fan of the band, and did get to see Joe on a couple of occasions. However, the one thing that will always stick with me is my memory of doing a paper round circa 1986. A family friend, Paul Mould, had given me a copy of *Give 'Em Enough Rope* on cassette. Unfortunately, whilst my cheap Walkman would automatically play both sides, there was something that had broken inside the device meaning it couldn't be removed without damaging it. Until I was able to save up enough for a new personal stereo, I set off – come rain or shine – with 'Safe European Home' marking the start of my daily routine!

ODEON THEATRE
16 NOVEMBER 1978, EDINBURGH

LENNY HELSING

Following the Dunfermline gig in July, the next time I saw The Clash was on the *Sort It Out* tour with The Slits in support.

A small bunch of us showed up outside the venue in the late afternoon, and not too long after The Slits arrived in a battered van. I remember Ari Up saying to us that they were skint and that they were all really starving. A few of us who were hanging around clubbed together and bought one or two pie suppers from a nearby chip shop and shared it around.

I recall The Slits were great on stage, even though by then they'd already begun to leave their more primitive punk status behind and were rhythmically experimenting and deep into the dub style reggae sounds they were becoming renowned for. I remember Budgie's drum sound was massive.

I only remember a couple of things about The Clash on stage that night. They were loud, really energetic and the crowd was excited. The gig had to be stopped towards the end when they tried to play 'White Riot', which resulted in half the audience trying to get on stage. The bouncers didn't like this and started lashing out. Joe and Paul told them to stop being so heavy handed. I remember one or two of the group ended up getting involved in the fray, trying to fight off all the bouncers.

We went back to where the band were staying that night, the Barnton Hotel on the outskirts of town. They didn't seem to mind us all hanging out in the bar talking to them. After a while they started going off to their rooms and we thought they were going off for more drink, or maybe to get stoned or something. Somewhat naively in hindsight, we attempted to go with them, but I remember Caroline Coon saying something along the lines of like 'no guys, this is as far as you go.'

After that everyone started to leave the bar. Most of us walked back into town, all still elated about the whole evening.

TOWN HALL
17 NOVEMBER 1978, MIDDLESBROUGH

DAVE PRATT

I saw The Clash at Middlesbrough Town Hall a couple of weeks after the Banshees played the same venue. This performance was probably one of the best I have ever seen in my life. The energy, the passion, the movement on stage and the atmosphere that The Clash created were nothing short of amazing. They pretty much played the best tracks from the first two albums and their singles to date including 'I Fought The Law', 'English Civil War', 'Tommy Gun', 'Complete Control', 'Janie Jones', 'Garageland' and 'City Of The Dead'. I was exhausted just watching them.

The Clash weren't terribly tight or brilliant musicians. Some people would argue that they weren't the best songsmiths around either, but they just had this exciting charisma. That night they flew into their opening track 'Safe European Home' with such aggression and belief that the audience were sucked into their world immediately. I don't think I have ever seen a crowd like it at the Town Hall, either before or after this gig. It was absolutely staggering. Before the term 'mosh-pit' was ever invented, this was the epitome of it. The crowd at the front moved fifteen yards to the right and then pushed back to the left in waves throughout the entire set.

The band were relentless, delivering a barnstorming gig that has become historic. It was one of those concerts where about ten thousand people claim to have been present at a fifteen hundred capacity venue.

I got backstage. When talking to Joe Strummer, I explained that I was learning to play the guitar, and he showed me how to play bar chords right there and then. So, from that moment onwards, my claim to fame would always be that the legend that is Joe Strummer taught me how to play guitar.

When I left the backstage area, I made my way to the bus stop to find my mates and, on arrival, discovered that most people who'd exited the venue via the front door had been beaten up by a large gang of skinheads, who had been waiting outside. I was completely bemused by the sight of Peter Harrison, Barry Redden and even some of the girls

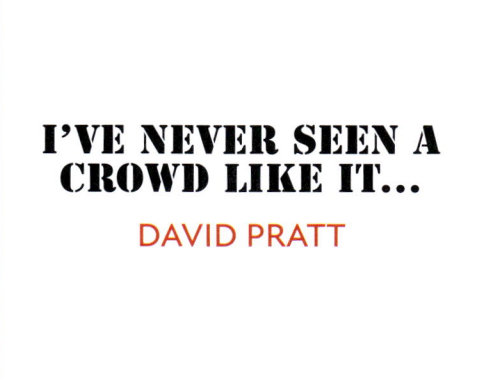

I'VE NEVER SEEN A CROWD LIKE IT...

DAVID PRATT

like Claire Cowans staring at me, strutting along like the cat who'd got the cream, with their fat lips and bleeding noses. I had missed all the excitement whilst meeting the band. A lucky break.

LEEDS UNIVERSITY
18 NOVEMBER 1978, LEEDS

DAVID GEDGE, THE WEDDING PRESENT

I've always been fanatical about pop music. I used to play my parents' singles from the fifties and sixties obsessively and listened to BBC Radio 1, Radio Luxembourg and Piccadilly Radio. *Top Of The Pops* was genuinely one of the highlights of my week. I loved the glam rock era in the early to mid-seventies but then one of my best friends at school, Dave Fielding (who later went on to be one of the guitarists in The Chameleons), introduced me to progressive rock. Discovering bands like Genesis, Yes and Emerson, Lake & Palmer when I was 15 felt like stepping into a whole new world. But then he introduced me to punk rock. I remember going round to his parents' house and sitting in his bedroom playing records. He'd say, 'There's this band called the Sex Pistols' – which sounded like a bizarre name – and he'd play me their single. I loved it all. I immediately felt like it was thrilling and different. I didn't start hating progressive rock, but this seemed more *me*. I know much of it was recycled from earlier rhythm and blues bands – The Stranglers had been going for years, Dr Feelgood had done something similar a bit earlier, and you also had Chris Spedding and all those kinds of people – but it sounded like a new form of music to me.

At the same time, another school friend said, 'Have you heard about this DJ called John Peel? He's playing bands like The Clash and the Ramones on late night radio.' So I started listening to Peel too and really got into punk, although I still liked pop groups like ABBA. (In 2018, my two bands each recorded a song from 1977 for a seven-inch single, The Wedding Present covering 'White Riot' and Cinerama 'The Name Of The Game'. Both of those songs meant a great deal to me when I was 17, and still do now.

I didn't go to many concerts during my school years in Middleton (North Manchester) – although I remember seeing the Tom Robinson Band, XTC and Mink Deville. Everything changed when I went to university in Leeds. It was such a brilliant time, because punk bands would tour the college circuit regularly. We'd see the Buzzcocks and Siouxsie and The Banshees at the university, and less popular groups like Wire and local bands at the smaller city centre venues. It felt like a music revolution was happening. It felt like people were picking up a guitar and forming a band.

I loved the music but I didn't dress like a punk. I still had quite long hair, and me and

A PEOPLE'S HISTORY OF THE CLASH

my student mates used to stand watching from the back; keeping well away from the mosh pit. The idea of people at the front of the crowd spitting particularly put me off. Our parents were slightly concerned. They would say, 'You're not involved with any of this punk stuff, are you?' because the media had blown it all up; 'Punks have been banned from Middlesbrough because of the problems they're going to cause,' and all that. I didn't see any violence at concerts, but it could feel a little threatening at times.

David Gedge of The Wedding Present pogoed for the only time in his life

But that was kind of one of the points of punk. It was shocking and extreme. It wasn't just the energy and the ferocity of the music, it felt like the whole culture was anti-establishment and, that by just being fans, we were being rebellious too. It was a revolution of fashion, of culture, like rock 'n' roll in the fifties, psychedelia in the sixties and disco in the seventies. It had more of an impact on me because I was the perfect age for it. But if you listen to those records now, they don't sound quite as outrageous as they did then. I'm not saying that they haven't aged well, but ultimately it just sounds like a more dangerous version of rock 'n' roll.

The Clash were one of the punk groups that came to Leeds University. They were an amazing live band and, probably because of that reason, I finally found myself down the front at a gig. I was this geeky student kid surrounded by a load of massive skinheads. They started pogoing and I got taken along with them. Actually, I didn't have much choice because I was crammed in the middle of them, so I just went with it. It felt a bit unsafe but that slightly intimidatory atmosphere was all part of the excitement. That Clash concert was the only time I've ever pogoed… before or since!

⭐ TOP RANK
19 NOVEMBER 1978, SHEFFIELD

ANDY ROTHERHAM, AGE 15

As I often remind my now grown-up children; I may be old, but I got to see all the great bands. Having seen hundreds of bands, and thousands of gigs, I can honestly say that The Clash were the most dynamic, vibrant and on-the-edge band that I have ever had the pleasure to see. The sheer unbridled energy that they exuded from the stage is something I have never seen again.

ALL THE YOUNG PUNKS

The first time I saw them was at the age of 15, when they brought their *Sort It Out* tour to Sheffield's Top Rank Suite. Sheffield at that time was a very exciting city, musically. Heavy rock bands would play the City Hall and punk/new wave bands would play the Top Rank.

I was introduced to The Clash when my elder brother bought 'Remote Control' and '(Get A) Grip (On Yourself)' by The Stranglers in a peak of curiosity about this 'punk' thing everyone was talking about. He quickly realised it wasn't for him and gifted me the singles. That simple gesture was to change my life course.

Andy Rotherham recalls scenes from the film *Rude Boy* being shot

So, there I was, at the age of 15, freezing in the queue outside the Top Rank Suite to see The Clash. It wasn't cool to wear a jumper or a coat, so I was in just a t-shirt and jeans. Exposed to the grim realities of late November Yorkshire weather. There was always an air of anxiety when queuing at Top Rank. The policy was for over 18s only. Looking back, there was no way I could ever pass for that age, so it was always a gamble as to whether we would get in or not.

The doors opened and we surged forward, to put pressure on the door staff, making it less likely that they would try to turn us away and against the crush formed behind us. We did what we always did. Quick visit to the merch. I was way too poor to buy a t-shirt, but I still own the badge I bought: blue police officers, a red band logo on a white background. Then it was a race to the front. As usual, we managed to get front and centre.

To our right, there was something going on, by the toilets. They had closed the toilets as a film crew were shooting something. I remember seeing Ray Gange and a lady being filmed exiting the gents. I am pretty sure this was part of the scene in the film *Rude Boy* where Ray receives oral sex in the toilets.

I have read that a band called The Innocents were on first. I honestly have no recollection of them. The Slits were on next, and I do remember them playing. My live introduction to music with a reggae dub feel. Mick Jones watched them from the side of the stage. I didn't realise until many years later that he was in a relationship with Viv Albertine.

The changeover happened. Some people drifted towards the bar, or the toilets.

A PEOPLE'S HISTORY OF THE CLASH

There was no way we were going to give up our prime spot though. I remember the excitement as the lights went down and The Clash burst into 'Tommy Gun'. The excitement and suddenness of the drum intro sent the crowd into a frenzy. From then on, it was a question of gripping the stage, so we didn't get knocked over by the pogoing surge all around us. In between songs, Joe Strummer was shouting at people to stop spitting as they and we were getting covered in the disgusting mess.

All too soon the gig was over. Time to check the floor for any stray badges that had been torn from people's clothing. Then it was time to run for the last train home. Now, getting to the train station and onto the train might sound easy, but times were very different then. The music and fashion tribes all fought each other. The bus station we had to traverse was known to be a hang-out of the re-emerging skinhead movement. Young punks, weighing only nine stone when wet, were an easy target. We had to pick our route down the hill carefully and at a run.

RICHARD PORTER

Richard Porter cut his hair & changed his clothes after seeing The Clash

I'm 61 now. I was born in 1962. The first time I can remember hearing The Clash was 'Remote Control,' their second single, which came out towards the end of 1977. I'd have been 14 or 15, and I loved that sort of football chant to it. I was going to football matches; I was a Grimsby Town supporter, and it caught my ear because I hadn't heard anything like that before on a record. The first thing I bought by The Clash was 'Complete Control' and then I went back and I got 'Remote Control' and 'White Riot'. By then I was also listening to other similar bands, but prior to that I liked things like 10cc, so it was quite a big change musically.

I got further into the scene and saw The Clash at Top Rank in Sheffield in November 1978, which really sealed it. I cut my hair, cut the clothes and eventually it led me into being in bands as well. The Clash were an inspiration. I wanted to look like Paul Simonon, and I wanted to drum like Topper. I ended up in bands until my mid-forties.

I used to work Thursday and Friday nights and then Saturday at Tesco. There was a guy there, Neil, who was a little bit older than me. He was 18 and used to arrange coach trips. I hadn't seen many bands prior to that. I think The Slits were support. When The Clash came on stage, it was like a bomb went off and the explosion just carried on for the next hour and a half. I had to get down the front. I was a little bit shorter then – I'm six foot now – but I can remember my head bobbing about on the shoulders of the people around me. There was a guy with a mohair jumper on in front of me and when I got out of the gig, it looked like my face had been taken to with sandpaper.

I learned very early on that you had to wear Doc Martens but to take your laces out. If your laces came undone in the middle of that mosh pit, you were dead meat. You couldn't bend down to do them up.

 DE MONTFORT HALL
20 NOVEMBER 1978, LEICESTER

RICHARD HOUGHTON

One of my favourite shows was seeing The Clash at 'De Mont' in 1978 on their *Sort It Out* tour. I'd first seen The Clash at Aylesbury Friars in June and sat up in the balcony, intimidated by the media insistence that punks were a threat to the established order and that I'd be taking my life in my hands by going to a punk gig as stabbings were routine, etc. This was despite my having gone to see Black Sabbath, Rainbow, Thin Lizzy and Status Quo without incident and whose audiences were

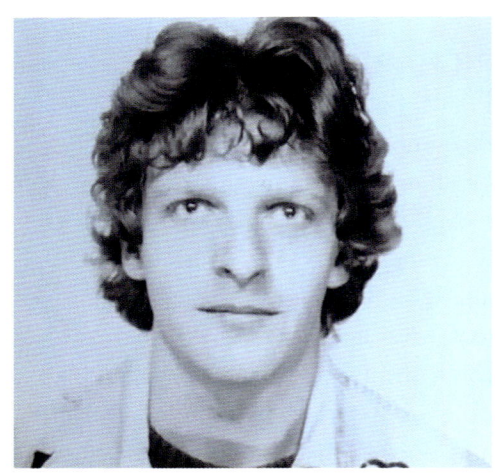
Richard Houghton had a vaguely Mick Jones hairstyle

populated by seriously threatening-looking biker dudes who looked like they would eat a safety pin-bedecked punk for breakfast. Watching The Clash from the balcony at Friars was like being a kid with his nose squashed up against the sweetshop window. I wanted to be in amongst the action, so when I got tickets to see the Clash at De Mont, I was determined to be down front.

In November 1978, they'd just released the album *Give 'Em Enough Rope* to mixed reviews, with CBS Records having appointed Sandy Pearlman (who'd produced Blue Öyster Cult) to allegedly clean up their sound. The music press were suggesting that The Clash had sold out. If that was the case, you wouldn't know it from their performance.

They opened with 'Safe European Home' and the crowd was up and bouncing from the off. I wasn't a punk sporting a mohican, but a traditional rock fan with curly hair almost down to my shoulders and wearing a leather jacket that owed more to John Travolta and *Saturday Night Fever*. But I was in the mosh pit from the beginning and stayed there until the end, bouncing around with all the other idiots. No spitting by me, though.

I can't recall everything they played, but 'Tommy Gun' and 'English Civil War' from the new album got airings, as did 'White Riot', 'Clash City Rockers', 'Complete Control' and various other of their early gems. Joe Strummer was completely in command of his audience centre stage, and Mick Jones was running up and down, doing his best Keith Richards impression (not that Keith ever ran around too much). It was semi-controlled chaos from start to finish, with a non-stop barrage of fast songs and an audience full of kids in their teens and early twenties who knew they were seeing a band at the peak of their powers.

Even though some of the details are hazy, I remember leaving absolutely bursting with adrenaline. It's in my top ten all-time favourite concerts.

LOCARNO
21 NOVEMBER 1978, BRISTOL

SUE TERRY

The next time we saw them was at the Locarno in Bristol, on the *Sort It Out* tour with The Slits supporting them. That was another mind-blowing event. Ari Up was talking about things like menstruation that had never been spoken of before, the experience of being female, etc. The front cover of (the album) *Cut* was so outrageous for the time and such a positive thing to do, and that all came out of the punk thing.

When The Clash appeared they just rushed out on stage. They had a backdrop with flags from various nations. They were all wearing different coloured shirts, very visually arresting, very different from anything else. Then we were hit by a wall of noise. It was just incredible! It really did knock you backwards.

London Calling of all The Clash albums remains my absolute favourite. It's a superb record. It introduced you to lots of different things… jazz, R&B. It showed the things that the band themselves were into. Being such a massive reggae fan, the fact that Mikey Dread was the support on the *16 Tons* tour was interesting. The band came on in disguise when he was doing his set. I absolutely loved it.

My husband and I moved up to west London around 1980 and lived there for quite some time in the eighties. We'd often see Joe Strummer and Paul Simonon around the Portobello area and places like The Grain (health food shop). We were on nodding acquaintance terms with Joe simply because we were in the same place at the same time so regularly. There was no security. Joe would be in the market buying an orange and an apple, and the same thing would happen to him as was happening to me. They stayed pretty close to the street and close to reality.

When you go back to those late seventies and early eighties days, there was that whole thing of everyone being in it together. I've met people in later life – people who I now think of as my friends – who were all at the Anti-Nazi League gig in Victoria Park and you just think 'oh yes. I was there!'

APOLLO THEATRE
23 NOVEMBER 1978, MANCHESTER

ALLAN NICOL, AGE 16

In 1978 I had just started sixth form. In the first term there was a coach trip organised to see The Clash at Manchester Apollo. We arrived at the venue, which was populated by punks of all descriptions. We were a little more conservative in our dress. I didn't know a lot about The Clash. I had borrowed a few singles from a mate but nothing more.

The build up to them coming on was electric. The anticipation filled the smoke-filled venue. Around 9.30pm The Clash arrived on stage. I will never forget that moment. The passion, the energy was incredible, and that one moment will live with me forever. I think they opened with 'Tommy Gun', but I could be wrong. All the seats were ripped from their fixings and passed to the front.

Allan Nicol and his wife are still punk fans, here at Blackpool's *Rebellion* festival

Completely transfixed, I couldn't take my eyes off Joe. I stood in awe. The gig has never been bettered in my life. The fans took to the stage when the encore of 'White Riot' began, which put a slightly premature end to the gig. I was exhausted. I was hooked.

I saw them a few times after that, and they were always incredible, but that first gig was the pinnacle of live shows for me. Musically it was a life changing moment.

I continued my obsession by seeing Big Audio Dynamite in the 1980s, who were also superb. I remember going back to Manchester Apollo around 1991 to see Joe front The Pogues when Shane was elsewhere. They covered 'London Calling', which blew my mind. I also saw Joe with the Mescaleros in Blackpool in the month before he passed.

They were such an underrated band, and musically so talented. Joe's writing touches so many different genres. His first two albums with the Mescaleros are works of art.

I'm now 62 and have a few friends who are in their early fifties and love The Clash. They are very jealous that I got to see them live, in a similar way that I'm jealous when people older than me tell their experiences of seeing The Beatles at the Cavern (namely my father-in-law!)

GARY HOUGH

The Clash's November 1978 show at the Apollo was the last time I went to see them, mainly because I felt they had shifted away from being the band I'd liked and who were accessible. The energy and vibe was different now. They were more polished, and all a bit too showbiz for my liking. The gig still had its moments, but I couldn't shake the feeling that the raw, anarchic spirit of punk I'd loved was fading. I knew then that my path was diverging, and it was not long after I was ready to move on to the post-punk sounds of Howard Devoto and Magazine, and bands like Warsaw and The Fall.

JIM FRY, EARL BRUTUS

I used to hang around this brilliant guy called Dave Connors. Dave was nuts. He was a Manchester City fan and his dad was a policeman. Dave would go out and kick over hot dog stands at City games, a bit of a football casual. I went to technical college with him and we formed a band together.

Dave got through the toilet window the night The Clash played the Apollo. By the time I'd got to the Apollo, I also had mates – Clash mates – who were all from Stockport College and we went to the gig en-masse. It was just fantastic! It was important that we all got in. I had a ticket, but others got in this way!

To get to the Apollo you had to get the train to Piccadilly and then walk down towards Ardwick. There were always a few lads lying around waiting to hit people getting off the train, and for no reason. I was quite tall, so I generally wasn't the one that got hit, but it was always a bit weird. You felt like you were running the gauntlet.

I caught some of Suicide's set. I knew about them; I'd heard them on John Peel. A keyboard player and a mad rockabilly guy with all this delay. They were just getting canned; it was just brilliant. It was so fucking hostile they left the stage.

I've seen a lot of gigs at the Apollo but when The Clash came on the place exploded. People started ripping out seats and chucking them and bits of shit everywhere. People literally filled the area at the front of the stage. The Clash just carried on.

It was just after *Give 'Em Enough Rope* had come out. They opened the show with 'Safe European Home' and had flags behind them. It was wild, but to be honest, at the time, that was normal. Not violent in the gigs, just a riotous atmosphere in the air.

ALL THE YOUNG PUNKS

CARL ROE, AGE 15

The Slits came on and (bearing in mind I was only 15) the opening line from their singer, Ari Up, was 'what a fuckin' time to come on', looking between her own legs.

I was rather excited by the atmosphere prior to The Clash coming on stage. The dub reggae, the smell of weed, the anticipation, that feeling when the band make an appearance and – boom! – 'Safe European Home' to open, just exceptional.

In November, it had become a little boisterous. Apollo security weren't known for their diplomatic skills. So there's a fight, Joe's trying to calm it down and eventually he jumps into the crowd. He returns to the stage and says, 'It's only four fuckin' idiots you are looking at… Let's wreck the joint. 'White Riot'!' Bedlam ensued, with flying seats.

PATRICK MOORE, AGE 15

I saw The Clash on the *Sort It Out* tour promoting *Give 'Em Enough Rope*. I came across The Sex Pistols first; I remember seeing them on *So It Goes* on Granada TV. I was 13 years old and hadn't seen or heard anything like them before. After that I heard 'New Rose' by The Damned. Soon after, on a trip to my school friend's home at lunch, he played me 'White Riot' and its B-side, '1977', and I was hooked.

The Clash at the Apollo was the first punk concert I'd been to. I wasn't disappointed in the slightest. The Clash were raw, with flags

Patrick Moore was hooked after hearing 'White Riot'

sewn together as a backdrop. That was the set, real punk, no special effects. There was nothing slick about The Clash, just raw power with a message that meant something to us in Manchester.

Other generations had The Beatles vs the Stones or Oasis vs Blur. In my case it was the Pistols vs The Clash, and it was only ever going to be Joe and the boys for me. They were my favourites then and have remained one to this day. I still play their albums now.

'TOMMY GUN'/'1-2 CRUSH ON YOU' RELEASED 24 NOVEMBER 1978

IAN MOSS

From The Clash album *Give 'Em Enough Rope*, which was indeed, er… ropey, apart from two excellent tracks, both of which were thankfully released as singles. The first of

Ian Moss recalls 'Tommy Gun' as reflecting when the shooting of bullets was the best way to make a point

The seven-inch UK release of 'Tommy Gun' came in a picture sleeve

these was 'Tommy Gun', a song reflective of a time when peaceful protest was being abandoned and the shooting of bullets was perceived to be the best way to make a point.

Joe Strummer, as the song's narrator, adopts the position of a gunman reading his own press with all the satisfaction of an actor perusing a flattering review; he is sarcastic and sardonic and echoes the stance and sentiments of The Beatles on their song 'Revolution' – something of an irony considering Strummer's 'No Elvis, Beatles or Rolling Stones' pronouncement in '1977'. Still, one could not doubt his sincerity as he hoarsely spat-out his invective over buzzing, over-loaded guitars and rapid-fire snare drum flurries from the highly impressive Topper.

★ VICTORIA HALL
29 NOVEMBER 1978, STOKE-ON-TRENT

TONY BODEN

It was utter chaos. The energy from the band just oozed off the stage and that made you want to give 100 per cent back to the band. They always had time to talk and sign autographs for fans waiting outside.

★ WIRRINA STADIUM
30 NOVEMBER 1978, PETERBOROUGH

GARETH THOMAS

The last time I saw The Clash in 1978 was at the Wirrina Stadium. My diary entry for this gig reads: 'Saw the Slits and the Clash at the Wirrina Stadium, Peterborough. The Slits were good, but the Clash great. Really good lighting. As I told Joe afterwards.'

POLYTECHNIC
2 DECEMBER 1978, NEWCASTLE-UPON-TYNE

PETER SMITH

By 1978 The Clash were established, popular and the darlings of the music press, and as a result the gig sold out almost immediately. There was much anticipation for this concert. The students had come to see what punk rock was all about, and fans to experience their new rock heroes. The local people, those who managed to gain entry, were there to spit at the band and (for some) to fight with the students.

A group of people outside were trying to force their way in, getting angrier and angrier, and ended up waiting outside to attack students as they left. Although I enjoyed the gig, I was scared on both occasions. I had very long hair and looked out of place at a punk gig. The fact that the gigs took place in a students' union building offered a level of safety. I could blend in with the students, although I was also the subject of taunts from local punks. It was leaving the venue which was the most frightening aspect of the evening. We had to run the gauntlet of a large group of punks and skinheads who, having been denied access to the gig, were determined to vent their anger and frustrations on students leaving the hall, many of whom were the worse for wear from alcohol. Some people were seriously hurt. A heavy police presence minimised the violence and the danger and we survived both gigs unscathed.

CIVIC HALL
20 DECEMBER 1978, WOLVERHAMPTON

DAVID NEWTON, THE MIGHTY LEMON DROPS

December 1978, Wolverhampton, England. Christmas was approaching, which meant a two week break from school for us 14/15-year-olds. A lot was changing in our young lives; puberty, facial hair, our voices had broken, some of us even had girlfriends. In addition to football and the telly we also had music, and most importantly for a lot of us we had punk, spending our pocket money on the latest singles (none of us could afford albums) and dreaming of one day maybe even seeing our heroes playing live.

You can imagine our excitement when we all heard that our teenage heroes The Clash were to be appearing at Wolverhampton Civic Hall on Wednesday December 20th and what a day it was. During the daytime, as we all sat at our school desks in our classes eagerly awaiting the final 3.50pm bell, it snowed… and it snowed and snowed. When we all finally left school on what seemed like the longest day ever, we noticed that, due to the snow, that there was no traffic moving on the roads, most importantly on the main road from our school that led to Wolverhampton town centre, almost two miles away. We walked, and it was still snowing, and I think it took us over an hour! Maybe two?

We eventually arrived at the Civic. It wasn't my first time there. Almost two years previously I had seen Be Bop Deluxe supported by Steve Gibbons Band (my first gig, age 12). This time things were different. It was packed and the crowd was louder and there were no seats. It was exciting. First on were The Innocents, new to all of us (and just about everyone else), four women and one man (who we later learned was Greg Van Cook from The Electric Chairs). They were good but sadly were literally showered with gob by young provincial 'rent-a-punks'.

Next up The Slits. We all knew of The Slits but had heard little other than a John Peel session (they hadn't released any records at this point). We noticed that they had a new drummer, a man (Budgie, later of the Banshees etc). They were great but again sadly had to endure the wrath of spitting teenagers (who had no doubt read in the *News of the World* that this was the thing to do if you were at a punk concert). Kids, eh?!

This wasn't the first time that I had seen The Clash. A group of five of us were fortunate to have a cool schoolteacher that chaperoned us down to London earlier the same year to see them at that (now famous) Anti-Nazi League rally in Victoria Park. Quite a lot had changed since then, both in the UK's musical climate and in the band's sound and appearance (Mick Jones's hair was considerably longer for one). They were great, a lot of the material was drawn from the then just released *Give 'Em Enough Rope* album, including the current single 'Tommy Gun' along with the 'older' faves.

The only downside was, again, that the band were spat at to the extent that at one point Strummer halted the set mid-song, demanding that the spitting stopped, declaring, 'I just hope that the next person that spits doesn't end up in the hepatitis ward like I did' (a reference to the fact that Strummer was indeed hospitalised with hepatitis after being spat at onstage). The idiots in the crowd then got the message (finally) and the rest of the show was gob-free and fantastic.

MICK JONES' HAIR WAS A LOT LONGER...

DAVID NEWTON

FRIARS
22 DECEMBER 1978, AYLESBURY

IAN WEST

My third Clash gig of 1978 was once again Friars. Historically, the Christmas Friars gigs always seemed to fun-filled belters so I knew this was going to be a good one!

Admittedly, my strongest single memory of that evening is of the two all-female support groups, The Innocents and the wonderfully fun Slits. Although when I say 'all female', Greg Van Cook was on guitar for the Innocents. (Incidentally, many years later Greg would become the partner of a friend of mine living in New York and by coincidence she often used the name Janie Jones as her alter ego.)

It was when The Innocents came on stage and were announced that one of my mates commented, 'They don't look very innocent to me!' Amused by this, Ari Up from The Slits, who was immediately in front of us in the crowd, relayed the comment to the singer. For the remainder of the set, Ari stayed in front of us dancing delightfully in her own manner.

Specific memories of The Clash that night are a bit clouded but once again it's the overall memory of that special energy that they brought to a gig that remains, and an observation that Paul Simonon always looked way too cool to possibly be a bass player! It was a very enjoyable and electrically charged night once more, as so many Friars gigs were. The Clash would go on to play Friars a further two times before they split, ensuring their place in Friars history.

Why I never got to see them again I don't know. My best friend, Bob, who plays bass to my lead/rhythm covering the punk catalogue, worked at the famous Stoke Mandeville Stadium where they played for the last time under the Friars banner on 12th July 1982 and with Terry

> **PAUL SIMONON LOOKED WAY TO COOL TO PLAY BASS...**
>
> IAN WEST

Chimes back on drums. The stadium sports hall was apparently chosen as it had a much larger capacity than the Civic Centre. Bob often regales me with tales of that evening such as the concerns beforehand from the people who ran the stadium of the violence associated with punk. Such fears were completely unfounded as it was a very peaceful gig – as most Friars gigs were – and Bob said that they had far more trouble whenever they hosted darts nights! The hall was absolutely packed to the rafters and Bob remembers the walls dripping with damp. Being very technically minded, he told me how impressed he was with the set-up of the PA as the acoustics in the hall were normally appalling and not suited to music! Yet he could hear the hi-hat clearly and crisply cutting through the other instruments.

A PEOPLE'S HISTORY OF THE CLASH

ALL THE YOUNG PUNKS

PEARL HARBOUR US TOUR

CIVIC AUDITORIUM
9 FEBRUARY 1979, SANTA MONICA, CALIFORNIA

GORDON SKENE

When The Clash first showed up on the West Coast of America, playing the Santa Monica Civic auditorium, the scene of hundreds, if not thousands of concerts, it was a revelation. It was the energy, and the conviction and America was finally getting around to noticing.

It was a far cry from the way it was only a year earlier when I returned from London with a box of 'Anarchy in The UK' singles by The Sex Pistols. It was my assumption that Los Angeles, of all places, would embrace Punk and welcome this Second British Invasion the same way it did in 1964. Didn't happen – a friend who was a disc jockey at KROQ, the station which later prided itself as 'The Rock of the '70s' and who I persuaded to put on the air ran it one morning. Midway through the needle skidded across the disc and the very audible sound of 'Anarchy In The UK' being snapped in half, live on the air accompanied by a few choice comments asking why 'that crap was on the air'.

Punk was going to be a tough sell, especially in L.A. We were still knee-deep in Hotel California and Led Zeppelin. The Ramones were considered something of

a joke band, and it was clear New York was leading the way as far as American acceptance of Punk as a viable alternative was concerned. Any acceptance from the West Coast was going to come from the underground minority.

But when Punk finally did take hold in L.A. it didn't have the same social implications it did in the UK. You had Thatcher and we had Reagan and by its sheer size, America is a big and sometimes an unwieldy place and things take time to catch on.

The Clash, by comparison brought a political edge to the music that simply wasn't happening in America in the late '70s. America embraced the hair, the safety pins, the ripped clothes, the snotty cynicism and didn't really know why. The Clash played music that was about something – it was about confronting issues that were affecting people on a deeply fundamental basis. America liked the stance, but it didn't quite 'get' the reason.

What probably broke the ice was *The Cost of Living* EP and The Clash version of 'I Fought The Law'. It started life on the West Coast in the mid-60s by The Bobby Fuller Four and made its way into legend over the years.

But I think the other thing that changed some minds was seeing The Clash live. The UK was already quite used to the band by the time they came to the States, so we were seeing and experiencing for the first time which most people in the UK had been seeing for at least two years. But seeing them in concert made a big enough impression so that everything the band put out after was met with a goodly degree of anticipation.

Even KROQ, who had snapped 'Anarchy In The UK' in half on the air less than two years earlier were playing The Clash regularly. 'London Calling' became a staple on most car stereos, and it was now time for L.A. to follow suit in attempting to cultivate their own Clash (which they never came close to) but instead embraced the skinny tie and 'My Sharona' sentiment – at least it wasn't climbing to the top of a Tequila bottle and overdosing on 'peaceful easy feelings'.

What appealed to the larger audience, as opposed to the Punks who were slowly emerging, except for 'Holiday in Cambodia' by Dead Kennedys, were for the most part a-political, was the 'outlier' appearance – that sort of '50s Gene Vincent meets Link Wray. Slicked back hair rolled up shirt sleeves and kill-you-if-you-look-at-me-sideways vibe.

America was catching on, not yet catching up. Britain was still a couple of genres ahead of us. No sooner had we settled in to ripped t-shirts, hurling beer bottles and safety pins, but then The Jam came along.

Talk about switching gears.

At least The Clash made a lasting impression.

RON FAST

I saw them at the Santa Monica Civic with Bo Diddley. There was a hell of a pit there with anyone with long hair being smacked up. I'd first heard of them in '76, '77 when a friend who had just come back from London and worked at a record store with me told me about the Pistols. We started ordering all the import punk stuff. The Clash were one of my early favourites. At the time I was playing guitar in a band called Publik Enema. Me and the drummer from that band, Thumper, went 200 miles down to the Civic for that show. Belinda Carlile and Jane Weidlin (of The Go-Go's) were in Black Randy's band as The Blackettes. I took 'em both home after the show and one of 'em stole my copy of the first Clash LP. (I had one of the first import copies.) Me and Thumper tracked them down to the Canterbury Hotel in Hollywood and kicked in doors until we found 'em and retrieved my LP.

Then I saw them at the Palladium the second time around. I was up front for that one. That was the 'matching shirt' tour. 'Safe European Home' was memorable, as was 'Tommy Gun'.

THOMAS CHARTIER

The Clash were the first big British punk band to play Los Angeles. The Sex Pistols skipped LA, and we were all disappointed, to say the least. The Clash played at the Santa Monica Civic Auditorium, an old building with a wooden floor. Everybody in the LA punk scene was there.

The Dills opened and were scared shitless by the big stage and crowd. Second was Bo Diddley, who got a rather lukewarm reception and between acts they had a British DJ who played seven-inch punk records. All but one were British bands – no Ramones, no Dead Boys, etc. However, in the gap between Bo and The Clash they played our single, 'Sit On My Face Stevie Nix'! My band was The Rotters, the song was making waves and was banned in LA, and this was the only time I ever heard my own song played anywhere. We were not part of the cool Hollywood Masque scene (the Masque was a small punk rock club in Hollywood) and some of them were resentful.

The Clash opened with 'I'm So Bored With the USA'. I thought that was very apt and brilliant. The wooden floor was bouncing from all the people. They played a great show but to be honest, they never quite regained the same energy of that opening. Really, and place they had set the bar too high. I'm not sure I've ever seen quite the same sort of powerful rock moment since.

JANET HOUSDEN

The Clash's show at the Santa Monica Civic in '79 was a huge fucking deal to the tiny handful of punks in our little beach town, and missing it was not an option. When we ran out of gas on the way, Ron Reyes, who had generously packed his little car with a probably-illegal amount of kids, was willing to do whatever it took to make it to the show. Basically, he siphoned gas from some poor citizen's car, swallowing a fair amount in the process. We also, as was customary at the time, got absolutely shitfaced on cheap vodka.

When we got to the show it was absolute mayhem, like the biggest gathering of punk rockers I'd ever seen up to that point, and like the teenage philistines we were, most of us missed Bo Diddley in favour of hanging out in the lobby and mingling and gawking at the huge collection of People Like Us. Also, I spent most of the set hiding in the bathroom from a guy I had punched at another show and who was rumoured to be looking for me.

Anyway, the Did's set passed in a blur (the sound at the Civic was absolute garbage – even the Buzzcocks sounded shitty there!), but when it came time for The Clash, we sort of pushed our way up front because this was, as I mentioned, a Huge Fucking Deal, and pits weren't a thing yet so girls could stand in the front without getting the shit beat out of them by goons from Orange County.

THE CLASH WERE A HUGE FUCKING DEAL…
JANET HOUSDEN

The sound was still shit. It was hard to even tell what song the band was playing, but the crowd went wild and were bouncing around and generating lots of heat, and when I looked at Ron, he was green. The gasoline and vodka were sloshing around inside him and we were seriously concerned he might actually explode, like something out of a David Cronenberg movie. Thankfully he survived to drive us home.

A few years later, I went to the *Combat Rock* tour at the Hollywood Palladium, and all the spray paint fumes from the guy painting a mural behind the band practically made me hallucinate, and gave me a hell of a headache. So, basically, I associate The Clash with being poisoned! The Palladium had shit sound, too, so I feel like I never really heard The Clash live, but I sure smelt them!

ONTARIO THEATER
15 FEBRUARY 1979, WASHINGTON, DC

JOHN SHIPLEY

I was working the summer of '77 in Ocean City, Maryland between college semesters when a guy where I worked told me about the punk scene and what was happening in England. He let me borrow some Ramones albums to listen to until I headed back to college in late August. My next semester started and I never gave punk rock another thought. January of 1978 came around and I was bored of listening to Thin Lizzy and Bruce Springsteen. I headed to the nearby record store to try and pick up something new. Browsing through the LPs, I spotted a section called 'Punk'. The store manager said 'it's what's happening in England', so I picked up five punk LPs to take home and listen to: The Boys, The Vibrators, The Damned, The Stranglers and The Clash. I spun all five albums that evening. It was a totally different sound to what I was accustomed to listening to, but The Clash blew me away. And that January evening began my love affair with 'The Greatest Rock 'n' Roll Band'.

In the States in early '78, there wasn't much of a way to follow punk rock in England. There was no internet and no place local to get tabloids such as the *NME*, *Sounds* or *Melody Maker*. The only way was to hit the record stores and pick up singles and LPs to keep up with the current punk music. Finally, late in '78, the local record shops started getting heavily into carry punk rock records and magazines from overseas. It was then that you could follow your favorite bands much more closely. And of course, The Clash released *Give 'Em Enough Rope* which pitched my fever even more to see the Clash as a 23-year-old punk rocker.

January 1979 rolled around and I heard that The Clash were coming on their first American tour. I bought two tickets and couldn't wait to see my favourite band. February 15 finally arrived and it was a sleety and snowy evening. I was attending college in Towson, Maryland, about an hour's drive away. Because I liked to have a drink (or several), my girlfriend drove us to DC and we arrived in the nasty weather in plenty of time.

It was an old movie theatre turned into a concert venue so there were seats to sit in for the show. After we got our seats, I told my girlfriend that I had to use the restroom. As I hit the urinal, I turned to my right and two urinals down was Joe Strummer. I was in awe and too baffled to say anything, not even 'hello'. I came out and told my girl what had happened and was still awe. The one thing about my first meeting with one of my rock idols was how short he seemed. I am six feet tall but even today, my first recollection of Joe was he seems small for such a powerful frontman. I still remember the song that blew me away that night was 'Safe European Home'.

THE PALLADIUM
17 FEBRUARY 1979, NEW YORK, NEW YORK

MARC MIKULICH

I saw The Clash the first time they came to the United States. They played in New York on East 14th Street at a venue that was then called the Palladium. It had previously been known as the Academy of Music. It no longer exists, but it was a wonderful old hall. It probably held around 3,000 or so people and dated back to vaudeville, music hall times. When the Rolling Stones first came over that's where they played, but it was just a music venue in those days.

The opening acts for The Clash were The Cramps, followed by Bo Diddley. The Cramps were very big on the local scene. Lux Interior managed to have his fly unzipped by the first tune! It was the first probably the first time they'd ever been seen on such a big stage. I used to see them play at CBGB's and Irving Plaza all the time. They were an entertaining band to watch.

The Clash opened with 'I'm So Bored With The USA', which made us all laugh loudly. They had a banner behind them with flags from different countries. It was a great night. 14th Street is at the north end of the Village, so pretty much anybody who was part of that environment was there that night.

 THE REX DANFORTH THEATRE
20 FEBRUARY 1979, TORONTO, CANADA

IVAR HAMILTON

I jumped into punk from the start, having lived in the UK from the summer of 1975 for a year and then going back for six weeks in the summer of 1977. That summer I had some money from working various part time jobs whilst living at home. I was just turning 18 and graduated from High School, on my way to radio school at Humber College. CFNY was the station in my hometown of Brampton, Ontario and they were wild, taking all kinds of chances with music of all genres but whole heartedly embracing punk.

Ivar Hamilton's US tour poster from 1979 - he saw them in Canada

The punk scene in Toronto was miniscule in 1977. It had started with a few small events at Ontario College of Art where local acts such as The Viletones, Teenage Head and Diodes had played, as well as an appearance from Talking Heads. Plenty of bands were coming together, but most were terrible and couldn't play their instruments and didn't last long.

In that short period between the spring of 1977 and the start of 1979, you would see the same 250 – 300 people at every punk show. The only exception being when Iggy Pop and Blondie played two nights at Seneca College Fieldhouse. They had about 5,000 fans each night. That would have never happened had David Bowie not been on keyboards helping his pal Iggy out!

When The Clash first appeared in Toronto, in February of 1979 it was at the Rex Danforth Theatre, located at 638 Danforth on the south side at Pape Avenue. Let's clarify that. The Clash did not play the now better known Danforth Music Hall. The Rex was slightly smaller, and held around 900 – 1,000, depending on the event. It was short lived and has been a gym for the last 25 years or so.

I felt that the first show from The Clash was still one for the die-hard punks and some curious new music fans. Things moved quickly from then on. The show was oddly presented by the classic rock station Q107 and not CFNY, who played more Clash than anyone else and went deep on their music.

I remembered hearing that the band were not only choosing their own opening act but also bringing their own DJ from England with them. This I thought it was exciting. Usually, a local band would be the support, and the pre-show music would be supplied by a local roadie with musical taste not befitting the event. Not this time. We got local band The Curse followed by Bo Diddley and the DJ was Barry Meyers aka DJ Scratchy, who still DJs to this day. It really changed the atmosphere of what we were would usually see.

The Clash did not disappoint, delivering a blistering set. We had finally got to see one of the premier UK punk acts in Toronto. I loved the Pearl Harbour back drop and was very happy that The Clash were finally in Toronto after a very long wait. Simultaneously, I was hired in the Music Department at CFNY where I stayed until the end of 1988. I was able to ensure that all The Clash and their spin off projects always got on the commercial airwaves in Toronto!

'ENGLISH CIVIL WAR'/'PRESSURE DROP' RELEASED
23 FEBRUARY 1979

PETE BOYLE

I've thought up several songs for the terraces at Manchester United over the years and 'Johnny Goes Marching' is one I'm particularly proud of. Many people presumed it was from the 'The animals go marching two-by-two' tune, but it's from The Clash's 'English Civil War'.

When I used to be a DJ, I made a compilation from a cassette player; a 90-minute tape of Indie bands' B-side songs. A lot of them weren't hits that people had heard. I was driving through Marple to work in Stockport, bored in the rain, and that was on the cassette and it just sort of came to me.

A PEOPLE'S HISTORY OF THE CLASH

I went in The Bishop Blaize, a pub near Old Trafford, around September 2002 and started it up. Most people just started laughing, thinking 'Boyley's a nutter, that'll never take off,' but I persisted and persisted, and by February/March of 2003, it really started to take off at away matches.

We played Charlton at home the penultimate game of the season. We'd nearly won the league and literally all four sides of the ground were singing 'When Johnny goes marching' for 15 minutes. During a break in play, Nicky Butt went over to John O'Shea as if to say, 'Look, this is for you this. Look around, this is your song.' It was a real proud moment, because it started off with literally just me in the Bishop's trying to get a few people going, and it gradually took off until it became the song of the moment.

'English Civil War' inspired a Manchester United football chant

In town that night, there were people pissed up people all over Manchester who must have been to the game and who were pissing in doorways, singing 'When Johnny goes marching.' I went to about three different pubs and could hear people outside wandering down the street looking for taxis singing it. Some bloke, who looked ten years older than me, came up to me in the Peveril Of The Peak and said, 'It's got to be yours, Boyley?! What an anthem!'

It's just a shame that John never bettered that first season.

MARTIN BLENCO

Most bands use B-sides as somewhere to dump tracks that are cast offs from a studio session. Or you'll get an instrumental version or extended take on the A-side. The Clash always put something on the B-side that was worth a listen. And of all the reggae numbers The Clash performed, it doesn't get any better than this cover of Toots and The Maytals' 'Pressure Drop'. If white boys are going to play reggae, this is what you want. Attack-minded guitars and a rhythm that gets you moving. And makes you wonder what on earth all the fuss was about The Police and the brand of white man's reggae that they concocted.

ALL THE YOUNG PUNKS

⭐ THE COST OF LIVING EP RELEASED
11 MAY 1979

BRIAN YOUNG

In May 1979 the band took another leap forward with the *The Cost Of Living* EP, embracing slicked back American greaser rockin' somewhere along the way. The standout cut, their version of the old Crickets/Bobby Fuller staple 'I Fought The Law', was simply incendiary and boded well for the next album. Much as I love the original version(s) The Clash's version has since become acknowledged as the definitive recording of this classic and deservedly so!

The Cost Of Living EP included an 'incendiary' version of 'I Fought The Law'

Granted, it wasn't 'punk rock' by any stretch of the imagination, but by 1979 all the rest of the original first wave of bands had folded and/or self-destructed and punk itself was pretty much on its last legs, having degenerated into toothless self-parody.

For all their faults and to their eternal credit The Clash refused to stand still or rest on their laurels and alone amongst their contemporaries they seemed to have the ability and imagination to keep moving relentlessly forward embracing and drawing inspiration from other musical genres like ska, rockabilly, jazz and reggae. It didn't always work out, but they weren't afraid to take chances

⭐ NOTRE DAME HALL
6 JULY 1979, LONDON

JONNY DIAMOND, AGE 14

The Clash I remember the most was a 'secret' one at the Notre Dame Hall off Leicester Square. There were two gigs, early in July on a Thursday and Friday. I assume it was the Friday I went as I was only 14 years old and still at school! I grew up in West London and had seen a few punk bands already, but The Clash were my favourites as me and my mates identified with them the most. This had a lot to do with seeing various members of the band on a regular basis around our neighbourhood. They felt like 'our' band, and I'd seen them play on quite a few occasions up to this point.

A PEOPLE'S HISTORY OF THE CLASH

I was at school one day when rumours of The Clash doing a secret gig started to circulate. This was not unusual as there were frequently rumours of gigs. Most of these rumours turned out to be just that, but when it came to The Clash, I wasn't going to miss a chance to see them, especially as I hadn't seen them for a while. I knew they had been recording a new album and so the prospect of hearing some new material was a big draw. I loved their last album, *Give 'Em Enough Rope*, despite a lot of people dismissing it.

After a few days of frantically trying to find out details of the gig I got hold of an A4 flyer advertising the gig, picked up at either Rough Trade or BOY on the Kings Road. On the day of the gig, excitement was reaching high levels amongst me and my friends as we wished the school day would end so we could get ourselves down the West End. We may have even 'left' school a bit earlier than usual, which wasn't that unusual!

As we didn't wear a uniform at our school there was no need to go home and change. We were not part time punks! We dressed and lived the lifestyle. A bunch of us jumped on a double decker bus (top floor obviously) and made our way to the West End. We got to the venue where there was a bunch of people hanging about. The venue door was nondescript, just a plain door down a side street off Leicester Square.

We got there early as we were keen to see the support bands too. One of these were The Mo-dettes, whose lead singer we all fancied. The other support was The Low Numbers who none of us knew anything about.

Inside the Notre Dame Hall was what you'd imagine a church hall to be like, pretty small with a raised stage at one end, and with wooden floors, velvet curtains, etc. The first thing I remember was the band looked a bit flashier in what they were wearing, a look that we would get accustomed to. We got ourselves down the front of what wasn't a big crowd, maybe a few hundred or so. I remember feeling lucky that we were at this secret gig, which in turn made us feel special and like 'real' Clash fans.

They kicked off with 'Clash City Rockers', a massive favourite and followed it with '(White Man) In Hammersmith Palais' which is still one of my all-time favourite records. I don't remember all the songs played but there were some that we didn't know or recognise. It was one of the first times they performed 'London Calling'. It was a great mix of familiar tunes and ones that we didn't know but sounded great. For energy and excitement, you couldn't beat The Clash live. They were an assault on your senses and really felt like they cared.

It was over too soon but they played a great gig. Jimmy Pursey came on for the encore. The Sham 69 singer was making a habit of crashing Clash gigs, and not always a welcome addition to be honest! As the lights came up in the hall, we reluctantly made our way to the exit and out into the night, buzzing about talking about the new songs, what they'd been wearing, etc. We made our way through the West End, mucking about and poncing cigarettes off tourists, with a feeling that London belonged to us...

RAINBOW THEATRE
14 JULY 1979, LONDON

MARC MIKULICH

In 1979 I was in my final year at New York University, which is in Greenwich Village. I signed up that summer to do an NYU in London programme, which meant me travelling over the UK and doing two courses for eight credits. It was a way of getting over to London and helping to get through college while having a good time. My two courses were British drama and British art. I was getting college credits for going to plays and museums. It was a scam. I was there with a guy named Tim Schaffner, who was a fellow student, and we were both musicians and music fans and very excited to be there. We went and saw everybody we could see that summer.

The was the summer of the Mod revival. We saw The Merton Parkas, Secret Affair, Tom Robinson, Madness, The Pretenders. There were two nights at the Rainbow in Finsbury Park, which was a Rock Against Racism benefit event. It was specifically around a few protesters who'd been unjustly incarcerated. One night was headlined by Pete Townshend, who I believe supplied all the gear for the gigs, and the other headlined by The Clash. We went to both nights and they were just explosive.

I'd seen The Clash at the Palladium gig in New York and it was all seated. It was an opera house. But at the Rainbow, we were all just standing around.

The support included Aswad. By the time The Clash came on, you could have taken the roof off the place. The energy levels were just unbelievable. When we came out at the end of the show, there were police outside in the streets and access to the Tube stations were blocked off. It was a chaotic but exhilarating night.

TAKE THE FIFTH US TOUR

MASONIC TEMPLE
17 SEPTEMBER 1979, DETROIT, MICHIGAN

JOHN MORYS

My first time was in Detroit after I'd cut my long hair and ditched the bell bottoms. It was spikes and straight leg Levi's with Beatle boots. I was sold! I played that first album so loud it disrupted my parents' prayer meeting. Oops! In 1980 VCRs were costly. My parents would go away some weekends and I would rent a VCR for the weekend and have a little party. We would watch *Rude Boy*, which someone had taped for me. They were fun times.

SKOTT RUSCH, AGE 17

I saw The Clash twice over the span of six months. The first time was September 1979, at the Masonic Temple in Detroit. Six months later, on 10 March 1980, they played the Motor City Roller rink.

I was a high school senior, living about an hour north of Detroit and we had probably the only record store in the whole Southeast Michigan region that sold import records. They had all the magazines – *Rolling Stone, Creem, New York Rocker, Crawdaddy* – all that shit. You couldn't open one of those books or magazines without seeing The Clash, Sex Pistols or New York Dolls – all that punk stuff – so The Clash were on my radar. As soon as the record store got that first Clash record in, I gobbled it up just like all the other early punk stuff.

When they came to the Masonic Temple, they were touring *Give 'Em Enough Rope* which was absolutely my favourite Clash album. I loved it a million times better than the first record. It was just more American rock sounding. The Clash had a huge stage, and they had this enormous backdrop. They were great. I mean, I was just like 'fuck yeah, this is The Clash.' It was like my head was exploding. I don't remember any difficulties, but I read later that they apparently didn't have a good time with that show. There were some gear issues, but as a 17-year-old, I was floored. I thought it was the greatest thing I ever saw.

The Motor City Roller rink show was a completely different experience. My brother and I, a friend and maybe a couple of girlfriends drove down. We skipped school in the afternoon so we could get to Detroit on time because there was bad weather. Outside the venue there were maybe a couple dozen people standing around. This would have been late afternoon. It was so bitterly cold out and windy.

ALL THE YOUNG PUNKS

We were standing outside and we could hear the band playing inside. We were young and stupid, thinking, 'Oh fuck, we're late,' then somebody swung the front door open and waved us all in. We rushed in and there was The Clash playing. I found out later that they were obviously doing their soundcheck. I heard that their road manager claimed he let everybody in because the band said, 'There's people waiting outside, it's freezing, let them in.'

They were playing an instrumental, Booker T and the MGs' 'Time Is Tight', and looked like they were having a good time. All the lights were on in the venue. They waved and shook some people's hands and then retreated to the back. The show had been promoted on local radio as a surprise gig. It was a benefit for the singer Jackie Wilson, who was ill in the hospital.

Lee Dorsey was an opening act. I can guarantee you most people in the audience barely knew who he was until he started playing some of his songs like 'Ya Ya' and 'Working In A Coal Mine'. I was stoked. He was just playing to backing tracks. He was this old dude who seemed pretty hip. Mikey Dread was also on the bill. He did a kind of a DJ toasting set. I thought it was cool though I'd never seen anything like it but I don't remember him being well received. I think it was your typical Detroit rock, sick-headed response to him, with a lot of rude shit shouted at him like 'where's the fucking Clash?'

The Clash came on and mostly did stuff from *London Calling*. In that venue there was the stage, and the backdrop was a huge wall. I guess they did theatre there. The wall had these doors and windows that opened. Somebody took a shot from there, behind the band and you can see a photo online of my buddy Billy right in the front row, just over Mick's shoulder. They seemed like they were having a great show, having fun. When they did an encore, Pearl from Pearl Harbour and the Explosions and Mikey Dread came out for it and they did 'I Fought The Law'.

That was an intimate show. It wasn't a huge place. Like I said, we got there so early that we were close to the front. They sounded amazing. *London Calling* was still fresh at that point. It was a

THE CLASH WERE DOING THEIR SOUND CHECK...

SKOTT RUSCH

completely different experience to the Masonic Temple where I was a distance from the stage.

 THE PALLADIUM
21 SEPTEMBER 1979, NEW YORK, NEW YORK

MARC MIKULICH
After spending time in the UK I returned to the US and was at the Palladium when The Clash came back to play. Sam and Dave were the opening act for that show, and they were great. I can still close my eyes and see them doing 'Hold On I'm Coming'. Then The Clash came out and once again they were amazing. And we all know what happened…

A little over an hour into it, Paul takes off his bass. The story goes that he did it out of frustration, because the crowd wasn't responding enough but I remember the crowd being very into it, but in the way New York crowds were, which is always a little laid back. Having seen what happened in London at the Rainbow, I understood where he was coming from. It was not the same kind of thing.

DAN BRUNING
I saw the Palladium show when Joe wanted people on stage and security held them back. Paul was pissed about that and smashed his guitar in anger. The album cover shot for *London Calling* was from that show. It's probably the most recognisable album cover of all time.

Later I also saw Joe Strummer and the Mescaleros at my work, in 2001. I worked at a casino in Atlantic City. I had a choice to either meet Joe and serve food and drinks or go see the show… I went to the show, and it was amazing. He was spot on. He broke out into a 20-minute Clash medley. I went wild.

Sadly, Joe passed just a few months later…

RONNIE BEE
I probably saw The Clash ten times, either in New York, where I lived from '75 to '90, or in Boston, where I went to college between 1976 and 1980. I saw the famous Palladium show that features on the cover of *London Calling*. I saw six or seven of the Bonds, New York shows – it was just a casual walk-in, straight to the bar – and I also saw a show on Long Island in '83 or '84. I saw them at Pier 84 in NYC, which was very cool due to the retired battleship converted to a museum on the next pier over. The Clash were fantastic, and a rollicking good time was always had by my friends and me. And I saw the Shea Stadium show and hated it, because of the show traffic. The band looked like ants – and sounded even worse!

O'KEEFE CENTRE
26 SEPTEMBER 1979, TORONTO, CANADA

IVAR HAMILTON

The Clash at O'Keefe's was a show that felt like when The Police played at the Horseshoe Tavern. There were maybe 150 people at that show, and in subsequent years about 150,000 claimed to have been there. It was much the same with The Clash returning to play seven months on after their Toronto debut at the Rex Danforth Theatre in February.

The venue up until that point had never hosted any punk shows and was better known for hosting

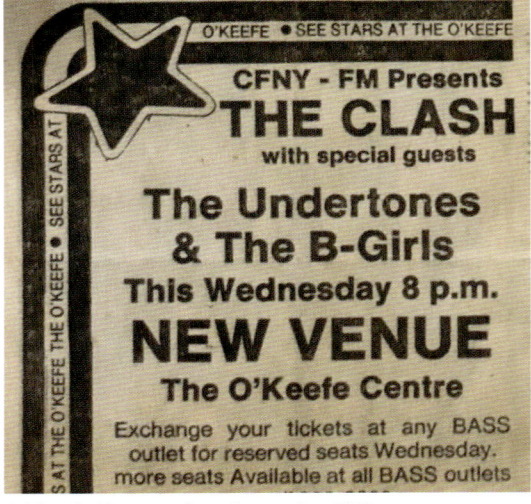

Ad for the Toronto show September 1979

musicals and plays in the 1960s as well as a lot of premiere jazz and progressive acts (the kind you sit down for!). The show was originally advertised to play the International Centre on the northwest side of Toronto across the street from the International Airport. At the last minute, it was moved to the O'Keefe which was a good move, since most fans would have had trouble getting there with limited public transportation available.

The show this time was presented by CFNY, although unfortunately the band did not make it out to the radio station for any interviews. Neither did the band diss the station like they had Q107, who presented the debut show February. (The station had some specialty programmes that featured The Clash but if you turned it on, the regular playlist was full of Meatloaf, Rod Stewart, Steely Dan, Supertramp and Led Zeppelin.)

My memories are that the B-Girls were not received well, but The Undertones were absolutely the right kind of act to play with The Clash. It was their one and only appearance in the city.

The ushers and security staff had a tough time handling the crowd, who were hell bent on pogoing and not sitting down for any of the show once The Clash hit the stage, especially since the band encouraged people to come down to the front. It's well documented that a couple of rows of seats were completely trashed, and you can find film of it online.

We didn't get The Clash back in Toronto until 1982. However, what we did experience that night was the magic to come with new tracks from *London Calling*, three months before the album was released including the title track, 'Brand New Cadillac', 'Koka Kola' and 'Wrong 'Em Boyo'. Every time they were here proved to be worth the wait!

CLARK UNIVERSITY
28 SEPTEMBER 1979, WORCESTER, MASSACHUSETTS

BRIAN GOSLOW

There's many Clash shows I saw, all with their own unique memories (including one where we broke down about an hour from the RPI Fieldhouse in Troy, New York and friends had to come get us – all made better by getting supper compliments of the band after the show).

I hopped on the Number 21 bus across town and arrived right at the appointed time to be greeted by DJ Scratchy who I knew, and we talked as The Clash were doing their soundcheck with Joe singing something along the lines of, 'We don't like no Howard Johnson's.' That's where they were staying, a few

Brian Goslow & friends broke down on the way to one Clash show

miles down the road in West Boylston, across the street from the West Boylston Drive-In, where Penny Smith captured Paul Simonon in an image included on the jacket of *London Calling*.

DJ Scratchy dedicated and played Sham 69's latest 45, 'Hersham Boys' for me before The Clash played. Strangely, of the times I saw them live, it's the show I remember the least, other than being psyched to see how excited the local kids were to have them playing in their town.

Later on, up in the dressing room, where the band greeted a parade of fans, Scratchy recorded a station ID for WCUW, 'after a stormy night in Worm's Town,' as he called it, that aired for several years, as did one by Topper, who told me that along with the material that would comprise the not-yet-released *London Calling*, there was another album's worth of covers. Still waiting for that one!

RITCHIE COLISEUM
29 SEPTEMBER 1979, COLLEGE PARK, MARYLAND

JOHN SHIPLEY

My girlfriend and I were attending the wedding of the guy who hired me after I got out of college. I had no plans to go to the gig and hadn't bought tickets. Whilst the couple were exchanging their vows I said to myself, 'I'm going to see The Clash tonight. I can't miss them.' At the reception afterwards, I said to my girlfriend that I was going to see The Clash with my friend Mark, who was also at the wedding, that I had to leave right away and that I had arranged for someone to give her a ride home. We had been dating for a year. She said to me, 'If you leave, you will never see me again.' I looked at Mark and said, 'Sometimes a man has to do what a man has to do.' Five minutes later, he and I were in my car heading to Ritchie Coliseum. We arrived at the concert with no tickets but, after a quick explanation of what had transpired in the last few hours, we were let into the venue and I saw The Clash for the second time in eight months!

KEZAR PAVILION
13 OCTOBER 1979, SAN FRANCISCO, CALIFONIA

ERIC WEITZMANN

My first Clash show was at the Kezar Pavilion in Golden Gate Park. The inside of the venue looks like a basketball gym and holds about 4,000 people. It had bleacher (bench) style seating around what would be the hardwood floor which was spring loaded for more give to the game of basketball. The reason I mention that is because when The Clash played, the floor was moving so much during the set due to the energetic crowd that the lighting columns were swaying back and forth, almost ready to come down!

   The Dead Kennedys opened the show, followed by Ray Campi and his Rockabilly Rebels, and then The Cramps. A damn good line-up. There was a long delay after The Cramps, because Mickey Gallagher's Hammond B-3 organ was having issues, and they had to track down another one. Once that problem was solved The Clash came out ready to rock. *London Calling* wouldn't be released stateside until January 1980, but they played quite a few songs from it. A very memorable show, with four good bands!

'LONDON CALLING'/'ARMAGIDEON TIME' RELEASED
7 DECEMBER 1979

IAN MOSS

After the horrible production sheen that had made their second album sound like a desperate love-letter to American hard-rock audiences, The Clash got their mojo back by aligning themselves with maverick producer Guy Stevens – no doubt at the behest of Mick Jones, an uber Mott the Hoople fan, the band which Stevens had been instrumental in putting together and nurturing.

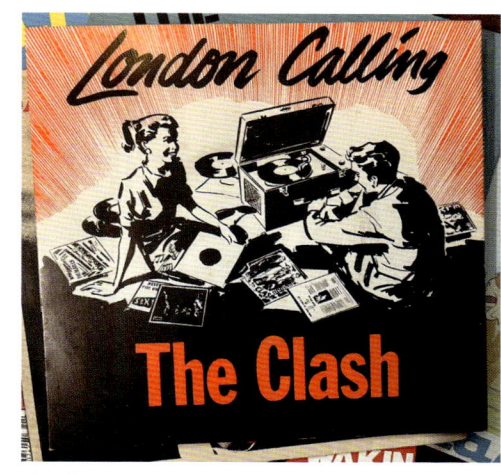
The Clash got their swagger back with 'London Calling'

'London Calling' (the title alludes to the tag-line used by announcers on BBC World Service) touched on several issues such as police brutality, drug use and the commercial repositioning of what, by now, were ex-punk bands... including The Clash themselves but the central and overarching theme of the song was the fear of an impending catastrophic nuclear accident, or a war that would see the rising tide swamping and sinking central London.

Played at a confident, mid-paced tempo, there is a swagger and swing to this track that only bands with a fine-tuned musical chemistry can conjure up and the vocal from Joe Strummer contained compassion, along with a sincere, heartfelt quality that seemed to address each individual listener personally.

LONDON CALLING RELEASED
14 DECEMBER 1979

HI, THIS IS AMERICA. WE'RE NOT HOME RIGHT NOW, BUT IF YOU LEAVE A MESSAGE AFTER THE BEEP, WE'LL GET BACK TO YOU AS SOON AS WE CAN

GREIL MARCUS

London Calling is a two-record Clash album with nineteen songs and an in-store price of about eight bucks. Pointed toward the future, it's also full of history - but the sleeve design, lifted from the first Elvis Presley LP, is almost a false clue. History here includes the history of times barely left behind, a history left unmade.

Always classicists – the 101ers, the band singer Joe Strummer left in 1976 to join

ALL THE YOUNG PUNKS

The Clash, just after seeing the Sex Pistols for the first time, was something of a rock 'n' roll revival outfit – The Clash meant to occupy the gap the Sex Pistols had suddenly opened in the rock tradition. For a moment, anything seemed possible, that the strangest noises could sweep the world, or that Western society was so corrupt its own fear and guilt might send it spinning off its axis. None of that happened. The moment passed, the punk no quieted, but for those who'd been part of it, things were not the same. After Johnny Rotten's negations, some could not go back to the false pop promise of – to use a phrase by Norman Mailer – an unearned freedom from dread.

The Clash's promise has been that a sense of dread, far from something to get free of, is a purchase on reality that must be sought out, constantly tested and renewed; the Sex Pistols 'no' has always been the Clash's 'yes'. Dread puts the edge on. It shapes fear, gives a laugh weight, strips away any mystification, and reveals paradox; song by song, *London Calling* does the same. History – pop history, political history – has closed around The Clash; they seem to have found a place in it. They play with a new confidence, with joy, a swagger, a casual look, as if with so many songs a half dozen you don't like could matter less *(My hair may not move you, but what about my clothes?)*, with the time to tell every side of any story.

The title song, a doomsday scenario stoically chanted to a clattering martial beat, opens the set, there's been a 'nuclear error,' the result is a new Ice Age, the river is rising (with an Ice Age, it would fall, but a smash-up of all disasters is the point), there's panic in the streets. It's silly at first, but after a verse the fantasy gathers its charm. As music, the prospect is too exciting to resist, the tale-teller too human. As the only one left with the presence of mind to warn the rest of the world, Strummer is back in 1938, in Orson Welles's *War Of The Worlds* broadcast, and crying out from 1956, in Hungary, the last revolutionary at the last open microphone, refusing to believe the rest of the world won't ride in like the cavalry she's seen in too many John Ford movies.

The song ends in suspension, everything in doubt; without a pause we're into 'Brand New Cadillac,' a borrowed swath of rockabilly so modern in its sound and so Presley-ish in its lyrics ('Baby, baby,' Strummer sings with naked glee, 'won't you hear my plea?' that the tune stands both as an affirmation of the timelessness of a beloved style and as a celebration of female nerve. When you get down to it, the singer knows he simply doesn't measure up. Punk once went from the smallest provocation to the biggest demand; now the road can run the other way too. The band moves to the smoky gin-joint blues of 'Jimmy Jazz', where Strummer, drunk but suddenly alert, draws an encounter with a cop into a coolly staged one-act play that moves from running sweat to an evasive shuffle to relief. The politics in each number are inescapable but natural – they're the politics of ordinary life, heightened by that sense of dread, that sense of history. *Baby, baby, can't you hear my plea*, says the Hungarian revolutionary as her mike goes dead; Soviet troops arrive; *Hey, I just work here*; she says; they let her go.

Strummer is the key. From track to track (or within a track) he can be pleasantly conversational, horror-struck, crafty, damned, burning with lucid outrage or quite lucidly soused. He uses four, maybe five different voices in 'The Right Profile', a hilarious account of the last days of Montgomery Clift. The listener is jerked from one view to another (after his 1957 auto accident, Clift, scarred on the left side of his face, permitted photos only of the right), now thinking of a star's betrayal of his talent, now of the indelible image of a character whose toughness came from his lack of hope. Clift swallows a roll of Nembutals; Strummer throws up all over the song. Without missing a beat, he pulls himself together for the chorus:

And everybody say
'What's he like?'
And everybody say
'Is he all right?'
Everybody say, 'He sure look funny'
'That's... Montgomery Clift, honey!'

Which means, who cares what he looks like? We saw him!

On *London Calling*, images of pop culture of stardom and images of political culture – of stardom – and images of political culture – in The Clash's spectacle, of anonymity are not at war with each other. The album finds its idea in simultaneity and multiplicities. You're reminded of the horn riffs from 'Sea Cruise', then of the hands of Robert Mitchum's mad preacher in *The Night Of The Hunter*, then of Spanish freedom fighters emerging from four decades of oblivion. Men and women of different classes, races, nations, and times appear and move on.

What I hear most of all is the conviction that the job of the band is to present life in all its parts, that conviction always playing against the fear that no action matters at all. The result is a faith that more is at stake in any choice (*Do I dare speak into this microphone? How are my clothes?*) than is ever apparent – and you can hear this best in 'Death Or Glory,' the most obviously important song on *London Calling*, and in 'Revolution Rock,' seemingly its most trivial.

'Death Or Glory' follows a reggae version of 'Stagger Lee,' here carrying a Jamaican title, 'Wrong 'Em Boyo.' The easy, happy beat, for a song about murder, cuts into 'Death Or Glory's scattered, then building fanfare, music of such passion

ALL THE YOUNG PUNKS

and force the sound seems to close around you. The band locks into the tune, and Strummer lashes out with the first verse.

'Every cheap hood,' he says, as if he's thought about this for a long time, 'strikes a bargain with the world.'

And ends up making payments on a sofa or a girl
Love 'n' hate tattooed across the knuckles of his hands
The hands that slap his kids around 'cause they don't understand
How death and glory
Becomes just another story
Death or glory
Just another story

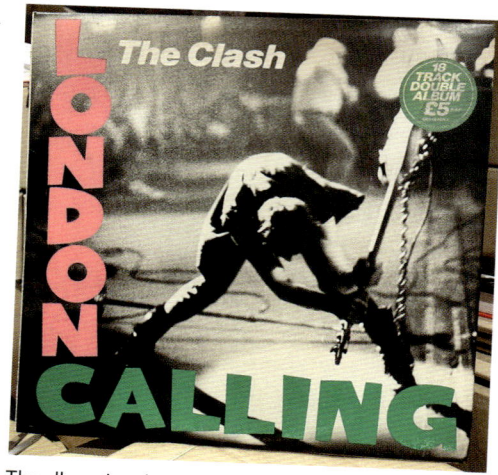

The album *London Calling* is widely regarded as one of the best double albums ever released

So Stagger Lee, the embodiment of black rage who lives in a world so fettered he can take out his hate only on his own kind, reemerges as a white man, the punk rebel of any era, the poor-white Elvis, selling his blood for fancy black pimps' clothes at Lansky's in Memphis; the London Edwardians of the 1940s and their 1950s Teddy Boy progeny (never vanished, still present in the Cashing onion, ready to fight over the wrong suspenders, the wrong shoes); the early-seventies London skinheads, moving out on a summer night to beat Pakistanis, who, unlike the Jamaicans whose ska sounds the skinheads loved, were the wrong shade of black. But this is a Stagger Lee one has never met before, Stagger Lee grown up, middle-aged, fat, balding, Stagger Lee denied his flaming death and made domestic, afraid to leave home, beating his wife to the floor, then looking at his children as they cower, quiet, as they've learned to be quiet when this happens and then Mick Jones steps out to take the vocal from Strummer, to run the squalid reality off to the fantasy behind it, to celebrate Death Or Glory! Alright! The stupid, risky promises of the rebel's youth can make you sick or break your heart. The dead Hungarian revolutionary (the Soviets were fooled only for a minute) is replaced by the Light Brigade; the no is turned again into a yes, and it's up to you to weigh the one against the other.

'Revolution Rock' wraps up the album; another reggae number, and, like 'Wrong 'Em Boyo', picked up from an obscure 45, an old skinhead favourite. Nearly sobbing with delight, Strummer rings the eternal changes of the lines:

Everybody smash up your seat and rock to this brand new beat

A PEOPLE'S HISTORY OF THE CLASH

This here music mash up the nation
This here music 'cause a sensation!
Tell your ma, tell your pa, everything gonna be all right...

'Revolution rock'- that was what the Clash started with, and 'revolution' was more than a joke then, so long ago, three or four years ago. Here, a joke is all it is, Strummer sounds as if he's waited all his life to sing something so dumb. The song, though, hangs in the air. Coming out of the fear and self-loathing the rest of the album has played through – half of it about the heroism of youth, half of it about the perversion that follows – the trashy, irresistible song says that while revolution made by music is a joke, rebellion sustained by music might not be, though it has room for plenty of jokes, what is a revolution, especially one that's failed, without humour? Up on the bandstand, crooning 'Revolution Rock' – you can hear him promise he'll sing anywhere, weddings, Bar Mitzvahs, and the way he sounds he should – Strummer is having the time of his life.

BRIAN YOUNG

In December 1979, when double album *London Calling* hit the racks, The Clash were simply the greatest rock 'n' roll band in the world – whatever that means – whether they liked it or not!

Nowadays, *London Calling* is regarded by many as The Clash's best work. I'd not go quite that far but it certainly contains some of the most ambitious and consistent material they ever penned. Strummer's lyrics are more poetic and ambitious than before, and Jones seems equally adept at mastering every genre of music he turns his considerable talents to. Simonon and Headon never played better or more cohesively too, and both had emerged as talented songsmiths. It's a stunning achievement and illustrates just how far the band have come in a short time.

It's impossible for me to pick a favourite track but the ones that always hit the spot include 'Guns Of Brixton,' 'I'm Not Down', 'Clampdown' and for obvious reasons 'Rudi(e) Can't Fail'. As a longtime fan I was delighted to see Vince Taylor's 'Brand New Cadillac' dusted off and revved up, introducing a whole new audience to the genius of that troubled black leather icon – though I much prefer the original!

Why sure-fire hit 'Train In Vain' wasn't issued as a UK 45 remains one of the great unsolved mysteries of this era. Critics argued that many of the raw edges of the band had been smoothed off to appeal to a wider mainstream market. I'm not so sure of that, but it's undeniable that around this time, our once proud spiky punk rock rebels are well on the way into becoming the 'new' Rolling Stones, which certain members of the band had wanted all along.

DARYL EASLEA

Punk came along when I was eleven. Being in the younger wing of the music's fan club, the Pistols terrified me (but then, so did Den Hegarty of Darts), as did The Stranglers, who looked like dangerously seedy old men.

The Clash, however, always looked like the Rolling Stones to me. They seemed bigger, more louche, unconfined by any labels they could be given. Weren't these the sort of people this new lot were supposed to be at war with? I read, still not quite knowing, that they had sold out by getting an associate of Blue Öyster Cult along to produce an album.

Older friends adored them and repeatedly went on about seeing them at, especially, Victoria Park, a Billy Graham moment for all concerned. Many lives were indeed changes. But then. Then. *London Calling* came.

DAVE WATSON

I love The Clash! Although I was too young to be 'there'. When I got into them, I immersed myself and fully embraced everything they did. It goes without saying that the savage beauty of the first LP metamorphosing into what came later was unparalleled. It was the poetry too, just read the lyrics to 'Car Jamming'. Lines such as:
The ragged stand in bags soaking heat up through their feet
This was the only kindness, it was accidental too
are beautiful.

One of my favourites of all Clash lyrics reminds me of when I decided to become a mature student which eventually resulted in employment by the local university and my subsequent attendance at numerous team-building development courses. One such hideous event was staffed by some truly unspeakable twerps. As an icebreaker on Day Two they asked, 'Does anyone have any favourite life quotes they'd like to share with the group?' It was such a proud moment as I recited, from 'Death Or Glory':
I believe in this and it's been tested by research
He who fucks nuns will later join the church

Funnily enough, I wasn't asked to contribute again. Thank you, Joe, you utter legend!

ACKLAM HALL
26 DECEMBER 1979, LADGROVE GROVE, LONDON

I WAS THERE: MIKE HERBAGE

In 1979 I saw them three or four times at The Lyceum. *Rope* had been released and they were now singing about world issues and had a League of Nations flag as a back drop. I thought maybe half of the album was good. 'Safe European Home' must be as good an opener as any album has had. But other acts had started appearing at the clubs – Bunnymen, Teardrops, Cabaret Voltaire, etc. Post punk was starting to develop and was producing interesting stuff. I'd ditched the punk look by now and had started going to clubs like The Blitz/Billy's. Punk was starting to look decidedly old fashioned. But at Christmas 1979, The Clash did a couple of secret gigs at the Aklam Hall under the Westway. A mate phoned and said his dad had said he could use his car. This was Boxing Day. It was great because there were only about 200 people there. It felt like at the beginning, when you saw the bands in a small club.

The Clash played two Christmas shows on home turf in 1979

I was captured in a photo that turned up in a Bob Green book of his pictures of The Clash. I couldn't believe it when I opened the page and there was a picture of me at the Aklam Hall gig, gob wide open and holding onto Mick Jones' mic stand! I emailed Bob immediately and explained that it was me in front of Jonesy and would he mind sending me a jpeg of it? The fucker wanted to charge me $400! I told him that I hadn't fought in the punk wars to pay $400 for a picture of myself and – bless him – he sent me it anyway! It has been on my wall ever since.

JOHN DANIEL, AGE 17

I had been a Clash fan since the first time I heard the first album. It changed my life. It was raw, aggressive, politically and socially aware. I had seen the band before a couple of times in my home town, Manchester, and at the Music Machine in Camden in 1978. In 1979, we went down as a family to Camden Town to stay with my auntie and uncle.

My cousin's boyfriend, Mol, worked at Fifth Column t-shirts in Camden Town. They screen printed the Clash tour merchandise and I would sometimes go down in the holidays on the train, pick up some 'seconds' t-shirts from the factory in Camden and sell them for £5 back in Manchester to my friends. (This included some iconic t-shirts such as 'Clash Take The Fifth' and 'London Calling', with the Post Office Tower backdrop.)

ALL THE YOUNG PUNKS

On Boxing Day, Mol said he had seen The Clash in Ladbroke Grove on Christmas Day for 50p, that he was going again tonight – Boxing Day – and he had got me a ticket for 50p, along with a poster and a pin badge from the gig (which I recently sold for an eye watering price).

We met up in my cousin's squat in Chalk Farm and were picked up by Christian Townsend, who owned Fifth Column t-shirts. Next stop we picked up Johnny Green (the Clash roadie, who Chris knew because of his merchandise connections) from his flat in Hampstead. Johnny had a bottle of Southern Comfort and he poured one half into an empty milk bottle and passed it to the back of the car.

The night was set. I listened to tales of the gig the night before from Johnny Green and my cousin Mol. Johnny talked about the band and improvements to the sound that he needed to set up – and how he hoped the gear was still there!

Ladbroke Grove was buzzing, the Westway a bit less so because it was Boxing Day. Johnny and Mol couldn't believe the amount of people outside Acklam Hall, compared to Christmas night the day before. There was a massive queue but we managed to get in because of Johnny. The hall was only small and the DJ, Scratchy Barry Myers, was playing some fantastic stuff. There was a real festive feel and an air of teenage expectation.

The hall was filled with the smell of marijuana and the floor crunched with the sound of Red Stripe cans. I couldn't believe we were going to see The Clash play in a tiny venue like this for 50p. I had tickets for the *16 Tons* tour at the Apollo in Manchester the next month and had paid a lot more for those.

The Clash walked on the stage to a homecoming cheer and 'Clash City Rockers' crashed out of Jones's guitar. Wow, The Clash on Boxing Day. I couldn't believe it.

The first part of the set was heavy with new songs from *London Calling* which had only been released a month earlier and being played here for the first time. When they played 'Stay Free' about halfway through the set, the audience all joined in as if it was a story of an old friend. The highlight of the gig for me was 'Armagideon Time'. It was followed by 'Police And Thieves'. The whole hall was moving up and down and sweat was dripping from the walls. They finished with 'White Riot' and 'London Calling' and then all mayhem occurred. Everyone got on the stage and the local punks were dancing away.

Then we were back out into the Boxing Day night. It wasn't a late night so we talked to other fans outside, sipping on cans of Red Stripe. It was a magical evening for sure. I couldn't sleep that night, as I relived the evening in my head song by song.

The Clash, Boxing Day Acklam Hall 50p. A Christmas present never forgotten for this 17-year-old punk rocker.

A PEOPLE'S HISTORY OF THE CLASH

ALL THE YOUNG PUNKS

16 TONS UK TOUR

FRIARS
5 JANUARY 1980, AYLESBURY

GARY CONNOLLY

I saw the band at Aylesbury Friars on the *Sort It Out* tour in late 1978, after first seeing them earlier that year at Queensway Hall, and got to appreciate how good they really were live. *Give 'Em Enough Rope* was out, and I remember being stage front watching Mick Jones play and move about the stage in another captivating performance. From then on, I saw them every time they played Aylesbury Friars. Over the years they had some great support bands including The Slits and the Coventry Automatics, who later changed their name to The Specials. A favourite for me though was back at Aylesbury for what was billed as a Christmas party in early 1980 following the release of *London Calling*.

The January 1980 show was billed as a Christmas party...

Also on the bill were Ian Dury and The Blockheads, who Mick Jones joined the band on stage for their song 'Sweet Gene Vincent'. After the gig, me and a mate managed to get backstage and meet the band. I will always remember Joe Strummer asking us, 'What's it like living in this town?' A great night all round spent in their company, if only briefly.

I must have seen The Clash over a dozen times during that period and every time they were amazing. I went to Hammersmith Palais and three of the seven nights at the Lyceum, all of which were wonderful. The Clash were in their prime. The last time I saw them was on 20 June 1982 at De Montfort Hall, Leicester.

The Clash were a great band live and on record a band that left a huge impression on me and opened my eyes to lots of other different types of music. I am so glad I got to witness some special moments in music and time.

TOP RANK
8 & 9 JANUARY 1980, BRIGHTON

JOHN TOMSETT

When The Clash released *London Calling* it was a seminal moment in rock and roll history and a life-changing experience for my 15-year-old self. Less than a month after the release date I was queuing outside the Brighton Top Rank to see the band play on their *16 Tons* tour. They were promoting the new album. As my mates and I shuffled from foot to foot to keep the January chill at bay, critical opinion was divided about *London Calling*'s eclectic musical mix. No one understood 'Jimmy Jazz'. 'Train In Vain' was pure disco. There was so much reggae! The title track was great, for sure, but 'Lover's Rock'? *Really*? Before the gig, the proverbial jury was still out.

Once in the venue, it was a matter of downing as much Pernod and black as you could afford and then getting to the front of the stage. There were no safe gaps, they were all filled with bouncers. If you were brave, you'd get a front row spot early and then just hold on. The crush was dangerous and exhilarating. The night The Clash played I ended up swaying around in the mosh pit, just a few feet from the front.

There was nothing quite like being in the mosh pit as The Clash began their set. The support had been finished for some time as chants of 'Clash… Clash… Clash… Clash' bounced around the Top Rank's sweaty walls. And just when you thought they would never appear, the lights fell. In the blackness torches scattered. The lyrics of Tennessee Ernie Ford's '16 Tons' floated out of the PA system and as they faded a voice announced, 'Ladies and gentlemen, I would like to welcome back to Brighton…THE CLASH!' And a nanosecond later… pandemonium!

They began with 'Clash City Rockers'. Mick Jones' opening chords growled out across the Top Rank and the surge of energy was raw, elemental and purifying. A lad next to me grabbed my shirt and hauled himself up to crowd surf into the swirling mosh. I gasped for breath. Before I knew it, we were straight into 'Brand New Cadillac' followed by 'Safe European Home'. One track, then another, then another. 'London Calling', bang! 'Stay Free', bang! '(White Man) In Hammersmith Palais', bang!

It was absolute chaos. I found myself laughing at the perilous thrill of it all. I loved it. And the thing was with The Clash, they loved it too. It was a night of heady celebration. They knew their new album was *bloody great*. As Andy Kershaw, who heard them a couple of weeks later in Leeds, said: 'They were at the absolute peak of their powers, the fully finished article… the last word in rock and roll bands.'

ALL THE YOUNG PUNKS

In those days the last bus home left at 11.05pm from Churchill Square. Miss the 729 to Tunbridge Wells and you were stuck in Brighton all night, 20 miles from home. We never saw a full set. We left as Simonon thumped out the 'Police And Thieves' bass line, Strummer snarled Junior Murvin's lyrics, Jones struck the jarring reggae chords and Topper orchestrated the whole thing with drum-machine precision.

It was 11.00pm on 8 January 1980. Margaret Thatcher was in power, and unemployment was on the rise. Unbeknownst to us, the Falklands War and the miners' strike lay ahead, soon to ambush our remaining teenage years. But that night, walking up West Street, sweat-ridden and frozen, we didn't care. We had seen The Clash. And *London Calling* would become the soundtrack of our lives. We were changed forever.

MARTIN JONES

The next time I saw The Clash was at the two nights they did at Brighton Top Rank as part of the *16 Tons* tour. *London Calling* had just been released and so this was the start of the band moving up to a new level. The tour continued and the next one I recall was Portsmouth. The second of these was memorable because Pete Townshend of The Who joined the band on stage for the encore which included a version of 'Louie Louie'.

GAUMONT THEATRE
14 JANUARY 1980, IPSWICH

PETER STRIKE

This was a great gig. I managed to get backstage afterwards and was totally starstruck. What do you say to your heroes? I had a chat with Joe and Mick and tried to explain just what they all meant to me but I probably just sounded like a groupie. I managed to get their autographs on the only piece of paper I had, an old green one-pound note. Joe signed it 'Spend Me, Joe Strummer.'

Joe Strummer wrote 'spend me' on Peter Strike's pound note. He didn't

STEVE HANSELL

My early adolescence had a glam rock soundtrack of Slade, Alice Cooper and T. Rex. Somehow these musicians seemed to have a mythical status about them, untouchable, a higher form of human being. It never dawned on me back then they were just hard-working normal blokes with a talent and aura that most people don't possess.

By the late seventies I began to hear of a new type of more street level music that was emerging predominantly from London and New York. I was 15 and living in Norwich. Like many I was in my last year at school in late '77 and early '78 and couldn't wait to get out of the place. The first punk records I heard were 'God Save The Queen' by the Sex Pistols and the first Ramones album. I just knew I had to be involved in all this in some way.

One afternoon I was at a friend's house. He'd just bought the first Clash album and from the first bars of 'Janie Jones' we were both instantly hooked. The Clash and many of those early bands changed people's lives for the better. We had our bullshit detectors switched on after that. I got to see The Clash live for the first time in 1978. We crossed the border into Suffolk, where they were playing in Bury St Edmunds at a venue I can't recall the name of (Corn Exchange). It was a totally amazing night only slightly marred by some skirmishes by people from different towns, which would often happen back then.

It was round about the time they released '(White Man) In Hammersmith Palais', to this day the greatest single ever recorded. I caught The Clash live again a couple of years later, at Ipswich Gaumont in 1980, a flea pit cinema with seats. It was not the ideal venue for a punk gig but it had a decent-sized stage. The place was rammed. When The Clash took the stage, they launched straight into 'London Calling' and the place erupted. It was an amazing atmosphere. Despite the fact there was some room directly in front of the stage for people to jump around, it wasn't anywhere near big enough, so people were clambering around and dancing on the first few rows of seats, which all collapsed. I've a vivid memory of a group of stressed-out bouncers trying to remove the rows of seats by lifting them above the heads of the crowd, trying to get them out the building.

Quite a few years later, I was spending a few days in Dublin and coincidentally Joe Strummer and the Mescaleros were in town. I managed to get hold of a couple of tickets. That afternoon I was sitting near the window of a bar having

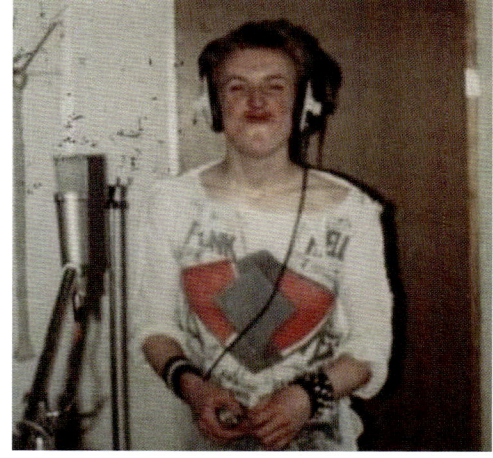
Steve Hansell recalls the Gaumont in Ipswich being rammed

a beer and spotted Joe and a couple of his entourage walking by. I'm not great at meeting my heroes so didn't rush out to shake his hand or ask for an autograph, but I did give him a little nod as he got level with the window and got one back.

DE MONTFORT HALL
16 JANUARY 1980, LEICESTER

RICH BARTON
My band, The Newmatics, were a big local draw, so when The Clash came to town and wanted a local band to support them, we got the gig. I thought they were anti-establishment punk princesses. I sneaked a look in their dressing room. Mick Jones had five Les Pauls in a semi-circle, all ready to go, more rock star than punk, but the energy they created on stage was awesome. I had no idea what was coming out of Strummer's mouth, but it was heartfelt. They were great after the show, chatting, sharing drinks and a spliff. Topper did seem on edge though.

PHILIP MULLETT
I was born in London, lived in Leicester and then we moved to Worcester when I was eleven. Punk rock came along and I was in a gang of little hooligans. We liked the Pistols and The Damned because they were more outrageous, but for me it was The Clash. When I first heard those drum beats, it was like this controlled aggression I hadn't heard in the other bands.

I wasn't very good at school, but I was always quite bright and loved history and things. So when I heard songs about certain things, like Montgomery Clift or whatever, I'd go and find out who these people were.

My sister, who's five years older than me, was going out with this guy, Malik. His band, The Newmatics, supported them in Leicester so I got the train to Leicester and, because I had a backstage pass, I watched them sound check and met them. That night, they started off with 'Clash City Rockers' and the place went mental. One of my abiding memories of that gig is the end of the night and the leads from the guitars being in a huge knot in the middle of the stage from where they'd been running around, crossing over and jumping on the drum risers.

After that I went to the Lyceum for a couple of nights when they did that big stint there. I was slightly disappointed by them. They just didn't seem to be that interested. Then they came back and did the *Casbah Club* tour and I went to Birmingham to see them at Bingley Hall and that was a good gig.

Then me and my mate heard they were doing an extra night in Brixton so we bunked the train down to London, went straight there, got a couple of tickets and got a bit pissed on Special Brew. And we went in to see them and it was like the best gig; it was just amazing. The other nights they'd always opened with 'London Calling', but this night they just came on and went 'one, two, three…' and straight into 'White Riot' and the whole place just went absolutely mental.

They played in Brighton the next night so we went down to Brighton and Terry put us on the guest list, so we went into that gig and that was another cracker. And we went backstage and that night we slept on some park benches and then went home for a couple of days and then it was Bristol, so we went to Bristol for a couple of nights to see them.

The funny thing is, I remember nearly everything about the Clash gigs I saw. The other bands I saw, I used to get pissed a lot at the time and don't really remember. But I never used to get pissed at Clash gigs because I always enjoyed it and I always wanted to see them so much.

I saw Mick's ever last gig for them in Britain. 'Complete Control' was the last song they ever played with that line-up.

I saw the Mk II version four or five times. I sort of enjoyed it, but it was like a nostalgia thing really. It was a case of hoping that they would be something rather than them actually being there. They missed something without Mick because he had something about him that was different. He wasn't playing to be hard or anything; he was always smiley and you know a bit more amenable looking. He wasn't trying to pretend he was cool all the time.

I was working in Soho, because I'm a carpenter by trade, and I was doing up some offices for solicitors when the news came on the radio that Joe had died. The guy who was with me said 'oh no, oh shit' and we went out and had a drink. The more it sunk in, the sadder and angrier I got, because I should have gone and seen him more often. On the way home, there was the *Evening Standard* billboard that said 'Punk Rock God Dies' and I ripped it off the news stand.

I didn't really like that world music thing he got into, but he was definitely a force for good in the world, with those ethics and that curiosity he had. Who'd heard of the Sandinistas? I hadn't. That made me more interested in the world and I still have that interest now, to this day.

They're the most important band for me. I don't like this almost evangelical hero worship that people have about them, because ultimately it was fun; it was a great time to be around. And I don't think that Mick or any of them would really want to be worshipped like they're gods and that everything they ever said was holy scripture. Joe got slagged by some people for having a house in Somerset. What was he meant to do? Live in a squat for the rest of his life? So I don't like the way that's gone.

ALL THE YOUNG PUNKS

But the memories are great. They're some of the happiest moments of my life. I look back at those times and I wouldn't change them for the world. The Clash gave me an education.

⭐ APOLLO THEATRE
21 JANUARY 1980, GLASGOW

STUART MACKELLAR, AGE 17

I saw The Clash at Glasgow Apollo. I had previously been to a few gigs before, but this was the first time seeing them. The Apollo was quite an intimidating place in those days. I don't think the bouncers liked the punks that much. (Do bouncers like anyone?)

You had to sit in your seat before the band came on but, as soon as they did, everybody just made for the front. The Apollo stage was high, so if you were down the front, jumping about and pogoing about like we were, you couldn't see the band. It was around the time *London Calling* had just come out, so they were playing most of the album. I remember 'Jimmy Jazz' the most. I didn't expect people would have taken to that song, because it was so different, but the whole place was singing along, which really pleased Joe Strummer.

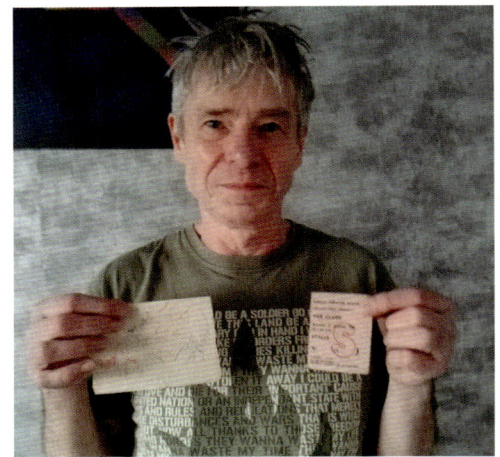

Stuart McKellar got The Clash's autographs

At the end, before we were going out, we sat down to let the mob disappear. Everyone was getting squashed, and the exits were two alleyways that led you out, so we stayed back until everybody left. Then this young lass come over and said, 'If you want to sit back down, the band are coming down and you can meet them.' We stayed sat down in our chairs with about 20 or 30 other people. Sure enough, the band came down and they were brilliant. They signed my wee bit of paper and they signed the back of my ticket. They couldn't have been nicer. We hung around for a good hour or so and we missed the train coming home. I had to get my dad to come and pick us up!

The Clash were pure heroes. I never saw them again, although I saw Joe at an Amnesty International gig in 1988. It was just him playing on his own.

KING GEORGE'S HALL
25 JANUARY 1980, BLACKBURN

PAUL BURROWS

I had a cousin that was really into music, and he picked up on the punk movement around 1977, '78. At first, I wasn't too keen on it but then started seeing bands on *Top Of The Pops*, although not The Clash because they refused to appear. I got into punk music and new wave. I lapped it up! I was listening to The Stranglers, Buzzcocks, The Clash, the Ramones, lots of stuff. My cousin John's favourite band was The Clash. He'd play the first album, *Give 'Em Enough Rope* and a few singles, and I got into them too.

The *16 Tons* tour was my first experience of seeing them live. They had played at Lancaster, my nearest venue, but for some reason, we ended up going to Blackburn. One of the

Paul Burrows' cousin was into punk and got him into it

support bands was a local band called The Not Sensibles. They were a bit funny as well. They had a single called 'I'm In Love With Margaret Thatcher' and went down reasonably well.

When you went to see The Clash (and other bands at that time) loads of reggae would be pumped out before the band came on and as the crowd was building up. You could smell marijuana in the air. The Clash also had Mikey Dread playing as the main support. It was a brilliant gig; the energy was incredible. Strummer epitomised the band with his energy and hyperactivity on stage. I can't recall the specific songs they played except that they opened with 'Clash City Rockers'.

After the gig we hung around King George's Hall. I'd bought the programme, which they called *Armagideon Times*, and decided to get their autographs. There was a little queue in front of each member of the band and when you got to the front you exchanged a couple of words with them, and they signed. I've still got that programme and the photo of them in it is signed by them all.

DEESIDE LEISURE CENTRE
26 JANUARY 1980, QUEENSFERRY

NEIL CRUD, AGE 13

My dad was a photographer for the local press and got me two press pass tickets for The Clash live at Deeside Leisure Centre, who were on their *16 Tons* tour. Me and childhood sweetheart Lynda Jones sat on the balcony with the other dignitaries as thousands of punks swayed on the covered ice rink below us. Just seeing the size of the audience below was breathtaking. The pre-gig music was a lot of reggae and people seemed bored. Then 'Problems' by the Pistols came on and everyone got warmed up, pogoing away!

Deeside Leisure Centre was the sixth largest indoor venue in the country and local band The Jiving Daleks from Chester had the honour of opening the show. The female singer, Maz, noted to the crowd that she had never seen so many people before and pleaded with the crowd to 'stop spitting at me or I will catch hepatitis.' I thought The Jiving Daleks were great and still remember the song 'Two Faced Bitch'.

Much to the dismay of the punk fraternity, Mikey Dread alighted the stage next. A reggae artist, and not the best of reggae artists either, was perhaps not the correct choice to entertain us heathen punk rockers brought up on 'Anarchy In The UK' and 'New Rose'. The influence behind the yet-to-be-released 'Bankrobber' became target practice for the front five rows of gobbing punks as they sprayed the performer with more liquid per minute than a top of the range power shower. The Clash came out in sympathy and, dressed in long coats and dark glasses, skanked onto the stage and joined Mr Dread, gobbing back at the crowd.

The Clash were simply brilliant, even if I didn't know any of the songs off the *London Calling* album. They also played quite a lot of reggae. My memory is somewhat jaded of any key points of their set because of events that took place afterwards.

The gig had finished and the crowds were trudging off home. Me and Lynda stayed in our seats waiting for my dad to finish chatting at the bar. We approached Maz and Sven of the Jiving Daleks who were milling around and asked them if they knew where we could get a concert programme. Maz apologised but said she could get us to meet The Clash if we liked. Our mouths fell open and she led us down the corridors past a queue of fans and into The Clash's dressing room. My little notebook was open, pen eagerly poised. Paul Simonon obliged with a smile as did Mick Jones. Topper Headon was busy being talked into bed by a young lady and quickly signed the book whilst Mikey Dread was in the corner cleaning his gob-ridden coat.

JOE ASKED WHERE WE WERE FROM…

NEIL CRUD

Joe Strummer was different. He took the time to ask us where we were from. 'Denbigh! That's just up the road, isn't it?' Wow! Joe Strummer knew where Denbigh was! Although, in hindsight, me being so young, I'm not going to be too far from home! He kept winking at Lynda and put kisses after his autograph for her. I would have taken him outside and given him a good kicking for messing with my bird, but I was only 13!

My dad got some ace pics of the gig, but the negatives were the property of North Wales Newspapers, and they'll be long gone now. He did give me a fantastic ten by eight print showing The Clash in full flow on stage, and I have an inkling it's in his attic with my school stuff. I've tried to get that stuff off him for 30 years!

TRISTAN CONOLEY

The date was January 26, 1980. It was The Clash's *16 Tons* tour. The friend I went with (we called him Manuel, but his real name was Steve) was two or three years older than me. But let's go back a couple of years…

I discovered The Clash by default. I had heard 'Keys To Your Heart' by the 101ers and loved it, by which time they were no more, and The Clash were the new force. Songs like 'Complete Control' and 'White Riot' now had me totally captivated. The band had played in Chester about a year before, in a club called Quaintways, but I was too young to go, so when the Deeside gig came up wild horses were not going to keep me away. My first real concert – The Clash!

They were supported by the late Mikey Dread (RIP) but although I thought he was great and was my first true introduction to reggae, he didn't go down too well with the congregation (which always troubled me, although at 14 I didn't quite know why). Also on the support list was a local punk outfit called The Jiving Daleks and their big-voiced female lead singer, Maz. Being a local band, I followed them to a few gigs over the next year, although they soon split up. (Years later, I am friends with their lead guitarist.)

During The Clash gig, two massive punk lads with Mohicans got in front of me.

Being considerably shorter than both, I now couldn't see my heroes on stage. Being 14 and unaware of the correct concert etiquette, and despite my friend Manuel's reservations and obvious upset, I simply told these two massive lads I couldn't see... The result of which was that, for at least one song, I was hoisted up onto a set of shoulders and had the best view in the house (a favour I have since paid back). It is a night I will never forget.

PETE STEVENS

The Clash played Deeside Leisure Centre, Queensferry on the *16 Tons* tour and we braved one of the coldest nights of the year – something like -5°C outside and dense fog – to watch them perform new songs from *London Calling*. If memory serves, it was also the first time 'Bankrobber', recorded in Pluto Sound in Manchester around the time of the Deeside gig, was played live. No bootleg audio recording or setlist has ever surfaced from this gig to confirm or deny my shaky memory.

After skanking around the stage in red and black bandanas, crombies and pork pie hats behind a toasting Mikey Dread, the tension built, lights dimmed and Tennessee Ernie Ford's 'Sixteen Tons' blasted out of the PA... The Clash exploded onto the stage in a barrage of light and sound and straight into 'Clash City Rockers' and, sadly, showers of gob from some mindless cretins close to the stage. The sound was appalling, the venue being a cavernous metal shed with a pretty thin carpet spread over the ice rink. To this day it's still the coldest gig I've ever been to! They finished with 'Tommy Gun', one of 'Topper's Boppers' – his drumsticks – landing agonisingly close to me in the crowd.

SHEM SHARPLES

I was 19 in 1979 and after spending my first year at university in Canterbury and having seen a huge number of inspiring bands while I was there, including Joy Division, Magazine, Wire, The Rezillos, The Undertones, The Jam and many others, I decided to drop out from my electronics degree and form my own band.

I went back to Chester and practised my guitar for a while. I got together with my friends, Nick and his girlfriend Maz, and they liked some of my made-up guitar riffs. Maz was a musician and started singing some of her lyrics to my riffs. We liked the sound of what we were doing and another friend, Earl, joined in and so we became a four-piece. We called ourselves The Jiving Daleks.

Word got around and Sven Harding and Simon Lewis jumped ship from another Chester band named WSS and filled in spots on bass and drums respectively. Nick stepped aside and became our guide, inspiration and manager, although it was Maz who really managed the band herself. We played a few local gigs – at Chester Arts

Centre, Smartyz night club, Chester College, and Chester's Gateway Theatre – each gig successively getting bigger towards the end of 1979. After the Chester Arts Centre and Smartyz gigs, Simon left to go to college to do an art degree in Brighton. We found Paul Williams (Gazmo) to take over on drums, who slotted in well.

Shem Sharples with his band The Jiving Daleks

The Clash put out an announcement for local bands to apply to support them on their upcoming tour. Maz jumped at the chance and contacted them, took a reel-to-reel tape recording of one of their gigs to London and landed us a spot at Deeside Leisure Centre in January 1980. Exciting times!

We were a very tight band. We practiced a lot and were very focused, although I was also a bit druggy and stoned a lot.

We played The Clash gig at Deeside to around 12,000 people. We were on first before Mikey Dread. We went down well – lots of our fans were there – and the energy was high. It felt like it was over in a flash. We played for around 30 minutes or so. We were cheered, gobbed on (those times were still full of punky gobbing) – one solid specimen landing on my cheek. Some of the audience wanted The Clash to come on and were less enthusiastic. But all-in-all it was a successful show. The thing is that it was only our sixth ever gig, and I'd only been playing guitar for about 18 months at that point. Punks welcomed and encouraged minimal skill levels. Remember 'One Chord Wonders' by The Adverts? I did make a good sound on my guitar, and Maz was a powerful singer and frontwoman. Paul's drumming was great too!

The Clash were very supportive, and I could see them watching from the balcony. It was a great thing for them to offer the opportunity for local bands. It was a taste of stardom before we were really ready for it – or maybe that was just me.

That was our high point. Paul said he couldn't handle it anymore and left. We never did find a replacement – although we practised with a couple of other drummers who just didn't fit in. Disillusion set in for me. I think I was too heavily stoned by then and I didn't feel committed any longer. To be honest, my mental health was suffering due to drug abuse. The band split and that was the end of a brief but exciting dance with stardom. Our 15 minutes of fame.

A local newspaper put out the headline 'JIVING DALEKS HAVE LANDED!' and wrote a great review of the event. We were also reviewed in *Zig Zag*, a popular fanzine of the time.

The Clash played a great set by the way, they were on fire. All credit to them. It was the one and only time I got to see them live. They'd always been heroes to me.

I've never given up with music however and I've always been writing songs and recording ever since. I formed a band called Rev Rev who were ongoing for 30 years on and off. More recently I've been playing and recording under the name Shem Sharples with a bass player – Thor Brown. So, I'm still in the game and very much alive.

DAVID WILLIAMS

When the Bill Grundy thing happened with the Pistols, I was only twelve. Me and me and my mates thought all the swearing was cool. A lot of punk stuff was banned but gradually you could listen to stuff on John Peel. My mum and dad weren't happy about it, but I'd stay up late in bed listening to punk and reggae on a little radio.

Me and my mate used to do paper rounds. When we were collecting the paper money off people, we'd nick the milk money they'd left out. We'd go from Holywell to the train station in Flint and then jump the train all the way to Chester and then to Liverpool.

There was a club in Liverpool called Eric's. We found out in *Sounds* that they started doing matinee gigs for kids who weren't old enough to go in the evenings. I became a regular there. The first band I saw was Penetration with Pauline Murray. She was my teenage crush. We came out all buzzing after Penetration. And a couple of weeks later it was Magazine. And just as we were going in, the guy who ran Eric's, Roger Eagle, said, 'Look lads, The Clash are coming but it's going to be a secret gig.' Because they were supposed to play the Empire but Liverpool Council had banned them after all the trouble in Glasgow. So they played gigs on the Friday night and Saturday daytime.

The place was absolutely rammed. About 5,000 people claim they were there, and there's no way you could get that many people in Eric's. They were one of the loudest bands I've ever seen in my life, and I've seen Motörhead. It just blew my mind. It changed my life.

We didn't go and see them for a while after that. They were getting bigger but they never, ever sold out. We next saw them at Deeside Leisure Centre. Me and my mate went there early and sat around the back, drinking cans. The next thing we saw this little mini bus with blacked-out windows coming and The Clash get out. So we stood around talking to them and then, because it was a leisure centre, we played football with them in one of the five-a-side courts.

We got inside and my mate, who's a drummer, had a go on Topper's drum kit. We chatted with them some more and they were absolutely lovely guys. Then the security said something like, 'Come on lads, I don't think you're supposed to be fucking in here. You've got your tickets so can you leave?'

They were good but not as good as that first one.

There wasn't a bad track on the first two albums. But *London Calling* wasn't really punk anymore. The ideas stayed the same all the way through to *Combat Rock* but the music changed. There's a couple of tracks on *London Calling* that I don't like, like 'Jimmy Jazz', and that 'Lover's Rock' is shit. I could never be done with that. So I was thinking, 'Well it's not perfect, like the first two.' Then *Sandinista!* came out and I thought 'what good value', but it shouldn't have been three LPs. They should have squashed that down into one. Obviously, there's all different styles going on, with the reggae influence, and some cracking stuff on there but some of it's shite, to be honest.

Then we saw them in the 'Radio Clash' era for three nights at Manchester Apollo, with Theatre Of Hate supporting them. I like 'Radio Clash', because I'm into the hip-hop music as well. And I got into rave music. The punk and rave cultures were very similar, and I was lucky enough to grow up in between the two. They were both anti-authority.

I saw them a few more times, with the last one being at Liverpool Royal Court, but there was only Paul and Joe and the other three by then, the Mark II version. It had finished when they got rid of Topper and Mick Jones, but we still went to see them.

I was in work in 2002 and my mate said, 'You're into that Clash, aren't you? Or you were.' He said, 'Joe Strummer's dead, like.' I said 'fuck off!' He said, 'Yeah, yeah, yeah.' Oh God, what a nice guy. What a shame.

I saw what I think was the last time Joe played in Liverpool, with the Mescaleros at Mountford Hall. He was still good even though he was getting on. Me and my mate went over there and it was sold out. We said we'd blag our way in. There was a student on the door and I said, 'Mate, I'll give you ten quid to get in.' 'No mate,' he said, 'tickets, tickets, you've gotta have your tickets.' And this old school bouncer came along and said, 'What's up, lads?' I said, 'Look mate, we've come all the way from fucking Wales here, got on the fucking train and we can't get in. Any chance, me and my mate? Score?' He said, 'Yeah, go ahead lads.' And we gave him 20 quid and he let us in.

I still try and jump the train now if I can. The punk thing is in my head and always will be. But I don't pinch the milk money any more.

 TOP RANK
27 JANUARY 1980, SHEFFIELD

ANDY ROTHERHAM

London Calling had been released the month before. I was finding the double album unwieldy and difficult to process. The many influences and different styles of music were challenging to me. I was to learn that it was a slow grower and would lead me on my own path of discovery through the different genres it introduced me to.

The *16 Tons* tour was underway and heralded The Clash's return to Sheffield Top Rank. Once again, we braved the Yorkshire winter, in just a t-shirt and jeans. We really wanted to look tough. How naive we were!

We got through the door. Being slightly older, now just turned 17, I wasn't as anxious about being turned away. I was also working, so had a little money in my pocket for merch. I bought a t-shirt and a badge. The t-shirt was the Bonds' portrait of the band on a white shirt. The badges were a *16 Tons* logo on a green and a yellow background.

This time we couldn't get to the front. The surge was too much. I do remember Mikey Dread coming on as support, doing toasting, and The Clash and their crew appearing masked behind him, to dance at his grooves. The other change was that a Hammond organ had appeared at the side of the stage. This would be ably played by Micky Gallagher from The Blockheads.

The band had grown into a much tighter and more musical unit now. No longer shy about their influences, their musicianship was truly emerging. Mikey Dread joined them for 'Bankrobber'. The gig was spectacular, Joe constantly throwing himself about, dropping to his knees, laying across his monitor and singing in the faces of the crowd. Paul too was animated, but his bass playing abilities had improved markedly. He was really nailing it by this stage of their career. Mick was his usual aloof and stroppy self. After the band left the stage, there was a seemingly interminable wait for the encore. I was later to find out that they were arguing in the dressing room.

As they returned to the stage there was still a tangible friction between Joe and Mick. As they came on stage, this boiled over and fists were thrown between them. I am told that Mick didn't want to end the show with 'White Riot', and the rest of the band did. To me it was an early sign of the break up to come.

The Clash did return to Sheffield, on their tour supporting *Sandinista!* Unfortunately, I found a lot of the music on it to be self indulgent and impenetrable to my young brain. I boycotted the gig. What a stupid decision that was!

RICHARD PORTER

After seeing them at the Top Rank in November 1978, I saw The Clash again in January 1980. I remember it being cold. Me and a friend went on the train to Sheffield, but we didn't have tickets and it was sold out. We were sat on the steps of the Top Rank when the band and roadies turned up and start loading gear in. This guy came up to us and asked what the matter was. We explained we'd not got tickets and were hoping we could buy one at the door. He then introduced us to Johnny Green, the road manager, who said if we gave them a hand, we'd get a 'Lumper's Pass', which we hadn't realised first meant we got in the gig for free.

As we'd done the roadie thing, we sat up in the back and were able to watch them soundcheck. After they'd finished, we had a chance to speak to them, but we chickened out. We were a little bit in awe.

I didn't find out till years later that Joe and Mick had an argument before coming out to play an encore because Mick Jones didn't want to play 'White Riot' and apparently Joe punched him. When they finally came out to play it, Mick pointed to somebody in the crowd and swore at them after about a minute and a half and with that, he just took his guitar off and walked off stage leaving the other three to finish on their own.

Another time I saw them was at Bridlington Spa. For that we end on a coach. On the way back we wrote down all the songs that we could remember them playing, and it was over 30! People talk about Bruce Springsteen and others giving value for money. With most punk bands, you were doing well if you got an hour. The Clash played for nearly two hours!

LEEDS UNIVERSITY
31 JANUARY 1980, LEEDS

MARK JOHNSON, AGE 17

To this day, even after seeing thousands of bands live, this Clash gig is still my favourite of the lot. They were at their peak both musically and aesthetically. They sounded magnificent and looked incredible. This was the *16 Tons* tour and they were promoting the release of arguably their greatest album, *London Calling*. That

ALL THE YOUNG PUNKS

was quite a week because the Ramones had played the same venue a few days before, and I went to that too. I only saw The Clash that one time because nothing they did after that came close.

They started with 'Clash City Rockers' and it just kicked off; it felt like everything was going at 100mph. They played all my favourites, including 'Safe European Home' and '(White Man) In Hammersmith Palais.' I kept trying to guess the encore but then that song would be played. I was certain that they would play 'White Riot' last, especially being in Leeds, who play in the famous all-white kit, but they didn't play it at all! I was too elated to be disappointed. I think the last song was 'London's Burning'.

The Clash in Leeds in 1980 remains Mark Johnson's favourite ever gig

A few years later, I was in the queue to see The Alarm play at the same venue (by that time I was getting into university gigs for free, so I went to all sorts of shite) and quite unbelievably Strummer, Simmo and Co showed up and started busking to the crowd. They did a couple of songs and then someone chucked a bucket of water over Strummer, allegedly as a protest at them 'selling out'. Funny really, cos even though they were only busking and wet through, they were still better than The Alarm.

JOHN PAYNTER

Me and my mates had been listening to what our friends' older brothers were feeding us – stuff like Slade, T.Rex and Bowie – so when punk happened, it felt like it was something of ours. We used to go to gigs at Leeds University. We were school kids and we didn't have any money so we'd blag our way in as best we could. And the first bands I saw there were The Clash, The Stranglers and the Ramones. We'd go up straight after school and just sort of hang around while the band was sound checking. We'd usually try to hit on a support band and get on the guest list with them.

The Clash were great. I saw The Clash a few times at Leeds Uni. They used to just let people in for sound checks and so this was like a mini-gig in the afternoon. Leeds Uni held about 1,500 people and there were probably about 30 or 40 of us in there watching them sound check. The one track that stood out was 'The

Israelites', the Desmond Dekker song. I later found out they used to do it in sound checks and never recorded it. It was a song that you used to hear it on the radio as a kid. So when The Clash started playing it in this punked-up version it was just like 'wow'.

I've always been a massive record collector and we were in Bleeker Bob's record store in Greenwich Village, New York in 1993. It was February and it was freezing, with snow everywhere. Me and my partner were just going into shops to keep out of the cold really. It was midweek and there was absolutely nobody in there. There was a lot of old soul stuff in there – Lee Dorsey, Allen Toussaint, that sort of thing. There was loads of Clash memorabilia behind the counter and the glass-topped counter had loads of Clash picture sleeves, like 'White Riot', on display. They were all signed.

I was flicking through some records when the bell over the door rang. I looked over and Joe Strummer had walked in, accompanied by a woman. I was just mesmerised. I couldn't concentrate on looking at the records any more. Joe went to the counter and I saw him chatting with the guy behind the counter. He bought a Clash single off the guy and gave it to this girl (who I later found out was his future wife).

My missus was saying 'go and have a chat with him'. And I was like, 'No, I can't do that. He's with somebody.' I've since read that he absolutely loved it when people were talking about The Clash with him. But it just didn't feel right, invading somebody's privacy.

I don't have many regrets in life. But that's probably the one that jumps out every time. He still looked great.

APOLLO THEATRE
4 FEBRUARY 1980, MANCHESTER

GERRY DALY, AGE 15

I saw The Clash twelve times in all, though a couple of them were with the post-Mick line-up. The first time was on the *16 Tons* tour at Manchester Apollo. I had only been to a couple of gigs – Stiff Little Fingers at Manchester Poly and Showaddywaddy at the Davenport Theatre in Stockport!

The first glimpse of Strummer and Jones came during the set for the support act, Mikey Dread. They came onstage in Crombies with red hankies

Gerry Daly saw The Clash twelve times in all

covering their faces and trilbies on their heads. I grabbed my mates Jacko and Carl and shouted 'it's them, it's them'. I've read accounts of this evening that have other people on the stage from The Clash entourage like Johnny Green and Baker. Maybe they were but it's over 40 years ago and I only remember Joe and Mick.

JONNY PAUL, AGE 13

It was the *London Calling*, *16 Tons* tour, two months before my fourteenth birthday. My dad dropped me off and picked me up. I don't remember too much from the gig other just being in awe. I still have the ticket, which cost £3. It was a huge privilege to see them at their peak.

I also went to Joe Strummer's funeral and wake at the Paradise Bar in West London. I remember going for a pee and looking up – and there was Rat Scabies peeing next to me!

STEVE HIGGINSON

The Clash, the greatest rock 'n' roll group, and still the greatest to this day. I first heard the debut album, *The Clash*, in the summer of 1977 in my neighbour's bedroom one day after school. We listened to it over and over again. It was amazing and fresh and within a week we knew all the words, riffs and guitar intros. After the release of *Give 'Em Enough Rope* in late 1978, it inspired the guy next door, his punky friend and myself to form a band of our own, much to the dismay of my parents and neighbours down the street! We were obviously heavily influenced by The Clash and the social changes coming out of punk rock.

My friend had seen The Clash a few times in London with his cousin, but as the time came for me to go and see them, the excitement became euphoric. The weekend before, I played all three albums back-to-back, but was loving the new and varied songs on *London Calling*.

The day of the concert came – a school day! Do I bunk it off or sit in lessons daydreaming? We were blessed with Theatre Of Hate as the support act, Kirk Brandon's operatic voice resonating out into the venue's bar that was a-bustle with testosterone.

The time had come. The Clash ran on to the stage, a rimshot from Topper and we were up and running. It was absolutely mind-blowing, the sheer energy and adrenaline of the band hit every corner of the auditorium and hastily spread through the eagerly awaiting audience.

The presence and magnitude of these four guys rhythmically dispersed and filled the entire room with adrenaline. Strummer and Jones's duelling guitars, Topper's one-man percussion section and Simonon's thumping bass lines… sheer poetry in motion.

With *London Calling* being released the previous December, the set list included many tracks from this 'pay no more than £5' double album but we knew every word and boy did we belt them out! The night finished with 'Train In Vain' and the crowd went berserk.

The whole evening went far too quickly. Before we knew it we were on our way home, each one of us reminiscing about our favourite tracks and the highlights of the show. It was just as much a visual treat as a musical one, and one I will never forget.

I saw The Clash a number of times after this, each one just as magical as the first. By the way, the garage band we started became a local success. Now that wouldn't have happened if I had never heard of The Clash!

SIMON WOLSTENCROFT, DRUMMER

I think I first saw them not on the *White Riot* tour but the one after, in late 1977. I could be wrong, but I think between 1977 and 1980 I saw them about 30 times!

John Squire and I were classmates as was Ian Brown. John Squire and I were really into The Clash, and we started going to the Apollo Theatre. We were going there all the time because we knew a guy who was a promoter called Mike Henley. He used to let us in the back of the Apollo when there was no health and safety, and we helped him carry the boxes in and out of the truck. We let onto Joe and Mick Jones in particular. He was always smiling; he was a very funny guy.

I sort of gave up my education because I liked The Clash so much. I bought the first album and all the singles. I followed them around on tour, not every night, but when I should have been studying at college, I was spending all my money on National Express coach trips down to Bristol, London, Wolverhampton, Birmingham. I went to quite a few places to see them, as did John.

One time at the Apollo, Manchester, I think on the *16 Tons* tour, Topper didn't turn up and they wanted somebody to play the drums on the soundcheck (not with the band, although I was hoping that would happen!). I was in the soundcheck as I always was when the road crew asked 'can anybody here play drums?' and I just stuck my hand up and thought 'go on, you do it.'

They did offer me a roadie job, although The Baker was their full-time drum roadie. That's when I got a real taste of music. I wanted to be in a band myself, as a full-time thing. It was fantastic hearing that kit, the massive silver custom Pearl kit. It was a lot louder back then. We liked the style of their clothes. John and I would try to emulate them. They had handmade clothes made for them. We tried our best to convert whatever we had to look like The Clash.

I didn't ever get to play with the band, but I did get to meet Mick Jones and have a great chat with him for about 40 minutes at the Ritz a few years ago. There

ALL THE YOUNG PUNKS

was a Hillsborough fundraiser with The Farm. Ian Brown invited me down to the soundcheck and John Squire came along to do 'Bankrobber'. I did get to play this with Ian and John, and it was the first time we'd played together since we were 17 or 18, which was amazing. Unfortunately, nobody had a camera to film it.

Later, I found myself in the dressing room at The Ritz with Mick Jones. He liked a bit of a smoke, like I did. We just laughed and laughed. I said, 'Do you remember when you came up here and recorded Bankrobber?' 'Oh yeah', he said, 'it was Strawberry, wasn't it?' I said, 'No, it was in Pluto Studios.' Ian Brown was lucky enough to witness them recording it on Granby Row...

The Clash have been a big influence on me and my daughter. I'm glad I put her on to them too.

JEFF DAWSON

I first saw The Clash before my 18th birthday. I'd been going to a few low-key gigs around Bolton since the age of 16 but hadn't been to any massive gigs. I was still listening to ELO and that kind of thing, but my mate was into Buzzcocks, Magazine and Wire. I absolutely loved it, and one day he played me The Clash. We went to the Apollo for the 16 Tons tour. It just blew my mind; I still get goosebumps thinking about it now. Mikey Dread was supporting. We were about halfway back near the mixer. The Clash came on and

Jeff Dawson's Manchester Apollo ticket

the first track they did was 'Safe European Home' and the place just exploded. I hadn't passed my driving test at the time, so going to a gig in Manchester was a big thing, because if you were late out of the gig, you'd be on the last bus home which would have been a bit of a nightmare.

⭐ TOP RANK
6 FEBRUARY 1980, BIRMINGHAM

JOHN MITCHELL, AGE 15

My older sister was into The Commodores, The Stylistics and things like that, but that wasn't my music. All the kids at school walked around with Pink Floyd albums under their arms. Around 1976, friends started bringing those little mono tape recorders into school. When we moved into 1977, it was The Stranglers, Buzzcocks, The Clash and 'Anarchy In The UK', and suddenly *this* is my music. I got to hear 'Janie Jones' and all that stuff. A friend lent me a copy of the first Clash album, which I then immediately bought. The first single I bought was 'Clash City Rockers.' I have a great affection for *Give 'Em Enough Rope*, because that was the first album that we bought when it first came out. A lot of people were disappointed when *London Calling* then came out, but I loved it. I saw it as strong. Joe was portraying the person he thought he ought to be, rather than the person he was. I think he found his voice during *London Calling*.

My first Clash concert was on the *16 Tons* tour. We had a minibus up from school to Birmingham Top Rank, which apparently was The Clash's least favourite venue.

When they opened with 'Clash City Rockers' the whole place went mental, and then they launched into 'Brand New Cadillac' and threw in 'Jimmy Jazz'. The whole floor was bouncing, something you never saw usually for a punk band. It was fantastic. I loved that period of The Clash. They look fantastic with the greased-back hair.

I missed seeing the shows in 1981. I wanted to go but I was 16 or 17, and my dad didn't want me to bother my uncle in taking me. I had a ticket to see them at Bingley Hall in Birmingham, just when Joe Strummer did a runner.

SOPHIA GARDENS
11 FEBRUARY 1980, CARDIFF

DOMINIC HALL, AGE 17

I'd got the *London Calling* album for Christmas '79 and played it to death. I was gutted when I couldn't get a ticket. Luckily, my uncle managed to get me one from the touts who ran the fruit barrows in Manchester city centre near Tib Street. It was for the first of the two nights planned at the Apollo.

The Apollo is a fantastic venue and I had been there several times for gigs in the past. I would usually stand downstairs in the stalls but I ended up with a seated balcony ticket, mid-centre and halfway back. On this night the place was absolutely buzzing when I arrived. Even down by the merch stand in reception, the atmosphere was electric. When the band came on, the place just went wild and from my vantage point upstairs I could see it bouncing down in the stalls.

The newer *London Calling* songs were well recieved but when the 'Tommy Gun' drum intro started the chaos erupted, as loads of fans rushed forward and tried getting on stage. Security were pushing fans back to stop them from getting on the stage and it started to turn into a bit of a brawl. Joe Strummer could see there was a problem and he stopped the gig and asked for the house lights to go up so he could see what was going on. He told the security guys to drag some of the trapped fans off the floor and onto the stage.

The rush of fans had resulted in some of the seating in the stalls area collapsing and so they asked fans to form a chain and pass the damaged seats over their heads and onto the stage area to be cleared away. This went on for some time. The gig then resumed with 'Tommy Gun' with 50 or 60 fans still on the stage and all bouncing around while the band played on.

It was an amazing end to an amazing night, and how lucky was I to see them, as the following night's gig was cancelled due to the damage caused.

This was the first (and only) time I saw The Clash live. Even now, I get hairs on the back of my neck when I think about it.

GREGG JOHNSON

Me and Daz Brickell nipped out of school at lunchtime to jump on the 192 to the Apollo and got our tickets from the box office (£2.50). We went back to school but arrived late and the headmaster was on the door with a cane in his hand. We didn't care as we'd got the gig tickets and were off to see the mighty Clash! It was February 1980, the *London Calling* tour with Mikey Dread supporting.

The night of the gig I was all set to go. My mum was taking us to the Apollo and I think we'd agreed we get the bus home. I'm all punked up and good to go when Mum starts going on about me wearing a big coat as it's February and pretty fucking cold, but I don't want to as 'I'm going to see The Clash'. We're in the middle of this when there's a knock at the door. I'm pleading with Hylda not to show me up in front of Daz and I open up the door to find Daz stood there in his snorkel parka and his mum is shouting at him to keep it on as he'll catch his death.

The gig blew me away. I bought a t-shirt and programme, *The Armagideon Times*. The t-shirt went past my knees. (I've still got it.) I remember the show getting stopped as the first six rows in the stalls went mental and they ripped the chairs up. Needless to say, it was a game changer.

The very next day in woodwork at school, Daz started making a bass guitar. Me, I didn't bother… I think I said something along the lines of 'what's the point? We just saw The Clash, it doesn't get any better than that.' As The Hold Steady sang 35 or 40 years later:

Save a toast for Saint Joe Strummer
I think he might've been our only decent teacher
I'll always be a Clash fan.

A PEOPLE'S HISTORY OF THE CLASH

PETER METCALFE

It was a former aircraft hangar. When The Clash were on, there were several fights down the front and they had to stop a couple of times and calm things down. It was still a great show and after the usual two encores, some people left but the lights didn't go up. Eventually they came back and played 'White Riot'. The place went mad and people who had left came running back in. Sophia Gardens closed two years later, when the roof caved in after heavy snow.

SARAH WELLS, AGE 17

I saw The Clash in Sophia Gardens a year or so before the Pavilion came down in a storm. I've seen loads of bands although I can't remember them all, but I remember this one. The venue wasn't great but obviously The Clash were. It was a nice walk out of town, crossing the River Taff and across the park to the Gardens. I went on my own but met up with the crowd of punks I knew and we all walked over together. It was cold so a mate lent me his leather jacket. I was a very straight accounts clerk, but I loved punk music, especially The Clash and Stiff Little Fingers.

The gig was great although the venue was very dull. Most bands played Cardiff Top Rank or pubs around that time, but I guess this was bigger. The Cardiff scene was pretty good generally. Later it was the anarcho-punk scene was where I really found my place, but those gigs were unfortunately frequently attacked by the far right.

MIKE JONES

Just when everybody was leaving, the band returned to the stage and did a storming version of 'White Riot', which I missed three-quarters of due to the stampede back into the venue!

STATESIDE CENTRE
12 FEBRUARY 1980, BOURNEMOUTH

SIMON BOXALL

The concert was not that well attended, which surprised me, and the band were dressed up in 2-Tone clobber. Mikey Dread was great! They weren't very good, though, and I always thought their musicianship, except for the drummer, was poor.

London Calling was their best album, and had *Sandinista!* been shorter it would've been just as good.

ALL THE YOUNG PUNKS

NATIONWIDE TV PROGRAMME
18 FEBRUARY 1980, DURHAM

PAUL HUTLEY, AGE 14

1979. London was calling to the faraway towns.

My town, a city by dint of its magnificent Norman cathedral, lay the best part of 300 miles from the capital by road or rail. I couldn't drive and I had no money. I was 14 years old. London cared not and was calling to this Durham lad regardless. It was calling through the speakers pulsing high on my bedroom wall. A clarion call – loud, urgent, compelling – The Clash! The Clash! The Clash! The Clash were calling to the faraway towns. Nothing would ever sound as important again. Nothing.

Paul Hutley recalls seeing The Clash on TV

The sounds exploding from the vinyl's hairline grooves made your heart pump and your head spin. When you had fallen this hard you wanted more and you wanted it now, but long-distance love would prove a frustrating affair when communication was scant, and detail was missing. Beyond the vinyl, every available slice of it racked beneath my suitcase-sized music centre, the nation's music papers were my only other source of intelligence. The internet was years away, radio was in tune with nothing new or exciting, music video was yet to flourish, and a paltry three TV channels offered minimal music programming. To top it all, my boys had decided to boycott the weekly music show, *Top Of The Pops*. A decision I defended in the playground while detesting in private. Selfish bastards!

The music papers teased with black and white stills and the printed word. The gig reviews and interview questions I would rather were mine were devoured and digested but proved inadequate morsels to an insatiable lover. Those inanimate images implied electrifying on-stage action, the words striving to paint that rock and roll movie in my mind. Mick the leaping livewire, Joe with his pneumatic leg, Paul's effortless cool and Topper the one-man engine room. So, it read, but however well crafted, the words fell short and left me wanting. I NEEDED TO SEE THIS FOR MYSELF! The band spent most of '79 touring the US. Selfish bastards!

Then, a new decade dawned, the clouds parted and maybe the rock gods looked down and took pity? What drew me to our living room and BBC 1's *Nationwide* on the evening of 18 February 1980, I really don't know. What I do know now is an epiphany was imminent.

Four familiar faces were on screen as I entered the room, only this time, for the first time, animate, breathing, ALIVE. Then, as the opening to 'Clampdown' swelled towards its thrilling head of steam, the narrator declared, 'The Clash don't sing soppy songs about teenage love,' and the camera panned across a seething crowd before a side stage angle revealed the molten, liquid movement of a band about to ignite. It was in that single incendiary moment that I felt for the first time what hundreds of words had tried and failed to deliver – the breath-taking, spine-tingling, heart-pumping joy of witnessing The Clash on stage. In an instant, in a living room in a faraway town, the most exciting twelve minutes of my short life had arrived.

LEWISHAM ODEON
18 FEBRUARY 1980, LONDON

PAUL HOOD

I bought the first album as soon as it came out and loved it. It was the great songs, the honesty and that almost melancholy tunefulness that Jones added, at least in later recordings with 'Stay Free', etc. They were a big influence on fashions in London, with the writing and stencils on clothes and particularly the zip trousers. There were quickly efforts to manufacture and sell items like that, to cash in really.

Lewisham Odeon was a huge Art Deco venue (since demolished in 1991) that had featured The Beatles, the Stones, Little Richard, Ziggy-era Bowie, Queen, Carl Perkins and dozens of others. There was a real local buzz about this show, even though The Clash and its audience had changed since 1977. It featured a set by Joe Ely. US roots rock and country was not heard too much then, at least not by punks, so it was an adventurous booking choice of (I presume) Joe's. Mikey Dread was a very popular reggae DJ 'toaster' (a term not used so much nowadays) so another cool support choice. Mikey was very popular with his *African Anthem* album. I can't quite remember how he was presented, but he definitely did a track with The Clash. It was an exciting and rich gig, hot and sweaty, but most gigs were like that then.

When working at a famous London museum I met Jiving Al of The Vultures, Joe's first band in Wales. We had a short chat. He was a lovely guy and he said that, even then, they knew Joe was a bit special and would go on to greater things.

At the same workplace, I was lucky to serve Mick in the museum shop. He was really nice. I said, 'Oh I've been going back to your old lot recently,' meaning The

Clash of course. I was actually immersed in the band again as I had been reading *Passion Is A Fashion*, so it kinda felt like I knew Mick! He was smiley and friendly. He always spoke about Mott the Hoople looking after the fans, and punk also broke down barriers between band and audience. It was great to meet the man, albeit briefly.

The Pistols and The Damned were brilliant, but The Clash managed to have an emotional and philosophical dimension the other bands lacked. My favourite tracks? 'Complete Control', 'White Man', 'Cheapskates', 'Stay Free', 'Garageland' and so many more…

READING UNIVERSITY
20 FEBRUARY 1980, READING

SUE TERRY

I was at Reading University and we had lots of bands come and play. This particular evening, Ronnie Lane and Slim Chance were the band. I was with a friend of mine called Lucy and I said, 'Oh, Ronnie Lane, I quite like him but I'm not bothered. It's not The Clash or reggae or something like that, but let's go to the bar anyway.' And we were in the bar having an orange juice or something and my friend looked at me and she said, 'See that bloke at the bar?' There was this very interesting looking hippie deluxe-type bloke with a waistcoat and long black hair and stuff. She said, 'I think that's Mick Jones.' I said, 'Don't be daft. What's Mick Jones doing at Reading University with Ronnie Lane?' Anyway, it was Mick Jones and I don't know why I didn't take the opportunity to go and say hello. I'm still kicking myself about that. I might have waved ineffectually from the background when his back was turned or something.

Ronnie Lane did his show and it was a really good show. He did some Faces numbers and Mick Jones was invited onto the stage – he just so happened to have his guitar with him – and he joined Ronnie and co for at least one number. I could see some of the people in the audience going 'who the hell's this person who's just come on?'

LE PALACE
27 FEBRUARY 1980, PARIS, FRANCE

MICHEL GARCIN

I'd been in London in the summers of 1976 and 1977 practising my English. During these two years London was incredibly animated, with warm months, the Silver Jubilee, Freddie Laker and the Skytrain, and of course the beginning of the punk movement. For me punk was both a revolution and revelation. The Clash, The Stranglers, the Sex Pistols, Sham 69, Buzzcocks… there were so many bands I discovered.

Back in my native France, I had to wait for the coming of The Clash in Paris, to see them in Le Palace on in February 1980. Fortunately, I knew the security team of these gigs and they let me in. I also assisted at the concert, but it was so crowded that I was unable to get next to the stage as I always tried to.

The gig was fantastic and recorded by French TV (like some other gigs that year at Le Palace). I later saw The Clash on 27 May 1980, when they performed an incredible gig at Palais des Sports, Porte de Versailles à Paris in front of thousands of people for another spectacular and memorable show.

16 TONS US TOUR

★ WARFIELD THEATRE
2 MARCH 1980, SAN FRANCISCO, CALIFORNIA

ERIC WEITZMANN

My second Clash show at the Warfield Theatre, which holds about 2,300. It was all fixed seating, so you couldn't get quite as wild as you could at the Kezar Pavilion. Nonetheless, this was The Clash in their prime during their *16 Tons* tour (the title borrowed from the Merle Travis song). Lee 'Ride Your Pony' Dorsey opened the show and made a point of telling the crowd 'I still got it for an old man!', which he did.

Before The Clash appeared, 'Mighty' Mikey Dread came out with his beatbox. He was joined by two fellas by the name of Jones and Strummer who started dancing beside him in their Rude Boy suits and Ray-Bans. They were laughing so hard that they could only get through one song with their prank. It was hilarious!

 TOWER THEATER
6 MARCH 1980, PHILADELPHIA, PENNSYLVANIA

SHEVA GOLKOW

I missed The Clash's first show here in 1979 but there was no way I was missing this one! The opening acts were Lee Dorsey, Mikey Dread, and the 'B' Girls; all great. We even got Ian Dury providing guest vocals on 'Janie Jones'. I had a front row orchestra seat, which had been fine for the openers, but when The Clash came on stage, I jumped up and joined the folks in the standing only pit. After all, I loved this band so much; their albums and singles were almost constantly on my turntable. They were glorious live – all that raw energy blasting, all those fantastic songs with the audience singing along. What can I tell you? If you ever saw them, you know.

Not even the discovery after the lights came up that someone had walked off with my coat, leaving me to shiver my way home on the freezing cold subway, could put out the fire.

 MOTOR CITY ROLLER RINK
10 MARCH 1980 DETROIT, MICHIGAN

BRUCE JESSOP

I saw The Clash at a roller rink that was about the size of a high school gymnasium. It was one of only a handful of dates on the *16 Tons* tour of the US following the release of *London Calling*. The gig was a benefit for Detroit's own 'Mr Excitement', Jackie Wilson, who'd been in a coma for at least five years at this point after collapsing onstage. Lee 'Working In A Coal Mine' Dorsey opened, as did Paul Simonon's future wife, Pearl Harbour, as vocalist of The Explosions.

MARC MIKULICH

In 1980, I'd just graduated and I got a job working at Electric Lady Studios on 8th Street in Greenwich Village. I was what you'd call a gopher. It was an interesting time to working there. The Rolling Stones were up in Studio C finishing *Tattoo You*, Lou Reed and Hall & Oates were doing demos in Studio B, and in Studio A, The Clash were recording *Sandinista!*

Going to work was interesting. I remember seeing The Clash coming and going at Studio A. Mick Jones was carrying a copy of the Keith Richards book by Barbara Charone. It was the UK print because the US edition had a different cover.

A year later and they had the residency at Bond's which came about through some kind of booking fiasco. They were as big as they would ever be in the US.

I didn't have a chance of getting a ticket, but it turned out a friend of mine somehow got a job as being a cook, preparing food for them. He got me in one night as his assistant!

16 TONS UK/EUROPEAN TOUR

PIAZZA MAGGIORE
1 JUNE 1980, BOLOGNA, ITALY

TESKIO RAMONES, AGE 20
I was on the left side, far from the stage. We all had to wait for the gig to start because Topper, they said, had 'troubles' on the way to Bologna. But nobody believed that. We now know what kind of 'troubles'. The first part of the gig was played by another drummer. Then Topper arrived, but I didn't notice any difference (and I used to be a drummer). The sound of the band was not the best, but they were THE CLASH!

COLSTON HALL
10 JUNE 1980, BRISTOL

DAVID PENBERTHY
Rock has been my mother and father from the first day I placed a vinyl on a turntable. I was born in 1962 and fed on post-hippy, early Vietnam rock from an early age. I had no problem embracing punk. Boom! It arrived and I swam deep within it. I must admit that I first fell in love with The Clash, then out of love, and finally, after a few years divorced, found part of them I loved intensely.

I bought 'White Riot' the day after hearing it at a friend's house, on an old beaten-up record player with two duff speakers and a well-worn needle. I played it to death. All the way up to 'Tommy Gun', I followed them like a sex-starved teenager at a local disco looking for thrills.

I was working in a youth and community centre in Taunton and, as you do, borrowed the centre's van. I bought tickets for all the best gigs in Bristol and saw a ton of bands for free. The Clash came up in the paper (this is before online booking, kids!) and I was straight in like a bullet. However, I'm ashamed to admit I wasn't completely ready for their reggae path. It was a Tuesday. The hall was heavy with anticipation and strange, exotic smells. The only other time I felt this depth of tension was at a Stiff Little Fingers gig. The political situation in Britain wasn't simple and these groups were throwing everything at it.

THE GIG WENT OFF AT A MILLION MILES AN HOUR...
DAVID PENBERTHY

The gig went off at a million miles an hour. Bejesus, I remember being swept up in a wave of fury and leather. The first three songs finished before I'd got my jacket off! The vibe was magic and angry. 'Clash City Rockers' and 'Brand New Cadillac' flew by. 'Jimmy Jazz' was never one of my favourites, so I remember feeling the energy drop in me at this moment. The dub bass lines that blended with punk guitar fucked my head up a bit. I was craving something simpler and straight forward. I was seventeen and lived on a mixture of Thin Lizzy, Motörhead, The Undertones, etc. I only found an appreciation of ska and reggae later in life.

Later in the gig, Mikey Dread and some other Rastas joined the Clash on stage. I can't remember the songs, but the cultural mix was fascinating and invigorating. However, I needed years to fully get what was happening to my beloved rock 'n' roll.

After a short while, I felt pulled back into the gig again by the second crescendo. I remember being chucked around to 'I'm So Bored With The USA', one of those mental moments never forgotten! Then up we all went to the song 'Complete Control', wooooo… Waving fists, spitting, moshing. So much youth energy being streamlined.

My honest opinion of The Clash is this, they were a major crossover band. They mixed so many styles and did it well. As I developed as a musician, their lack of fear about adding a bit of basic rock 'n' roll to mainstream punk, or a reggae bassline here or there, made sense. I have no shame in saying that 'Guns Of Brixton' and 'Spanish Bombs' are timeless and massive pieces of music for me. 'London Calling' is world class. It's the Real Madrid of Clash songs.

The Clash developed in front of our eyes. They passed barriers. They pissed people off. They are a super memory, disregarding the politics. RIP Joe.

ROB PURSEY, SKEP WAX RECORDS

The Clash at the Colston Hall in Bristol was the first gig I ever attended. Me and Tim (Rippington, my best friend and Five Year Plan bandmate) were still at school. In fact, we had a Physics O-Level exam the next morning, and my main memory of that is that my ears were still ringing with the aftermath of guitar noise while I struggled to remember Boyle's Law in a hushed classroom.

I guess we were the perfect age to be Clash-worshippers. We were already politicised and getting good at picking fights with older, more conservative relatives and neighbours. This attitude was as much thanks to bands like The Au Pairs and The Gang Of Four as to the teachings of any political party. We were obsessed with independent music, we didn't like the mainstream, and the righteousness of The Clash appealed to us. Here were four impressively angry grown-ups, telling it like it was, rousing us to a kind of conviction that the Tories were shit and that the charts weren't worth listening to. Also, Paul Simonon was the coolest bassist I'd ever seen.

The Clash were on to *London Calling* by now – we were too young to have witnessed the early punk gigs – so this was a very efficient rock band we were watching. They could switch genre, from punk to reggae to dirty blues, without missing a step. But there was nothing too slick about it. Joe Strummer broke most of his guitar strings. Other things went wrong. But the sheer whirlwind of the band just swept up all these mistakes into its angry, swirling core and converted them into extra fuel. It certainly made for a much better show – I remember noting that. Played live, the songs didn't sound anything like they did on the records, and they were all the better for it. Joe Strummer's vocals were all over the place. He sounded – and looked like – an angry polar bear shouting from a melting iceberg. It was mesmerising.

My other educational experience of the night was taking a good look at the leather jackets of the older punks all around us. On their backs, in white paint, were the names of bands I didn't know much about: Wire, Six Minute War, Killing Joke. I committed them all to memory so I could investigate them later. It was more productive than revising for a Physics O-Level.

I wonder now if those old punks at the Clash gig were thinking, 'Hmmm, I preferred their earlier stuff.' Some of them probably were. But what was the point of preferring the earlier stuff if there's no way you could have been there for it? I just felt incredibly excited to be there at all. Anyway, as far as I could tell, everyone was into it. I reckon I was lucky to see the band at the point where the punk energy hadn't

> **PAUL SIMONON WAS THE COOLEST BASSIST I'D EVER SEEN...**
> ROB PURSEY,
> SKEP WAX RECORDS

waned, the songwriting was getting more ambitious, but their apparent destiny as the biggest rock band in the world hadn't yet seduced them into self-consciousness and eventual self-destruction.

ANDY MARKHAM, AGE 14

I bought 'Tommy Gun' when it first came out. I remember it playing at a youth club that we used to go to back in the day. One day, one of my sister's friends asked if I wanted to go and see The Clash with her, because she knew I was into that music. She was a couple of years older than me and we convinced my dad to take us to Bristol, to the Colston Hall. She bought the tickets for us. It was when they brought out *London Calling*. The original show had been postponed for some reason.

We got there and there were two support bands, Holly and the Italians, who were pretty good, and Mikey Dread, who was really good. It was a seated venue and the seats were like church pews. As soon as The Clash came on, everybody picked all these chairs and threw them up against the stage at the front. For a youngster like myself, aged 14, it was absolutely amazing. It was a brilliant gig and I'll never forget it for the rest of my life.

I saw them a couple of times after that, at the Cornwall Coliseum in St Austell in '81 and at Poole Arts Centre in '82. Again, they were absolutely brilliant, probably one of the best bands I've seen over the years.

My first ever gig was The Jam at Bath University in December 1979. I remember that because we went in a school minibus from Ilfracombe in North Devon and it snowed all the way there. It was quite a trek back then. One of the lads at school used to organise all the trips to go and see different bands.

I remember seeing Joe with the Mescaleros on the *Later… With Jools Holland* show and thinking 'they're not bad'. Then he died and it's like, 'Well, there's no going back from that.' It would be nice for the others to get together and reform but I don't think they ever will. They could still do a good show, I think.

The Clash and The Jam were probably the top two bands in the country at the time. All the other kids I knew at school loved those bands as well. And if I had to choose between the two? I'd choose The Clash.

MAYFAIR BALLROOM
12 JUNE 1980, NEWCASTLE-UPON-TYNE

PETER SMITH

One of those all too familiar nights where I was torn between two gigs. Rush were playing at Newcastle City Hall and The Clash were playing at Newcastle

Mayfair on the same night. I already had a ticket for Rush when The Clash gig was announced. What a dilemma for me! I hadn't missed a Newcastle gig by either band, but what could I do?

I decided to buy a ticket for The Clash and try and time things so I could see both bands. On the rare occasions I had tried to do this in the past, it had not worked out very well, and I usually ended up having not enjoyed either gig. On the night of the gig(s) I went along to the City Hall with my mates to see Rush as originally planned. This was the *Permanent Waves* tour, and my mates were big Rush fans who couldn't believe that I would even contemplate leaving the gig early to see The Clash, but that's exactly what I did.

The norm at The Mayfair was for the band to take the stage around 10pm, so I watched around one hour of Rush then, once 10pm neared, drove down the road to the Mayfair to see The Clash. I had missed support act Joe Ely but arrived in the venue just as The Clash had started the first song of the night.

I always find it strange entering a gig late. It's like coming into a party uninvited when everyone is already drunk. Picture this. I enter a packed ballroom, The Clash are playing 'Safe European Home' and the place is going wild. I stood on the balcony and wandered around the place, taking it all in. The Clash played much longer that night than the previous times I'd seen them. They had a much larger repertoire of songs to draw from by 1980.

They were great as usual, but I didn't see as much passion and energy as at the Newcastle Poly gig a couple of years before. I thought the gig dragged at times, but picked up towards the end, and the place went crazy when they finished with 'White Riot'.

So, my aim of taking in two gigs on the same night sort of worked, although I didn't see that much of Rush, and couldn't really get into their set as my mind was more focussed on getting my timings right to catch The Clash. I'm so glad I did!

JIM BURNS, AGE 14

My first recollection of punk is listening to the Sex Pistols on *Top Of The Pops* singing 'Pretty Vacant'. I was twelve years old and it just changed everything. Kids were looking for something and all we had in Newcastle was punk and football. We were just young kids growing up, playing football every day and talking about football and music. When punk came along, we just latched onto it.

A bloke who lived near me used to like to paint and he used to always drink Snakebite. He would say, 'James, go to the shop for us and I'll give you a record.' So I used to nip the shop for him, and he used to give us a record for going into the shop. That's how I used to get my singles.

I had a tape of the *Bollocks* album off my pal, Robert Balmer. He gave us that towards the end of '77. I used to listen to it on a cassette in my bedroom. The first album I bought with my own money was the Buzzcocks' *Love Bites*. I earnt money working with my dad on the weekends or in the holidays. He was a plasterer, and I'd give him a hand knocking the plaster up.

I used to go to gigs with Robert. He's the one that recorded the *Bollocks* album for us and he was the one that got us into it. He had that and he had The Jam's *The Modern World* album. We used to just go into his house and play it hour after hour. His mother must have been up the walls with it.

Before I even started going to concerts, I remember hearing on the radio about a riot in Newcastle when The Clash played the university. They wouldn't let the normal kids, just the students, and they tried to break down the doors.

I've never experienced energy like when I saw The Clash. They hadn't played in Newcastle for two years. I remember getting a ticket off a girl at school called Tracy Gibson for a fiver because it had sold out.

It was an over-18 venue and it was two days before my 15th birthday, but my sister, Christine, worked in the box office so she got me in. It started off with 'Clash City Rockers' and within a minute there were three thousand people just heaving. They were smacking each other all over. It was like a fight at a football match, when a big gap open ups. It was just hell from the beginning to the end. I was right at the front and now, when I look at some of the footage, I think you could literally get crushed to death. And I remember – and I'm not proud of this – when they first came on and started 'Clash City Rockers', I spat on Mick Jones' face, above his left eye.

When I met him after the gig, I didn't tell him I'd done that or he probably wouldn't have signed some of my stuff. But I met them backstage and they signed my t-shirt, poster and programme.

My all-time favourite gig would have to be The Clash. I didn't think that could be so much going on in one place. It was chaos. There was trouble, the gig had to be stopped several times. It was just life-changing. It's something I think about all the time, that gig. It was just the energy.

HAMMERSMITH PALAIS
16 & 17 JUNE 1980, LONDON

DAVID WALLACE

I saw The Clash, probably once, but may have seen a second time in the same week at Hammersmith Palais where they played several consecutive nights. I was earning good money by this time working in Leadenhall Market and living in Islington. I was going out to see bands nearly every night.

There were many aspiring stars and liggers in attendance at such a high-profile gig. I was hanging around with some Scottish lads who were a bit older than me and who were in a band called The Trendies. It may have been then that some very delinquent young punks tried to nick my leather jacket on the way to the concert.

My memory may be a bit hazy as I'd started to drink a lot by then, but my clearest memory is still to this day of Mick Jones standing atop a very rickety swaying stack of speakers while they did an elongated version of 'Armagideon Time'. I was near to stage for this one as were the proper punk fans, rather than the 'Tufty Club' lot (ie. the skinheads) who were wrecking Sham 69 and Madness gigs.

The Clash by then had gone more Americana in image and album content, much to my disappointment, but the live shows were still exciting and raucous. They saved their best for Hammersmith Palais.

STEVE EVERETT, AGE 17

I first saw The Clash at Hammersmith Palais, probably the most iconic venue possible to see them in. I was 17 and trying (as usual) to impress a potential girlfriend. I knew Karen was into them and so I suggested trying to go see them. As I lived in Holborn in central London, I walked to Premier Box Office in Charing Cross Road. They sold gig tickets in the shop – I remember the elasticated bundles – and I was chuffed to buy two. We were in.

On the night, as Karen was quite short, we decided to go up to the balcony where we got a great view. First up were Holly and The Italians who had a hit called 'Tell That Girl To Shut Up'. They were cool but it was The Clash we wanted. They came on and just tore the place apart. I'd never witnessed power and energy like it, and haven't since by any other band!

I secretly wished to be in the mosh downstairs but enjoyed being squeezed tight to Karen. They played 'Clash City Rockers', 'White Riot', 'Tommy Gun' and the most iconic moment of the night, '(White Man) In Hammersmith Palais'. I can still feel the buzz!

ALL THE YOUNG PUNKS

Despite a cheeky snog on the way home it didn't work out with Karen. The next gig we went to was Thin Lizzy at Hammersmith Odeon, but her boyfriend accompanied us on the Tube there and back! She did tell me a couple of years later that she regretted it, but by then it was too late.

GRAHAM PATTLE, AGE 17

I'd have been around 17 years old when I saw The Clash at the Palais. I always felt that they were so much better live than on vinyl. Their sound was so much rawer and packed a real punch, which was somewhat lost in the studio recordings. The Palais had the stage along the longer side of the rectangular dancefloor, so it was wider than it was deep. People were jostling to get into prime close and central position but every ten minutes, there'd be a surge from the back, and you'd suddenly find yourself spat out the side by the speakers and having to start again to get a decent spot!

PETER STRIKE, AGE 19

Hammersmith Palais was an event; I was 19 and couldn't really hold my drink back then. I got drunk and fell asleep upstairs feeling sick and ill. I woke up to The Clash's intro music just as the black and yellow barriers lifted and the band came storming onto the stage. I was awake and feeling great again, the hairs standing up on the back of my neck. It's my all-time favourite Clash gig in such an iconic venue and I still have the ticket to this day...

'BANKROBBER'/'ROCKERS GALORE' RELEASED
8 AUGUST 1980

IAN MOSS

This was lightweight, fun stuff, even with the inclusion of a myth-building rebel lyric that Joe Strummer quite simply could never resist. A more accurate 'Daddy was a Foreign Office secretary' didn't scan as well!

The Clash, from the start, were poseurs at heart. Even if their hearts were in the right place, their political affiliations and manifestos made them a hugely contradictory outfit. I learned to take their propaganda with a pinch of salt and simply enjoy the music, because if you could do that, the music was very good and

'Daddy was a Bankrobber' scanned better than 'Daddy was a foreign office secretary'...

often capable of stirring emotions.

'Bankrobber' isn't one of their famed rabble rousers but a gentle lilting cod-reggae piece. With a debt to Bob Dylan's 'Knocking On Heaven's Door' in its DNA, it somehow comes together as a piece of great sing-along pop in the manner of Mungo Jerry's 'In The Summertime' from one era or Culture Club's 'Karma Chameleon' from another.

'THE CALL UP'/'STOP THE WORLD' RELEASED
28 NOVEMBER 1980

ROBERT CASSON
The single, which clocks in at over five minutes and would languish midway through the fourth side of *Sandinista!* upon release a couple of weeks later, had the odds stacked against it being a hit despite following the successful 'Bankrobber' which had stalled just outside the Top 10 during August.

'The Call Up' managed to reach No 40 in the UK charts before beginning a downward trajectory over the following five weeks.

The cover of the track by Chris Whitley, on his 2004 album *War Crime Blues*, is eerie and chilling and captures something that The Clash couldn't as he delivers a pointed commentary on conscription and the human pain it leaves in its wake, evoking a mournful and regret-laden pathos.

SANDINISTA! RELEASED
12 DECEMBER 1980

MARTIN BLENCO
Critical opinions oscillate wildly between whether *Sandinista!* is the greatest Clash album (even the greatest triple album ever released by anybody, not that it's a crowded field) or a bag of shite from which a decent single album could have been extracted if someone had exercised a bit of quality control. I remember buying it on release and after a couple of listens being quite adept at lifting the arm on my stereo and dropping the needle onto the tracks that merited repeated listens. Years later, it's the lyrics of 'Washington Bullets' that still ring most true, especially with the ongoing Israel-Palestine conflict. 'Career Opportunities' re-imagined by Mickey Gallagher's sons I could happily never hear again.

DAN ANKLIN
The one Clash album most people don't talk about is *Sandinista!* although it didn't need to be a triple. It should have been a single album. It wouldn't have been as good as *London Calling*. But 13 or 14 songs? That would have been fantastic.

 'HITSVILLE UK'/'RADIO ONE' RELEASED
16 JANUARY 1981

ROBERT CASSON

An oddity in The Clash's catalogue, being a duet between Jones and his then girlfriend Ellen Foley, which underlines the experimentation on *Sandinista!*

The track pays tribute to the post punk Indie scene in UK during the late 1970s and early 1980s, referencing: Lightning Records disco, dub and reggae specialists, the initial home of Althia & Donna; Small Wonder, who had released The Cure's first single, 'Killing An Arab'; and Fast Product, whose first release, ironically, had been The Mekon's 'Never Been In A Riot', alongside the legendary Rough Trade and Factory Records highlighting that whilst the band were soaking up sounds in New York, they still had an eye on what was happening at home!

MARTIN BLENCO

You couldn't get further from the sound of The Clash than this record, and the chart-buying public didn't much care for it as it only reached No 56. But you wonder if it might have done better if it had been credited to Ellen Foley and The Clash's involvement just been hinted at.

 *BLACK MARKET CLASH* RELEASED
1 MARCH 1981

ROBERT CASSON

Black Market Clash was initially a budget compilation for the American market and a rarities collection in the fact that it included the exclusive track, 'Time Is Tight', a cover of Booker T & the MG's Top 10 from 1969 (on both sides of the Atlantic).

Side 1 revisited The Clash's punk past with songs like 'Capitol Radio One', 'The Prisoner' and 'City Of The Dead' whilst Side 2 pointed to the future, with three extended reggae jams showing where the band was then heading.

Later expanded as *Super Black Market Clash*, initially just on CD, to include other rarities such as the 1977 *NME* freebie version of 'Capital Radio' plus later B-sides, thios was essential if you couldn't afford to purchase the *Clash On Broadway* boxset or the later *Sound System* mega box.

A PEOPLE'S HISTORY OF THE CLASH

⭐ 'THE MAGNIFICENT SEVEN' (EDIT)/'THE MAGNIFICENT DANCE' RELEASED
10 APRIL 1981

RICHARD HOUGHTON

'Vaccum cleaner sucks up budgie' has to be one of the most memorable lines in any pop song. I'm surprised Joe didn't get shit from the animal rights movement for seemingly trivialising the suffering of that poor creature.

MISSION IMPOSSIBLE TOUR

⭐ JAAP EDENHAL
10 MAY 1981, AMSTERDAM, NETHERLANDS

LUUK VERSLUIJS

The third time I saw The Clash was the first time I went with other people, my girlfriend and a friend from the army who, like me, had just finished 14 months of compulsory military service. This was one of the first concerts I went to following my studies and military service.

Luuk Versluijs' ticket from seeing The Clash a third time

The Clash had graduated from the Paradiso in Amsterdam to the much bigger Jaap Edenhal, an arena built for ice hockey games with a capacity of 4,000. In the seventies and eighties, the building had also been used as a concert venue for big acts as The Doobie Brothers, Little Feat, Bad Company, Uriah Heep, Neil Young, Bob Marley and The Wailers, Rod Stewart, Fleetwood Mac, ABBA, Status Quo, AC/DC, Judas Priest, Thin Lizzy, Dire Straits, John Denver, Peter Gabriel, Eric Clapton and Lou Reed. The Clash was a big act now and the show was almost sold out. The Belle Stars were the support act.

From the opener, 'London Calling', until the last song, 'London's Burning' (aptly retitled 'Amsterdam's Burning'), it was a great show, probably the best Clash show I attended. The set list drew heavily on the albums *London Calling* and *Sandinista!* It was a long show, almost two hours. Despite the Jaap Edenhal being notorious for bad acoustics and a cold atmosphere, The Clash succeeded in turning the ice hockey arena into a hot club!

⭐ IDROTTSHUSET
14 MAY 1981, KÖPENHAMN, DENMARK

PER SJÖBERG

The day I went to see The Clash is the day that changed my life forever. It's the best show I have ever seen. It was incredible, it was brutal, and it was at an extremely loud throughout the whole show.

I took the cover of *Black Market Clash* with me, hoping to get it signed. My friends were laughing at me, saying, 'There's no chance you'll get it signed.' After the show I was waiting closely by the stage. A security man came down and asked, 'Who is a journalist? Put your hands in the air!' About 15 people put their hands in the air. Then he asked, 'Who is a fan of The Clash? Put *your* hands in the air.' I was one of them and he said, 'Fans of The Clash? Follow me!'

There was a long staircase up to the dressing room. In the middle was a long board with food and drinks for the fans, and the band was sitting there, all sweating with towels around them and with cigarettes and beer in their hands. I was just staring at them.

I was attending a clothing design course at college in Malmo at the time and I was wearing a shirt with no arms and a leather cartridge belt round it. It had a very special type of font on the

Per Sjöberg had Paul Simonon admiring his outfit when he met the band post gig

Photo Per Sjöberg

Joe in action

side, with 'THE CLASH' embroidered on it. It had taken me ten seconds to make it. Paul Simonon looked at the shirt, asked where I purchased it and said, 'Do you want to swap with me?' Stupidly, I said no, which I regret so much because if I had, that shirt I'd made would now show up on some pictures of Simonon somewhere. I explained that I'd designed it, and he complimented me on this. I got my copy of *Black Market Clash* signed, and they were so nice to me. It was the greatest moment of my life.

Paul Simonon astride his motorbike

That summer, I went to London for a holiday and spent a lot of money on Clash bootlegs and merchandise. One day I was standing at a red light when a motorbike pulled up close to me. I was thinking, 'I remember this fellow', so I lifted my camera and whistled at him. It was hard to see who it was because he had his crash helmet on but I snapped a picture of him. I only took the one, because it was real film I was using and I didn't have a lot of money. The motorbike parked 100 metres away right outside Harrods so I ran up to it. The rider had taken his helmet off and it was Paul Simonon! He didn't have long to talk as he said he was on his way to buy a vacuum cleaner and he had a mess to clear up, either at home or in the studio (I can't remember which!).

 VIGORELLI VELODROME
21 MAY 1981, MILAN, ITALY

GIOVANNI TAVERNA

I was born in 1966 and raised in Italy, in Milan. I started to listen to music around 1979, 1980. My first introduction to punk rock was a Ramones concert, them being supported by UK Subs in Milan at the end of February 1980. I was in the third year of middle school, so not quite 14. I very impressed by music, especially very loud bands. I really dug punk, but the Sex Pistols had already gone by then. But I found The Clash.

My first introduction to them was *Black Market Clash*, the ten-inch album released between *London Calling* and *Sandinista!* I'd been too young when *London Calling* came out, but I was already into reggae through Bob Marley. I liked The Clash's approach to reinterpret reggae music and reggae songs whilst writing their own tracks like 'Bankrobber'. I was also impressed by their approach to dub.

The Clash were also very political. Italy was in the middle of some strong political conflicts and many people, especially kids my age, were attracted by their image, their almost guerrilla warfare look and their support for international liberation movements, like the Sandinistas in Nicaragua, and their approach to social issues.

I was too young to see their first show in Italy, in Bologna in June 1980, when they played a free concert for the Italian Communist Party, but the following May they finally came to Milan on the first Italian date of their *Mission Impossible* tour. The concert was organised at the Vigorelli Velodrome. Built in the twenties or thirties, it used to be used for bicycle racing. The concert was in doubt until the last minute, because the authorities in Milan didn't want to give the go ahead to use the structure due to safety reasons.

Sandinista! had come out five months earlier and was a very popular album. The whole city was completely covered with posters of the concert. Very simple posters, just saying, 'The Clash - Mission Impossible'. Even the name of the tour was evocative.

I went to the concert with my older brother. The velodrome filled with people very quickly. The audience was 30,000 people, a very big audience for The Clash. Many people believed entering concerts without paying for a ticket in Italy and so there were people who entered but had to fight with the police to get in. Outside the stadium, the police reacted with tear gas but inside we didn't notice this, and only heard about it later.

Before the concert The Clash played a disco music tape, which was a big surprise for the crowd. I remember Diana Ross's 'Upside Down' and other disco/funky rap songs. After the sunset, the lights went off. The stage was very simple, very naked. From the speaker came 'For A Few Dollars More' by Ennio Morricone. Hearing that introduction music, which probably lasted three minutes, created a growing atmosphere in the completely dark stadium while the band was entering the stage and getting into position.

I think even the band were

> **THE BAND WERE SURPRISED AT THE SIZE OF THE CROWD...**
>
> GIOVANNI TAVERNA

surprised by the crowd being such a big one. They seemed quite tense up to the point when the Morricone song finished. And then they immediately crashed into 'London Calling'. If you listen to the recording of that concert, until the line 'the Ice Age is coming', the guitar sounds completely different live to how it is on the record.

The second track was 'Safe European Home'. They did many songs from *Black Market Clash*, *Sandinista!* and *London Calling* before they closed with 'White Riot' in the encores. The Clash were at the pinnacle of their career. They probably used those three Italian concerts in 1981 – Milan, San Remo and Florence – to warm up for the Bond's gigs in New York.

STADIO COMUNALE
23 MAY 1981, FLORENCE, ITALY

MASSIMO PRUDENTE

The second time I saw The Clash was during the *Mission Impossible* tour of '81 at the Stadio Comunale in Florence. I'm listening to the recording of the show whilst writing this and even now it gives me goosebumps. They took to the stage to Ennio Morricone's 'Il Buono, Il Brutto e Il Cattivo' and went straight into 'London Calling' which was the apotheosis.

The third and final time I saw The Clash was on September 7, 1984 at the Festa dell'Unità, ex Velodromo, Rome, Italy. Some years later I had the privilege of seeing Joe Strummer and the Latino Rockabilly War at The Tabernacle in West London on June 17, 1988 and on the 19th at the Milton Keynes Bowl in support of Amnesty International, documented by Don Letts, whose film also showed Mick Jones on stage in the background. In the late eighties I was working for AZ Music in Rome. We booked Joe Strummer's final Italian tour and what came to be my final Joe Strummer gig. It was October 27, 1989 at the Teatro Tenda Pianeta in Rome. I remember, amongst other things, the day after when I had to accompany Joe to the local mechanic as they were having mechanical trouble with their van that we managed to resolve.

The Clash, the only band that matters!

BONDS INTERNATIONAL CASINO
28 MAY-13 JUNE 1981, NEW YORK, NEW YORK

DAN ANKLIN

Bonds was right in the middle of Times Square. It was an old department store at one point, and they turned it into a club for a short time around the time when

The Clash played. I went the night when Grandmaster Flash was opening for them.

My friend and I were living in Syracuse and took the train down to meet another friend of mine who was living in New York and who got the tickets. We were that excited we'd been up for 24 hours, so by the time we got in there, it was just explosive. They hit

The Clash played Bond's & brought NYC to a standstill

the stage, and it felt like we'd just plugged ourselves into the electricity. They were so good. The sound wasn't great, but I felt their live sounds was never great. That wasn't the thing. The thing was the show, the experience.

People just went nuts! I know people who saw all the shows, I had no idea how they pulled that off. I was lucky to see one of them. It might have been $15 or $20 a ticket. Not a lot nowadays. If you were able to see The Clash now in a club, it would probably cost you $500.

I was supposed to see The Clash again in 1980 at something called The Heatwave Festival outside of Ontario. They pulled out at the last minute, leaving Elvis Costello and the Attractions to headline. If The Clash had been there that would have been the icing on the cake for me, but it was a great show anyhow.

Then there was the show at Rich Stadium, Buffalo opening for The Who. That was *Combat Rock* era. That wasn't one of my favourite records, they were going downhill at that point in my opinion. My all-time favourite record, not just The Clash, is *London Calling*, and my second would be *Give 'Em Enough Rope*.

DAN BRUNING

I'll never forget waiting outside Bond's Casino for tickets. There were thousands waiting outside down the blocks to score Clash tickets. The cops on horses tried to control a bunch of punks and it didn't go so well. I remember seeing people being forcefully pulled back by the horses. The scene was electric. Everywhere you looked around Times Square there were Clash posters, and as ironic as it was, The Clash

A PEOPLE'S HISTORY OF THE CLASH

were on the rooftops recording the crowd.

I saw the opening night with Grandmaster Flash and the Furious Five, who got booed pretty much since us punks hated disco. But Joe liked the disco sound!

I went on night number three as well. But the New York fire marshal shut it down. So what did Joe do? He announced that all ticket holders would still get a chance to see the band and they added ten shows to make it a total of 17 and with very inexpensive ticket prices, at $10-$12. Joe had a heart of gold. I went twice more, so four shows in total. They were very small crowds in a very intimate setting. Those shows were legendary.

SHEVA GOLKOW

I was 23 and living in Philadelphia. I'd only seen the band once, the year before, and was crazy about them – and Philly was just a two-hour train ride away from NYC. I bought tickets for a couple of shows and made plans. On May 30 my buddy Frank and I had tickets for the matinee, which seemed funny – rock and roll in the afternoon? – but fine with us. We rushed to Bond's from the train, but when we got there, we couldn't get near the place; the street was swarming with would-be concert goers, lots of them – and lots of cops. *Uh-oh*. We asked people what was going on and learned the show had been cancelled. Cancelled? Turned out the shows had been oversold, to the tune of twice the legal capacity, so the fire department stepped in.

We stayed there a little while, partly stunned by the bad news and partly curious to see what would happen next. At some point we got the idea to head over to the Gramercy Park Hotel, where we knew the band was staying. Sure enough, when we got there, Joe was in the lobby talking to a handful of unhappy fans. He was apologetic and assured us that the band was going to try to make it up to us.

Sheva Golkow's ticket signed by Joe Strummer

Some of the kids were angry and started yelling at him; we could see his anger and frustration with the situation, but he stayed calm. As unhappy as we were, it was still exciting to be there with Joe and his lovely girlfriend Gabby. Eventually we headed for home, clutching our unused tickets and wondering what would happen – would the band really make it up to us?

They did indeed, adding several more shows, which more than doubled the run, and a few evenings later I was there for the first of what would be three shows for me. Bonds was a big club, and it was both exciting and a relief to finally see The Clash. The opening acts that night were The Senders and the Treacherous Three. I confess I don't have many memories from that night – I had such a great time and being thrilled to see this band I loved right in front of me. It was a Wednesday night, which meant I must have gotten back to Philly in the wee hours on the train. Whatever I did the next day, I'm sure I was smiling.

Three days later, and I was back for show #2. This time the opening acts included Funkapolitan and The Brattles, a wonderful, perfectly named band of twelve-year-olds. I managed to get up close every night, banging on the rail in time to the music. I also leant on it as the show wore on – these long nights were endurance tests – and even, I blush to admit, oh so briefly dozing off during 'Charlie Don't Surf' (no reflection on the song, just my weariness). But it only lasted a few seconds; the rest of the time, you can be sure I was wide awake – dancing, singing, cheering. It was incredible watching this powerful band, especially Joe Strummer, who put his heart, soul and guts into every performance. No wonder I was so nuts about him.

When the show ended, I ducked into the ladies' room, still dazed, where I saw two of the most breathtakingly beautiful young women I'd ever encountered. Tall, slim, blonde, wearing fabulous rocker/cowgirl outfits – they were dazzling. I recognised one as Gabby, Joe's girlfriend, who I'd seen the week before at their hotel; I wasn't sure who the other one was but suspected she, too, was some rocker's girl. Sure enough, while I washed my hands, eavesdropping as subtly as I could, I learned she was Joe Ely's girlfriend. I'd only recently discovered Ely and thought he was marvellous. At this point, they both became aware of me, looked over, and smiled. I fought back my shyness and decided to start talking. I told Gabby how much I loved the band and loved 'her' Joe, and told the other woman how great I thought '*her*' Joe was. They were both very sweet and gracious; well, I wasn't exactly a threat to them, so why not. Gabby was charming, and after listening to me babble a bit more about how crazy I was about Joe and the band, she put her arm around me and said, 'Well then, you simply must come with me and tell him!'

A PEOPLE'S HISTORY OF THE CLASH

Before I knew what was happening, I was swept backstage. And there he was – Joe Strummer. He was drinking a beer, just hanging. He looked gorgeous, practically glowing. Gabby took my hand and presented me to Joe, telling him, 'This is Sheva, and she loves you!' I could feel my face turning bright red. I expected Joe to smile, put out his hand, say something; instead, he looked at me, threw his arms around me and hugged me tight for what felt like several long lovely minutes. Had I been a less sturdy lass I think I might have fainted. When he let go, he gave me a grin and asked me how I liked the show. We talked for a few minutes, then he signed my ticket stub. I thanked him, thanked Gabby, and stumbled out of the club. I don't recall how I got home that night, but I would not rule out the possibility of having floated all the way back to Philly.

June 9th was my third and last Clash show at Bond's. The opening act on this night was The Fall. I'd seen them before and didn't care for them at all (in an example of 'how life works', I've spent the last 33 years with someone who absolutely loves them). Oh, these shows were so damned good. I tended to hang back after the shows were over. I'd speak to Baker, the band's adorable young roadie, and their road manager Johnny Green, both of whom were always friendly and willing to chat with fans. On this night I just sat for a moment after those chats. These shows were an emotional experience for me – I loved the band so much, and of course had that crush on Joe; the end of the night was as likely to find me crying as cheering, and between all that, the late hour, and knowing it was the last show I'd see; this was a crying night. I heard a soft voice ask, 'Are you OK?' and looked up to see a somewhat older woman standing there wearing a fabulous thrift store dress, a look of concern on her face. I told her 'Yes, yes, I'm OK – just filled with emotion.' She understood immediately, and we commiserated for a bit. She didn't make fun of me for getting weepy; she got it.

As we spoke, I realised I'd seen her before. She was the woman who had

The Clash's Bond's dates were massively oversold

once materialised next to me at a Pretenders show, grabbing my hand and dancing with me when they did the Small Faces classic 'Whatcha Gonna Do About It'. She was the one I would spot in the front of the line for so many shows at Stars, in the days when the first 15 or so got in free. I didn't know her name or where she was from, only that she was clearly a rock and roll kindred spirit who had this way of simply appearing now and then. We didn't exchange names that night either; she stayed with me a few minutes more, then said good night. A little over a year later I was in an almost empty hotel bar outside of Philadelphia. It was well past midnight, I was with my gaggle of Squeeze girls, and we'd just said good night to the band, having hung out after their show. Two women joined us, the kind yet mysterious woman last seen at The Clash, and her adorable friend, both decked out in yet more thrift store splendour. The conversation drifted from Squeeze to Elvis Costello, with yours truly saying, 'Oh, I *love* him! The two strangers looked at each other and smiled, 'You love Elvis, do you? You love seeing him?' Murmured agreement and nodding heads all around. 'Would you like to meet him?' An enthusiastic, unanimous 'Yes!'

At this point the two smiled broadly, assured us this was something that could be arranged quite easily, and proceeded to introduce themselves. Finally – the mysterious stranger, now casually offering me my heart's desire, would have a name. And what a name – Cynthia Sagittarius. Cynthia Sagi… OHMYGOD! I fell, realising that the woman before me was none other than the Cynthia Sagittarius immortalised in Robert Greenfield's book *STP*, about the Rolling Stones' 1972 American tour. I loved that book! And now here before me – Cynthia, who hitch-hiked across the country and in and out of Canada, following the band. Cynthia, who saw every single show on that tour. Who refused to be interviewed by Dick Cavett, because she didn't want any fame, she just wanted to see the shows. That Cynthia! It was surreal; until that moment I hadn't thought of her as being a real person, let alone one with whom I'd previously danced, and on whose shoulder I'd shed a quick tear.

We went on to become friends and travelling partners. And yes, thanks to her, I got to see and hang out with Elvis many times over the next few years; we went to see The Clash together, too. Cynthia lived on the outskirts of life, with few of the conventional trappings – no social security number, no job, no bank account. She was devoted to music and to seeing the musicians she loved as often as possible, in as many places as possible. Smart, funny, argumentative, loving, generous. We drifted apart after several years and a few disagreements, but she always stayed in the back of my mind. I learned a few years ago that she passed away. It's hard to believe that I'll never see that shining freckled face or big sunny smile, hear that soft voice which could get so loud when she laughed, or watch her move gracefully in one of her fantastic old dresses.

RIP dear Cynthia. Thinking of you and all the wonderful moments we shared. Stay free.

GEOFF HOOVER

I saw The Clash a few times, twice at Bonds, once at the Pier, and once at Shea Stadium. I stood for several hours on that line for Bonds that wrapped around 45th Street with my friend John Engle and that was relatively inconsequential. I believe we bought a bunch of tickets for night four, but of course the oversell happened, and our night got pushed back.

When our show did happen it was good, although during 'Washington Bullets', someone came out to rap about stuff and some assholes in the crowd weren't having it and started throwing shit at Mick. To his credit he came up and stood right next to the guy rapping and his eyes meant business. He protected him just by staring at the crowd intensely. It was damn cool.

I returned to Bonds a few nights later. My friend Dorothy came up from Philly and said we should go. We didn't have tickets, but she had met Ray Jordan from the band's security team earlier in the run and he let us in the side entrance for free. No blowjobs or lines of coke to get in! If you were a true believer, they welcomed you with open arms and no expectation of reciprocity. The band was on fire for that show. No crap from the audience.

The *Combat Rock* show at the Pier was a bit weird. Joe was on Terry's ass a bit. I think he was having a time with pace. Joe kept pumping his arms at Terry. It was a sluggish show. Alan Ginsberg came out and recited his bit from 'Ghetto Defendant' which didn't seem as cool then as it does in retrospect. Kurtis Blow opened and did 'The Breaks', which was awesome.

It was a crap rainy night at Shea Stadium, but they were unstoppable. The Clash destroyed The Who. I was 500 feet away, no video screens. It was only as loud as a ghetto blaster from where I was but holy fuck it was intense! The live album doesn't capture how amazing they were that night. They were the best band in the world, I can tell you that. Whatever problems they were having with Terry at the Pier were gone and his drumming like it was 1977 all over again…

ANTHONY RAO

When I was 15 my friend used to play The Clash and *London Calling* constantly. I thought they were good, but when I saw them at Bond's everything changed. As Joe would say, it was year zero. The set was blazing with old songs and the newer ones as well. The crowd rushed the stage and towards the end of the show I was on stage with The Clash. It was a religious experience! I never walked out of a show soaked and wet before.

RACHEL FELDER, AGE 13

I bought *London Calling* the week it came out, although I wasn't into them enough when they did the Palladium shows, the ones where Pennie Smith shot that famous picture of Paul for the cover. By the time the New York Bond's shows came around I was obsessed with The Clash and so excited they were coming to town. The concept of Bond's was so unusual that it was a true event. Bond's had been a big, bustling Times Square department store. It was before my time but my parents remember shopping in there. A very big sign still hung outside.

In 1981 I was living in Manhattan. New York was a very rough city with a lot of tension. There was a general feeling of edginess, especially at night. To go to a show in Times Square, with me being just 13-years-old, was an odd thing to do. CBGBs was in a posh neighbourhood but Times Square had a lot of pornography movie theatres and there was a tension at night that meant you wouldn't feel great about strolling through it at night. It was a neighbourhood to be avoided.

The Clash were doing such a long run of nights it was a big deal, so I bunked off school one day to buy my tickets and wait in the queue. That was an incredibly wonderful experience because I was surrounded by kindred spirits. I bought tickets for three nights. The night before my first night, I was at my gran's apartment and we turned on the local news to learn there were riots outside the venue. I went into a bit of a quandary of whether I was going but my gran encouraged me. My uncle, her son, was a songwriter, so she understood the whole milieu.

I went to three shows, but I honestly don't remember whether any of those were rescheduled shows. One had a band called Blue Angel opening, Cyndi Lauper's original band. The opening acts were super diverse on purpose. They echoed The Clash's eclectic tastes. We hated Blue Angel. We couldn't believe how bad they were. I can remember The Clash all three times, but not the other opening acts. With The Clash I remember feeling the ground move, all of us dancing in unison, and then there was the power of that band. The beauty of the three voices together - Mick and Joe, with Paul coming in here and there. They were brilliant.

I never saw The Clash again after that, because at the risk of sounding elitist, they got successful and I became a little less interested. To be honest, I was into my alternative bands. I knew what a big deal it had been to see those shows at Bond's. For decades, I knew that, and I still know that. They stuck with me very deeply

I BOASTED THAT I SAW SEVERAL BOND'S SHOWS...
RACHEL FELDER

because when I went to university here in New York, I had to write a thesis to graduate, and my thesis was about The Clash's first album. That thesis became the guts of my first book. My deep love, respect, admiration, and fandom of The Clash only intensified after those shows. They were memorable and incredible. I would boast years later, decades later, that I had seen some of the Bond's shows. That was a badge of honour for me.

Many years after those shows, like almost 20 years afterwards, I started dating the man I ended up marrying, Howie Weinberg, who I'm now divorced from. He is a mastering engineer, and unbeknownst to me, he mastered *Sandinista!* and *Cut The Crap*. On our second date I boasted, as I had become accustomed to doing, that I had seen several Bond's shows. Very nonchalantly Howie said, 'Oh, yes, I remember those shows, too. I was mastering *Sandinista!* so Mick would come to the studio in the daytime and we'd work on the record. Then I'd walk to soundcheck with him, and I'd watch some of soundcheck and then the gig.' I never boasted about seeing those shows in the same way again!

DAVE DENFIELD, AGE 20

I saw The Clash three times in NYC: one of the Bond's shows, at the Pier in 1982 and at one of the Shea Stadium shows with The Who. I grew up in Queens and was dating a girl who was a huge Ramones fan so it was a short trip to other punk bands. At the time I was interested in almost any rock bands and we would check out shows practically every weekend. The Bonds shows were all over the news in the city for like a month. I remember mostly being surprised by how well the *Sandinista!* songs played live. Bad Brains opened, and were booed when they played a reggae song.

The 1982 shows seemed a little off. I don't know if it was Terry Chimes or something, but it seemed to lack a bit of the magic from the earlier show.

PETER AARON

My family moved to Ohio when I was 16 but before that I grew up in a town in New Jersey that was about half an hour from New York City. I got into punk around 1977/78. It was my 'big bang'. I had a little bit of an awareness, but seeing Elvis Costello on *Saturday Night Live* was what really opened the door for me.

The Clash's first album came out over here in 1979. I was part of a gang with two or three other guys in high school who had gotten into punk. The Clash were our band. That first album was hard to find. The commercial FM rock stations that we knew didn't really start playing The Clash until *London Calling*, so there was a little bit of, of 'should I buy this record I haven't heard?' Obviously, there were college radio stations that were playing The Clash and other punk stuff, but we didn't know about those at that point. Seeing the debut in the rack, however, you could tell these guys were serious and were real. I bought it! In the US it also came with a bonus, the 'Gates Of The West' single.

My friends and I were too young and suburban to know how to get around and get out to gigs. Gigs were mainly happening in in the city, where being underage was less of an issue. We didn't drive, we'd have to take the bus, and we didn't know where we were going, we didn't know anything! We missed out on the Palladium show, but I remember the ads for it on the radio. We then started going to see shows at the Capitol Theatre in Passaic, New Jersey. The Clash played there in 1980 but for some reason – maybe we couldn't get a ride – it just didn't work out.

We finally got to see them at Bond's. That was a religious experience. We were originally supposed to be at the 30 May matinee. We took the bus in, having got all 'punked up' for the occasion. We waited in line outside, waiting and waiting and then there was a real big scene. People were selling stuff. People from the IRA were selling buttons and passing out literature and stuff. The Clash had an incendiary political reputation, and I guess that was why they thought they could connect with people. It was a sunny afternoon and then suddenly all these cops started showing up on horseback with helmets. There was a truck that had water cannon on the top of it. We were like, 'What the hell is going on?' It had been just a nice, pleasant thing, talking to other punks and other New Jersey suburban types like us…

Eventually someone came out of the side of the club and started handing out these flyers, which I still have, with 'The

For Peter Aaron & his friends, The Clash were 'their' band

Clash Will Play' on them with rescheduled dates. 30 May was changed to 6 June. We were like, 'Wow, it's cool. It's OK, well, so we gotta come back next week.' That turned into a lot of people yelling and shouting in the middle of Times Square. Traffic stopped for ten minutes. In Times Square that was a big thing. We felt like we were having a riot. This was like the back of *The Clash* album cover! It ended up making the TV news.

We went back the following week. The opening were The Brattles. They were all young kids, maybe nine or ten years old. I think Chris Stein was producing them. I don't know if anything ever got released, but they just did all covers. I remember they opened with a version of the Ramones 'I Just Want To Have Something To Do'. At first it was like, 'This will inspire kids or something.' They were too young for us; the cute factor was lost on us.

The second band was Funkopolitin but none of us dug them. We appreciated where they were coming from, what they were going for, but it didn't really do anything for us. And then The Clash came on and obviously it was just a huge, electrifying moment.

They opened with 'London Calling' and then I think 'Safe European Home' right after that. It was just epic, a wall of sound, even greater than I could have hoped. Up to that point, it was the best gig I'd seen. It was just so incredibly powerful. The records, amazing as they were (and are), hadn't prepared me for this. All the projections that they had were well done. They were doing a lot of stuff from *Sandinista!* 'Hitsville UK' I remember, 'Somebody Got Murdered' and 'Guns Of Brixton'. They did 'Career Opportunities' but it wasn't supposed to be in the set, it was a spontaneous decision. Joe had said to Mick something like, 'Hey, Mick, do 'Careers',' and they did it, so we got a bonus, something that wasn't normally on the programme. I loved that song.

At home I said to my dad, 'I saw the greatest rock'n'roll band in the world today.'

STEVE HANLEY, THE FALL

Times Square has undergone a peculiar transformation and is teeming with people from all over the States who've travelled here to see the original London punk band, The Clash, play live.

Apparently, they were booked to only play eight dates in New York, but the promoters sold three times as many tickets as the venue holds so fire chiefs shut the place down and caused a riot amongst the thousands of fans who'd paid but wouldn't get to see a show. Not wanting to disappoint anyone, The Clash have decided to play enough extra nights to honour all the ticket sales. Very fair-minded of them. And look at the results of it… people have taken up residence outside the club they're performing at: Bond's International Casino, which is an almost derelict, bombed-out department-store-turned-nightclub, without a roulette table in sight.

There's a huge, home-made Clash banner hanging from the roof. Down below, between the roadblocks and the riot police, is an impromptu festival that's been going on for days. There are people from all walks of life having their own Clash parties: bandana hip hop kids with roller skates and ghetto blasters; bald Hispanic men improvising percussion on bongos and empty beer cans; overweight housewives punked up in radical sleeve-shorn t-shirts and studded leather collars; long-skirted hippy mothers dancing with their flower children; mid-westerners in cowboy boots and swanky-shirted black guys, all being herded around by police on horses.

And now us. Here by happy coincidence, joining in all the fun.

Better still for us, The Clash are flying their favourite British bands over to support them – like The Slits and Aswad – but there's a civil service strike affecting passport applications and some of Aswad haven't made it, so we get asked to fill in. I spare a thought for the stranded musicians, and for my younger brother Paul, who'll be even more gutted when he hears about this. It's all over the local news: British punk bands taking Times Square. The Clash are getting new hip hop artists to remix some of their tracks. Would you ever think of fusing punk with hip hop? Seems to work though. It's being played on all the radio stations.

'Here's the difference between these boys and Iggy Pop's punks: as soon as they've finished sound checking, Joe Strummer walks straight up to Mark Smith. 'I bet you don't like me,' he says, in his exaggerated cockney accent.

'You're alright, cock,' says Mark, his North Manchester twang more refined than ever. 'It's your latest image I'm not sure about.'

Mark proceeds to spend much of our soundcheck gaps harping on about them being plastic punks selling out British art. 'They're rich boys pretending to be cockneys,' he complains. 'Grant, will you turn them keyboards down!' How does he do it? How can you find fault with something like this? We've spent hours sitting around his flat listening to *Black Market Clash* and now they've already done something to piss him off. What could it possibly be? Maybe he's just mad because we haven't created as much of a storm over here as they have.

After the soundcheck we've got a couple of hours to explore the Times Square party. Amid the garlicky aroma of the pizza parlours, the grease of the takeaways, the electronic bleeping of the amusement arcades, ticket touts and hustlers roam the crowds. Drug dealers sidle past murmuring their wares while desperados try to con a quick buck out of curious onlookers with card-game blags. Karl Burns and I are caught up in a surging crowd when several helmeted police push us to one side with their horses, truncheons and guns.

Somehow, they've still got to let the cabs get through! In the procedure we are crushed into a bunch of leather-clad girls. 'Sorry!' I deliver my polite apologies, underestimating the effects of my British accent. As the stumbling subsides, the girls take another look at me and Karl.

'Oh my God! It's Mick Jones! Mick Jones from The Clash!!' Obviously, they can't mean me. It'd be more accurate to mistake me for the edgy bass player, but no one is doing. It's never occurred to me that Karl bears a resemblance to The Clash's guitarist, but now that it's mentioned, on the litter-strewn pavement below the flashing lights of an amusement arcade, they do both share the moody air of an unjustly dealt-with fifties gangster.

'Awright, gerws!' responds Karl, dusting himself off with a degree of panache I never knew he had. I notice a small crowd of what could be boyfriends or pimps closing in on us and try to seek out an escape route while Karl capitalises on the girls. ''Ow are you all enjoying this little bit of Lahndon, then?' You've got to hand it to Karl. He didn't even pause for a beat before laying it on thick with a fake cockney accent, the sly old fox. Who'd have thought it? Karl as a groupie magnet! Having missed out on the States last year, he's clearly adapting to all aspects of tour mode with twice his usual level of enthusiasm.

It's the same when we're playing later. We go on stage to a typical support-slot scenario: people are more bothered about where they're going to be standing when the headliners come on. But this is the biggest venue Karl's ever played, and he does his best to make sure every single one of those two thousand people are aware of his drumming presence. It's a short set of our more commercial material and by the time we get onto the last song, 'Lie Dream', despite being rabid Clash fanatics, most of the crowd are paying attention. Karl and I lock

'OH MY GOD! IT'S MICK JONES!'...

STEVE HANLEY, THE FALL

ourselves into bass-drum combat like two snipers pitted against each other, both becoming profoundly aware that the best way to conquer is to join forces.

Back in the confines of our dressing room, before long we can hear the crowd start up a feverish chanting for The Clash. The haunting trumpet intro to the title track of Clint Eastwood's spaghetti western *For A Few Dollars More* begins to drift down the damp concrete corridor leading to the stage before the great Clash themselves stride past with purpose, guitars in hand. Joe Strummer in white jeans and red sleeveless denim jacket with the collar turned up, his right wrist heavily bandaged to protect it from its own strumming action. Lead guitarist Mick Jones with his slicked-back quiff, suit and t-shirt, strutting like a mean-looking Fonz. The bass player Paul Simonon: black leather pants, studded belt, black sleeveless jacket, dirty-blond quiff, cigarette hanging out of his mouth at a James Dean angle.

Now there's a style – what would I look like if I went on stage in black leather pants and a sleeveless top? Ridiculous probably, not super-cool like him. And sinewy drummer Topper Headon with his hair sticking up at naturally cocky angles and a look on his face that smacks of defiance. On they go, to a fired-up crowd shouting 'WE WANT THE CLASH! WE WANT THE CLASH!'

Because we can, we follow them down the metal fire-escape stairs, past the dirty bare brick walls through a flyer-plastered doorway and stop just short of the stage as they raid into 'London Calling', causing mass insurgence in the vast hall. Just as well Joe Strummer's got those strummer-guards on; he's thrashing that Telecaster with such vein-bulging intensity he really could do himself a mischief. Mick Jones, on the other side of the stage from me but well in view, is mincing somewhat, windmilling his low-slung Les Paul, indulging in some excessive headshaking and stamping around, but his guitar action is nonetheless grounded and groundbreaking.

Of course, my focus is pulled towards the rhythm section. When Topper kicks the bass drum it's like a glorious punch in the stomach, especially at such short range. Paul Simonon isn't someone I've ever particularly considered to be one of the world's greatest bass players, but I must admit the way he jumps into the air, does the splits, lands without a stumble and never misses a note is something to behold.

They can be hit-and-miss, live, The Clash, if they're too busy pogoing around to give the music the attention it requires. But this is different. In the middle of a two-week stint of two gigs a day, they're really on it. By the time Mick and Joe level into the classic '(White Man) in Hammersmith Palais', watching from the side of the stage isn't what this is about, so I head down the corridor to join the crowd for the rest of the set, a searing two-hour epic. The whole effect is like being in the epicentre of a major explosion.

MOGADOR THEATRE
23-30 SEPTEMBER 1981, PARIS, FRANCE

BOB ADCOCK

I did one tour with The Clash. I was working with The Scorpions and they were doing some recording so I had some time free. A friend of mine, Ian Flooks, owned Wasted Talent which was The Clash's agency. They'd just come back from New York and were looking for a tour manager and my name was put forward. That said 'the tour' was a residency in a club in Paris!

As a tour manager, it's all planning and arranging things – crew members, travel and hotels as well as anything to do with the gig itself. Once the gig starts, that's your job finished really, unless anything untoward happens during the show. So, it's an advisory role which doesn't vary that much between bands. I got on well with Joe Strummer. I didn't think I would, because it wasn't my kind of scene, but then again when you're working it's different.

It was Bernie Rhodes, the manager of the band, who arranged for me to do the job not the band themselves. I guess they had a different tour manager for each tour because they weren't touring regularly. The gigs they did directly before Paris were in America, where they played in New York City. They had an American tour manager for that one, so they didn't bring him back to England.

Bernie was great. I got on well with him. I met him at the ice cream parlour opposite the Roundhouse in London. He said, 'You can see the whole history of British music on those advertising hoardings.' In other words, all the bands who played there, because there were old posters there. In those days, Camden Town was like San Francisco. In London, all the freaks and people like that used to hang out in Camden Town. It was pretty much Bernie Rhodes' patch. He had great ideas. He seemed to be non-stop with ideas in those days, when he managed The Clash.

I don't think they were an easy band to manage. They had their own ideas which and didn't necessarily tie in with what management wanted. I didn't find Bernie to be any kind of trouble at all. I found that he was great to work with. I didn't see much of him after The Clash. I got really fed up with the whole punk thing, even after just a few weeks.

RADIO CLASH UK TOUR

 **APOLLO THEATRE**
5 & 6 OCTOBER 1981, MANCHESTER

GERRY DALY

Me and my mate, Jacko, got right down to the front before support Theatre of Hate came on and stayed there waiting. The Apollo was all seater, but they used to take the first few rows out for The Clash, otherwise they'd get trashed. Gobbing had pretty much died out by this point, but one idiot scored a direct hit on Joe who was obviously not too happy. Mick looked across at him with that distinctive grin.

After the gig we queued up to go backstage to meet the band. Mick pointed at his picture on my t-shirt and asked, 'Who's that funny looking geezer?' and carried on rolling possibly the first spliff I'd ever seen. Mick, Joe and Topper signed my t-shirt, but the signatures unfortunately didn't survive my mum's washing machine. We would have liked to speak to Paul, but he was sitting cross-legged on the floor, surrounded by girls.

JOHN YOUENS

I was 14 years old when I first heard about The Clash. I was into the kind of second-generation punk bands like The Undertones, The Members and Stiff Little Fingers that were touring regularly. A classmate had seen them on the *16 Tons* tour in 1980, but I didn't see them until October 1981 at the Manchester Apollo.

I grew up in Wilmslow, Cheshire which is part of the leafy commuter belt. I was a suburban middle-class punk. I didn't really have much to rebel against, to be quite honest. I had a regular upbringing, but it wasn't very exciting.

By the time I saw The Clash, some of my contemporaries had gone off them as they had strayed away from being 'pure punk'. *London Calling* was obviously a very sort of diverse record which I grew to love. *Sandinista!* which I absolutely loved, and still do, was even more diverse and it was the entry point

for me. It was reggae and hip hop and punk and soul and all these different genres. It was a real eye opener.

The Apollo was their first UK date in 1981. They'd been around Europe before that and done a three-week residency in New York. I wish I'd seen those! This was my first opportunity, and I was tremendously excited. My dad drove me and my friends to the gig and waited outside the venue for three hours. I didn't thank him or anything. I feel very guilty about that.

Theatre Of Hate were supporting, and they were good. I remember the massive sense of anticipation that I was going to see them. In the setlist there was a lot from *Sandinista!* Not all the old punk stuff, and it was a long set, maybe two hours.

The intro music was the theme to *A Few Dollars More*, but as the band came on, these sirens went off and all these yellow lights came on. It was powerful. I was tremendously impressed by that, to the point that when I got home, I painted yellow and black stripes across my B&Q wardrobe in my bedroom, much to my parents' dismay!

This was the beginning of that military chic thing that they had on *Combat Rock* as well. They just looked fabulous and very cool. It was an important gig to me. There were coachloads of people come from all over the country, with a load of coaches outside the Apollo. It was an important event.

The next time I saw them was at Victoria Hall, Hanley, Stoke-on-Trent in July 1982. There were coachloads travelling down from Manchester for that!

DAVID GLEAVE

I loved The Clash. Iggy from the Naughty Boys loved 'em too. I bought *London Calling* and we played it every night at Naughty Boys HQ at 12 Seymour Grove, Sale. We learned every song on guitars. I saw them at the Apollo in '81. The Clash were my favourite band from that era.

JEFF DAWSON

By October 1981 I'd been to see loads of bands: Stiff Little Fingers, Stranglers, Devo. I was just lining them up. They only used cost around £3 a ticket. Some weeks I was at gigs two or three times a week, and once I got my driving licence I was there all the time. We'd often get the tickets from the Apollo on a Saturday morning when they went on sale, because you'd better tickets from the box office than if you went to Piccadilly Records. The Clash were doing two nights and we got front row tickets for both nights (even though there were no seats – they'd taken them out after earlier gigs where they'd been ripped out and trampled on!).

ALL THE YOUNG PUNKS

MICHAEL CLARE

I was only twelve in 1977 but had a brother who was 18 and a bit of a punk. We shared a bedroom, so I was exposed to John Peel and my brother's record collection at an early age! I immediately fell in love with The Clash, The Damned, etc. (not to mention The Fall and Ivor Cutler via JP), but as I got a bit older it was The Clash that I became obsessed with, preferring *London Calling* and *Sandinista!* to the earlier stuff. I didn't get to see them until October 1981 at the Manchester Apollo.

They played two nights, supported by Theatre of Hate. I can't remember which night I went to, or much about it to be honest, except being awestruck (and very sweaty).

The next time I saw them was at Leeds University in 1982, on the *Combat Rock* tour. I seem to remember it being postponed when Joe 'disappeared' for a while. We managed to get backstage afterwards, got posters and tickets signed (sadly, no longer in my possession as I had to sell a lot of stuff off in the early 2000s due to some not-so-groovy times). I remember Joe was talking to someone about *Mean Streets* when he was signing my stuff…

SIMON WADSWORTH

Being from Manchester I was very fortunate as a Clash fan. Manchester was very much a Clash city. They played live there 13 times and recorded tracks there. I remember when *Give 'Em Enough Rope* came out in November '78, they were playing the Apollo and they came down to HMV on Market Street in the afternoon and met all the fans and signed stuff. There was no desk separating them from their fans. They just walked in and spent time with everyone.

I saw them many times but the gig I want to talk about is the one on 5th October 1981. The band had released *Sandinista!* and had done residencies at Bonds in New York and at the theatre Mogador in Paris. By the time they got to Manchester to open the *Radio Clash* tour they were on top form. They played on the 5th and the 6th and this was the last time that the classic line-up of Topper, Mick, Paul and Joe played Manchester.

On the first night we got there very early as we were determined to be down at the front. The doors opened and we rushed in and plonked

> **I DECIDED I WOULD REMOVE ONE OF JOE'S SHOES…**
>
> **SIMON WADSWORTH**

ourselves next to the stage centre. The support act was Theatre Of Hate who had a lot of psychobilly fans who insisted on slam dancing and throwing themselves into us in an effort to move us from the stage. Bruised and battered, we stood our ground and, boy, was it worth it.

As the lights went down and Ennio Morricone's 'Sixty Seconds To What?' from *For A Few Dollars More* struck up, the place went ballistic. Then I found myself stood at the feet of Joe Strummer as they played for over two hours. At one point, I decided for some bizarre reason that I would remove one of Joe's shoes. They were white winkle pickers with a crepe sole and as he stood with his foot on the monitor in front of me I took my chance and grabbed it, removing it from his foot. I would love to tell you that I still have that prized item but after a minute one of the roadies came running up to me and asked for it back. That was not the end of interacting with Joe though, as when they played 'Bankrobber', he knelt down right in front of me and shoved the microphone in my face for me to blast out my best version. Topper handed my mate one of his 'Topper's Boppers' drumsticks, which he had to quickly hide as many hands attempted to relieve him of it. The Clash were the greatest rock 'n' roll band there has ever been. On that night, they were at their very best.

FRED HEIS

I was 14 when I first became enthralled which was 1980, so a little late on. I went to a strict grammar school and cool kids were few and far between, but a couple of fashion leaders affected about six of us in our year. The Clash were without doubt the coolest band, whose sound, philosophy and presence just felt different to the others. I became a fan of a load of bands, all the usual suspects and some others as well. But The Clash actually spoke to us. The others were just bands that you liked. Whether it be Rock Against Racism, or their views on fascism, or fighting capitalism or poverty, they told us how they felt. We could identify, and believe in them. They weren't just in it for fame or the money.

And clearly, knowing what I know now, a lot of this stance was from Strummer. It was Strummer who made sure that the fans were always, always considered. If it was corporate it would be called 'platinum customer service'. Whether it be ensuring that anyone wanting to go backstage got to see them, or allowing people without tickets in through the door (we'd not done this but we heard the legends), or releasing double and triple albums at the same price as a single LP. I can well imagine the arguments with Bernie and CBS – yet incredibly he won.

That being said, Mick was our favourite. He just exuded cool. And my favourite tracks were generally those that Mick sang – 'Train In Vain' and 'Stay Free' especially (and both have such good origin stories as well). But that was because we were star-struck teenagers. Without Joe, it wouldn't have happened, and it was Joe that made The Clash the absolute stand-out band of our generation.

I'd been to Stiff Little Fingers and then The Damned a week later in November 1980 and they were amazing, I was properly overwhelmed by the whole experience. But then in 1981 I saw The Clash at the Manchester Apollo. I was so excited and needed new apparel so I bought a white boiler suit as it was cheap and wrote 'The Clash' on it in marker pen. Along with my Docs and donkey jacket, I felt I could fit in (not sure I did, but it created a story!).

And I don't remember it much to be honest. I was a little drunk and a little too excited, but I remember the feeling – this time it was real. It was my third ever gig and it was on a different plane, as I knew all the songs inside out and most of the lyrics. They were the best, most important band then, and now.

As a punk I'd always wanted a tattoo and could never think of anything. It's only two years ago that I finally realised, and was amazed that I'd never thought of it back then – a Clash star, followed by a Zounds 'Z', an *Unknown Pleasures* graphic and finally a Nine Black Alps motif – the four most important bands to me, in chronological order of awareness and it's appropriate that The Clash start the order for both reasons.

Unfortunately, they didn't tour again before the split, and I remember buying the *NME* and phoning my mate from a phone box with the news, cos it couldn't wait and I needed to spend the 2p to tell him. I felt sick.

I got to see them on the *Cut The Crap* tour, but it was a shadow of the band that meant so much to me. They really were the only band that mattered.

PAUL HEXHAM, AGE 13

I'd been to see The Clash a few times when me and my mates went along aged 13 for the *Radio Clash* tour at Manchester Apollo. We went round the back after the gig as we knew that they let people in to have a chat with the band. We were there to around 3am with Joe pouring very generous measures of rum and blackcurrant to a 13-year-old! Being a bit cheeky we asked if we could get on the guest list for the Lyceum shows, and Joe called Kosmo Vinyl over who took our names and addresses.

On the second night at the Apollo, we did the same again. I took along all my singles, all picture sleeves, albums… everything and got them all signed. They were great.

My brother was living in London, so we thought we'd chance it and went down for the Lyceum shows, no tickets or anything. We rocked up at the venue at 3pm, popped round the back and banged on the door! I can't remember who came out but we got let in for the soundcheck.

There were about half a dozen people watching while they played for an hour. Then we got told we'd have to leave. I asked the crew what we should do now, and they just said to go round the front… When we did Kosmo was stood there. I told him my name and he remembered me from Manchester. I asked if my brother could come in too and he said yes…

I asked what to do if the bouncers asked for our tickets and he just said, 'You're on your own!'

We did that again the second night too. It made my life. The Clash had passion, commitment and integrity. As a 13-year-old, that was amazing. Joe Strummer made me the man I am today

⭐ APOLLO THEATRE
7 & 8 OCTOBER 1981, GLASGOW

PAUL HILL

I travelled down to meet my pals in Manchester, one of whom – Mettas – had actually roadied for them in Europe. We were in digs across the road from the Apollo. It was basically a doss house stinking of piss, as we found out after the gig. We met this Theatre of Hate fan with a Mohican who was from London. He had Chelsea and West Ham tattoos on each arm. We asked him 'what is the crack with that?' and his explanation was 'it's just in case I run into one of them one day!' We got

Paul Hill met Mick Jones at the Apollo

to meet the band in the bar next door to the Apollo. I was star struck but my mate Kieron got the autographs on his ticket, although he lost it years later.

Glasgow Apollo was next with two nights there. We had a posh B&B in Kelvinbridge and the owner must have thought 'what the fuck?' when five punks rocked up, but we were all good lads and he liked us. The gigs were unbelievable, and the Apollo was massive with two or three tiers and both dates sold out. I remember Joe saying to everyone in the balconies 'what is it like up there in the summer house?'

ALL THE YOUNG PUNKS

ALLAN MARSHALL

As a sixteen-year-old who had previously been introduced to punk and new wave thanks to my older brother, Robert, via his Stranglers, Sham 69 and Dr Feelgood records, I was now starting to go to more and more gigs at the legendary Glasgow Apollo and at Tiffany's aka the Locarno Ballroom (then Discotheque).

Having started with The Stranglers in October 1979 and after seeing The Clash on their *16 Tons* tour in January 1980, I was really looking forward to

Allan Marshall's ticket for the Glasgow Apollo

this gig, having saved up my pocket money for a ticket at £3.50. This did seem a lot of money!

Despite having been to numerous gigs already at the Apollo, the venue was not only legendary for the acts that played there but for the 'penguin-dressed' bouncers. There was one bouncer that I always remember due to his small but rotund physique. On several occasions he'd have altercations with fans who tried to run down the front of the stalls to get closer to the ten-foot high stage. He was always shoving them and telling them to get back to their seats.

As The Clash finally came on stage to a backdrop of colourful flags, my cousin David and I decided to try and get closer to the front. We sneaked along our row, which was quite far back, to the far-left aisle of the theatre and then proceeded to move down two or three rows at a time until we got close to the front. Unfortunately, as we were in mid-flight our progress moving forward was spotted by the said small rotund bouncer, who appeared at the end of the left aisle at the front and was now staring at us.

Much to our astonishment he waved to us to come forward and pointed us into a space just a few feet back from the stage where we got a great view of the band. I remember him saying, 'You'll be okay here, boys.' What a result! Why there was no altercation we will never know. Maybe punk/new wave audiences had mellowed or perhaps finally the bouncers realised that the fans just wanted to see the bands without any punch up?

The highlight of gig was when Mick Jones was right at the edge of the stage mid-guitar solo and looked down at me and David and proceeded to give us the 'thumbs up' and a big smile. We went home extremely happy and relieved that we hadn't got thrown out after getting caught sneaking down the front.

SPA ROYAL HOTEL
10 OCTOBER 1981, BRIDLINGTON

GARY CUNNINGHAM, AGE 16

As a 16-year-old lad coming from the deprived city (well, deprived of anything exciting), music became my escape to another world, which seemed very alien to what I had experienced and what was expected of my life. Too young for the start of punk and just old enough for new wave, I started to buy seven-inch singles by bands such as The Ramones, The Jam, Buzzcocks, The Clash, etc. Their songs aligned to my teenage anger and sense of despair, the lyrics understanding what I was going through. 1980 was the time of one in ten unemployment, coming after the despair of the seventies with its strikes and blackouts, music gave me a sense of hope in a bleak world. My mate and I shared our record collections, and as our love of music developed, we wanted to see these bands live in concert.

The Clash gig at the Bridlington was, and still is, one of the best I have ever experienced, from seeing the support act Theatre of Hate (later Spear of Destiny) to the actual performance from The Clash. As we were both 16, going to a gig out of town was, for us, very daring and a little crazy. We'd hatched the plan of what to tell our parents, or rather what not tell them. We'd got the ticket money and train fare from our paper rounds and spent the day in the town waiting for the gig. The excitement was intense.

I wanted to watch the support band, but my mate wanted to get a beer like the older kids. He was a few months older than me but smaller in size. I was quite tall and had some facial hair, so it was down to me to get the pints in. I was surprised at my success in getting served! One drink each was all our meagre funds would cover so after consuming them we just waited for The Clash to come on. Song after song was delivered with the energy, anger that we anticipated. The audience pogo-ing. Sweat, beer and other smells battered two young lads' senses. We were in a place that wasn't bleak anymore.

After about two hours of playing, Joe started speaking again. 'Is there anyone from Hull?' he shouted. The crowd roared back. There were a lot of people from Hull there that night. 'Well, the last train is just leaving, and we are playing on,' said Joe. Me and my mate looked at each other with shock and horror. 'Fuck, how are we going to get home?' We both said 'ah, fuck it' and stayed to hear the rest of the songs and the encores. Walking out into the cold January air woke us from our delirium, and we then had to find a way home.

We decided that my dad was not going to be as big a problem as my mate's dad. We would still be in big trouble, but the best option would be to call for a lift home, which meant finding a call box to reverse the charges as we had no money left. Dad came up trumps. He didn't ask too many questions, I guess him understanding that part of growing up means to push boundaries, break a couple of rules and take risks, but to enjoy life.

The whole build up to seeing The Clash, the actual gig itself and the time of it, meant it left me with an indelible memory of what live music should be about. I still attend live gigs, but today they seem very safe and sanitised. The last live music which moved me was seeing Shed Seven and Ocean Colour Scene. We need another music revolution, but in this PC controlled world I don't think it will be allowed to happen.

JOHN MURRAY

I remember this day well considering it took place when I was less than one-third of the age I am now! Five of us crammed into an overloaded Vauxhall Viva, setting off on what seemed like a big trip (80 miles!) from the small town of Darlington to the smaller town of Bridlington. A trip to the seaside to see the Westway Wonders. How did 'The Only Band That Matters' end up playing in an art deco ballroom in the Lobster Capital of Europe? This was before the advent of the arena of course, and The Clash's reputation has only increased in the intervening years.

What we saw immediately entered my top ten gigs of all time, and has remained steadfastly there ever since (despite how many gigs I have seen since), alongside Josef K (twice), The Wedding Present's first ever outing, Radiohead playing a pub, The Smiths at the GLC and the Bunnymen at their early days best.

Jon Murray's *Nag! Nag! Nag!* fanzine reviewed the Bridlington gig

I even wrote the experience up in my teenage fanzine – *Nag! Nag! Nag!* – so my memories are likely enhanced by reading it through my seventeen-year-old enthusiastic writing. Without reading those words, I remember the hyped-up anticipation, literally dripping from the ceiling as the perspiration condensed. Theatre Of Hate had set the scene, but there was only one band everyone had come to see.

Automatic barriers striped in black and yellow raised, sires blared and The Clash took the stage in a haze of smoke and evaporating human moisture and stormed through a set which seemed to be about two hours long. The energy, the sound and the fury ripped through the Victorian ballroom in a seething wave of ungeniality. This ain't no Tea Dance! My vivid memories include witnessing the power of Strummer closeup – his guitar as a weapon – crashing amongst hundreds of young punks. It was a communal experience!

Against a backdrop of political slides – newspaper cuttings and photos of US scenes and the political figures of the time (Ronald Reagan being front and centre stage there) – they delivered all the classics: 'Janie Jones', 'Clash City Rockers', 'London Calling' and the brilliant 'Magnificent Seven'. There must have been an encore of eight or nine songs. They knew how to please the adoring crowd.

Then it was back in the Vauxhall Viva, sweat-soaked, exhausted and, unknowingly, with memories to last a lifetime.

MALCOLM HOPWOOD

1979 to 1982 was a great time to be a teenager who was into punk and new wave. Growing up in the heart of West Yorkshire there were a great variety of venues to choose from to see our favourite bands. We saw The Jam play Leeds Queens Hall, The Skids at Bradford University, Pete Shelley at Leeds Warehouse, U2 at Leeds Tiffanys (before they became global) and The Southern Death Cult at Wakefield Town Hall. I even ventured over to Liverpool Royal Court to see the Dead Kennedys and U2 again.

Malcolm Hopwood went to Bridlington with his twin brother & his best mate

In October 1981, The Clash were playing Bridlington Spa. Along with The Jam, The Clash were my favourite band at that time, so me, my twin brother Graham and best mate Andrew devised a plan to get there. Luckily, Andrew's grandma lived in Filey, so we arranged to stay at her house for the weekend and bought our tickets for the gig.

The gig was brilliant. We'd never seen a band give so much on stage. Strummer put himself on the same level as the fans. He made us feel so important and the band and audience had a rapport as one unit, something I'd never seen before. The only one to come close was Richard Jobson of The Skids.

The gig was electric, but it still didn't prepare us for what was to come. Most bands at that time did a couple of encores, maybe playing two songs in each one. I think we got The Undertones to do four encores once. The Clash didn't do that. They'd already played an extensive set but when they came back for the first encore, I distinctly remember it lasted 55 minutes. I kept saying, 'Bloody hell, they're still going, this is brilliant.' It was hit after hit, the mosh pit was on fire, or pogoing as we called it then. Then they came again, another two songs. My memory is hazy, but I think they finished with '(White Man) In Hammersmith Palais'.

ROYAL COURT THEATRE
12 OCTOBER 1981, LIVERPOOL

ANDREW BRASH, AGE 15

In 1976 I was a ten-year-old schoolboy living in the suburb of Garston in South Liverpool and a choirboy in the local church, St Michael's. One of my closest friends and fellow chorister Andrew Williams told me about a TV appearance by a group called the Sex Pistols that he'd read about in his father's newspaper. They'd sworn profusely, vomited to order and spat their way through anything. My interest in punk was born right there and then.

It was nurtured partly by a late-night television programme in the North West called *What's On*, hosted by TV presenter Tony Wilson who would go on to be part owner of Factory Records and the Haçienda nightclub. The programme aired up-and-coming new wave and punk bands such as Joy Division and was the fuel that fired my interest in this alternative world.

1978 saw my interest in punk soar. I was now attending a former grammar school, Hillfoot Hey in Hunts Cross, South Liverpool. Hillfoot still operated like a grammar school despite it being a comprehensive and was something of a hot bed of aspiring wannabe punks. One individual (whose name escapes me) was the real deal and a bit of a hero to many of us. He had the spiked hair, was thin as a stick insect and wore his uniform adapted to make him look just like Paul Simonon.

My usual dress in 1978 saw me in a biker's jacket, black (what were called) Clash kecks with zips all over them and a pair of Doctor Martens. I even had a replica black Nazi armband, the wearing of which could be very tricky. I would like to point out that this was nothing to do with my political leanings, as I was only twelve at the time.

And I was acquiring single records via music press adverts.

Around this time, Eric's – a music venue in Mathew Street, Liverpool that catered for the punk genre – was running into very serious trouble. Magistrates had decided to remove its license due to some not particularly violent or really serious incidents. I attended three of five marches that were arranged to oppose this. The first one was the most memorable. It ended relatively peacefully although there was the odd scuffle or two with a couple of arrests. A friend and I managed to get ourselves photographed standing next to a high-ranking policeman with a megaphone who was leading and directing the march. The photograph appeared in the *NME*. Mother was horrified!

My slightly older cousin Colin also liked his punk and new wave music. He had a rather impressive Les Paul copy and his record collection included the first Clash album. That was it. An instantaneous addiction occurred. This lot were the real deal. Political, raucous and rebellious all rolled into one, whereas the Sex Pistols were something of a travelling circus.

My first gig was in 1978 at the age of twelve; Howard Devoto and his group Magazine at the Empire Theatre in Liverpool, a brilliant gig made all the better by a superb support band – Simple Minds. I attended more gigs throughout the late seventies and early eighties including the Undertones, Stiff Little Fingers, Ultravox and The Stray Cats, on one occasion supported by the Ramones.

Approaching my sixteenth birthday, I and a couple of school friends including a lad called Paul Turner had managed to get tickets for the *Radio Clash* tour. The Clash were probably close to or at the height of their fame, and demand for tickets was so high that we ended up on the balcony of the Royal Court Theatre, when normally we were right down at the front, in the thick of the action. However just to be there was a privilege and we made the most of it.

My lasting memory of this night is not necessarily a good one. I'd arranged for my father to give me and my two friends a lift home. He was coming off shift at 10pm and we were to meet him at about 10.45pm in a side car park at Liverpool Lime Street station, close to the venue. As

> **DEMAND FOR TICKETS WAS SO HIGH WE ENDED UP IN THE BALCONY...**
>
> ANDREW BRASH

the clock got closer to 10pm, it inevitably started to speed up and the hands moved faster and faster as they approached 10.30pm. There was still no 'White Riot' and it was now 10.40pm and we really had to go. That was it. The night was over and still we had not heard that iconic song. We eventually met my father, who insisted that we should have stayed and that he would have waited. Never mind. It was too late. But at least we had made the effort and seen The Clash, which not many others had. It was quite a turning point for me in my life, as only days after the Clash gig my father suffered a massive heart attack and died aged only forty-nine. He was very close to the age that Joe Strummer died from the same thing many years later.

 LYCEUM THEATRE
18-26 OCTOBER 1981, LONDON

GERRY DALY

The Clash announced a seven-night run at the Lyceum in 1981, so I sent off my postal order for a ticket for each of the first three nights. Unfortunately, I got sent three for the first night so took my sister and her flat mate. They played a two and a half hour set, opening with the unlikely choice of 'Broadway' from the *Sandinista!* album which worked brilliantly, starting quietly then bursting into life in the middle, to an ecstatic response. This would be the last time I saw the classic line-up, with Topper being replaced by his predecessor Terry Chimes. Terry was a more than competent drummer but Topper was on a different level, and it would never be quite the same again.

MARTIN JONES

I did six of the seven nights at the Lyceum, only missing the second night. On the Tuesday I even missed a Fulham home game to see The Clash. (For the record they beat Exeter 4-1 and eventually won promotion that season.) I didn't drive so would get the train up to London but wouldn't be able to get a train back to Bognor, so I would have to spend the night at Gatwick Airport and get the first one back in the morning. For midweek gigs, I'd cycle to the station from my job on the sewage works to get the train and then go straight to work the following day. I kept enough clothes in my locker to do this on repeat, through the residency, three nights in a row.

The only band that mattered? Yes!

GARY LONGDEN

Almost exactly four years after seeing The Clash in Leeds, in October 1981, everything had changed. They had released their fourth album, but they comprised no fewer than seven vinyl records, an output that matched The Beatles, Rolling

Stones and The Who in their heyday.

Their repertoire was considerable, diverse, critically acclaimed and well digested by the fans. They were playing on their home turf, London, at the Lyceum Ballroom, for a seven sold out nights residency. Their last album, *Sandinista!* had delighted, intrigued, outraged and appalled in equal measure, but for every old fan they lost, they gained four. The Lyceum was a great venue, but artistically it was a million miles from the 100 Club. On the Strand, distinguished, not a punk gig, but ideal. They had made it – but on their own terms.

It was a long, sprawling, majestic set. 'Broadway' an audacious jazz-infused opener in London's West End, before the thunderous reggae stomp of 'One More Time'. Musically they were on another planet from that Leeds Refectory gig. Light and shade, changes of pace, space between the notes, with Joe's vocals now a plaintiff, soulful roar rather than a hoarse howl submerged by a wall of sound.

Those bands that had previously been ahead of The Clash were now well and truly in their slipstream. The Jam were namechecking Michael Jackson as Weller edged towards soul, The Boomtown Rats had gone down the commercially successful 'I Don't Like Mondays' blind alley never to return, the Buzzcocks struggled to escape their formula, The Stranglers found their groove as a rock n roll band and the Pistols had imploded. Welcome to the Last Gang in Town.

What set The Clash apart was their ability to adopt, adapt and improve upon the constantly morphing musical landscape around them, combined with listening to the astute image guidance of manager Bernie Rhodes till he left in late '78.

Somehow, they were still hip, even though the setlist was a distant cousin of 1977. '(White Man) In Hammersmith Palais' and 'Clash City Rockers' still blazed, but the lighter touch of 'Somebody Got Murdered' and 'Spanish Bombs' sounded just as good. There was no room for 'White Riot'. 'Complete Control' gloriously wrapped things up. It would never be better for the Clash.

On 22 December 2002 I was driving to our office Christmas party when the radio broke the news that Strummer had died of a heart attack, aged 50. You never know how you are going to react when you learn of the demise of your heroes. I pulled to the side of the road, stunned. A small part of me had died too. I reflected how cruel life was, just when his talent was re-emerging for a new audience, he was gone.

I'm the White Man in Hammersmith Palais, only looking for fun

JED MEEKINS

I'd just turned 17 and was living the dream working in a record shop on the Isle of Wight when I got talking to a couple of mates who were heading back to college

ALL THE YOUNG PUNKS

in Guildford. All obsessed with The Clash, we bought tickets at the heady price of £3.50, for the second night of their residency at the Lyceum in Londo. As none of us had even been to London before, this was an adventure of a lifetime!

Heading to Portsmouth via the ferry from the island we caught the train dressed only in jeans and Clash t-shirts, arriving at Victoria Station around midday. We went straight to around the stage doors of the Lyceum and waited an hour, but as soon as we realised no one was going to turn up we went hunting for food and beer!

We finally got inside the Lyceum with the first wave of fans and were greeted by a wall of bass pumping through the massive speakers. We all managed to barge our way to the first couple of rows, next to the stage, just as the support band, The Meteors, kicked off their set. Just then all hell started breaking loose just behind us and we were thankful that we were so close to the stage! About 200 Meteors fans were beating the hell out of each other (for fun) whilst shouting out inaudible chants! With their fusion of punk rock and rockabilly, The Meteors looked as demented as their manic fans. Avoiding most of the flailing arms and legs, one of my friends caught a blow to the head!

If the venue wasn't already hot enough, after The Meteors finished and the psycho fans had left, I was dripping with sweat but resisted a chance to get to the bar, preferring to keep my place at the front.

Finally, the lights went down and in the semi-darkness I could just see the band walking on and getting into their positions, with Joe in the middle, Mick on the left, Paul on the right and Topper settling down on his drum stool. Out of the corner of my eye I could make out a fifth member getting into position at the back of the stage, though not with an instrument in his hand, but a spray-can instead! This was Futura 2000, the graffiti artist befriended by The Clash, who through the duration of the gig painted a giant backdrop of New York City while the band played, stinking the venue out with spray paint fumes!

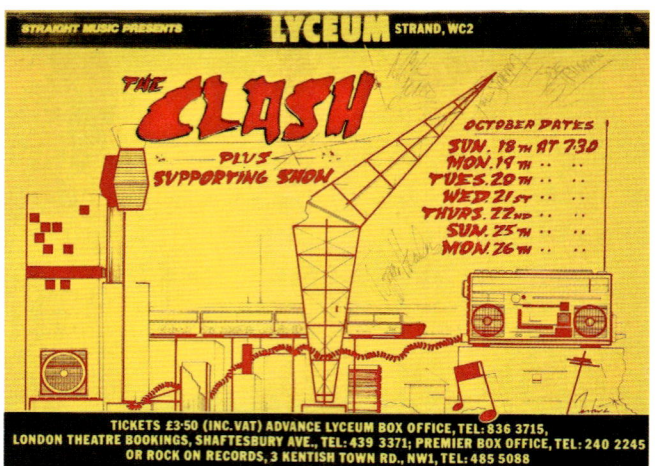

The Clash started with a powerful version of new song 'Know Your Rights', sounding raw and with what I thought were different lyrics to the final vinyl version. The sheer power, energy and pace of the music just blew me away. I had been to a handful of gigs before this, but this was in another league. Paul strutted around the stage and in his 'god-like' stance towered over us, whilst Mick danced around on his side, acting like the guitar hero he was, staring at the crowd. Joe had total control of the crowd, as he always did, spitting out the words. Topper in the background was thundering out the beats like a machine. The set was decked out as a construction site with yellow and black chevron road barriers matching Topper's drum kit.

Time stood still as the songs reached our very souls, with no time to catch a breath. I remember thinking I was part of something very special, and that the whole world should be seeing and hearing this! A fantastic version of crowd (and my) favourite 'I Fought The Law' filled the hall with pure energy, and then Joe introduced Futura to the crowd. He did a short history of graffiti rap which went down well. Near the end of the main set 'London Calling' belted out, now fine-tuned to become a great addition to anyone's set. When the main set was over, they came back on for three encores, as song after song, new and old, graced our ears.

With very little time to catch our train back south we ran as fast as we could and just about made it. Halfway through the journey, my two mates got off at Guildford and headed back to college campus, while I travelled on to journey's end at Portsmouth, shivering in the cold October air in the early hours in just a sweaty Clash t-shirt.

I had to wait a whole nine months before I could catch The Clash again, this time in Portsmouth. It was a long nine months!

MARK FREEMAN

Whilst I was too young to socialise during the first years of punk, the Clash albums were constantly being played in my house, especially with an older brother two years my senior. Having managed to see many other punk gigs prior to my sixteenth birthday, I was finally able to witness The Clash in person at the week-long set of gigs at the Lyceum. I managed to attend both the first and last nights, with Tenpole Tudor (with a full band at that time) and Anti Nowhere League as the respective supports. These were the gigs with the artist Futurama spray painting a backdrop behind the band over the week. These shows were mind-blowing but sadly were not repeated in quality in future years. Two more Clash gigs at Brixton Academy in 1984 with a much-changed line-up faded into insignificance before the band finally split.

The eighties did, however, spawn Mick Jones' new band Big Audio Dynamite. BAD went onto have a number of hit singles and a very different live sound to the earlier Clash. I managed to see BAD in London a few times. They were exciting and different from other bands at the time, but they did not have the same raucous energy of The Clash.

Meanwhile I continued to witness the energy and stage presence of Joe when he stepped in to fill the shoes of Shane McGowan as frontman of the Pogues. I also saw gigs with the Mescaleros, including at the Town and Country Club in 1988 and Glastonbury in 1989.

I was gigging with a band called World By Storm in the late eighties and, having supported the likes of 999, we secured a support slot with Havana 3am at the Pink Toothbrush in Rayleigh in late 1990. This was a massive gig for me, playing support to one of my teenage idols, to have his bass tech set up my rig on the night and to meet the band in the pub next door pre-gig.

Mark Freeman saw The Clash more than once

WAYNE BEAN

I was in art class at school in November 1978 and a mate of mine got the record on the day after its release. He brought it to school and played it on a small portable record player that was there. I had never heard of The Clash and that day changed my life. From then onwards I was hooked.

In early October or late September 1981, I got a ticket for The Clash at the Lyceum Theatre. I remember it clear as day, walking up the stairs and at the top seeing two framed posters promoting the band's week-long residency. The support was from Theatre Of Hate, who I'd not heard of. They were great with some thumping tunes. When The Clash came on stage, they seemed to play for ever...

'The Magnificent Seven' seemed like the longest song in history. 'London's Burning' started in a blaze of flashing lights. Other highlights were 'Janie Jones', 'This Is Radio Clash' and 'Clash City Rockers'. Watching Joe Strummer knock those riffs out was electrifying to both see and hear, as was Paul cracking that bass out which just sounded so solid. With Topper on drums and Mick on guitar, all four of them were working together in this solid rock machine that was The Clash.

On the way home, I ripped the top half of a 'Radio Clash' poster off a wall (I thought I'd got it all but then it ripped... better than nothing.). One of the best gigs of my life.

This was my first major gig. Previously when I got paid, I'd spent my money on records or posters. I couldn't afford gigs too. Once I'd seen The Clash, I worked more. I also lived 60 miles away in the Kent countryside and didn't drive, so had to rely on jumping trains, hitchhiking and walking a lot to get home!

 'THIS IS RADIO CLASH'/'RADIO CLASH' RELEASED 20 NOVEMBER 1981

ROBERT CASSON

1981's standalone single, the bridge between *Sandinista!* and *Combat Rock*, 'This Is Radio Clash' was much derided at the time. *Record Mirror* called it a 'stinking rotten record' which was 'definitely best forgotten' whilst the *Melody Maker* described it as a 'ramshackle disco mess'. However, since then has been called 'a magnificent, daring, challenging record that was years ahead of its time; one of the great rock records of the 1980s.'

To this day The Clash fan's own brand of Marmite.

FAR EAST TOUR

CAPITOL THEATRE
11-14 & 16-18 FEBRUARY 1982, SYDNEY, AUSTRALIA

KEVIN ALLAN WHEATLEY, AGE 24

I saw The Clash in February 1982 when the band came to Australia. It was the *Magnificent 7* tour, with seven concerts in Sydney. My musical tastes were Australian centric. I gobbled up punk and new wave, bands such as The Saints. They were probably one of the first 'home grown' punk-type acts, not in terms of fashion but in their attitude and music.

I would have heard about The Clash through music programmes on the radio and in the press. We didn't miss out on anything. Australia was in a unique position to get the world's music.

I was there for the second night. Australian Aboriginal group No Fixed Address supported, a rock/reggae band mainly from South Australia. The gig was a revelation for me. I was expecting the pre–*London Calling* songs but those from *Sandinista!*…? Wow. The band played five genuine encores that night too.

The only negative was so-called punks spitting at Joe. Spit was running off his face.

MATTHEW WILLIS

Back in 1981 I was a kid living in northern Sydney, hovering around the edges of 16 years old and the edges of a musical awakening. I was becoming increasingly dissatisfied with most of what I was hearing on popular radio and starting to connect with music that was finding its way from the post punk world across into more mainstream success. The occasional band like the Sex Pistols and the Boomtown Rats had made it onto my radar, and I was getting the sense of there being a world of music I was yet to discover.

Leafing through a magazine one day, I came across an ad for the CBS Record Club. The deal back then was that you could sign up and get six albums for something like 99 cents for the lot, in exchange for buying a few at full price in the coming year. Going through the list of records on offer one really caught my eye – The Clash's *Give 'Em Enough Rope*. I had just been reading an article about the band in a music magazine and even without having heard any of their music, it piqued my interest. I honestly can't remember what else I chose from the list, but I sent off the form with my 99 cents and waited.

In due course, my little batch of new records arrived and I went straight to The Clash. I put the record on with curiosity but no expectation. Two bars into 'Safe

A PEOPLE'S HISTORY OF THE CLASH

European Home' my world changed forever. I had never heard an opening so emphatic, so powerfully raw, so connecting. The whole album left me stunned, enlivened, engaged.

Not long after, I was thrilled to see The Clash were coming to Australia, playing seven nights in Sydney on the *Magnificent Seven* tour. I managed to get a ticket for one of the nights and waited for the first international gig of my life.

In February 1982 I got the bus – on my own, as I didn't yet have the Clash-connected friends who came later – to the Capitol Theatre, a grand old venue in the heart of Sydney. I can still picture the scenes outside: the throng of people, the punks with their leather and rainbow mohawks. At one point the police swooped in and arrested a few random people seemingly for the crime of just being there – a show of force to keep the crowd under control.

Eventually I made it into the theatre and found my seat in the middle. The support band came and went, the tension built. All of a sudden, four figures took the stage and I remember wondering if it was really them, the band I now knew so well. The opening bass notes of 'London Calling' thundered through the air and I wondered no longer.

Joe Strummer once said The Clash had two types of gigs – the magnificent and the dreadful. Surely, this was one of the magnificent. The band powered through a deep and wide setlist from across their first four albums, highlighting the sheer range of their talents. An enduring highlight was the appearance of legendary Aboriginal activist Gary Foley during, as I recall, 'Armagideon Time', whose passionate call for land rights found a natural intersection with Strummer and The Clash's worldview. An enduring highlight in a gig that, to this day and hundreds of gigs later, remains the best I have seen.

More than 40 years on, my first hearing of The Clash is still one of the defining points of my life. It has influenced my musical directions, my friendships, my politics and beliefs since that day and even now – through friendships formed in Clash-centred social media groups – helps shape the person I am.

'KNOW YOUR RIGHTS'/'FIRST NIGHT BACK IN LONDON' RELEASED
23 APRIL 1982

IAN MOSS

Here we go… The most contradictory act of all time were The Clash. On one level, 'Know Your Rights' is simply glib hippy sloganeering about how bad 'the man' is, played in a punk-by-numbers style – pure populist posturing. On the other hand, Joe Strummer invests the song with all the deranged energy and passion of a true believer, so that it is imbued with spirit and is unquestionably exciting due to the adrenalised performance, to the point you find yourself dragged along, convinced of the sincerity being displayed.

COMBAT ROCK RELEASED
14 MAY 1982

PAUL CHEETHAM

It's May 1982, I'm 13 years old, bunking off school with three classmates and we're missing an apparently essential English exam. But we have much more important things to do. My mate's older brother has just got home with a copy of the newly-released *Combat Rock* album, and we must spend the whole afternoon listening to it. Over and over again. Not quite old enough for punk itself, we've played catch up on previous Clash releases and *Combat Rock* is the first album we get to absorb in real time. The jagged new wave, trippy dub-dipped fare is right up our post-punk street and the raw political messaging acts as genuine motivation for a gang of young northern teens increasingly needing savvy heroes to follow. It makes us feel different. It is the start of our first steps to becoming worldly wise and steadfast.

Back at school, we're in a world of trouble. We take it like men. It had all been worth it. We tell our English teacher the truth behind our absence. He immediately softens. He's a good one. He'd got us into The Police and The Jam during a school trip to Germany. He tells us to write a one-page review of the album by the end of the day. We do and he gives us an A for it and lets us off with the exam.

Years later, June 1999, and I'm a concert promoter living in Helsinki. We've brought Joe Strummer and the Mescaleros to headline the second stage at Provinssirock. The crowd is massive. Suede are headlining the main stage and refuse to go on until Joe has finished his set next door. So much is the respect for him. Joe plays on and on, and Suede go on late.

That night, we're at the after party. There's a group of people sitting in a circle on the lawn, under the midsummer midnight sun. Members of Suede, The Cardigans,

HIM and other assorted acts are mixed in with the crowd. And in the centre of it all is Joe Strummer. Sitting cross-legged, acoustic guitar in hand, playing around and telling stories to this impromptu audience.

For hours, everyone listened in awe, breathing in every word, every note, every last bit of the essence of the man.

 LOCHEM FESTIVAL
20 MAY 1982, LOCHEM, NETHERLANDS

LUUK VERSLUIJS

This was my fourth and final Clash show. Later I read it was also drummer Topper Headon's final show too. A few days after the festival he was sacked. The Clash were headliners at this annual festival in Lochem, a town in the east of the Netherlands. The year before there were 30,000 people attending and it had sold out. This year it was far from sold out. I guess at the most 10,000 people were there, despite the line-up of The Undertones, Bow Wow Wow, local band Normaal, Tenpole Tudor, Carlene Carter, Saxon and The Clash. The Pinkpop festival in the Netherlands that year also suffered from a drop in ticket sales compared to 1981.

The organiser of that festival blamed this on the three stadium shows The Rolling Stones were playing in Rotterdam early June. These shows were sold out and most people had not enough money to go to festivals in addition to going to The Rolling Stones, was his explanation. This explanation did not apply to me as I went to see The Rolling Stones two weeks after I saw The Clash!

I went to the Lochem Festival with a friend, in his car. It was two hours' drive from the city of Hoorn, where we lived. The weather was very bad. It rained most of the day and during The Clash's set there was a short thunderstorm. Joe Strummer invited the audience to come on stage and a lot of people knocked down the fences and climbed onto the stage. It was very chaotic, but the band kept playing with a few interruptions. They played a lot of songs from their new album *Combat Rock*, which I had bought a couple of days earlier. It was a great show and worth the long drive.

COMBAT ROCK US TOUR

CIVIC CENTER THEATRE
25 MAY 1982, EL PASO, TEXAS

ALFONSO QUIÑONEZ

I am from Juarez, Mexico, and grew up on the Mexican border, listening to American music as a kid; rock and roll, country, big band, jazz, blues, rock then soul, R&B, funk, pop, prog… and a little punk. But since we were down in the southwest, there wasn't much of a punk or reggae movement. New wave and eighties electronic music came by too.

   I was a student in a southern university in Guadalajara, México between 1980 and '83. Punk wasn't very popular there either. I came home on vacation and heard that The Clash were coming to play in El Paso, Texas. We crossed the border, bought the tickets, had some beers before the gig, smoked some pot, got into the concert and sat down and they started playing. It was the Combat Rock tour, and they played some popular songs like 'Rock The Casbah', 'Should I Stay Or Should I Go' and the rest of the album. At the end of the set some people started to invade the stage and throw themselves at the front rows. It was crazy. I was in the mezzanine upstairs, smoking a joint and watching the police trying to catch us smoking. They had a guitar guest, Jiménez from Austin, and he played some songs with them. It got wild.

CONVENTION HALL
29-31 MAY 1982, ASBURY PARK, NEW JERSEY

DAN BRUNING

I sat up front. During the gig some asshole threw an M80 firecracker right at Joe during 'Straight To Hell'. Many people thought it was staged because of the timing, but soon enough Joe just cursed, and they all walked off. They did return but he was obviously shaken and very pissed off. It had landed right next to him.

ANTHONY RAO

When The Clash played Asbury Park on Memorial Day in '82, me and my friends rented a limo. For a show without Topper, Joe later said it was one of the best shows they ever played without him. They didn't miss a beat.

JOHN SHIPLEY

The Clash were finally coming back to the States, kicking off their *Casbah Club* tour with three nights at the Convention Hall in Asbury Park, New Jersey over Memorial Day weekend. I bought two tickets for all three shows as my friends all now knew of my Clash mania and wanted to see 'The Only Band That Matters' with me.

After spending time on the 29th with my girlfriend (the same one I abandoned at a wedding reception in 1979 so I could go see The Clash that day), a friend and I drove 250 miles to Asbury Park to see The Clash and then 250 miles again afterwards, arriving home around 4am. I did the same on the next two days. At the end of that I was exhausted, but I would do it all over again today, at the age of 69, just to see them again.

BRONCO BOWL
6 JUNE 1982, DALLAS, TEXAS

DANNY EATON

I promoted a handful of shows for The Clash in Texas in 1982. I remember we did Dallas at the Bronco Bowl, El Paso, Wichita Falls and one other city. They were the first rock show at the Bronco Bowl, where hundreds of bands have since followed. Outside of picking them up at the airport, I didn't have much interaction with them.

When I picked them up at DFW Airport, Joe came up to me with eyes about as big as half dollars and almost yelled at me 'are you the promoter?' I said yes and before he even asked my name he said, 'Give me 20 dollars!' I complied. He took the 20 bucks and almost ran to the gift shop and bought a pack of cigs. It was long enough ago that I think he lit one up right there and finally got around to a 'thanks, man.' We had four killer shows with them. In El Paso, 'I Fought The Law' tore the place down. These guys deserve all the accolades they can get. They were the real deal!

'ROCK THE CASBAH'/'LONG TIME JERK' RELEASED
11 JUNE 1982

IAN MOSS

With music written in its entirety by Topper Headon, all that was needed was a lyric to match the tune's quality. Topper's original idea was dismissed out of hand as soppy and sentimental, which left Joe Strummer to disappear into the studio toilets to pen 'Rock The Casbah', inspired by the banning of Western music in Iran following the Islamic revolution. Topper's original track was piano-led and grooving. Guitars and bass were overlaid along with sound effects and Strummer sang in a playfully exaggerated fashion, the combination of which created perhaps the most pop radio-friendly single of The Clash's career.

DOWN AT THE CASBAH CLUB TOUR

BRIXTON FAIR DEAL
10 & 11 JULY 1982, LONDON

STEVE EVERETT

I saw The Clash five times in total, all in London. After Hammersmith Palais in 1980 I next saw them at Brixton Fair Deal in 1982. My then girlfriend, Mandy, begged me to take her American best friend, Jenny, who was visiting her for a holiday. She was small, being just over five foot tall, and adamant that she wanted to experience the full gig, mosh pit style, and despite my advice that apart from seeing nothing, she would get squashed. I reluctantly got two downstairs standing tickets.

It was a hot summer evening to add to a heavy crowd but we managed to get central and front stage. After the Drummers of Burundi supported, the boys came on to an Ennio Morricone track and launched straight into 'White Riot'. Cue absolute bedlam! I looked to my left and Jenny was upright but unconscious. I dragged her to the side, near the ladies' toilets, where I saw a security guard and said I had no idea who this woman was and that I had just brought her out for her own safety. I left her there. I wasn't going to miss a moment for her…

It was the most frantic gig of my life, and how I lasted the full two hours I don't know. I guess I was 19 and fit. I found Jenny once the crowd begin to drift away. She was okay, as a couple of girls had looked after her, and she had a story to take back home to the States!

42 years later, still the only band that matters!

CITY HALL
14 & 15 JULY 1982, NEWCASTLE-UPON-TYNE

DAVE PRATT

The Casbah Club tour in Newcastle would be the last time I saw this incredible band.

They opened the show with 'London Calling' and played a blistering set including songs from all four albums; 'Clash City Rockers', '(White Man) In Hammersmith Palais', 'Safe European Home', 'Guns of Brixton', 'Stay Free', 'Bankrobber', 'Complete Control' and 'Career Opportunities' all featured that night. These days, Strummer and Co are referred to as 'the only band that matters'. I can't say that I wholeheartedly agree with this statement, but if someone was to ask which bands they should listen to gain an insight into this brilliant musical era, The Clash would be at the top of the list.

A PEOPLE'S HISTORY OF THE CLASH

PETER SMITH

The Clash returned to Newcastle in 1982 to play two nights at the City Hall and by this time they were starting to disintegrate. Topper had left to be replaced by Terry Chimes, and it was the beginning of the end for the band. *Combat Rock* had just been released and although my ticket shows the gig as having taken place in May 1982, all the gig listings show the gig as being in July 1982. I guess the tour must have been rescheduled. A group of us went along to the gig and we were sitting close to the front. It was a shame to see that the venue was by no means full and the gig was not on the same level as earlier Clash gigs I'd seen. This was the last time I saw The Clash.

ST GEORGE'S HALL
17 JULY 1982, BRADFORD

JOHN YOUENS

St Georges Hall was good. For the *Casbah Club* tour they weren't playing massive shows. Topper had been sacked by then. It was a standing venue so quite chaotic. I was only about five feet tall and surrounded by big old hardcore punks. It was exciting and quite terrifying at the same time.

Southern Death Cult supported and were unbelievably just wild. They had Ian Astbury dressed in his Native American outfit with a massive headdress on, jumping around the stage. It was great.

I was a huge fan of *Combat Rock*; I absolutely loved it. I was decorating my school textbooks with iconography from the tour. The famous 'Know Your Rights' red star and the pistol, the coat of arms, all that stuff. Obviously, something was lacking because they didn't have Topper. You could tell it didn't sound quite as good. Topper was just a superb drummer, and it was sad what happened to him. In a modern set up, they would probably just take a couple of years out and got him back to health. I think The Clash felt that if they stopped, they wouldn't have achieved anything. Topper was a casualty of that. He was ill and he needed looking after. Regardless, it was a great show.

MALCOLM HOPWOOD

Me, my twin brother Graham and our best schoolmate Andrew set off to see The Clash at St George's Hall in Bradford. The venue was the ideal size to attract the names of the time in an intimate venue, including The Undertones, Stiff Little Fingers, XTC, Ian Dury, Elvis Costello, The Teardrop Explodes, the Pretenders and even the Kinks. The venue had been close enough for our parents to come and pick us up but we were now 18 years old and I could now drive, which gave us a bit more leeway on getting back from gigs. The Clash's final album as the original four-piece, *Combat Rock*, had just been released so we had some new material to hear.

They opened with 'London Calling' and the atmosphere was electric from the start. The gig was brilliant and was up there with the previous year's Bridlington gig. We were treated to long encores again, although not quite the 55 minutes of our first taste of The Clash live.

After the gig we were determined to meet the band. We'd brought our *Combat Rock* albums in the car to be signed. By the time we got back from picking up our albums the backstage doors were just opening. There must have been only 15 to 20 of us diehard fans there when Joe Strummer and Mick Jones invited us into the dressing room. There were a few cases of Heineken cans on a table and Joe told us to help ourselves. They were so on a level with their fans. There were no airs and graces. They just wanted to chat with us about the gig and about the new album. It was my first close-up face-to-face with my heroes and they just seemed so ordinary, which made it even better and put three nervous teenagers immediately at ease. There was no Topper Headon as I think he was doing a stint in rehab, so we had Terry Chimes (Tory Crimes) on drums, the former Generation X drummer.

I still have my signed copy of *Combat Rock* with all four signatures, plus all four also signed the free poster inside which was included in the first press of the album. I had it valued recently at an auction house. The music expert said it was more valuable with Terry Chimes' signature as that would be quite a rarity. I was moving to Spain in 2021, and I'd decided with a heavy heart to auction off my vinyl collection. *Combat Rock* went in a separate lot with a reserve of £350. Thankfully, it only reached £320 in the bidding, so I was very happy to bring it with me to Spain. I won't part with it now.

DE MONTFORT HALL
20 JULY 1982, LEICESTER

PANOS PAPAS

Aged 15 in 1977, I used to listen to *Your Mother Wouldn't Like It* on Capital Radio with presenter Nicky Horne. I'd heard about punk rock from the news and the Grundy interview but the first punk I heard was when Nicky Horne played The Stranglers on his show.

I'd become interested in left wing politics, taking part in anti-National Front marches. The lyrics of punk songs interested me as well. Over the coming year I listened to all the punk bands on the radio, but The Clash weren't one of them.

A PEOPLE'S HISTORY OF THE CLASH

I'd heard of them but never heard their music until April 1978. I persuaded my mum to let me leave a family Greek Easter gathering to go to Rock Against Racism. I arrived late. Tom Robinson was performing 'Winter of '79'. There was an encore where members of different bands who had already appeared performed a song. The refrain was 'Black White together Unite'. Some members of The Clash were on stage and that was my introduction to them.

For Christmas 1978 I got *Give 'Em Enough Rope* which changed my way of thinking completely. I became focused entirely on punk music and listened to nothing else. Their political message meant a lot to me and when I got the self-titled debut album a few months later, I was amazed how brilliant it was. I adopted a punk image – skinhead haircut, Doc Martens, biker jacket. I even bought bondage trousers. However, deep down I knew I was too middle class to be a punk, much as I loved the music and attitude.

I started going to gigs like The Damned, Angelic Upstarts, Stiff Little Fingers and XTC, but didn't get a chance to see The Clash until 1982. By then I was a student in Leicester and had given up trying to look like a punk, but was still enjoying the music. The University had a great gig circuit. Bands were on all the time, either at the University itself or the Polytechnic or De Montford Hall. I saw pretty much every punk band that visited Leicester. I also met my future wife Caroline there and we went to all these gigs together.

Panos Papas (above) was at Leicester's De Montfort Hall in 1982 and made a note of the setlist in his diary (below)

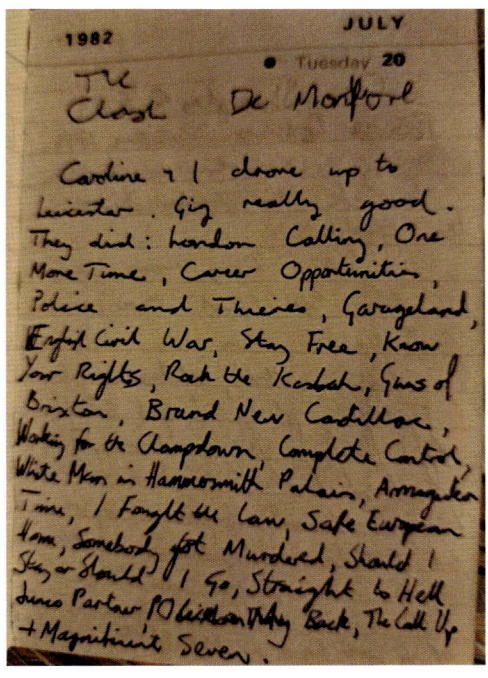

ALL THE YOUNG PUNKS

When the Clash date was announced for May 1982, I was 20 years old. Caroline was 22. I got us a pair of tickets. Then about two weeks before the gig Joe Strummer went missing. No one knew where he was or if the gig would take place. Thankfully, next thing we heard he'd turned up and the gig was rescheduled, though it was now a date after the end of term when we'd be back in London. No way was I going to miss seeing my favourite band, so Caroline and I drove up to Leicester on the day of the gig.

The Clash were superb. Joe Strummer with his Mohican haircut but wider, like Travis in *Taxi Driver*, a film referenced on the Combat Rock album. The stage had backdrops with projections of urban scenes riots and police. 'Know Your Rights' got everyone jumping up and down. I was pleased the audience were keen on the new material as it was now five years since the first album. All the music was brilliant. We got near the front to be part of the dancing. It was all good natured from the audience too. I remember someone in the crowd shouting 'Broadway', a song from *Sandinista!* and thinking no chance they would ever play that. I was right, but I thought it was cool to call out a less obvious song than say 'White Riot' or 'London's Burning'.

We had a brilliant evening and I'm so glad we went because a year later they split up and I never got another chance to see them perform.

POOLE ARTS CENTRE
27 JULY 1982, POOLE

JOHN MITCHELL

After living in Birmingham and seeing the band at the Top Rank my parents moved south. I made a new friend there who had a spare ticket to see The Clash at Poole Arts Centre. They came on stage and the first song was 'White Riot' and then 'Safe European Home' and '(White Man) In Hammersmith Palais' followed. By the time they played 'Complete Control', the place went absolutely fucking mental. They played a lot of stuff from *Combat Rock*, like 'Car Jamming' and 'Straight To Hell'. It was an amazing concert, even with Terry drumming rather than Topper. I think Terry is very underrated. I thought he had the perfect tone for the first album. The sound obviously expanded with Topper, but listen to some of those shows from 1982, particularly the Boston shows from later in the year.

After the Poole gig we went backstage to meet The Clash. I always say they broke up because of me. Paul and Terry were absolutely charming, signing everything, speaking to everybody. Then I found myself, 18 years old, with Strummer on one side and Mick on the other. I'm literally in a triangle with them. All I wanted to say was 'please hold it together', but being 18 years old, I didn't say anything and they just stared daggers at each other. And so this stupid 18-year-old doesn't say anything much, just 'can I have your autograph please?'

MARK GRIFFITHS, AGE 17

17 years old, I went down on the train from Southampton with my mate Peakey and a few special brews. We did enjoy a glass or two of malted beverage, the effects of which were magnified by the movement of the floating floor

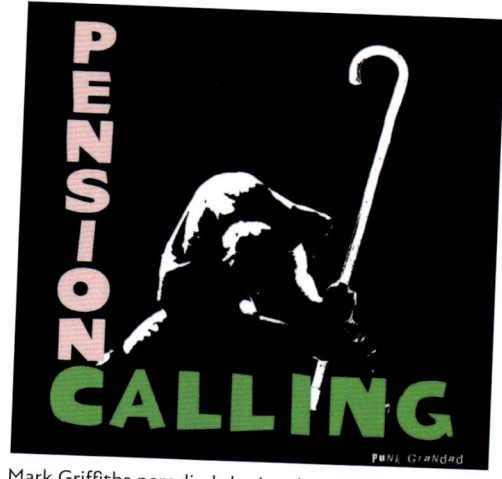

Mark Griffiths parodied the *London Calling* cover for a t-shirt design

in the venue! My favourite song back in the day was 'Clash City Rockers'. I later fell in love with the *London Calling* album. When I got old I had a t-shirt company with a mate for a while called Punk Grandad.

BRIXTON FAIR DEAL
30 JULY 1982, LONDON

GERRY DALY

The summer of '82 brought the band to Hanley Victoria Hall (a strange gig with no bar, just a table selling chocolate bars like a youth club) and to what is now Brixton Academy. In 1982 it was called The Fair Deal but the people selling the beer clearly didn't get the memo. £1.30 for a pint was astronomical at that time and Joe nearly got the 'White Riot' he'd wanted five years earlier. That was one song they never seemed to play any more so when they started the last night at Brixton with it, I dashed down to the front, probably spilling half my premium-priced lager. Nobody had any idea that this was turn out to be Mick's last London gig.

PETE STEVENS

The summer of 1982 was an incredible period in my life. You only leave home once and that's what I did on 11th July 1982, arriving in Kensington, London in the afternoon sunshine, leaving my hometown of Chester for good. My first impression? London looked really nice.

Some may recall this day as that of the FIFA World Cup Final between Italy and West Germany – 3-1 to Italy in case you're interested – but I had more pressing things on my mind. This was when Joe Strummer went 'missing' prior to the *Casbah*

Club tour, disappearing to Paris on the boat train on 21st April. The original May dates for the UK tour, including the two Brixton gigs, were delayed until July. This was fortunate for me, because in May and June I was still sitting my 'A' Levels and waiting for the Falklands War to finish…

I'd followed the news of Joe's disappearance in the weekly music papers and by the time I arrived in London, the dates had been rescheduled after he'd reappeared, the second night at the Brixton Fair Deal being 11th July.

> ## AN EVEN BIGGER SHOCK WAS TOPPER'S SACKING…
> **PETE STEVENS**

An even bigger shock to many fans was Topper's sacking and the return of Terry Chimes. Reports said that Topper Headon had quit the band over 'political differences' or 'musical differences'. At the time I was blissfully unaware of Topper's drug addiction, but in hindsight I can understand why they couldn't carry on with him behind the kit. It was something they'd all later regret, as we've witnessed in numerous documentaries since about the eventual demise of the band. Whether Terry was chosen for his innate drumming skills or as a matter of expediency, he was certainly familiar with their early back catalogue and a damn fine sticksman.

The Fair Deal was turned into a live music venue in 1981, albeit briefly, as it closed again at the end of 1982. (It would later become very successful as the Brixton Academy.) Brixton in 1981 and 1982 wasn't like it is today. Riots in the previous April and the Clash song 'Guns Of Brixton' had given it an edge and an air of danger, especially for a skinny white eighteen-year-old kid from up north.

By contrast with the very cold Deeside Leisure Centre gig I'd seen in January 1980, the Brixton Fair Deal gig on 11th July was incredibly hot and the additional 30th July gig an absolute scorcher. I was now working in Hammersmith and had travelled down to the Fair Deal box office as soon as this extra gig was announced. I had a fiver in my cheap grey suit pocket, enough for the gig ticket (£4). I recklessly spent a further £1 on a full-size gig poster – the 'Join Pimps, Punk, Hustlers, etc.' in red… Originals of this poster now go for thousands at auction, but I managed to misplace mine within a couple of months when moving to a squat above The Elgin's pool room on Ladbroke Grove/Westbourne Park Road.

A PEOPLE'S HISTORY OF THE CLASH

Some gigs you remember, some you don't, but some etch themselves indelibly on your mind that you can recall in minute detail the whole experience. The Clash at The Fair Deal, Brixton on 30th July 1982 was one of those gigs…

I left work in Hammersmith at lunchtime to get to the venue really early. I wanted to try and get in for free, somehow acquire a backstage pass and re-sell my ticket. Naive? Yes, but it had worked at a 999 gig at the Lyceum the previous week, where Tenpole Tudor were supporting and I'd got chatting to the complete madman that is Ed Tudorpole. We'd sat around in an empty Lyceum drinking tea (very rock 'n' roll, eh?) and I'd found out that they might be supporting The Clash. Potentially this was my way in. When I arrived outside the venue, I could physically feel the music through my feet. The iconic bassline of 'One More Time' was vibrating through the paving slabs into my soles and my soul. Some serious bass from Mr Simonon and I stood stock still, just soaking it up. The soundcheck over, I decided to go to the stage door and wait.

There were comings and goings, but no sign of the band. Kosmo Vinyl and Ray Jordan were both there and Ed Tudorpole arrived about an hour later; his rumoured support slot had obviously been confirmed. He remembered me from the Lyceum and I asked if I could get in with him on the list. It turned out that he wasn't on the list and it required a significant amount of pleading for him to be admitted. Standing just behind Ed, attempting to appear like an indispensable best mate or a vitally important personal assistant, I glanced at Ray Jordan and he shot me that very calm, slightly smiling look, that said, 'Nope, you're not coming in this way son, not tonight.' I've since met Ray many years later and he's always had that calm demeanour about him. Security without any aggression or menace.

For me then it was Plan B. Get in first and bag a space centre stage right in front of Joe, which is what I did as soon as the doors opened. Gigs like the Fair Deal had no pit, no secondary barrier, no 'golden circle', no exclusive access, no backstage official meet 'n' greet. You paid your (in this case) four quid and got entry to the building. After that it was a free-for-all. I did get that all important spot centre stage and, being six foot tall, could get my arms comfortably on the stage for some stability. Tenpole Tudor did an absolutely spectacular, wild support slot, and when they'd finished the venue was getting seriously hot, loud and crowded. It was all going on behind me, the crowd surging around, forward, backward, left and right. The only crowd comparison I can make is The Kop at Anfield; but Liverpool was never this hot!

I wasn't wearing a watch and neither were any of the others in the crowd with whom I'd been sharing spliffs, passed along what was the front row, so when the lights dimmed and the strains of Ennio Morricone's theme from *For A Few Dollars More* came through the PA, we knew The Clash were only moments away… Time didn't matter. What we were about to witness did, seeing Joe walk up to the microphone right in front of me, say, 'Good evening, welcome!' and Mick, Dee Dee Ramone-style, shout 'one, two, three, four!' and then straight into a screaming version of 'White Riot'.

The place went absolutely ballistic and I clung to the front edge of the stage as the whole crowd turned into a riotous, seething mass behind me; beer, cans, drinks and clothing flying around. By now the venue was way beyond capacity – later estimates put it at over 6,000 (official capacity 4,500) and most of them seemed completely mad. There was an intensity from the band and the crowd that night, perhaps from being in that venue, that I've never experienced anywhere else. The atmosphere was absolutely electric, the volume incredible, the heat intense, with sweat dripping from the ceiling. To this day, people who were at this particular gig just *know*. The press had frequently given The Clash a hard time, but this gig just showed that they were still the greatest live band in the world, with a breadth of material second to none and all in less than six years.

It turned out to be Mick Jones' last gig with the band in London and a year later he would be fired from his own group. The pressure became too much for a group with this much intensity. That they made it as far as they did genuinely still amazes me. At the time I was absolutely devastated, because I'd only been able to see it from a fan's point of view and had no inkling of the internal politics and power struggles within, or of Topper's addiction problems. I'm also very glad that they didn't reform. Mick was miles down his musical track when BAD began touring a couple of years later – always moving forward.

I did see The Clash Mk II about six times in Brixton in 1984 at the five March dates and then finally at one of *Scargill's Christmas Parties*. They were a great live band, very polished, with an amazing catalogue from which to choose a setlist, but they were missing what today would be known as (excuse me please) the 'X Factor'. There were some new songs and this was many months before *Cut The Crap* was released – essentially

> **IT TURNED OUT TO BE MICK'S LAST GIG WITH THE GROUP…**
>
> PETE STEVENS

a Bernie Rhodes murder victim. Nick, Vince and Pete really were on a hiding to nothing and all but erased from the album's final mix.

I was very lucky to see all three Clash line-ups, albeit with Terry in the *Combat Rock* era. I was even luckier that Joe gave me his 'Strumguard' at the end of this 30th July gig, just as it was falling off his arm, a cut up piece of towel which was always gaffa-taped to Joe's right forearm to prevent him shredding said forearm on his trusty, battered, old Telecaster. A great souvenir! One very strange memory is reaching forward tapping Joe on top of his black Doc Marten boot to alert him to the fact his boot lace was undone. The most touching experience came years later, when I was personally delivering some of my *Strummer Of Love* photographic books to Joe's widow Luce at Yalway Farm in Somerset. I sat around his kitchen table chatting with her; quite surreal. We even walked down to his stone circle at the end of the garden.

Mick and I became friends many years later, after I did a self-published book on Carbon/Silicon, then photographed his various rock 'n' roll public libraries. I was regularly invited up to his studio/bunker in Acton to photograph private gigs there and met some of his heroes and many of his close friends. I'd also supply a photo I took of him for the top of his birthday cake one year. Life is strange indeed!

THE LOCARNO
3 AUGUST 1982, BRISTOL

JOHN BRITTON

My introduction to The Clash as a thirteen-year-old was in the summer of 1977.

My then future brother-in-law lent me what was a state-of-the-art stereo tape player with two cassette tapes, *In The City* by The Jam and the eponymous debut LP from The Clash. I have loved both bands ever since.

One of my favourite gigs around that time must be The Clash at Bristol Locarno on a hot night in August 1982. The atmosphere in the room was highly charged and the anticipation, for what would be Mick Jones' last UK gig with the band, was high. The support sticks in my mind, a Sikh guy called Peter Singh - AKA The Rocking Sikh - resplendent in a jumpsuit like Elvis wore in his later years.

Keith Allen was on stage at some point. I can't remember what for, possibly introducing The Clash or doing a stand up routine? What I do remember is the crowd erupting when Joe, Mick, Paul and Topper's replacement, Terry Chimes, walked on stage. Two things really stand out in my memory, the band leaving the stage for what seemed like an eternity after Mick remonstrated with some people at the front for spitting at him, and Joe Strummer throwing his guitar some fifteen feet to a roadie who plucked it out of the air with perfect precision. Nights like that are just pure adrenaline rushes for both band and audience. Halcyon days.

KNOW YOUR RIGHTS TOUR

PENN RINK
26 & 27 AUGUST 1982, PHILADELPHIA, PENNSYLVANIA

SHEVA GOLKOW

Man, what a wonderful show! I was smack in the middle of following Elvis Costello's 1982 tour; much as I loved each night, there wasn't much loud fast music going on. A Clash show was just what I needed, and since Elvis had no show that night, my friend Cynthia and I took a little break and went from The Imperial Bedroom to Garageland. Boy, did they deliver the goods. They blasted into the first song and blew my glasses right off my face! But no worries, thanks to the wonderful Philly punk crowd, who created a protective circle around me so I could find them. Glasses firmly in place, we all resumed dancing and going mad for Joe and the rest of that fantastic band we loved so much. What a joy!

JOHN SHIPLEY

I got solo tickets for the two shows at Penn Rink. It was just tremendous to see them again and I was fascinated by how great they were every time they played. My ride from my house to Philly each night was only about an hour and a half. I played my Clash cassettes on my ride home, as you can never have enough Clash.

PIER 84, HUDSON RIVER PARK
31 AUGUST–2 SEPTEMBER 1982, NEW YORK

ANTHONY RAO

When they played The Pier in NYC, we went every night. Curtis Blow and Gregory Isaacs opened those shows. On the last night, it started pouring and they ended with 'White Riot' in the rain. The harder it rained, the harder they played. These were the greatest shows I ever saw in my life.

   I went on to see BAD so many times and Joe as well, plus Havana 3am. One time in NYC, I got to meet Joe and Mick, and I tell you they were the humblest guys. I never felt starstruck. Joe was the reason I picked up a guitar and started a band and because of The Clash and their DIY attitude I never did covers – all originals, warts and all. I've seen a lot of bands but when The Clash came to NYC it was always an event!

A PEOPLE'S HISTORY OF THE CLASH

JEFFREY DIAMOND

Trying to pinpoint your favourite Clash gig is like trying to pick your favourite kid or pick your most-liked pizza topping. For those of us old enough to have been present at even one Clash gig makes the current grey hair and sore joints in the morning worth it!

Circa 1980, I was straddling the two worlds of prog rock and punk. The previous few years saw my Roger Dean wall posters being replaced by *In The City* and *London Calling* wall art. My Peter Gabriel records were then in rotation with the *Gates Of The West* EP. While I missed out on the earlier tours, I still consider myself so lucky to be there at the end.

How to choose? I was there when The Clash opened for The Who at Shea Stadium. A lifelong NY Mets fan, seeing the juxtaposition of my favourite bands at my most beloved sports venue was a dream! The Mets were awful in the late seventies and early eighties and, appropriately enough, the ushers who worked that gig were about that same age, in their late seventies and early eighties! Even though our seats were in the upper 100 section, it was no problem joining a gang of rowdy, young, enthusiastic fans storming the field past the ushers to get closer to the stage. You can see me on the official video of 'Should I Stay Or Should I Go', about tenth row centre left. This was an amazing gig that later had me about 100 feet from the legendary Pete Townshend, but it is not my favourite Clash concert.

I saw The Clash at Asbury Park Convention Hall, on the Jersey shore. Another great gig, except some moron threw a cherry bomb at the stage. I remember confronting the guy I thought threw it after the show, not realising until I started yelling at him that 1) I had no idea if it was the guy, and 2) he stood about seven feet tall and was built like a brick wall. Luckily my friend whisked me away before I lost some teeth.

My most memorable and insane Clash gig must be the one in NYC at the Navy Pier. An outdoor venue under the stars, the concert area was set up literally in the shadow of the USS Intrepid warship, at anchor just 100 yards away. To see bands there singing about anarchy and punk rock while backdropped against this massive machine of naval power was always so surreal.

The area for the fans was just a long slab of concrete, so when bands played, the concert organisers set up rows and rows of folding metal chairs, the kind meant for parent-teacher meetings or marching band practice. From the opening chords of 'London Calling', we all started pogoing on these chairs, and every one of them caved in in the middle, forcing us to stand balanced on the left and right edges of the chairs.

The Clash played with such intensity, but for some reason that night seemed extra charged. To their credit, they always dipped back into their early album gems, so songs from *Combat Rock* were bracketed by songs like 'Janie Jones' or 'English Civil War'. As the show progressed, a severe thunderstorm was coming fast. The sky was lit up with lightning flashes that dwarfed the light show onstage. This must have added to the urgency as the band sped through 'Brand New Cadillac'. Rain was

> **IT'S THE SINGLE MOST MEMORABLE MOMENT BY ANY BAND I'VE EVER SEEN...**
>
> **JEFFREY DIAMOND**

sheeting down from the skies, the audience was soaked through, and still the band played on through '(White Man) In Hammersmith Palais'. The rain was coming down horizontally, and the band were as wet as we were. The lightning strikes were now so close the thundering boom of the thunder might as well have been the cannon fire coming from the Intrepid!

I remember seeing Joe saying something to Mick, to Paul, and over to Terry. Without a break between songs, they launched into the most frantic, energetic live version of 'White Riot'. It remains the singular most memorable moment by any band I've ever seen. The four horsemen on a stage being washed away in a storm of biblical intensity, thrashing out the chords and Joe screaming out. They exited the stage for their lives as the last chords were still echoing in our ears.

In the years that followed, out of loyalty I hung in there for Big Audio Dynamite. Out of love for Joe, I kept up with the Mescaleros. I was fortunate to see Joe also play with the Pogues but there was no band like The Clash, and no four-man live act that could do what they did on a stage.

And when I see another grey hair, at least I can say I saw The Clash.

KEN FRENCH

I saw The Clash live three times. Twice in 1982 (Pier 84 in NYC in September and Shea Stadium in October) and post-Mick at Rutgers University in New Jersey in 1984. The Pier 84 show was the best of the three.

I became a fan of The Clash in early 1980, shortly after *London Calling* came out in the US. I was a senior in high school and a classmate of mine, thinking I would like it, made me a tape of his copy. I hadn't paid much attention to punk prior to then, but hearing The Clash changed my life. I bought my own copy of *London Calling* right away and got both the first album and *Give 'Em Enough Rope* shortly after.

I really wanted to see one of the Bonds shows in the summer on 1981, but unfortunately, I got very sick that month and was even hospitalised for a week, so I was in no shape to attend. I still regret it because I never got to see the band with Topper.

I attended many shows at Pier 84 in the eighties and knew the venue well. I decided to go to the stands that were adjacent to the stage rather than in the

Ken French saw The Clash three times in total

crowd in front because I figured I'd have a better view and wouldn't get crushed! As you might have heard, it started raining during the show. I have to say, seeing Joe Strummer putting on an amazing performance while being pelted by rain convinced me that he is the greatest frontman ever. That image will stay with me my whole life.

The second time I saw them was just a month later, opening for The Who at Shea Stadium. I was quite a bit further from the stage. The Clash put on a great, high-energy show. I was there to see them more than The Who (nothing against The Who), as were many others in the crowd, and they performed as if they were the headliners.

The last time I saw them was in April 1984 at Rutgers University in New Jersey, where I was a student. I had friends on the concert programming committee, so I got in early and was very close to the stage. This was post-Mick and the energy was different. Joe and Paul were still great, but the band had lost some of its edge to me. The low point of the show was when one of the new guys sang 'Police On My Back'. I know it's a cover, but it just seemed wrong having one of the new guys sing a song that Mick had sung on *Sandinista!*

⭐ CNE EXHIBITION STADIUM
5 SEPTEMBER 1982, TORONTO, CANADA

IVAR HAMILTON

This was the biggest date on the North American tour prior to the band joining The Who later that month. Over 20,000 attended the Exhibition Stadium to see

The Clash and Black Uhuru close out the summer in Toronto. With *Combat Rock* wildly successful, 'Rock the Casbah' was all over the radio as well as 'Should I Stay Or Should I Go'. Simultaneously the opening act, Black Uhuru, had also begun to break through and were arguably the biggest reggae act.

The Clash's original following had never gone away and had grown in leaps and bounds since their visits in 1979. For probably 90 per cent of the attendees, this would be their first time seeing The Clash. Toronto had a reputation in the 1980s, whereby many of the UK alternative acts were far bigger than anywhere else in North America. New Order, Simple Minds, OMD and The Stranglers had graduated from clubs to major concert halls and arenas. It was the same for The Clash, only bigger! Once again, the band did not disappoint.

In 1987, I interviewed Joe when he was in Toronto, filling in for Shane MacGowan playing with The Pogues at the Palais Royale. Despite the immensity of that CNE show, he couldn't remember anything about it! To me the CNE show was when punk and second-generation reggae came of age and broke through to the mainstream in Toronto.

Beyond The Clash, I made a point to see Joe Strummer and the Mescaleros every time they came back to Toronto and met Joe a couple more times. I was always grateful for his kindness.

In 2019, I was invited to sit on a panel at an event at the Rivoli Tavern commemorating The Clash in Toronto hosted by Nick Smash. We each told our Clash stories, but the main attraction was the playback of the full unedited interview I did with Joe in 1987.

After he passed, I was able to hear some of the magic audio engineer and Grammy winner, the late Peter Moore, was able to put together on the Strummer box sets which he had worked on.

As I sit here in 2024, I proudly have a 1979 US Clash tour poster hanging in my house and continue to play the band on my 'Teardown' radio show on nythespirit.com that I have hosted for the past decade.

NEIL HUNTER

I was 17 and living in a small town north of Toronto, Canada. I didn't have much of a record collection, money always being a bit tight, and the radio played disco and the pop songs of the day. I liked music and was in the school band but there was nothing that felt like it was my music. I first heard The Clash in a friend's car. He had made a mixed tape of various bands and when I heard '(White Man) In Hammersmith Palais' it sounded different than anything else I had heard. Something in it resonated with me. The lyric, Joe's voice, the rhythm.

On my next trip to town, I went to the record store and found there were a couple of Clash records out. It wasn't really surprising I didn't know that. There was no internet or 24-hour music video channel back then. There was a show that played videos late Friday night but we could only get that channel if the weather cooperated and even then it was really fuzzy. But that's where my friends and I got our first glimpse of The Clash, playing 'Tommy Gun'. I bought their first two albums (the *Clash* album I had was the North American release with 'White Man' on it), got home and heard them for the first time. That was the music that woke something in me. I felt it in my soul, it meant something. It was so different from anything I had heard before.

I started looking for articles on the band in book shops. I'd stay and flip through any music magazines I could find until the store owner kicked me out. Then came *London Calling*. I couldn't understand why The Clash weren't everyone's favourite band.

I started going to live shows – local bands like Teenage Head and the Forgotten Rebels but also the Ramones and the Dead Kennedys – but there were no Clash shows. I had missed their 1979 stop in Toronto but did go to the Heatwave Festival where they were supposed to play but ended up cancelling, the news reaching the crowd as Elvis Costello and The Attractions came out on stage and said they were The Clash. *Sandinista!* came out but no Toronto shows. I would have made the trip to New York for the Bond's shows as daunting as that seemed at the time, but didn't hear about them until they were over.

Some friends and I formed a band and played a few parties. I learned some chords and bought a Telecaster because that's what Joe played. We hung out at my friend's basement practising and writing our own songs, and we got drunk watching a bootleg copy of *Rude Boy*.

Combat Rock was released and finally a date to play in Toronto was announced. I was in college by now and so excited to finally see this band that meant so much to me. Why did The Clash mean more to me than any other group? I listened to their music, wore their t-shirts (ok, I only had one) and flipped my collar up like a true rebel youth. It gave me the courage to look at the world around me, ask why things were the way they were, to question authority; basically to start to think for myself and not be afraid if what I thought wasn't the same as everyone else. They helped me grow up.

There was a bit of turmoil before the show with Joe disappearing and a suggestion the show would get cancelled. That seemed like my kind of luck but it was resolved. Myself and three friends drove the hour and a half to Toronto and spent the day at the CNE (Canadian National Exhibition) but the midway rides and carnival atmosphere couldn't match my excitement at finally getting to see The Clash.

We were seated in Row 37 in the Grandstand, looking down on a distant Black Uhuru on the same stage The Clash would soon be on. (How far away were we? I don't think I had heard of Topper leaving the band until I read it as part of the concert review the next day.) I knew I could not stay so far away from the stage, and that we would have to get to the front. The Grandstand was an open-air stadium, designed for football and baseball games, and there were all kinds of barriers, obstacles, security guards and literally several thousand people in my way if I was going to make it to the stage. But this was The Clash and I had every intention of getting as close as I could.

> **JOE DISAPPEARED AND THEY THREATENED TO CANCEL THE SHOW…**
>
> NEIL HUNTER

As the first chords of 'London Calling' rang out we were on our feet running down the Grandstand steps two or three at a time. The four of us vaulted over the railing and then jumped over another to get to the floor. I looked down going over one of these railings and saw a perilous drop of concrete stairs going to some subterranean secret. Had I slipped or misjudged the distance, it would have been a trip to the hospital if not worse. But we were all on the floor now and kept pushing forward. The crowd were on their feet but not too tightly packed in and people kindly let us slip by them.

By the time 'Know Your Rights' started I was three people from the stage. (I saw my head in the photo of the concert in the paper the next morning!)

The crowd was swaying and jumping up and down and my feet were barely on the ground. There I was in front of Joe. Then there'd be a big crowd surge and I'd be in front of Paul. Then back to Joe, and on and on for over half an hour.

It was intense, it was loud, it was crushing and exciting and everything. But it wasn't violent. If someone fell, they got helped to their feet. There was no pushing and shoving outside of the mass of people sardined together at the front, all trying to stay on their feet. All eyes were on the band.

Later on, we extracted ourselves from the front and found some space in front of the sound booth. The band sounded great. On the ground were flyers from people wanting to start a community farm (which I thought at the time a very weird thing to have at a Clash show). It was a fairly long show but it was timeless too. It seemed like it would never end and then it did. 'White Riot' faded out, replaced by the sounds of the midway rides just outside the Grandstand.

On April 30, 1984 I saw The Clash for the second time, the Mark II version at Maple Leaf Gardens in Toronto. I didn't know what to expect but it was still exciting. We couldn't get any closer than our appointed seats but the band sounded great (sorry Mick). The energy and intensity were still there but it was definitely a different group. It was clear the album lacked Mick's talents and I felt a void in the music coming out for years after they broke up.

'STRAIGHT TO HELL'/'SHOULD I STAY OR SHOULD I GO' RELEASED
17 SEPTEMBER 1982

ANA MARIA NAZARIO

Darling, you got to let me know. Should I stay or should I go?

This was the song that got me into The Clash. That iconic intro, and then 'Hola!'

As a teenager living in the Philippines, my reaction when I first heard this piece of music was, 'OH, MY GOD! Did they just shout 'Hola'?' Most music fans when they hear The Clash, immediately think of Joe Strummer. Mine's that video of Mick Jones in red overalls singing, with Joe Strummer doing the second voice in Spanish! WHOA! Talk about game changer!

You see, I was never a punk. I remember hearing the Sex Pistols' 'Anarchy In The UK' for the first time, and thinking 'this is an angry song'. Cool! But many teens in the Philippines, including myself, were new wavers. We liked the softer, more romantic side of music. The Clash's 'Should I Stay Or Should I Go' has an angry feel to it, but with lyrics like 'If you say that you are mine, I'll be here 'til the end of time' appealed to my teenage hopeless romantic self.

In the Philippines in the eighties, teenagers used to have this book we passed around to our friends called 'Slam Book'. Apart from basic questions like your name, your favourites, your likes and dislikes, it also had pages where the owner of the book put a collection of song titles, and you'd reply by putting names of people you'd like to dedicate these songs to. Most of these songs were mainly love songs, to be honest, but I remember answering a slam book where it had 'Should I Stay Or Should I Go' as one of the songs listed on it. I thought 'this has got to be the coolest slam book ever.' But I can't remember now who I dedicated the song to. There were at least two boys in my school who were giving me mixed signals.

Sadly, growing up in the Philippines, I never got to see The Clash live. But now that I live in Manchester, I'm hopeful that someday I'll get to see and hear Mick Jones sing 'Should I Stay Or Should I Go' live on stage. I'll keep my fingers (and toes) crossed for it.

All together now… This indecision's bugging me!

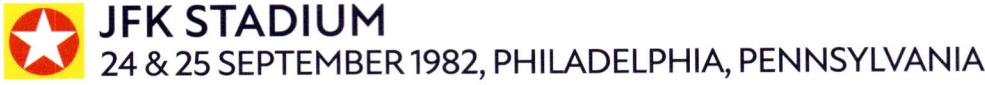
JFK STADIUM
24 & 25 SEPTEMBER 1982, PHILADELPHIA, PENNSYLVANIA

DAVID PERKIN, AGE 13
I saw The Clash opening for The Who in 1982 in Philly and the show changed my life. I was a big fan of The Who, but I had just become exposed to The Clash. Sadly, it was towards the end of the road for them, but the fact that I got to see Joe Strummer in the flesh wasn't lost on me. They were the first band I was really exposed to where they could move you musically as well as have something to say.

RICH STADIUM
26 SEPTEMBER 1982, BUFFALO, NEW YORK

ROSS MUNRO
Growing up in the snowy climes of Winnipeg, Canada (cold temperatures in the winter, always under attack by mosquitoes in the dry, hot summers), as your typical young teen I was feeding myself happily on a steady musical diet of Kiss, Queen, Cheap Trick, Aerosmith and Rush. But, along with the usual physical changes my body went through as I moved on to high school, I also underwent a musical transition. I left those previously cherished bands behind and followed this new, exciting muse called punk rock.

After getting my initial fix by buying the shrink-wrapped, behind the counter Virgin Records import seven-inch of the Sex Pistols' 'God Save The Queen' (for the then full price of a full-length record at $4.99!) at my favourite record store, I was full on hooked to this dangerous and primitive sounding musical force that made its way to my central Canadian prairie suburb.

Then I nabbed The Clash's first album, also an expensive import with the green UK cover. I later bought the blue North American version that included a few extra songs plus the 'Groovy Times' single as a bonus. Shortly after, now finding myself in my middle high school years, I went downtown and bought *Give 'Em Enough Rope* and was now a full-on disciple of The Clash.

Like many who were under the influence of this raw, important musical wave,

I then bought my first electric guitar and started jamming with a couple of classmates, inspired by the DIY, no-bullshit creed that anyone with passion and dedication can say something musically.

The real crowning glory of my love for The Clash then hit like a tidal wave, the release of *London Calling*. Looking back this was easily the most heavily played, groove-worn-out LP in my history of listening to music! From the powerful album cover of smashing-my-instrument punk attitude to the experimenting at the many forms of music that had only been hinted at previously, this was the LP that had me playing air guitar in my basement with 'Clampdown' blasting when I had the place to myself.

A few years after graduating high school, I moved to Toronto to go to film school and it was there, in the early 1980, that I first saw The Clash on the *Combat Rock* tour. It was a show opening for The Who at Rich Stadium in nearby Buffalo, New York, USA (I'm so bored there…. ha!). It was a big stadium show with around 70,000 people, probably mostly there to see the headliners, but I was in heaven as I loved both bands.

It was a steamy hot day in late September and The Clash came out. I remember being tightly packed in the crowd while my boys, Strummer sporting a cool Mohawk, ripped through many of their classics like 'White Riot' and 'I'm So Bored With The USA'.

This was near the end of the road for this version of the band as the next time I saw them was in 1984 at Maple Leaf Gardens in Toronto, where a couple of new guitarists replaced Mick Jones as Joe led the band through many cuts from *Cut The Crap*. Most of the tunes from this album played live came across as generic arena rock but it was great to see them, nevertheless. One song I remember from the show that stuck with me was a powerful rendition of 'Straight To Hell'.

Flash forwards all these years later and The Clash still occupy a place in my heart as my favourite band of all time. The passing of all this time has not diminished all the blazing music and influence this band has given the world… and the relevance of their lyrics and their songs are as potent as ever. Stay free!

STEVE SMITE

One of my all-time favourite concert memories is seeing The Clash live, so good in fact that my memories of the event are indelible. It was a stadium show in Buffalo, New York following the release of *Combat Rock* and supporting The Who. We all told our parents we were sleeping at each other's house and only one of us had a driver's license. When we got there, we went to the nearby 7-Eleven and noticed it was completely gutted and there was nothing in there but beer, pop and cigarettes.

ALL THE YOUNG PUNKS

We knew we could bring beer into the stadium but only in plastic containers. We bought two litre pop bottles and quickly replaced the soda with beer and headed in. David Johansson of New York Dolls opened, followed by Eric Burdon, The Clash and then the headliners.

We were up close to the stage when the first few chords of 'London Calling' hit, Joe Strummer running out on stage sporting a full Mohawk, wearing combat fatigues and screaming. It was exciting, intense, and terrifying. We were giddy. The Clash hated playing the stadium shows, however, as they felt they lacked the intensity and intimacy of small venues.

 MEMORIAL GYMNASIUM, KENT STATE UNIVERSITY
17 OCTOBER 1982, KENT, OHIO

JOEY BUCKLES

I saw The Clash twice, in Akron and at Kent State Ohio in 1982. I also saw Joe once with the Mescaleros. I had a friend who turned me on to them around 1978/79. I was learning to play guitar, and I used 'Police And Thieves' as one of my practice songs for rhythm and lead playing. I had been to NYC in May '81 and they were playing 'The Magnificent Seven' on a taxicab radio before the Bond's shows. It was an electric time.

Kent State was ferocious. I have never seen a more eclectic or dialled

Joey Buckles would practise 'Police And Thieves' on the guitar

in audience. This was clearly the better of the two shows I saw. Joe was either exhausted or sick in Akron and the band was off. I remember reading a quote from Pennie Smith about a Clash show where she observed the phenomenon where, when the band kicked off, there was an explosion of energy, and the crowd merged with the band. I'm sure it happened at both shows I saw, so I know exactly what she meant. It was a thing of beauty to behold.

A PEOPLE'S HISTORY OF THE CLASH

ALL THE YOUNG PUNKS

US FESTIVAL DATES

MARTIN BLENCO

This was a weird time in the life of The Clash. It felt like they were on the verge of becoming a stadium rock band, touring the US and only popping back to the UK occasionally, like they were Led Zeppelin or something.

MICK JONES SACKED
JULY 1983

MARTIN BLENCO

When I read that Mick had been sacked, I knew that The Clash were in trouble. Part of what made them so special was the whole Strummer-Jones thing, like Jagger-Richards or Lennon and McCartney. And Mick had written and sung so many great songs. How could they carry on?

A PEOPLE'S HISTORY OF THE CLASH

OUT OF CONTROL UK & EUROPEAN TOUR

APOLLO THEATRE
11 FEBRUARY 1984, MANCHESTER UK

DAN WORTON

Okay, so it wasn't the classic line up but witnessing The Clash at Manchester Apollo in 1984 amounted to my musical awakening. As a 12-year-old high on my older brother's record collection, we piled into my dad's Ford Cortina to make the journey north for this momentous occasion. They came on to 'London Calling' and that moment has probably permeated my musical career ever since. I was taking it all in, sat on someone's shoulders as I was too short to see, and it was amazing. This was it.

There was no weak link in The Clash, a rare characteristic in most bands, the musicianship progressively expanding until they recorded my two favourite albums, *London Calling* and *Sandinista!* Both were such experimental and genre-flitting works, timeless and massively influential. Still the best rock 'n' roll band ever. No doubt about it.

GRAHAM JONES, AGE 18

I was down and out in life, living in a bedsit. The world was a dark place, Britain's Rust Belt (now known as the 'Red Wall') was a wasteland of closed vandalised mills, tumbleweed, grey skies of desperation and misery. Depression, anger, poverty.

My life revolved around listening to all sides of the triple album *Sandinista!* until the early hours of the morning and then going to sleep until the afternoon to blanket out the misery and hopelessness. The Clash were long lost in the indulgences of stadium rock. Whilst the lyrics of the triple album spoke to young people, it envisaged a better world and took aim at political elites who'd destroyed communities across America and elsewhere. It was The Clash angry in words – but now lost on stage. From 1981 to 1984 The Clash were reduced to a musically unplayable indulgent mess; *Combat Rock*. The Clash had lost their way for too long, the world had moved on for the worse and The Clash didn't seem to care anymore.

Roll forward three years. This was Thatcher's Britain (Reagan's America). Five million unemployed, every factory closed, downsizing, YTS checkout jobs with welfare slashed. The odd job gone before the advert was up – captured by the lucky; friends, family begging for a favour. Not me. Like many, I wasn't lucky. I had no-one.

The Clash had gone from *Sandinista!* to a wilderness that wasn't The Clash. Stadium rock, stadium merchandise, stadium rock perspectives. Escapism and New

A PEOPLE'S HISTORY OF THE CLASH

Romanticism was the musical drug of choice. Electronica the new musical nirvana.

Music mattered, or at least *Sandinista!* did. But it couldn't mask the grinding misery of daily poverty in Tory cuts Britain, where everything was derelict, lost. It was either gritty reality or escapism.

Come late 1983, The Clash re-emerged, Joe captured by the impact this reality. The Clash were about to rediscover music, politics and purpose – much to the envy and frustration of a music media who shared their poison pencils. But was Joe who was in touch, it was The Clash who were to fulfil their ambitions as a project – to go out and embrace people. The concerts I wanted to go to sold out quickly. The Clash were back.

I caught the train to see The Clash that night in Manchester. The buzz was incredible. Like nothing I have felt since. The music wasn't enough now – this was the full deal. A band that mattered. The only band that mattered. Like many, I didn't need out of touch electronica or drugged up stadium rock. I wanted someone to speak for me and millions like me thrown on the scrap heap. Music, politics, life, anyone, someone. Joe Strummer.

The train pulled in and it was about a 30-minute walk to the Apollo. I could just about afford the ticket at £4 (an unbelievable £12 in 2024 prices). In those days it was tickets bought at point of sale and it had been a train over when tickets went on sale. Piccadilly Records on Piccadilly Gardens. That moment of realisation. The Clash are coming and they're back. Back to the people.

The self-indulgent music media said The Clash were finished. I presume by that they meant that it wasn't the same for them now the doors were opening to the masses. The band wanted ordinary people to be part of the journey.

That incredible vibe leaving the station that night cut through the air. As I approached the Apollo, I was stopped by endless ticket touts. The gig was sold out weeks in advance. Desperate for tickets and selling them at multiple times face value, the pavement was illuminated by scalpers: 'Any spare tickets, any spare tickets, I'll buy any spare tickets.' The car park next door was full of ticketless fans trying to work an angle to get in.

291

ALL THE YOUNG PUNKS

Vendors spread out huge carpets of various Clash t-shirts, lining the pavements from the entrance and the pavements nearby as fans approached. The buzz was immense, like nothing I've experienced before or since. Fans hung around seeking to buy or blag tickets, desperate to get in. And when the doors finally opened, the doorman fighting back a mass would open the door narrowly as the mayhem ensued outside, letting in one person at a time. It was mad. Desperate fans, desperate made-up stories just to get in.

This was now a band who in 1984 had made a leap from crappy stadium rock to a full musical and political aural onslaught. Corporates and yesterday's sulking green pen journos an irrelevance to the state of emergency that Britain and Joe saw people facing.

I had the chance to go in 1980 but that other escape, the terraces of Blackburn Rovers, were the place for me and I didn't go, much to my regret. This was 1984 and The Clash had reconnected with fans and it was again alive.

My stomach was churning as I hung out outside before finally squeezing in through the door, past a heave of heavy bouncers fighting back the crowd. I could hear fans spinning all sorts of tales just to get in.

This was it, only my bedsit awaited me. Tonight was my moment where I could take a journey out of Britain's rust belt misery. Where someone, Joe Strummer, would speak to me like no-one else could. This was my moment, my escape and it was those bastards, Reagan and Thatcher, who I hoped tonight would be in the firing line, cut and spliced with a back-to-basics energetic music. The last thing I wanted was the dreary stuff – or even the musical perfections of *London Calling*.

This Clash were the only antagonists that were standing up for millions like me. The only band that mattered, spokespeople for a generation, for generations. Tonight had to happen. Mixed in with the politics, angry power punk anthems.

I headed into the theatre. It was rammed. More had got in than had tickets. It was a crush so I stopped back a bit - I wanted to capture it all.

The house lights went down and the mayhem started all the way to the back, with those standing up in the packed gallery joining in. Unbelievable. I have never witnessed anything like it since that night. No band will ever capture so much, connect so closely and mean it whilst tub thumbing the audience into delirium.

Joe was on fire and it wasn't long before the politics kicked in. 'How many of you are registered to vote?' Every emotion went through me, emotions that I have relived many times. Emotions I have recycled many times. That constantly reenergise me and I'm sure many others there.

The songs kept rolling. The hall rocking, the pace frenetic. It never stopped. The new songs like the old songs.

And the sound was so loud, the political message from an angry Joe Strummer standing up for the people he represented even louder.

Years later, I got given the master audience tape from this night at Manchester which had been stored, left, lost, in a dusty loft in Blackpool. Discovering it had been recorded, to relive that aural record, brought back so many feelings from that night. It stands as testament to anyone just how exciting The Clash were during this period and on that particular night.

It took an age to get out and away from the Apollo running past the crowded parade of t-shirt sellers, who were still doing a roaring trade, just so I could catch the last train back.

That last train, that bedsit were now different places. My world changed forever. Someone had spoken for me, spoken to me, spoken about the pain of my generation. Someone cared about the future. That person was the legend that is Joe Strummer.

You can have all the musicians in the world, but none stand taller than Joe. I felt angry, inspired. 1984 ended with The Clash playing seminal concerts for UK miners whose historic strike had begun in early March 1984.

Today, I feel sorry for all the sad journalists who think The Clash belong solely to them, stuck in some 1977 London time warp. The Clash that took the stage at Manchester that night were The Clash that spoke for a generation, not to a few liggers holding on to past.

When I read journalists' retrospectives tomes about how bad The Clash were in 1984 I just think, 'You weren't there, you didn't understand Britain. You didn't like sold-out concerts with excited fans, you didn't understand the people going, and you don't understand how important Joe Strummer and The Clash were in 1984.'

In my view, it was the music press that destroyed The Clash – not The Clash.

PHILIPSHALLE
19 FEBRUARY 1984, DÜSSELDORF, GERMANY

MARK COATES

I saw The Clash in Germany whilst I was in the British Army, but it wasn't the iconic line-up. The thing I remember most is Joe introducing the band members and adding '…and I'm Mick Jones'. They were great.

ALL THE YOUNG PUNKS

The whole gig was standing only, and the mix of locals and squaddies made for a great atmosphere.

BRIELPOORT
21 FEBRUARY 1984, DEINZE, BELGIUM

PETER STRIKE

There was a coach and ferry package over to Belgium organised by MCP Promotions which had been advertised in *NME*. We had a rough crossing and a lot of seasick souls, especially those of us who'd drunk four bottles of brandy from the duty-free shop on board the boat. Passport Control boarded the coach to rifle through our drunken unconscious punks' pockets to stamp passports and drop them back into our drink-fuelled comas. With a coach full of drunk English Clash fans, the gig was good but no match to the original line-up of The Clash. (Mick and Topper had gone).

Some local lads took exception to us, so a massive brawl erupted. Strummer stopped the band playing while we battled in the crowd as he tried to calm the violence, with us foolishly singing 'England, England' for good measure.

Peter Strike recalls a brandy-fuelled xenophobic trip to see The Clash Mk II

PALAZZO DELLO SPORT
24 FEBRUARY 1984, MILAN, ITALY

GIOVANNI TAVERNA

I saw The Clash for a second time in 1984 during the *Out Of Control* tour. At that point the band was already without Topper Headon and Mick Jones. It was the day that Joe Strummer's father had passed away although I only found that out later. The new guys in the band were very young.

They did two concerts in Milan; the 1984 concert was very different to 1981 with a very different sound. And in 1984 there were a lot of visual, which had become very important in music. The background of the stage was TV screens which for most of the concert projected videos of ultraviolence, very, very violent short clips from movies and and a lot of war videos and battles.

They started with 'London Calling' and 'Safe European Home' again and did quite a few songs that would appear later on *Cut The Crap*. I remember the new songs sounding quite good live although many Clash fans are very critical of that version of the band.

You could see it was a different band without Mick Jones. Pete Howard was not a reggae fan. He was beating the drums very hard, and definitely in a different style. Strummer seemed quite nervous, very tense, but it made sense when I realised later that he'd lost his father only a short time before. There were a couple of songs where he had to restart the song and he was getting very angry with the band. But overall the concert was great.

The concert poster and the ticket used a beautiful picture taken during a riot in Budapest in 1956, with a guy throwing something probably towards a Russian tank. I was just 17 and the use of that image proved to me that The Clash were on the right side of history, supporting social justice, and were for oppressed people and against the injustice and corrupt of politicians.

The Clash are still important to me now.

They all did great things in the following years. I saw Big Audio Dynamite, Joe Strummer and the Mescaleros and even Havana 3am with Paul. But the best solo work from them in the years that followed was the album by Topper Headon, which had a soulful style. They were all great musicians.

I'm happy they never reunited. That way, we can keep the memories of what they were in our youth.

KING GEORGE'S HALL
4 MARCH 1984, BLACKBURN

PETE EASTWOOD

I was 13 when punk and new wave hit. Blackburn was blessed, as we had a venue in King George's Hall that hosted all the latest bands and artists on an almost weekly basis. I have always described myself as a Mod with a punk attitude. Mod was my calling, and I was Jam obsessed, but I liked most releases by The Clash, and absolutely loved *London Calling* from the moment I heard it. Unfortunately, I only ever got to see The Clash once, in March 1984 at King George's Hall. The ticket was orange and reads, 'MCP Presents THE CLASH 'Out of Control', ticket number 109.' It cost the princely sum of four English pounds.

The band's five-man line-up for the show was Joe Strummer, Vince White, Nick Sheppard, Paul Simonon and Pete Howard. I know that it would be cooler to say that I loved the gig, but to be completely honest, I almost walked out. I can't

ALL THE YOUNG PUNKS

remember the reason for this (maybe because they weren't The Jam, or because there was no Mick Jones) but I can't have enjoyed it that much, even though they opened with my favourite tune by them and blistered through an incredible 25 song set. I do though acknowledge that I would probably love it if it was now. But at least I can say I saw the iconic Clash, and that wonderful mint condition ticket is still in my possession.

JEFF DAWSON

After seeing The Clash in Manchester three times I went down to Hanley Victoria Hall in Stoke in 1982. And then the last time I saw them was a bit later, just before they disbanded. Mick had left. It was before they did the *Cut the Crap* album at King George's Hall. 'This Is England' was a bit hit and miss really. The gig was good though. I just loved seeing them. The stage looked like they were in the Haçienda, with all black and yellow striped tape, like 'police do not cross' tape and with loads of televisions on stage. It was a bit different, but it was still good to see them.

Jeff Dawson thought the stage looked like the Haçienda

I must have been to over a thousand gigs, but with The Clash you felt you were part of something special. I've never felt like that since about any other band.

★ BRIXTON ACADEMY
9 MARCH 1984, LONDON

WAYNE BEAN

Mick and Topper were gone and it was the new five-man Clash. People complain a lot about that line-up but live they were great. I also remember it well as I saw one person get up on stage at the side but quickly get back down. So I made my way to the front, went straight up to the middle of the stage (in '84 you could go right up to the stage, which was about chest high), saw that all the bouncers were in the wings on both sides and saw my chance. I pulled myself up and ran to the front of the drum riser and then waited until the bouncers were like six feet away from me on either side. I then ran like hellfire past Joe Strummer and dived off the stage back over and into the crowd, getting a cheer from the Academy crowd. After that, the bouncers would not let anyone else get on stage… Classic stuff! They played a bunch of new and old songs – 'We Are The Clash', 'Clash City Rockers', 'This Is England' and 'White Riot', which sent the Academy nuts. The album *Cut The Crap* is pretty poor, but live that line-up delivered.

ULSTER HALL
12 MARCH 1984, BELFAST

BRIAN YOUNG

When the unthinkable happened and founder and chief songsmith Mick Jones got his marching orders in September 1983, it was all over bar the shouting – though there was a lot of that on the first record they made without him, *Cut The Crap*. Tellingly, Machiavellian control freak Bernie Rhodes supposedly had more to do with the finished recording than many of the band members – several of whom promptly disowned the final product. It's a dreadful album and the least said about it the better. And don't believe the wishful hype about the original demos being much better – cos they aren't!

Live too, without Topper and Jonesy, even with an added guitarist, the Clash Mk 2 were a shambolic mess – a mere shadow of their former selves. Strummer's ugly ill-advised Travis Bickle Mohawk showed just how out of touch and desperate he had become. I saw them play here in Belfast at the Ulster Hall in March 1984 and was horrified and heartbroken at just how low my once favourite combo had sunk. The only saving grace was that ever reliable Paul Simonon still looked as cool as fuck!

OUT OF CONTROL US TOUR

GWU SMITH CENTER
8 APRIL 1984, WASHINGTON DC

JOHN SHIPLEY

I never thought The Clash would end. Through all the turmoil that occurred in 1982 and 1983 with Joe, Topper and Mick, I still thought they would always be around. When the 'new' Clash formed, I was still on the bandwagon and couldn't wait to see them again. 1984 brought them to the Smith Center at George Washington University. Again, I went stag (even though I was still with the same girlfriend). This was another awesome show. I certainly missed Mick and Topper, but the new members were excellent along with Joe and Paul carrying that punk rock Clash torch. I loved the new songs and Joe was at his best as always.

ALL THE YOUNG PUNKS

My five years of seeing The Clash in concert were some of the greatest times in my life. So were the times with the girlfriend who I spent six years with and who put up with me during my rabid Clash mania and which I carry with me to this day. I will always remember how The Clash changed my life in January of 1978 when I first played their debut album. To this day, I am an avid Clash collector. I just wish the live music would have never stopped.

DAVID BENDER

I never saw them live, but I met Joe and Paul, plus the other three that were part of The Clash Mk II, at a bar in Washington DC called Poseurs. It was 1984 and they were in town for a show. Joe was not friendly and in fact looked miserable.

That Clash Mk II mess certainly took its toll on him. It wasn't really The Clash without Mick in my opinion.

KIEL OPERA HOUSE
21 MAY 1984, ST LOUIS, MISSOURI

RICHARD KOCH

I was never able to see the original line-up, but I was still thrilled to see Clash Mk II in St Louis in May 1984. I heard about the show from a close friend who I had met when he approached me as I wore a Clash shirt. I wish I could still fit into the 'Jive after Five' t-shirt I bought that night instead of displaying it on my wall. Luckily, I was able to grab four tickets in the last row of the lower section for two friends along with a gal who was sleeping with all three of us. (We all remember her fondly.) At the time, I was very much into trading tapes so I knew I had to try to sneak a cassette machine in the show. I discussed the situation with my mother who used her sewing skills to create a jock strap device for me to hide the machine. I made it through security and was able to set up the machine on the arm rest. The show was awesome with Joe with his Mohawk. I recently found my recording on YouTube. I'm glad to see other fans can enjoy a truly hot show. It is funny to hear my buddies give me trouble about changing the tape on time to not miss a song. Since the seats were in the last row, we had a bit of backlighting. My favourite memory is Joe pointing our way and saying that he saw us dancing up in the back.

A PEOPLE'S HISTORY OF THE CLASH

BRIXTON ACADEMY
6 & 7 DECEMBER 1984, LONDON

BEN COOPER

I am the drummer in a band called Restless that supported The Clash twice in 1984. They were a bit of surprise for us and at short notice. The whole event was organised very hastily, leading to us and other support acts not being listed on the event poster. The events, called *Scargill's Christmas Party*, were held at Brixton Academy in aid of the Miner's Strike. We were first support on both nights.

The Clash played *Scargill's Christmas Party* to raise funds for striking miners

Restless were very excited to be supporting such a big band at such a prestigious venue. It was the biggest gig we'd done so far. The Clash were all extremely approachable and friendly. No prima donna type behaviour at all. We had a pleasant chat with Joe and Paul at the backstage bar, exchanging stories of gigs and what we'd been doing. They were also very helpful to us as our rhythm guitarist had a serious malfunction with his guitar, Joe lending him his iconic Fender Telecaster for our gig on the first night without hesitation.

The fans were very receptive to us too and we got a great reaction from them. The Clash were quite well known for having modern rockabilly-influenced bands like us supporting them and we gave our best possible performance, making the most of the amazing opportunity.

I've read over the years that the five-piece line-up of The Clash has always been contentious; diehard fans not thinking it the same band without Topper and Mick Jones. I thought they were awesome, the atmosphere was electric, and you could feel the love coming from the audience. The band were on fire both nights.

Following one of the gigs, the venue re-opened the main bar for the bands and crew after the audience had left. We'd never experienced anything like this before. It was cool to see the band relaxing with close friends and family and associates. This contrasted with the atmosphere in the dressing room after each, which was very subdued. Since then, I've learnt how much turmoil the band were going through, especially Joe Strummer. That turmoil didn't affect their performances at all.

ALL THE YOUNG PUNKS

During this Brixton Academy after party, I had a long chat with the then Clash drummer Pete Howard. I think I told him how great I thought his drumming was during their set and particularly on 'Radio Clash'. We also had a long conversation about the merits of Ludwig Speed King bass drum pedals. I guess I was still buzzing after our gig and went on a bit for too long. I'm sure I nearly bored Pete to tears, but he didn't show it. A nice guy and a great drummer.

Ben Cooper drummed for support band The Restless at *Scargill's Christmas Party*

When we did the gigs, I wasn't really a fan of The Clash. However, I have become much more of a fan since. My band never got as successful as we would have liked, but because of The Clash supports we at least got a taste of what it was like, and for this I will always be eternally grateful.

ANDREW FARMER

I feel a bit of a fraud really. I only ever saw half of The Clash. I saw them in 1984 at a Miners Benefit gig. Only Joe and Paul remained from the original line up, but even though I've seen hundreds of bands since this is still in my top three gigs of all time.

In 1984 England was in trouble. Along with social unrest, racism was rife, and the Tory government led by the evil Thatcher was determined to break the working classes whilst trying to defeat striking miners. As the saying goes, 'Nobody can do everything, but everyone can do something,' so what better way to help than to spend Christmas with your favourite band and favourite union leader, Arthur Scargill?

With tickets purchased it was off to London on a coach, a fiver for the ticket and a fiver for the bus – absolute bargain. Brixton was a culture shock. Shops were boarded up and even the KFC had a serving hatch that you passed your money through before they would give you your order!

The venue was completely unreserved so you could stand or sit where you liked. We chickened out and sat on the front row of the circle. A rockabilly band, Restless, were up first followed by Smiley Culture. After a brief interlude, the house lights dimmed and The Clash came on, individually. I seem to remember them playing the James Bond theme. Strummer entered last, looking about ten feet tall.

Before kicking into an exhilarating two hour set, he apologised for Scargill not being there as he 'couldn't get his hair into a quiff'. Thriving off the energy from the thousands in the mosh pit, The Clash played a high octane set with all that you'd want to hear. The whole of the downstairs was mayhem, the crowd never stopped dancing and the stage was invaded so many times. People were stage diving into the crowd, getting back up and doing it again. Complete carnage but probably the most joyous event ever.

Everyone came together for a great cause to see a great band led by the late great Joe Strummer, the likes of whom which we will never see again.

I miss you, Joe. The world misses you. The poster of that gig still hangs proudly in my hall.

PHIL DE JONG

I saw them around the *Cut The Crap* album at the Brixton Academy. My one abiding memory of the gig is the loudness of the bass. I'd never heard a sound system so loud, it was visceral, a felt experience. It felt like my chest was being punched in, it was that loud! But I was disappointed that Mick Jones and Topper Headon were no longer in the band, and it didn't seem like a 'proper' Clash gig to me.

JOHN YOUENS

There is dissent in The Clash world whether the band were The Clash when Mick left. I saw what's often called the 'dodgy Clash' a few times. At Colston Hall, Manchester and Brixton Fair Deal. You could tell that it was coming apart. It felt you were holding on to something that just wasn't there anymore, but desperate for it to be okay.

I saw the last two shows, *Scargill's Christmas Party*, at the Fair Deal in Brixton. It was December 1984; the miners had been on strike for nearly a year, and it felt like a civil war was in danger of breaking out across the whole country. Everywhere you went, there were miners collecting money and there were police roadblocks all over the country. It was an incredibly divided time, and you got the sense of that from those shows.

Joe seemed to be in an agitated state. Something massive had gone with Mick and Topper not being there anymore. At the very end, after they left the stage for the last time, Joe had a change of heart and decided that he wanted to play some more songs. They had to put the drum kit back together again to do a few more but it felt like the ship had sailed.

HANS PETTER SCHJØLBERG

I saw The Clash live three times. The first time was after the release of *London Calling* and then later the Mark II line-up. In 1984 my friend and I were at Brixton

Academy. The Redskins were opening, and it was a great night. Everyone was friendly and we ended up just in front of the stage jumping up and down. Then my friend, Geirr, lost his shoe! For the next ten minutes, Geirr and I were crawling on all fours through the mosh pit looking for his shoe. We eventually found it, boot-tracks on our backs…

JOHN MITCHELL
The third time I saw them was The Clash was with the same friend who invited me to go and see them in Poole. I was living in Exeter, so got a bus from Exeter to Bridport and we drove from there to London for the first night of the *Scargill's Christmas Party*. Like a lot of people, I wanted that version of The Clash to be good. I still had faith in Strummer. I think Vince White came on first, from down the big stairway, and they were doing 'One More Time'. So we had one guitar playing and then Nick Sheppard came on and he added his guitar. Paul came on and then Pete Howard, and finally Strummer.

They played all the hits this time. I did know some of the new stuff – it sounded pretty good in concert, but it wasn't the same. When Mick and Topper were there, there was that sense of chaos. You listen back to those bootlegs and sometimes the guitar playing was all over the place, but that sense of chaos is what you got with the classic four-piece line-up. This was like watching a traditional rock show. They were all good musicians, and you wouldn't turn down an opportunity to play with The Clash, but there just wasn't that excitement.

MARK GREATOREX
I went to see The Clash at Brixton Academy and went down the front with my small camera to take some photos. I'd been in the pit for a few minutes, then someone staged dived wearing Doc Martens. They went straight for me and hit me on my nose. There was blood everywhere. The last time I took photos at a Clash gig!

BUSKING UK TOUR

LEEDS UNIVERSITY & FAVERSHAM PUB
7 MAY 1985, LEEDS

IAN CORBRIDGE

It seemed like an average sunny Tuesday evening in Sheffield as I waited for my mate Nigel to pick me up and head off to see The Alarm at Leeds University. However, all that was about to change. A rumour emerged from the early evening showing of the *Old Grey Whistle Test* that The Clash might appear outside The Alarm gig for one of their busking sets, and that was a rumour we could not ignore! We headed at top speed to Leeds to see what was happening and whether there was any truth in this rumour.

We arrived to find what appeared to be the entire Alarm audience stood outside, looking like they were waiting for something to happen. Clearly the rumour had spread, but then again, maybe nothing would happen. Suddenly, a lot of commotion emerged from near the University building and we noticed Joe, Paul and the rest of the band with their acoustic guitars almost ready to play. This whole evening was taking a completely different turn!

This latest incarnation of The Clash proceeded to play three or four songs before seemingly getting hassled to move on from outside the University building. Amongst the large crowd that was gathered outside, it wasn't clear what had caused the problem although it was subsequently reported that a member of the then Leeds-based band Chumbawamba, Danbert Nobacon, had splattered red paint over the band and probably surrounding members of the assembled crowd in some form of protest.

A more recent conversation I had with Chumbawamba vocalist Dunstan Bruce, who is now with Interrobang!?, confirmed that their band were behind this disruption, citing the fact that they had been annoyed about The Clash signing for a major label like CBS. (The ultimate irony is of course that Chumbawamba subsequently signed to a major label.)

Anyway, we thought that might be it, short and sweet, but as the band started to march purposefully down the road from the University, we made the snap decision to follow them, and that was one of the best decisions we ever made.

We managed to catch up with Joe and even had chance for a chat along the way, talking nostalgically about their first ever gig at the Black Swan ('the Mucky Duck') in Sheffield that Nigel had attended back in 1976. Joe was very friendly and could certainly recall that gig, even though it was some nine years before.

Then as we reached the car park of the Faversham Pub, the band obviously decided this was a good place to set up, so they got into position to play a set which lasted around 45 minutes. This was an amazing experience, standing so close to the guys as they went through a classic set of both old and new numbers which included 'White Riot', 'Clash City Rockers' and '(White Man) In Hammersmith Palais'.

As Joe later documented, it was an attempt to get back to their rock 'n' roll roots and the performance certainly achieved that. It was one big Clash singalong, but it is one that will live long in the memory. I cannot confirm the rumours that members of The Alarm also came down to witness the event, but once The Clash finished their set, we just had enough time to head back to the University building before The Alarm came on stage.

My one regret is not having a camera to capture some images from the whole event. Both pictures and recordings of this tour are very scarce and it's a pity there aren't more images available to document this amazing evening in Leeds.

'THIS IS ENGLAND' / 'DO IT NOW' RELEASED
5 SEPTEMBER 1985

ROBERT CASSON

Is it OK to admit liking 'This Is England'? The only single from The Clash which didn't have Mick Jones involved? Released three years after the double A-sided 'Should I Stay or Should I Go' / 'Straight To Hell', it arguably contains one of Joe Strummer's strongest set of lyrics as he captures the state of England in the early 1980s.

Written in 1983 but not released until September 1985, it comprises a run-down of many of the problems the country was experiencing under the Conservative government which had come to power in 1979 including inner-city violence, a high unemployment rate and police corruption along with the wave of patriotism from the Falklands War.

A strong single which maybe would be better regarded if it had been recorded and released a year or so earlier, away from the *Cut The Crap* album.

The press didn't like it…

CUT THE CRAP RELEASED
4 NOVEMBER 1985

GREIL MARCUS

As the number two British punk band, The Clash began as the Rolling Stones to the Sex Pistols' Beatles, but good and bad were reversed in punk. As The Beatles, as those who set the terms of the new game, the Sex Pistols demanded everything and damned everything – knowing they would be left with nothing, they played and sang as if they didn't care. The Clash criticised, always leaving an opening, the Sex Pistols were wreckers, they were partisans. The Sex Pistols were symbolist, with every meaning left open and uncertain, utopia and hell in a single, unstable body; the Clash were rhetorical, voice to flesh. If the Sex Pistols – or, anyway, Johnny Rotten – truly were committed to the destruction of rock 'n' roll not only as myth but as fact, The Clash were committed to changing rock 'n' roll, to taking it over, to becoming the Number One Band in the World ('The Only Band That Matters', their American label said, after the Sex Pistols disintegrated).

The explanations the Sex Pistols offered when interviewers asked them why-are-you-so-angry turned into The Clash's songs, songs about boredom, autonomy, lust, power; The Clash took the true anarchy and the real nihilism the Sex Pistols offered and rationalised it, made it seem almost reasonable.

The Clash latched onto received ideas, but they soon made those ideas their own and were changed by them – or anyway, Joe Strummer was. It was never clear if he wanted to be a star or if he wanted everyone to hear him. In the rock tradition Strummer was so tied to, the difference between the one and the other was never clear. With a giant multinational corporation behind them, the Clash toured the USA (1977, 'I'm So Bored With…') again and again.

In 1982 they finally cracked the American Top Ten, made it twice, with *Combat Rock* on the album charts and the indelible 'Rock The Casbah' on the singles list. Most assumed that The Clash were working for nothing else, that the heresies of 1976 London punk were merely the old clothes of bad dreams, but the band's success seemed to shock Strummer. If The Clash had scored their hits, if large numbers of people were finally happy to listen to what the band had to say, Strummer seemed to have decided that that meant The Clash were no longer saying anything. With work on the boards, he disappeared in Paris, then reappeared with his head shaved. Drummer Topper Headon quit; the group was unravelling. Strummer called a meeting, got bassist Paul Simonon's vote, and kicked guitarist Mick Jones out of the band.

Jones had been a founder; he had asked Strummer to join him. As guitarist, singer, and co-writer, many saw him as far more central to The Clash's success than Strummer, but in a way that was the point. Jones's noisy love songs ('Train In Vain,' 'Should I Stay Or Should I Go?') had been the Clash's most effective bids for mainstream airplay before 'Rock The Casbah' (a sardonic, up-from-the-Muslim-streets reply to the Ayatollah Khomeini's ban on music in Iran, and written by

Topper Headon); Jones's voice lacked Strummer's rough edges, his promise that any song could go in any direction, anytime. Strummer detected a spiritual flaw behind the style, despite the punk attempt to destroy the star system. Strummer announced a pop star was all Mick Jones had ever wanted to be. He was a fake, a revisionist; he had to go.

Strummer and Simonon recruited three new members, drummer Pete Howard, rhythm guitarist Vince White and lead guitarist Nick Sheppard, the latter both twenty-three-year-old 'ex-punks' who affirmed they'd grown up on Clash music. As a band ('The Clash') they played a few shows; hope against hope, their American label even brought them back to the USA.

It was, for a night, a trip worth taking. 'This isn't *white* reggae,' Strummer shouted, introducing 'Police And Thieves', 'this is punk *and* reggae. There's a *difference*. There's a difference between a rip-off and bringing some of our culture to another culture. You hear that, Sting?'

It was 21 January 1984. It had been eight years since The Clash formed, six years and one week since the Sex Pistols played their last show in San Francisco, and The Clash were back in town not as 'The Only Band That Matters' but as the only punk band left. 'What we play now is what we can do,' Strummer had said in 1979. 'It wouldn't be fair to do ranting music because we've mastered a time change. So, there's just no point.'

'We started to think we were musicians,' he told Joel Selvin, a San Francisco critic, before the New Clash show. 'When we made the first record, we knew we weren't. It's a bad thing to think; it's irrelevant, not to the point.'

To a happy, not quite sold-out crowd in a dumpy, medium-sized hall, The Clash played ranting music. Keeping Strummer's promise to Selvin, they 'went back to where we went wrong, and then forward again.' Against an industrialist backdrop and eight television sets flashing images of present-day social disaster, Strummer shook, scowled, smiled, and sang as if he and his audience had a life to make within a world they'd already lost.

The band was ragged, Nick Sheppard played too many Mick Jones licks, and such rock-star flimsy as leaps from the drum riser or floodlights in the crowd's face was still part of the show. The only identifiable new song was the hopeless 'We Are The Clash,' which only added credence to the old rumour that the favourite song of Bernard Rhodes, the Clash's original and now returned manager, was 'Hey, Hey We're The Monkees.' Still, I'd never seen Strummer more exhilarated, or more convincing. In 1978 in Berkeley, 'I'm So Bored With The USA' was a gesture of contempt to a bourgeois audience; this night it was offered to the audience as their own, and they took it. Some of our culture to *another* culture.

Still, almost everyone was sure it was the end of the road. As time passed, Strummer gave increasingly confused interviews about 'rebel rock' changing the world, the special role he had to play in that change, England's turn to the right under Margaret Thatcher, the collapse of the punk community and the possibility of reinventing it, social injustice, fascism, the end of the world, and when there might be a new Clash album. He wasn't saying anything terribly different from what he and many more had said in 1976 and '77, but in London in '76 and '77, the old rock 'n' roll dream of 'taking over the world' hadn't meant topping the world's charts. It was supposed to mean making the charts irrelevant, and then proving that the charts and graphs and ledgers that governed the structures of everyday life the hierarchies of education, work, family, bureaucracy, politics could be made just as irrelevant.

Now, though, with Thatcher's brutal, popular Tory rule, the oppressions punk had fought when it gave birth to itself, the oppressions of false leisure, false work, false entertainment seemed like the playthings of childhood, and Strummer sounded like a crazy old man.

In May 1985, in the UK, the new Clash, the five of them, showed up in a parking lot outside of a hall where The Alarm, a newly popular group, were playing a sold-out show. Strumming acoustic guitars and tapping drumsticks against each other, they were busking playing for small change. Before 1976 Strummer had been a subway singer, a thick-fingered guitar banger – that was where he got his name. In interviews in the 1980s, he talked often about 'going back to the roots', but no one could have guessed he'd meant going back so far. It was a bizarre reversal, and a testament to how desperate Strummer was to dramatise that punk had meant what it said when it said it would destroy all heroes.

On their early tours of the UK, The Clash sometimes brought their fans back to their hotel and let them sleep in their rooms; now, playing the Isley Brothers' (or The Beatles) 'Twist And Shout', their own 'Garageland' (from The Clash's first album) or 'Stepping Stone', (The

Monkees again – the Sex Pistols had tried too, once), The Clash asked the curious who gathered to hear them, if the fans could, you know, put them up for the night. In this moment, you could see Joe Strummer's whole future; on some dank London corner, the drunken bum calls out to passers by. 'Hey, you wanna hear 'Rock The Casbah'? It was a hit, it was a hit in, ah, in...'.

As the band chanted in the parking lot, you could see The Clash's past. On the back sleeve of 'White Riot,' The Clash's first single, there was a rough collage of photos (ugly public housing blocks surrounded by rubble, cops, a band) and words. Along with quotes from the Brighton Beach youth culture riots of the mid-1960s (a Mod, 'I haven't enjoyed myself so much for a long time... It was like we were taking over the country'), one could read something more suggestive, that there is, perhaps, *some* tension in society, when perhaps overwhelming pressure brings industry to a standstill or barricades to the streets years after the liberals had dismissed the notion as 'dated romanticism,' the journalist invents the theory that this constitutes a clash of generations. Youth, after all, is not a permanent condition, and a clash of generations is not so fundamentally dangerous to the art of government as would be a clash between rulers and ruled.

Out of this blind fragment of a found manifesto, The Clash had made a career. In advance of any sort of pop career, the words took in the inevitable dismissal, or failure, of any attempt to use rock 'n' roll to dramatise a clash between rulers and ruled, as far as almost everyone was concerned, no band could signify more than a transient clash between generations, a present-day (now long past) version of a sixties beach riot between Mods and Rockers, new fans of The Who and the Small Faces beaten bloody by fans of Bill Haley and Gene Vincent, Teddy Boys who kept the faith, relics whose whole lives were based on the conviction of any they had heard the truth and would kick in the faces of anyone who suggested it might be incomplete.

In other words, with that old manifesto now playing against the idea that an old band could, make itself new, Strummer, well into his thirties as he spoke, as the new Clash made noise for coins, and then made a new record and asked people to buy it – was precisely what the old fart punks had dumped when 'White Riot' first hit the stores. *Cut The Crap*, the new Clash album was titled, and the words were thrown back in Strummer's face. *You* should talk, said the British reviews. Go away! Who wants to hear what a dead man has to say! Stop reminding us of what you failed to do the first time around!

On the terms punk set for itself, it would change the world, or it would be nothing. In a certain sense, Strummer was never a real rock 'n' roller, because he trusted neither fun nor money; thus, the chart success of the Clash had to mean nothing to him.

ALL THE YOUNG PUNKS

You could draw two different conclusions from the failure of punk to change the world and its sometime success on the charts, you could conclude that the punk critique of everyday oppression and spectacular entertainment was wrong - or you could conclude that it was more correct, and the enemy more invisible, than even the most conscious punks had dared to think. Drawing the first conclusion, you would, if you were Strummer, try to find a place in the record business; drawing the second, you would try to find a new way to say the same old things. And of course it is the second path Strummer has chosen.

Cut the Crap seems to be set in a riot - not the idealised 'White riot/Wanna riot of my own' of the Clash's 1976, not their 'LONDON'S BURNING WITH BOREDOM NOW!' but a far more prosaic affair, tired, too familiar, the everyday bad news of the New Britain. A new kind of riot, as the strict redivision of British society into capitalist and serving classes proceeds, it becomes plain that redundancy and civil disorder are not merely costs of this project, but linchpins. Under Thatcher, redundancy is not simply economies, it is social exclusion organized as spectacle. Those who are cut out of organised social life make up a third class, which is used to terrorise those who still retain their places into a thank-god-it's-them-instead-of-me acquiescence, which is silence, and that silence has no force without some noise in the streets.

This is power as culture, a form of speech that has answered all questions in advance. Behind the Labour government of 1977, which administered What Is as a final social fact, punk could discover a negative, welfare security as spiritual poverty.

With Thatcher, who administers What Could Be (you can be anything, she says, which means, you can lose everything), oppositional culture can only discover an affirmative. It can only agree, and agreement is a further silence. As the redundants riot, the ranter grabs a passing clerk by the collar and tells him the truth, 'You could be next!' 'Right, mate,' says the clerk. 'That's why I'm keeping my nose clean. Hey, aren't you Joe Strummer?' As public speech, both the riot and The Clash's new music have been contained before the fact.

Thus, The Clash's new riot, too, sounds like a kind of silence, an exhortation in place of drama, inspirational music for 'rebel rockers'. 'CLASH COMMUNIQUE OCTOBER '85,' it says on the inner sleeve. 'Wise MEN and street kids together make a GREAT TEAM… but can the old system be BEAT? Mo… not without YOUR participation… RADICAL social change begins on the STREET! So, if your looking for some ACTION… CUT THE CRAP and Get OUT there.' The new songs, the new music, aren't much more convincing. A wash of ambient mass media noise, an old-fashioned punk guitar sound communicating not as a revival of a period style but as a new discovery, an occasional rhythmic jump-too soon, it all seems lost in a shoving match between skimpy lyrics and football-match chants of vague slogans. More than anything, *Cut the Crap* sounds like a transfer from The Clash to Big Country – a band that scored a good, rousing hit with the self-titled 'Big Country', a teary approximation of early Clash – back to The Clash again. *Cut the Crap* sounds less like failed 'rebel rock' than like failed pop music.

And out of this comes one true moment, 'This Is England.' Released as a single, it had a strange jacket, on the front, a Mohawked punk couple wander through Piccadilly Circus, blank-eyed and scared of the sleaze, country mice finally arriving in the big city to find out what punk is, seven years too late.

24 HOUR ETERNAL SUNSHINE STRIP STRIP STRIP,' 'SEX STYLE SUBVERSION,' 'DISCUSSION DISCO.'

There's no one else on the street. On the back, there are lots of people on the streets, black-and-white shots of 1950s men and women finally shrugging off the privation of the postwar period and shopping, buying, smiling, 'IT'S NEW,' 'GET IT,' 'LAST FEW DAYS SALE,' and, square in the middle, a collage from old painted postcards, Buckingham Palace, the Queen in her carriage, a hand raised to hide her face.

'Who will buy my potatoes?' asks the voice of a small child; a drum machine kicks in, slowly, firmly; synthesiser chords lift the music, hold it in, refuse to let it move through any melody, to find any rhythm; a punk buzzsaw guitar rides down, sounding wonderful, alive, free, then beaten. Strummer begins to sing, to talk, walking through the riot like his own tour guide, nearly mute for all his words. As the riot takes place it's already over; he is singing the ruins, and the passion in his voice, the despair, the plain desperation to make you understand, is like blood frozen on a corpse. The corpse is the singer; it's the country. 'This is England,' an anonymous male chorus says over and over, and again and again Strummer comes off the chorus to try and tell you what it is, 'Land of a thousand stances.' Images of random violence, of official murder, pass by; nothing connects. The singer flees; he's trapped. An incident comes to life with detail, then vanishes as allegory.

On a catwalk jungle
Somebody grabbed my arm
Her voice spoke so cold at last
Weapon in her palm
This is England
This knife of Sheffield steel
This is England
This is how we feel

ALL THE YOUNG PUNKS

England is a nowhere, but all possibilities of feeling seem present in the way Strummer sings that last line, here in the voice of another, throughout the rest of the song in his own.

'THIS IS ENGLAND,' echoes the chorus, and then Strummer is solitary, bearing down on the following words so hard he makes them vibrate, the solitary 'we' so painful and strange, pressing with such force that all that's come before, The Clash's whole career, all the great songs, your favourite, seems trivialised by this quiet, still negation, the patent, physical gap in the 'this' of 'this is how we feel,' a frightened hesitation between the 'th' and the 'is,' a break in time that carries the full weight of what Strummer is saying, carries it, and suspends it, leaving you hanging, unready for the fact that after a few minutes the record, like other records, simply fades out.

Postscript, Shortly after the release of *Cut The Crap*, the three new members quit the band; it never re-formed. *Cut The Crap* was never released in the United States. 'This Is England' has been excluded from all Clash retrospectives, greatest-hits collections, and CD boxed sets.

A PEOPLE'S HISTORY OF THE CLASH

ALL THE YOUNG PUNKS

JONNY PAUL
Joe Strummer 1952-2002

You made growing up so much more bearable. You gave me definition when I struggled to find it. You gave me a purpose when I thought I was nobody. You gave me something to stand for and be a part of when I felt lost. You gave me sanctuary when I was hurting.

You helped rid us of the blandness of the seventies. You changed the face of music and brought us something real, something tangible, something to believe in and be a part of. You championed issues of racism, social deprivation, unemployment and inequality and gave a voice to the young and hope to an entire generation.

The Clash were one of the greatest and most critically acclaimed bands to emerge from these shores. You were at the forefront of a musical explosion that revolutionised music and became a mammoth influence on so many and so much.

My love of punk began in 1978; I was a disaffected eleven-year-old when I heard a Radio 1 session. I was overwhelmed hearing 'I'm So Bored With The USA', 'Janie Jones' and 'White Riot' on the radio. I progressed onto the debut album, *The Clash*, and the second, *Give 'Em Enough Rope*. I could not have had a better music apprenticeship.

One cold December morning I scurried into Virgin records on Market Street in Manchester on the way to school to buy *London Calling* on the day of its release, the excitement and adrenalin I still remember and feel today. It has since been my life's soundtrack, my bible, my best buddy. I still hear it the same way today; it still totally blows me away, it is so intelligent. Pure genius.

I saw you play Manchester Apollo a few weeks later. I don't think I fully understood or appreciated the moment. I can say proudly however that I have seen live one of the greatest rock 'n' roll bands ever.

Joe, your humility, honesty, conviction and integrity some would say were against the punk ethos but you defined it, embodied it and wrote the rules.

Joe Strummer is dead; I cannot believe I'm typing these words. My childhood icon, my saviour, my hero, my life.

Thank you, Joe, for your music, it made my world. Thank you, Joe, for your energy, it inspired me. Thank you, Joe, for your immense contribution. It gave me a springboard and a way to look at and embrace life.

Love you Joe. Go in peace Joe. Punk is not dead.

I'll never forget the feeling I got when I heard that you'd got home,
an' I'll never forget the smile on my face cos I knew where you would be,
an' if you're in the Crown tonight have a drink on me,

but go easy…step lightly…stay free
'Stay Free' (Strummer/Jones) 1978

SIMON BRETT

The greatest of modern music is alchemy. A combination of creative minds, timing and I suppose a smidgen of luck.

I don't really believe in talent as a thing in its own right. I do wonder whether the commitment, belief, hard work and focus of an individual paves the way for eventual brilliance. The mining of musical gold. It's not the virtuoso operators who make my heart sing. It's the bloody-minded buggers who bang their creative hearts and heads against the edges of conservative values. Over and over again, until the true 'talents' if there are any – judgement and taste – steer them to filter the chaos down into incredible, emotive music that means something more than just clever guitar tricks.

There's a sweet spot between established genres. When I first heard Big Audio Dynamite fusing sampling, electronic beats, dub wise reggae, cinematic coolness, dance and rock 'n' roll, it felt like Mick and the boys were doing exactly what you should have been doing with the emerging technology of the eighties. Suddenly, it started to feel like you could create any sound you wanted. And if you couldn't create it, you would steal it and make it your own.

At that point, I knew little of The Clash. I was aware of a few songs, not yet latching on to their brilliance, but liking them all the same. The singles of the early eighties popped up now and again on chopped up TDK Top 40 scratch-taped compilations. 'Rock The Casbah'. 'Bank Robber'. Christ, even 'This Is England'. (Don't shoot me.) But soon I got wise to the whole rock family tree thing. I began to work backwards, picking up cassette copies of *Combat Rock* and dare I say it, *The 12" Tape*. Remember that? Yes, I was a child of the eighties, not knowing any better.

But if anything was going to allow me to follow the threads that led Mick to create Big Audio Dynamite, it was those repackaged, remixed and yes, probably slightly sanitised offerings that helped me see that the melting pot philosophy of BAD had been there from the early days, never mind the eighties.

Man, *The Story Of The Clash* was really important to a bunch of eighteen-year-olds stuck in backwater Cornwall. Eventually, you only listened to Tape 1 to build you up to Tape 2. I'm pretty sure the old school purists thought it was a travesty, but for those of us who didn't know any better it was a training ground.

Fast forward a few years and I've done my homework. I've explored The Clash's output from finish to start, while BAD climbed their way to the mighty *Megatop Phoenix* before mutating into a new line-up with mixed fortunes of questionable quality. But, hey, the rock family tree technique works again, and I investigate Screaming Target and eventually the wondrous Dreadzone, following every band member's journey to other plains.

It all felt like things had travelled full circle when I was watching Dreadzone play at the Lizard Festival. I think it was the late nineties. I'm easily distracted and became curious when I noticed a man dancing just off-stage behind the speakers. He was bouncing a small child on his shoulders, their small arms caressing a slicked-back mane of glossy black hair. Whoever he was, he was obviously every bit the fan of the band as the rest of us. I like to think it was Joe. Just like I like to think of myself as a Clash fan. Even if I did get there backwards via shite CBS reissues. But I got there, nonetheless.

STEVE PALMER

I went to see The Cramps. I got talking to Joe Strummer who was on his own.

A homeless guy came up to us and said to Joe, 'I love your band,' and then sang 'Going Underground'! Joe – being Joe – played along and joined in with the song. What a guy!

ANDREW JOHNSON

I first got into The Clash via Big Audio Dynamite although I was vaguely aware of them before that through my sister who said, 'They're a bit like The Kinks'.

I couldn't get enough of Mick's voice and songs at first as I felt it was an extension of BAD but I gravitated more and more to the initially indecipherable garble of that other bloke that was singing (little realising there was a third too!). It was Joe Strummer's absolute commitment to the cause and the band's global political viewpoint that still managed to feel grounded that kept me a lifelong fan and shaped my own views also. Too many favourites to pick from but 'Spanish Bombs', '(White Man) In Hammersmith Palais' and 'Stay Free' are all up there.

PAUL CATTEN, DEAD SHEERAN

I must admit I got into The Clash late. Whereas my early eighties introduction to punk and the Pistols, Damned and Buzzcocks were all via fantastic debuts, my first Clash album was *Combat Rock*, the only one available in the long-deceased Ross Records. I listened, and other than the two singles, I hated it. I knew 'London Calling', 'Bankrobber' and 'I Fought The Law' off the radio and that was okay, but this? I took it back, claiming it jumped.

Back then we had no YouTube or Spotify to hear band back catalogues. It was the radio, mates – or fuck all. And that's how it stayed until 1986, when a local band played some Clash covers in their set. I liked the sound of those, especially

'Safe European Home'. I was still suspicious however, as I was very much into Crass at that point, who didn't speak too highly of them. Some music book in the library told me what album it was on, so off to Gloucester I trotted and buy *Give 'Em Enough Rope*, 'Tommy Gun', 'English Civil War', 'Safe European Home'. Shit, why did I leave it so long?

Right, so now I needed the debut album and the following week it was on my turntable. I can still remember the first time 'Janie Jones' came blasting out at me as I placed the needle down, Strummer sneering his on-point lyrics throughout. A life changing moment. This was real politics to me, and let's face it, the eighties were as bleak as the time they wrote the songs in the decade before.

And thus started my real love for The Clash. And it's never waned in the slightest. Strummer, along with Rotten and Ignorant, made me want to be 'that' sort of vocalist. Sneery, sweary and honest.

I even made it through all six sides of *Sandinista!* one day. Only once, mind you.

GARY MCDONNELL

I met Joe at some after show on the *Rock Against The Rich* tour, possibly at The Brown Cow in Salford. He defaced my copy of *On The Road* by autographing it, calling it 'my fav book'. Ray Lowry was around and some lad was claiming to be the son of Jimmy the Weed (a Salford gangster, formerly of the Quality Street Gang). I had to keep explaining to Joe who 'the Weed' was and the significance of his gang. He asked if it was anything to do with Thin Lizzy's *Johnny The Fox* album (which features a track called 'Johnny The Fox Meets Jimmy The Weed').

I said 'absolutely!' The Brown Cow was a Phil Lynott and George Best haunt and was probably owned indirectly by the Weed. The landlord used to have Phil's pictures on the wall, including his wedding photos. Bestie had a clothes shop a few minutes' walk away.

Joe was fascinated by how the various worlds collided; I told him that oddly enough it was probably Phil Lynott's mum who was the catalyst, as she used to have an hotel where various characters would drink together on neutral ground.

Joe had an absolute curiosity about wherever he found himself and in that, the wall between fan and 'star' would blur and then disappear and boil down to a couple of people having a meandering conversation that everyone could chip in with.

This was way before the Glastonbury stuff. The roots of Joe's campfire vibe of stories and storytelling, the ability to create a mini scene for the night or location, were already in place. It was that, I reckon, that meant so much to people. Yeah, he was Strummer the punk icon, but I'd bet everyone who ever found themselves involved in a long, ever-evolving conversation with Joe will recall it instantly, even if the gigs have blurred into one.

PAUL RYDER

I saw Joe Strummer and his band in the mid-eighties on his *Rock Against The Rich* tour. The gig was upstairs at the Lighthouse in Poole, with some kind of sprung floor. I can't remember the song everyone was jumping up and down to (as you do) but it created some kind of wave or ripple effect. There were tripod lighting rigs to the right and left of the stage and one toppled into the crowd, landing heavily on a few people.

They finished the song and stopped playing. A few people, mainly blokes, had cut heads, etc. with plenty of blood everywhere. Five minutes later, the tower was put back up and the set continued with two blokes holding each tower to stop it happening again. The bloodied guys carried on as before, if anything jumping around even more vigorously. They probably show their grandkids their scars of honour!

> **A FEW BLOKES HAD CUT HEADS…**
>
> PAUL RYDER

ROB FURS, DIABLOFURS

When I was in Birdland we went to a *Melody Maker* party in around 1990, when they'd invite bands that were in the press and doing all right. Me and Lee were there and so was Joe Strummer. We were upstairs talking to him about music and there were loads of posters. I looked over and there was a huge one of Morrissey. Joe muttered something and walked over, got his lighter out and set fire to the poster on the wall. Moz was going up in flames!

Joe just walked back and carried on talking to us like nothing had happened.

CHAS BLACKIE

At *T in the Park* I was at the backstage bar (I had worked in the industry) and Joe Strummer was there, on his own. It was a bit surreal as I was standing next to Kylie Minogue, as I noticed after the paparazzi started snapping her. What irony that the legend was generally unnoticed at the bar. I met Mick Jones while working with Big Audio Dynamite too, a really down-to-earth guy.

ROB ALLEN

My experience of The Clash that's most memorable is thinking how amazing 'Bankrobber' was when Audioweb played it at Leeds Town and Country Club in 1995. What a tune! How did they come up with that one? It was part of my musical education to learn that it wasn't an Audioweb original at all. You can probably file Manic Street Preachers rendition of 'Train In Vain' alongside that one. I was daft, but then I got the debut and *London Calling* on vinyl from Kingbee Records and corrected my course!

JAMES BONE

The Clash became a huge band for me as a young teenager in the late nineties. A particularly dire period for music, that first album seemed an absolute world away from the string-laden, bland indie bands and manufactured pop acts clogging up the charts. Raw, simple, and effective. The stubborn refusal to be stifled by the confines of what many thought punk was supposed to be. They became a template for so many groups that followed. The ultimate garage band.

ROB WATSON

I was too young to be a proper first-generation punk – I just caught on to the tail ends. However, the first time I heard the opening bars of 'Janie Jones' I knew that I'd found what I had been looking for. This was around the time that *Combat Rock* was released but I soon caught up. I listened to everything and read every word about The Clash that I could find… and, of course, I watched *Rude Boy*. I already knew that I didn't like bullies, and I didn't like racists – my dad had laid those foundations – but suddenly I had mates that thought like me. It was great. Even back in my school days, mates who were punks and Clash fans looked out for each other and took care of each other.

I didn't get to see The Clash live. I was a bit too young when the classic line-up split. I nearly went to one of the Miners' Benefit gigs just before Christmas 1984. I was sixteen and living in South Wales. I didn't have anyone to go with. I knew that there was an album coming out – there is bound to be a tour, I thought. Of course, there wasn't, and I was heartbroken. A few years later I discovered that my mate's older brother who lived next door but one had gone to one of the Miners' gigs

> **I HEARD 'JANIE JONES' & FOUND WHAT I WAS LOOKING FOR…**
>
> **ROB WATSON**

and would have been very happy for me to go along with him! I was heartbroken all over again.

Subsequently, I took every opportunity that I could to see Big Audio Dynamite, The Latino Rockabilly War and later, of course, The Mescaleros.

It hit hard when Joe Strummer died in 2002. I had met him once to get my copy of *Earthquake Weather* signed, still my most treasured possession. I have read enough about the band to understand that he was a complex character and could be hard work… but it really felt that the world was a sadder place without him.

I know that lots of people say it, but this band changed my life. They introduced me to so many other bands, artists and genres, particularly reggae, ska, rocksteady, etc.

The Clash have provided the musical backdrop to my existence and a moral compass. I shudder to think about what an awful person I could have turned in to without them. Punk and in particular The Clash gave me a sense of belonging and something to identify with when I badly needed it… and the courage to speak out and confront injustice.

I continue to find that the people I connect with, get on with and have shared values with are often Clash fans. Recently, I needed the services of a plumber. On arrival, he spotted a Mescaleros' poster on the wall and a conversation quickly ensued about how much we both loved The Clash and Joe Strummer. He pulled out his phone to show me what he had been listening to in his van on the way to my house… it was *Combat Rock*.

DARYL HUMPHREYS

My appreciation of The Clash began to diminish as I discovered new genres and started making my own music in the eighties. The Clash went on to produce some great new songs and conquer America but it is the early experiences, when they were just starting out, that bring back the most potent memories. Most of all Joe Strummer made a great impression. He was somewhere between laidback everyman geezer and socio-political philosopher, plus he really did walk the walk and talk the talk of punk rock.

I didn't fully realise the depth of the impression Joe made on me until I briefly met him in the mid-eighties. I'd been to an overnight party in the west country and had got up early to hunt down some breakfast. I was sitting in the kitchen when this bloke walked through the open patio doors. I thought I knew him from somewhere but it didn't click immediately until he ambled over, sat down opposite me and said 'hello, I'm Joe.' Then the penny finally dropped.

I've never been phased at meeting someone famous but I can honestly say that on this occasion I simply froze. I'd had no idea he was a neighbour and in the habit of dropping in when he felt like it. He lingered for a moment before heading off and to this day, I deeply regret not starting up a conversation with the man because there are so many things I would have liked to have discussed.

When he died unexpectedly in 2002, I was gutted at the potential loss of his legacy as a punk icon but I'm comforted by the fact that he lives on as the angry young voice of a generation. Joe was a thinker who dared to challenge the norm and stand up for what he believed in. He lived by a code of freedom of thought, fairness and equality and his influence on youth culture and music is immeasurable.

JOE KELLY

I saw Joe at a festival playing with the Mescaleros in '99. Afterwards, my mate swapped t-shirts with him, and years later he started cutting up that shirt and giving it to people who are true to Joe's vision and values. It's a pretty cool thing to do.

JOHN MITCHELL

I felt more loss with Joe Strummer dying than when my mum died twelve years ago, maybe because I'd been prepared for that. Even though I was in the Midlands, I was that kid, London calling to the far away towns. Growing up in the middle of town, buying the *NME* every week, reading on the bus, reading every Clash interview as if it was a missive from the front. I was that kid. Strummer had a great effect.

My son was born on 20 August 2006, I was hoping my ex would hang on for another day so it would be Strummer's birthday, but my son is called Joe.

I try not to buy into the Clash myth because I think there was a lot of posture and a lot of nonsense, particularly when you read the interviews from around 1978, and I think The Clash confused themselves as to where they were.

I remember when Mick Jones got thrown out the class and I was 19. The Clash were over, but I think the reason we still talk about them 40 years later is that, above any other band, The Clash were our band, even when they were in America. We felt an affinity with them, we wanted them to make it. I wanted the people to hear 'Complete Control', '(White Man) In Hammersmith Palais'… It's disgusting that it only got to 32 in the singles chart!

The Clash could have been bigger, but they were quality and we're still talking about them 40 years later. Their legacy now is bigger than ever.

STUART CLARK, *HOT PRESS*

Voyage Of The Damned. Or should that be The Clash? Well no, actually, cos there's no Clash, Damned or Pistols in 1999. But there's still Joe Strummer, who was there when Shane got his ear bitten off and, 22 years later, is back for his own second bite with The Mesacleros.

No disrespect to the Scottish port, but of all the Godforsaken places in the world to mistakenly end up in, the worst has to be Stranfuckingraer. Especially when it's 4.45 in the morning and you've just double-somersaulted down the steps of Joe Strummer's tour bus in the rat-arsed position.

The brief had been simple enough. Collar the former Clash man after his gig at the Belfast Limelight, and find out what's with this Mescaleros malarkey. We'd originally been due to meet the previous night when Strummer, obviously on a course of monkey glands, had treated the Olympia to the most athletic display of rock 'n' roll showmanship since Steven Tyler was last in town. The crowd responded by refusing to go home, even though the house lights had gone on, and the bouncers' famously sunny disposition was in danger of clouding over. The whooping and hollering continued for 15 minutes until Joe, now showered and changed into civvies, emerged from behind the security curtain and announced that if we promised to bugger off afterwards, he'd do 'London Calling'. The deal brokered, it was 1979 all over again as 1,300 pairs of feet pogoed in perfect unison.

It would've been the perfect time for a natter, except that Charles Shaar Murray from *The Sunday Telegraph* had got in there before me.

'You've got to look after the quality broadsheets', Strummer cackles 24 hours later. What, even if the bloke writing for them gave The Clash their first slagging? 'Shit, I'd forgotten that. After seeing us play somewhere, the cunt said that we should go back to our garage and gas ourselves, which was the inspiration for 'Garageland'. Y'know, back in the garage with my bullshit detector/carbon monoxide making sure it's effective. The next time I run into him we're going to have words.'

That'll teach him to nick our interview slot. The upside to us being gazumped is that I've been given another opportunity to see the man who changed my life. To understand how The Clash made the impact on late '70s rock that they did, you have to realise that prior to them and the Pistols erupting onto the scene, we'd been subjected to such indignities as Whispering Bob Harris and triple

> **THE CUNT SAID WE SHOULD GO BACK TO OUR GARAGE AND GAS OURSELVES…**
>
> STUART CLARK,
> *HOT PRESS*

Emerson, Lake & Palmer concept albums. When you've lived through those sort of horrors, you don't easily forget the people who rescued you from them.

It's precisely because the gig's so jam-packed that The Mescaleros fail to hit the same nosebleed high that they did in Dublin. With the only ventilation provided by a single Wild West saloon fan, Joe is soon asking for the back door to be opened. When he's told that's impossible because of the neighbours, he snaps. 'They'll complain even more when we smash the place up, and there are 36 ambulances outside.'

He's suffering so badly from the heat that halfway through he leads the band off for a break, and on returning, changes the middle-eight of 'Bankrobber' to 'Going to get all my friends in Belfast town/Bring 'em to the Limelight and burn the fucker down!' The roar from the front-rows is in direct proportion to the look of horror on the manager's face.

'I wasn't able to say it at the time cos, y'know, we'd have been banned from everywhere, but I loved it when Clash gigs ended up in a riot,' Strummer confides over an apres-show pint of red wine. 'I'd see what was going on in the crowd and think, Fuck, I'd much rather be down there smashing up chairs.'

'My five years with The Clash were just too intense,' he explains. 'After releasing 16 sides of long-playing vinyl in that time, I'd had my say. Imagine it was a party and I'd been talking for five days and five nights straight. At the end of that anybody would go, 'Wooo, I need a breather'. When you're young and your group takes off, you don't really have any life experience. I'd had a bit more than the others cos, y'know, I'd worked as a gravedigger and a toilet-cleaner, but there were times when I forgot what the world outside rock 'n' roll was like.'

Did he end up hating the business he was in? 'Not really, but when we supported The Who in America in '82, I remember looking at them and thinking, 'God, any day now this is going to be us.' I was also worried that no matter how hard I tried not to, I was going to become a phoney. How can you impart things to other human beings when you're not one yourself? There was a point around the time of *Combat Rock* that if we'd been prepared to become just another conveyor-belt rock band, we could've been huge. On one hand there was our dignity, and on the other, Aerosmith.'

MARTIN BLENCO

I remember reading in the *NME* about Joe playing a benefit gig for striking firefighters at Acton Town Hall, a few days after it happened. Mick had got up to play a few numbers with Joe at the end. Was a Clash reunion finally on the cards almost 20 years since Mick had left the band and The Clash had, to all intents and purposes, ceased to be? My hopes were up.

I was in the kitchen of my then girlfriend, in South London only a few weeks later, when the news came on the radio that Joe Strummer had died of a heart attack at home, aged 50. 50 seemed like no age then. Now I'm 64, it still seems terribly young and terribly cruel to rob Joe of life, his family of a husband and father, and all of us the chance of a Clash reunion. RIP.

JOHN YOUENS

I bumped into Joe at a few Glastonburys. I watched him enjoying himself. You could see how big a deal it was for him to have campfires, the whole unifying ethos of a way for human beings to come together and interact. I always think of Joe when we'd go on camping holidays and we'd all sit around the fire tell jokes and stories to each other. I thought that was a very Strummer-ish thing to do. I've been inspired by Joe to bring people together like that.

I don't listen to The Clash's music that much anymore. Probably I should. They had a deep, profound impact on me. I mean they opened so many doors for everybody and gave you things to find out about it. I learnt about the political situation in Central America and what was going on there. The lyrics to 'Washington Bullets,' I remember analysing them and going off finding out who Victor Jara was and what was going on in Nicaragua and with the CIA's dirty operations in El Salvador and what Pinochet had done in Chile. In pre-internet age they were important in terms of spreading those messages, those ideas about what was going on around the world. The lyrics to 'Straight To Hell' I remember as being amazing, not just great poetry but a real snapshot of what it was like in the early 1980's as heroin swept through the world.

The night I heard Joe died I was in floods of tears and in pieces. It was terrible. I'd just met my girlfriend, and I saw it on the TV. We went to the pub near where I was living in Bristol and just talked about Joe. It was seismic and at a point he'd found some peace in his life.

I'm grateful that I took time to go to Wales to see him play with the Mescaleros a few weeks earlier. It was the last one of the last shows he ever did. Joe looked at peace there, enjoying what he was doing. He had some wilderness years, but he seemed to be in a good place.

SUE TERRY

I saw Joe and the Mescaleros later on, at the 100 Club, at Brixton Academy and so on, and those were special gigs and special moments, but different. You're talking about a mature man with different things happening.

I'm always really glad that The Clash never reformed. There was that wave of bands having a second or third go round and being lured out of retirement and all those awful rock musicals using their songbook and things like that, and I'm damn glad that The Clash weren't part of all that. It keeps them relevant and it keeps them important

I would have been 42, maybe a little older, when Joe died and a little part of me was still hoping that they might get back together. I remember my mum was sad when Jim Reeves died but I never thought I would be affected by the death of a pop star. I worked for a local council and was on my way into the office when I heard the news that reports were coming in that Joe had died. We had a skeleton staff working over Christmas so I had to go in but I felt like I had been hit by a truck. It was just so weird. I went and sat at my desk for a while and I thought, 'I've got to be the professional, got to do this paperwork while it's quiet' or whatever the hell it was I was doing, but I was like, 'Oh my God, I don't know what to do with this stuff.' I just couldn't focus for a long time and I kept thinking, 'This is because Joe's dead. This is awful, I can't believe it.' It's the day the music died. It really, it really was like that.

One of my colleagues was a really nice bloke but a bit of a joker and he was joking a little bit about it, saying, 'Oh, let's have the funeral' and I just thought, 'Oh, actually you've really been a bit shit there,' because he didn't quite understand or appreciate what this meant for somebody of my generation, to actually suddenly turn around and think, 'Crikey, they're starting to die.'

The Clash were so important in saying 'the future is unwritten'. That's one of the things Joe said in later years, and it's one of those quotes of his that has always been very special to me as I've matured over the years. Joe would have done so much more if he'd lived. You can still do anything. You don't have to give up. You can still do it. And who knows what might happen next week. Next year. The next 50 years. All of this will change and something else will come in its place, and with luck, it'll be better.

When Joe died, I just thought, 'My God.' The one comfort I took from it was that

> **JOE WOULD HAVE DONE SO MUCH MORE IF HE'D LIVED...**
> SUE TERRY

he'd just been out walking the dogs or something. He seemed to be in a happy place when it happened. It wasn't dying in a hotel room as a result of a drug overdose or something. Healthy living got him in the end. Yeah, we'll never forget Joe. They're still the only band that matters, and that's what's important.

NIGE TASSELL, AUTHOR

I never met Joe Strummer. I never saw The Clash. But still…

I was a little late to the ball, a little too young to feel the white heat of the band in their pomp. Me and my friend Jonny (who, until that point, worshipped at the fonts of Hendrix and Van Halen) only properly got into them around 1985, by which time of course Jonesy was fronting Big Audio Dynamite and Joe was putting out the underwhelming *Cut The Crap*.

Nevertheless, the back catalogue was our soundtrack for the next few summers. And the winters too. We discovered hitherto unknown reggae artists through the roll-call lyrics of '(White Man) In Hammersmith Palais'; we pogoed around suburban front rooms to their cover of 'Pressure Drop'. 'Stay Free' remains redolent of our easy relationship in those carefree times of youth, even if the song's tales of school-days trouble-making and subsequent jail time were so wide of the mark when it came to our own life stories. Rebellion by distant association.

In adult years, I tried to make that association less distant. When I became editor of *Venue* magazine, Bristol's version of *Time Out*, I left a message on Joe's home phone; I'd got his number from WOMAD, with whom we both had connections. I wanted to do a cover interview with him for the mag. By then, he was living on the edge of the Quantock Hills near Bridgwater. It was about 40 miles from Bristol, but just about close enough for us to call him a local, to call him one of our own.

A few nights later, I was at home cooking, the kitchen door shut to the lounge so that my stereo didn't drown out the TV. The phone was ringing, but I didn't hear it. My girlfriend, my future wife, answered it and came into the kitchen. 'Joe Strummer's wife is on the phone.' I dashed across the kitchen to turn off the stereo; *London Calling* was playing and if Joe's wife Luce had heard that playing in the background, I'd have justifiably been suspected to have been some kind of Rupert Pupkin-esque stalker.

I remember my chat with Luce for two reasons, 1) She cut me off almost instantly, having dropped the phone. 2) After calling back, she explained that Joe was currently on 'walkabout', and she had no idea when he'd be back. Luce was talking days or weeks, not hours. That walkabout seemed to be a long one. The interview never happened.

(A quick aside, mention of my wife prompts me to divulge her first gig. It was… The

Clash. At the Rock Against Racism gig in Hackney in 1978. She was seven. SEVEN!)

Anyway, one day, towards the end of 2002, Joe phoned the Venue office as he wanted us to run something about a gig he was putting on in aid of his Strummerville charity. Normally, as editor, I'd have pulled rank and done the interview myself, but I was otherwise engaged, 12,000 miles away, on honeymoon in New Zealand. So, Cris, the music editor, did the interview instead. It turned out to be Joe's last-ever one. He was dead within a month.

When the news came through that Joe had suddenly passed away, it was the only time in my whole career that I've ever shouted, 'Hold the back page!' It was a couple of days before Christmas and there were just a couple of us in the office, nursing the new year issue to press before we disappeared for the holidays. The motorbike courier was about to arrive to take all the chromalines to the printers when the news about Joe broke.

I quickly dropped the back-of-the-mag column that was ready to roll (almost certainly a fairly asinine piece on the theme of 'new year, new you') and instead wrote a speedy, but heartfelt, tribute to him. The words just poured out.

I then spent much of the rest of the day doing radio interviews about Joe, explaining the importance of his songs, both personally and to a wider constituency. There was a touch of imposter's syndrome about it, what with me never having seen The Clash, and never having met him. Surely there were more qualified people to pontificate about him. Perhaps they'd all disappeared for the Christmas holidays. But, again, over the airwaves, the words just poured out of me. Thanks to his music, his lyrics, his stances, Joe Strummer wasn't a stranger. It felt like I knew him.

We all felt that way.

ANDY INNIS

I didn't see The Clash, but I did see Derek Forbes from Simple Minds and Mike Peters from The Alarm when they appeared as Los Mongo Bondo and played music by The Clash at The Cavern Club in Exeter.

My abiding memory is seeing The Cavern filled with young lads who were born 30 to 40 years too late with decent Mohicans and punk clothing. Not modern goth punk stuff, but proper 1977-79 stuff. They were in heaven in their mosh pit!

IAN FORTH

I've got a friend who gets incensed by the very mention of Joe Strummer. He thinks because his dad worked for an embassy, his left-wing views must have been a fake. I think that's to fundamentally misunderstand both Joe and The Clash.

For me, they're the opposite of fakes. At times naïve about complex political issues, at times over ambitious musically, they were always sincere, always authentic. Relentlessly curious and openminded, creating bridges from their parochial pub rock base to the lands of punk, reggae, dub, jazz, rockabilly, ska, R&B and pop.

Public Image Ltd get full credit for blending punk and dub on *Metal Box*, as they should, but The Clash had done exactly that on 'Armagideon Time' in the same year. Great lyrics too.

Charlie don't surf for his hamburger Momma
Charlie's going to be a napalm star…

CAFFY ST LUCE

The Clash are carved in culture, a thread in my life from a Black schoolgirl digging punk to the present day.

A memory of running the nib of my biro pen into the word 'CLASH' carved into a provincial school desk by the pupil from another form. We were never being taught in the same class, but we took it in turns to doodle the word deeper, as lessons droned on about war and royalty dates – but not how we could learn from them and improve the future.

Fast forward to end of the 20th century London life escapism. On a Tube train one more morning, out of millions of people, a familiar face from 'the sticks'. Tim Satchwell. We discovered that we were The Clash desk vandal kids!

From then we stayed in touch. He knew somebody at Rough Trade. They knew of a job going. I came a receptionist moving on to a regional radio promoter. One of my fave bosses, Jeff Barratt of key 1990s to now independent label, Heavenly, signed Manic Street Preachers. I loved working with them and couldn't believe my luck that they got me a position with Hall Or Nothing (who I still love/see/giggle with).

So The Clash improved my future. There's an education.

PETE EASTWOOD

In 2010 I attended Glastonbury with my friends and was determined to visit the mystical Strummerville cap fire area at the festival. It took me two nights and three attempts to find it (not easy) but I was so glad I did. There was a packed campfire the whole night (I don't even remember seeing anybody leave) and a very small stage. Known and unknown acts would simply just turn up and perform a few songs, with no advance warning, and maybe that's why nobody left, scared of missing a gem.

I remember sharing a randomly placed settee (that had seen better days) with The Mystery Jets, and a London band I knew (Depot) performed a handful of numbers around 5am in the morning. I was totally shattered walking back to my tent on my own, but it was totally worth the effort. Thanks Joe.

A PEOPLE'S HISTORY OF THE CLASH

GAVIN HASTIE

Having been fortunate to have worked (and sometimes socialised!) with several of Scotland's greatest musicians, I can't think of a single one who wouldn't give a quick, passionate and warm response when asked what they think of The Clash. If there's ever a time where this doesn't happen then I will have no issue in instantly correcting them and in looking forward to their imminent apology.

ERVIN SOON

We had a bunch of young so-called artistic people in a small town in russified Eastern Estonia: the most successful of which is Raul Saaremets, who as the leader of his band Röövel Ööbik (The Robber Nightingale) also recorded a Peel Session around 1990. A lifelong DJ and editor-in-chief of the alternative part of the national youth radio, Raul brought us all kinds of interesting records from the bootleg LP market in Tallinn during the Soviet era including The Stranglers, The Smiths, The Cure, The Pogues, Nick Cave, Siouxsie… and The Clash.

One guy from our group became a Lutheran church teacher. He loved The Clash and even had a t-shirt with the band's picture on it. He was nicknamed 'The Clash'.

GARETH GORDON-WILKIN

It's often been written and said that 'The Clash were the only band that mattered'.

Whatever your view no one can deny that The Clash were a great band. I saw them 70 times – all over London, as far north as Manchester and as far west as Bristol, from April 1978's Rock Against Racism in Victoria Park to *Scargill's Christmas Party* at Brixton Academy in December 1984.

Their first and self-titled album was amazing, Their second *Give 'Em Enough Rope* took me a while to get into, but I now think it's brilliant. Their third, *London Calling*, is a masterpiece with its iconic cover. Then and now, it is just fantastic. *Sandinista!* had the makings of a masterpiece with 'The Magnificent Seven', 'Somebody Got Murdered', 'The Call Up, 'One More Time' and many more, but a couple of duff tracks such as a re-worked 'Career Opportunities' with kids singing just clogged it up. If it had been released as a double album instead of a triple, people would speak about it in the same vein as *London Calling*.

Combat Rock released in 1982 was another masterpiece, and several years after The Clash called it a day it yielded a posthumous No. 1 with 'Should I Stay Or Should I Go'. This album made the top ten in America, and they always seemed to be in the news for something. Joe Strummer went AWOL, ran a marathon and on his return, Topper Headon was sacked. The single 'Rock The Casbah' did very well and is still a classic.

ALL THE YOUNG PUNKS

Paul Simonon was the coolest dude on stage. Mick Jones, who'd been to my school a couple of years before me, was a musical genius. Topper Headon is one of the greatest drummers of all time and Joe Strummer a great songwriter whose stage presence was electric. The Clash live, in their prime, were awesome and very few bands since, in my view, have ever matched them.

When Mick Jones left in 1983 the new Mark II line-up released the album *Cut The Crap* and it got slated by the press. There are a couple of good tracks such as 'This is England'. Live, they were good but the last time I saw The Clash they played a benefit gig raising money for striking miners. The press was cruel with quotes like 'It's time to quit holding out and draw another breath,' and 'This is crap Clash on pirate satellite.'

The Clash, yeah, they REALLY mattered.

STUART CLARK, *HOT PRESS*

How concerned is Joe that audiences get his new material?

'I don't wait for no reaction. I just get up there and do my thing. Even if they all turned round, dropped their trousers, bent over and farted, I'd still carry on with the song. We're not there to shag around. We're there to try and say something intelligent and communicate with the people who are in the room. If there weren't no people in the world, I'd still play my songs to a rock or a tree.'

Mick Jones and Paul Simonon have just finished compiling The Clash's first official live album, *From Here To Eternity*. Culled from such disparate sources as the Lewisham Odeon and Shea Stadium, it's guaranteed to not only storm in to the top 10, but have record companies offering them telephone numbers to reform.

'Never in a hundred million fucking years,' Strummer snarls in response to the R-word. 'You heard the crowd tonight shouting for 'Cheat' and 'Police And Thieves'. It'd be the easiest thing in the world for me to put The Clash back together again, but like shagging an old girlfriend, I'd regret it the moment we went on stage. Don't get me wrong, I love Paul, Mick and Topper, but we had our moment in time together.'

Is Joe Strummer proud of what The Clash achieved?

'Yeah,' he says after a thoughtful pause. 'As proud as a gnarly old lion. I tell you what I'm going to have on my gravestone: 'Here, not of his own volition, lies Joe Strummer. He could've lived his life differently, but he couldn't have lived it better. Apart from doing the 'Fat Les' single, that is.''

MOLLY WOODCOCK

Joe Strummer passed away before my first birthday, so I was never able to experience The Clash live. I've been fascinated by their music and story since my teenage years. Their most popular songs had always been on my radar, but as I went through college, I found myself listening to them more and more. I remember the first time I listened to *London Calling*, probably around aged 16 or 17, and being blown away at its innovation, range and lyricism.

I've also been into politics since a young age and discovered the Clash. I was beginning to listen to more and more political music from the period. I find it fascinating how spot on their message was and still is today. I felt like they spoke to me on a level that many other bands just didn't. They had an incredible passion and energy for music, people and life, and even though some of their songs are about serious subjects they're still somehow uplifting. Ever since, my love for them has only grown and their music is one of the most important things in my life.

I've accepted I'll never see them live (as a long-time Beatles fan, I'm used to this disappointment!), but I have managed to catch the tribute band London Calling a couple of times and they were top class, delivering incredible energy all night.

I've studied The Clash throughout my undergraduate degree, including in my dissertation, 'White Riot? An Analysis of Rock Against Racism', in which I looked at the impact that the band and the wider movement had in the defeat of the National Front.

Although they haven't been covered in my master's degree (focused on The Beatles, again!), I hope to perhaps come back to them from an academic perspective in the future if I decide to partake in future study.

In the last year, I have got a *London Calling* tattoo on my arm and visited Strummerville at my first ever Glastonbury festival. The night I spent in Strummerville was probably one of the best of my life – the positive atmosphere of love and life that surrounds the place is almost overwhelming. It was nice to just sit amongst peers around the campfire and listen to some excellent music, both new and old. I hope to visit again in the future, and to carry on keeping the spirit of the Clash alive for future generations.

PHIL FITZPATRICK, STRUMMERCAMP

The Clash have been a backdrop to my life for around 48 years. At the age of ten in 1977 and growing up in Droylsden, East Manchester, my 13-year-old sister Michelle was buying the early punk and new wave singles – 'White Riot' being one that stuck in my mind.

Later I would 'borrow' her records for repeated blasts on the family record player and start to buy my own with saved up pound notes from my paper round (three and a half years, seven days a week, morning and evening). Our house always had some kind of music going on, my parents being from the rock 'n' roll generation. We'd have

ALL THE YOUNG PUNKS

Elvis, the Everly Brothers and Johnny Cash but also musicals, opera and country, so I guess it had an influence in my developing a wide and eclectic taste in music.

I recall getting hold of a copy of *Give 'Em Enough Rope* and swapping it with a lad in my street for *London Calling* (my sister had it, but I wanted my own). This I think started my real interest in The Clash.

I started going to see live bands just around the time of leaving school, with my sister and her then sound engineer boyfriend. A small tatty venue in the centre of Manchester named The Gallery (where he worked and where she did bar work) was my introduction to all things live and close up. Being a bit late for the 1977 wave of punk, I was heavily influenced by the likes of New Model Army, The Redskins, Newtown Neurotics, The Three Johns, etc., whilst being open to all kinds of bands that weren't commercial pop!

I always loved the *Sandinista!* album, even though it was generally slated by the music press, and I think I learned to make my own mind up about what I did and didn't like.

I got to see The Clash Mark II including a trip to Brixton Academy for *Scargill's Christmas Party* and then through the eighties and nineties I'd see Big Audio Dynamite, Havana 3am, Joe Strummer with Latino Rockabilly War, Joe with The Pogues, Carbon Silicon and of course Joe with The Mescaleros.

A couple of times I had backstage passes for gigs including the *Rock Against The Rich* tour in Manchester and regret not heading backstage and meeting Joe, not for being nervous or in awe, but because it just felt right to not stick my nose in!

One sunny day in May 1985, as I worked in the Corn Exchange in the centre of Manchester, I nipped out to get some dinner and walked up Market Street past a small crowd gathered outside the HMV record shop. I took no notice, thinking it would be some pop personality signing LPs. I returned ten minutes later to see a slightly bigger crowd still there and carried on to work, thinking nothing of it. Around 7pm that I got a phone call from my dad informing me he'd read in the *Manchester Evening News* that The Clash had been busking in town. Well, you can imagine... I don't talk about that too much...

As the years have gone by, I have never tired of listening to all of The Clash's recordings and realised more and more how important they were to so many people all over the world. They had, and I think still do have, a far-reaching cultural influence. Their music stands the test of time. So many people have been inspired by the band's energy, positiveness and creativity that their story seems more interesting and relevant today.

Having put on a few gigs as a labour of love over the years, it seemed only natural to pay tribute in some way to Joe after his passing. Initially I put together a line-up of punk, cajun, folk and indie bands for the first Joe Strummer/Clash tribute night at the Witchwood in Ashton-under-Lyne. This was a great success with the venue sold out and an amazing bunch of people coming from all over the north west and beyond.

Around eight months later I did a second one at the same venue and around twelve months after that I put together another great line-up in the centre of Manchester at Satan's Hollow. By 2005, there were various events going on celebrating Joe and The Clash and I got talking with a few people which resulted in a decision to put on a Festival in Joe's name. Strummercamp Festival was born!

Many weekends and nights were spent working out what exactly was needed to put on a festival. A venue? Manchester Rugby Club in Cheadle Hulme. Bands? A chat with Ranking Roger from The Beat got us on the way. He was so positive and encouraged us to do it and said he would be there to play, along with Neville Staple and band, Attila The Stockbroker, Goldblade, Cheapskates, The Clash tribute Take The 5th and many more. Volunteers? Loads of amazing people got on board and made it a fantastic bank holiday weekend in May 2006.

Fast forward to 2024. Strummercamp now looks forward to 19 years of being an independent, not-for-profit, volunteer run, family friendly event with an amazing history including performances from Billy Bragg, New Model Army, The Damned, The Alarm, The Beat, The Selecter, Spear Of Destiny, Dreadzone, The Men They Couldn't Hang, Geno Washington, Ruts DC, Sham 69, Jah Wobble, TV Smith, The Blockheads, Bar Stool Preachers, Random Hand, The Members, Rory McLeod, The Undertones, The Three Johns, Newtown Neurotics, Hugh Cornwell, Tymon Dogg, UK Subs, Vice Squad, The Stupids, Ed Tudorpole, George Borowski and hundreds more.

We have the most amazing volunteers, stage crew, security, door staff and punters from all over the UK, Germany, Spain, USA, Iceland, Belgium, Netherlands and beyond.

Strummercamp has also been nominated several times as the friendliest small festival in the UK. It is a true testament that without people you're nothing. The festival has become a very special part of a lot of people's lives, not to mention my own! I'm forever in debt to all the people involved who make it what it is and I remain very proud to be paying tribute to Joe and The Clash, taking all the positiveness they gave me and hopefully creating something of significance.

The legacy of The Clash lives on.

ALL THE YOUNG PUNKS

AFTERWORD

RAY GANGE, *RUDE BOY* ACTOR

There was a buzz going around town about this new band, The Clash, but somehow I kept missing them until a gig in Harlesden. Up until then I'd thought Wilko Johnson was the most intense performer I'd seen but, fuck me, these guys were ferociously intense. I might not have understood many of the words Strummer was snarling but it was 'sit up and pay attention' intense. A few weeks later, the first album was released. Although it had that tinny, scratchy sound it also had an urgency that was unlike anything heard before. Sitting still wasn't an option.

The next gig I saw was on the White Riot tour in Brighton which again didn't disappoint. I was buzzing all the way home. That summer I went to a punk gig in Putney and was surprised to see Strummer at the bar on his own. I walked over and had a conversation with him and that encounter is summed up by the lyric in 'Cheapskates':

Cause London is for going out and tryin' to hear a tune
But people come poncin' up to me and say, 'What are you doing here?'

We hit it off and started going to loads of gigs together – at The Marquee, Speakeasy, etc. The first time I went round to where he was living, I made a negative comment about him having a Bob Dylan album on his Dansette which earned me a look of pity and disdain. (I wish I could go round and discuss the brilliance of Dylan with him today.) That house, which was round the corner from the Capital Radio building, was a hive of activity, with clothes being designed and made downstairs by the Conran Brothers and Alex Michon.

When Joe invited me to go to Rehearsal Rehearsals with him to meet the rest of the band I was made up, although nervous as not knowing what to expect. But I was largely welcomed into the fold although with suspicion from some. Going there, I had no expectation of anything grand which is just as well, as it was a freezing shithole!

But it felt magical, that I was standing in the heartbeat of something important even if it came to nothing. Getting asked by a filmmaker who was a customer at the record shop I worked in if I'd be interested in taking part in the film they were going to make about the band led me to spend the best part of two tours on the road with The Clash around the UK, as well as a few in France, Belgium and Holland. Experiences that were a mixture of the good, the bad and the ugly. I wouldn't change them for the world. I don't imagine any fans would.

They might not be The Only Band That Mattered but they were fucking great and seem to have affected a lot of people's lives for the better. I'm glad I got to spend a short period of my life in their orbit.

ABOUT THE AUTHOR

IAIN KEY is a recognisable face on the Manchester Music Scene from many years in the late '80s and '90s. Iain rediscovered his love of writing about music during the pandemic which saw him invited to join the team at *Louder Than War*. Since late 2020, he's written over 400 pieces including music, book and gig reviews, and also produced a weekly music show, *Indie Brunch*, featuring both music and interviews with new and established acts such as Kevin Rowland, Frank Turner, Amelia Coburn and Meryl Streak along with journalists and authors such as Daniel Rachel and Tony Fletcher.

Iain's love of music began with The Jam and The Clash as a 12-year-old in 1982, and over the next couple of years he was introduced to the likes of The Smiths, The Housemartins and Billy Bragg. Away from *Louder Than War*, Iain has worked in the telecoms industry for over 25 years, is a lifelong Manchester United fan and shares his home with three cats, Storm, Shadow and Thunder, and occasionally his son, McKenzi.

GOT A STORY?

Did you see The Clash? Or any other iconic band from any era? We're always looking for your concert memories for future volumes in the *People's History* series. Write to us at iwasatthatgig@gmail.com with your story.

ACKNOWLEDGEMENTS

Thank you to the following for permission to reproduce extracts from their publications or blogs:

Bruce Pegg & Glenn Williams (*Goin' Down De Mont: A People's History of Rock and Pop Concerts at Leicester's De Montfort Hall*, Spenwood Books, 2022); Ged Duffy, *Factory Fairy Tales 'The Remix'* (Empire Publications, 2023); Steve Hanley & Olivia Piekarski, *The Big Midweek: Life Inside The Fall* (Route Publishing, 2014); Ian Moss, *45: The Original Soundtrack* (Empire Publications, 2022); Ian Moss, *A Part Of No Tribe* (Empire Publications, 2023); Ian Moss, *Pre-Millenium Shake* (Empire Publications, 2024); Martin Ryan, *Friends of Mine: Punk In Manchester 1976-1978* (Empire Publications, 2018); Greil Marcus, *In The Fascist Bathroom: Writings On Punk 1977-1992* (Harvard University Press, 1999); Stuart Clark & *Hot Press* for extracts from https://www.hotpress.com/music/london-recalling-stuart-clark-stowed-away-with-joe-strummer-in-1999-21012563; Jo Bartlett; Gary Longden; Jonny 'Itch' Fox of the King Blues for the haiku; Peter Smith at myvintagerock.com; Tony Fletcher at https://tonyfletcher.substack.com/p/on-resistance-street; Neil Crud at http://link2wales.co.uk/1980/gigreviews/the-clash-mikey-dread-jiving-daleks-deeside-leisure-centre/

I'd particularly like to thank Graham Jones of http://blackmarketclash.co.uk. The site has been invaluable in fact checking information as well as providing illustrations. And thanks also to Paul Bedford (Kick Down The Doors PR), Ashley Shaw (Empire Publications) and Ian Daley (Route Publishing). And thank you to Karl Kathuria for proofreading.

THANKS

To my son, Mckenzi, who I'm delighted to say has a wonderfully eclectic taste and passion for music. Keep following your dreams.

To Paul, my best friend of 40 years, who's been telling me since we were 15 that I should do something creative with my love of music.

Thanks to my sister Cathy for introducing me to The Clash, The Jam and the bands who have shaped my life.

To John, Nigel, Audrey, Wayne, Ged, Nathan and everyone at *Louder Than War*.

To Debs and Jason for keeping me grounded in the 'real job'.

To all those who responded to my requests to get involved. You all know who you are. To Richard for giving me this opportunity.

And last, but definitely by no means least, to my fiancée Gill for her unwavering support, love, encouragement and belief.

SPECIAL THANKS

TIM JOYCE ★ PHIL CURME ★ PETER AARON
DYLAN WHITE ★ GARETH GORDON-WILKIN
SUE & JOHN TERRY ★ MICHAEL HERBAGE
KEVIN PIKE (CLASH ROADIE 1978 TO 1981) ★ DAVID PORTCH
PANOS & CAROLINE PAPAS ★ RICHARD PORTER
JANE DICKIE & JACKSON SHIRLEY ★ RICHARD MURPHY
JAMES CONNOLLY ★ GARY CHANDLER ★ LEE GOWING
STEPHEN HANSELL ★ PER SJÖBERG ★ JOHN MURRAY
ADAM PORGES ★ IAN WEST ★ GEOFFREY HOOVER
STEVE PALMER ★ DAVID BENDER ★ MARK JOHNSON
GERARD DALY ★ PETER STRIKE ★ MALCOLM HOPWOOD
JED MEEKINS ★ KENNETH FRENCH ★ BRIAN YOUNG
MARTIN JONES ★ NEIL GARRITY ★ IAN DALEY
ED & JOHN SILVESTER ★ NEIL BIRCHALL ★ HÉLÈNE GIB
PETER SMITH & ASHLEIGH SMITH ★ TADHG COUGHLAN
LUUK VERSLUYS ★ LENNY HELSING ★ KEVIN TANSWELL
THOMAS SWEENEY ★ MARGARET FARMER PRINGLE
MARGARET BURKE ★ EVELYN JACKSON ★ DAVE WATSON
NEIL HUGHES ★ SKOTT RUSCH ★ DAVID WILSON
GILL THOMPSON ★ DEBORAH WRIGLEY ★ ULF LYRAAN
CATHERINE WALKER ★ CARL SPARGO ★ DAVID WILLIAMS
BARBARA KNOBBS ★ EVELYN JACKSON ★ NICK KEEN
GIOVANNI TAVERNA, PIETRO TAVERNA & ROBERTO VOLPONI
ALAN JOHN ★ AARON MCCANDLESS ★ ÅKE KÄLLBACK
PAUL WOODMAN ★ SIMON NICHOLS ★ ALAN BURKE
ROSS O'MALLEY ★ IAN CORBRIDGE ★ PETER BESLEY